P9-DJA-812

THE FIRST WORLD WAR IN THE MIDDLE EAST

KRISTIAN COATES ULRICHSEN

The First World War
in the Middle East

HURST & COMPANY, LONDON

First published in the United Kingdom in 2014 by
C. Hurst & Co. (Publishers) Ltd.,
41 Great Russell Street, London, WC1B 3PL
© Kristian Coates Ulrichsen, 2014
All rights reserved.
Printed in the United States of America

Distributed in the United States, Canada and Latin America by
Oxford University Press, 198 Madison Avenue, New York, NY 10016,
United States of America.

The right of Kristian Coates Ulrichsen to be identified
as the author of this publication is asserted by him in accordance
with the Copyright, Designs and Patents Act, 1988.

A Cataloguing-in-Publication data record for this book is available from the British Library.

ISBN: 978-1-84904-274-1

www.hurstpublishers.com

This book is printed on paper from registered sustainable
and managed sources.

CONTENTS

ACKNOWLEDGEMENTS

This book could not have been written without the professional support, friendship and encouragement of Michael Dwyer and his colleagues at Hurst & Co. The value of a good publisher is inestimable and worthy of deep appreciation. A section of the research was presented at the annual meeting of the British Commission for Military History in Keble College, Oxford, in July 2012, and other parts drew upon the author's doctoral research at the University of Cambridge between 2002 and 2005. Academic colleagues at the London School of Economics and Chatham House provided further support and friendship, as did a small group of close friends who made the sometimes solitary task of writing a book a pleasurable experience. Finally, the book is dedicated to my parents and to my wife, in grateful recognition of their love and support.

ABBREVIATIONS

Anzac	Australian and New Zealand Army Corps
APOC	Anglo-Persian Oil Company
CUL	Cambridge University Library
CUP	Committee of Union and Progress
EEF	Egyptian Expeditionary Force
GHQ	General Headquarters
HMS	His Majesty's Ship
IEF	Indian Expeditionary Force
IOL	India Office Library
IWM	Imperial War Museum
LHCMA	Liddell Hart Centre for Military Archives
MEF	Mesopotamian Expeditionary Force
NAA	Northern Arab Army
NILI	Netzakh Yisrael Lo Yishaker (The Eternity of Israel will not lie)
OETA	Occupied Enemy Territory Administration
RAF	Royal Air Force
TNA	The National Archives

SERBIA

BULGARIA

Corfu

ALBANIA

GREECE

Imbros

Istanbul

Black Sea

Gallipoli

Mytilene

Ankara

OTTOMON EMPIRE

Chios

Izmir

Zakynthos

Athens

Samos

Aleppo

Rhodes

Crete

CYPRUS

Beirut

Damascus

Mediterranean Sea

Amman

Benghazi

Jerusalem

Port
Said

Gaza

Alexandria

*Suez
Canal*

El Arish

Qantara

LIBYA

Cairo

*Sinai
Desert*

N

EGYPT

0   125

km

Nile

Red Sea

The Levant - 1914

© Mapman.co.uk (2013)

RUSSIAN EMPIRE

Black Sea

ANATOLIA

Trebizond

ARMENIA

Caucasus Mts.

Kars

Erivan

Sarikamis

ASIA MINOR
(TURKEY)

Erzurum

Bitlis

Van

Tabriz

Caspian Sea

OTTOMON EMPIRE

Aleppo

Mosul

Mediterranean Sea

SYRIA

Deir ez-Zor

MESOPOTAMIA

Tigris

Teheran

Euphrates

PERSIA

Damascus

Baghdad

Ctesiphon

Amman

Kut

Amara

JORDAN

Nasariyah

Qurna

Basra

Abadan

ARABIA

KUWAIT

Persian Gulf

N

0   125
km

Mesopotamia - 1914

INTRODUCTION

A century on, the First World War continues to cast a long shadow across the Middle East. Two of the states that emerged from the legacy of the first large-scale, modern Western military intervention in the region lie in ruins. Iraq has been shattered by the baleful results of a renewed Western assault nine decades after a British commander assured Baghdadis that 'our armies do not come into your cities and lands as conquerors, but as liberators'.[1] Neighbouring Syria has been torn apart by civil strife as part of the post-2011 Arab uprisings that have shaken the post-colonial system of states and regimes to their core. Commentators and analysts alike have observed variously that the 'Arab Spring' represents a second 'Arab Revolt' or that it heralds the final unravelling of the Sykes–Picot legacy. In each case, the terminology hearkens back to developments during the First World War as it was this conflict, more than anything else, that determined the nature of the state-system which later emerged. Other, more recent, forces such as Arab nationalism, political Islam, revolutions, terrorism, civil wars and, not least, decades of superpower rivalry and Arab–Israeli conflict have all transformed the region and its place in international politics. Nevertheless, the legacy of developments and decisions taken during and after the First World War remains a source of bitterness, contestation and conflicting interpretation to this day. This reflects the fact that the war years represented a transition of the region from a crucible of competing empires to the emergence of the modern state-system with all that implied for the realisation – and crushing – of national aspiration, the recasting of loyalties and the birth of grievances that have come to occupy totemic positions in regional narratives.

This book explores the multiple conflicts that took place between August 1914 and November 1918 in the Middle East and North Africa. It examines the fighting that took place between the Russians and the Ottomans in the Caucasus, the forces of the British Empire and France and the Ottomans at Gallipoli, and British and Indian troops and the Ottomans in Palestine and Mesopotamia, as well as smaller outbreaks of fighting elsewhere in North Africa. Some of the battles have become immortalised in historical and national memories. Gallipoli is the most notable example and its centenary will be widely commemorated in Turkey, Australia and New Zealand in

2015. Other battles have mostly been forgotten, despite the terrible toll they exacted on participants and bystanders alike. A prominent example is the Battle of Sarikamis in December 1914, in which nearly one in two Russian and Ottoman combatants perished as tens of thousands froze to death in winter snowstorms at an altitude of nearly 2,000 metres above sea level.

Caught within the crosshairs of four empires vying for different aspects of regional supremacy, the Middle Eastern theatres of war were characterised by vicious fighting in treacherous conditions along extended and vulnerable lines of communication. In addition, the heavy logistical demands of sustaining an industrialised conflict in the largely pre-industrial terrain of the Middle East made enormous demands on host societies and local communities. The voracious demands for food and fodder, animal- and manpower necessary to supply and transport the vast imperial armies had a devastating impact on non-combatants already living close to or under the margins of subsistence. Greater still was the hardship caused by forced displacements and the economic dislocation resulting from the carving out of competing and hostile spheres of influence and control. Worst of all was the Armenian genocide of 1915, in which up to a million Armenians were slaughtered in an orgy of mass killings and death marches that continue to resonate to this day.

For the inhabitants of the Middle East – combatants and non-combatants alike – exposure to, and participation in, the war was therefore intense. Hardships ranged from the rampant spread of diseases to the forcible requisitioning of foodstuffs and natural disasters that could have been prevented. Their cumulative impact meant that much of the region was either in or close to a state of famine by 1918, as military requirements diverted scarce resources from threadbare civil supplies. Areas of Syria and Lebanon fared even worse, as a succession of harvest failures and a devastating plague of locusts in 1914-15 were compounded by exceptionally harsh Ottoman measures and heavy disruption to trading patterns. Up to half a million people died from the resulting famine which started in the cities and towns before spreading rapidly throughout rural areas of the Levant in 1916. Much of Mesopotamia and Egypt also were afflicted by food scarcities in 1917-18 and remained dependent upon emergency shipments from British-controlled India, itself nearing a state of economic breakdown by the autumn of 1918. For the over-stretched militaries operating throughout the Middle East, the relatively quick end to the war in November 1918 came not a moment too soon.

Many English-language and Western-centric works on the First World War treat the campaigns outside Europe as 'sideshows', draining much-needed troops and resources from the principal battlefields on the Western Front. It is undeniably the case that the war was won and lost in France and Flanders, and that the fighting elsewhere had at best a marginal impact on the final outcome. The cascading collapse of the Central Powers in 1918 led to the defeat of the Ottoman Empire in October, as the Anglo-French breakthrough in Bulgaria directly opened the way to Istanbul in a manner that the British advances in far-flung Palestine and Mesopotamia could never do. Yet, to dismiss the Middle Eastern theatre as peripheral to the conflict as a whole would do a gross disservice to the near-total impact of the war on its societies. Nor does it disguise the fact that the strain of sustaining the deployment of large-scale forces across the broader region (including the Caucasus) contributed to the collapse of two long-standing empires (Russian and Ottoman) and left the British and French empires dangerously over-extended.

More than 420,000 Ottoman soldiers died during the wartime campaigns in the Middle East, alongside an estimated 260,000 deaths suffered by British Empire forces, a roughly similar number of Russian fatalities, and around 50,000 French dead.[2] Non-lethal casualties from disease surpassed even these high figures. British and Indian forces in Mesopotamia recorded 207,000 casualties from sickness in 1916 alone, compared with a 'mere' 23,000 attributable to enemy action.[3] For the inhabitants of Turkey and the territories of the Ottoman Empire, the total human cost of the war was even greater. Recent literature has suggested that the population of Turkey decreased by more than 20 per cent in the decade of war that encompassed the 1912-13 Balkan Wars and the wars of Turkish independence that lasted until 1922. This figure compared to the less than 1 per cent decrease of the population of France, where most of the war's most iconic Western Front battles – for which the war is primarily remembered today – actually took place.[4]

The centenary of the First World War will provide an opportunity to reflect on the enormity of the four years of conflict that profoundly shaped the course of the twentieth century. The scale of the commemorations taking place between 2014 and 2018 testify to the public and political fascination with the war and its enduring ability to politicise national agendas. The British Government allocated £50 million to support a four-year programme of commemorations, events and educational initiatives, with one right-of-centre newspaper noting that 'Ministers hope the commemorations will harness the patriotic spirit which came to the fore last year [2012] with the twin celebrations of the Olympic Games and the Queen's Diamond Jubilee, when the country wrapped itself in the Union Flag.' With the initial commemorative events in August 2014 taking place just six weeks before Scotland's planned referendum on independence on 18 September, the same newspaper reported how 'senior figures in the government are also crossing their fingers that the First World War programme gives a political boost to the campaign for a "No" vote', while Scotland's First Minister announced an entirely separate campaign of events.[5]

Similar programmes of remembrance are taking place across the world. In many cases, they are likely to have less political resonance than the above-mentioned British events, although the Australian Government's dedicated 'Gallipoli 2015' website emphasises how the 'bitter eight-month campaign…helped to forge our young nation' and 'created a legend, adding the word "Anzac" to our vocabulary and creating the notion of the Anzac spirit, the ideals of courage, endurance, and mateship'.[6] The 'WW100' initiative set up by the New Zealand Ministry of Culture and Heritage expressed similar sentiments about the 'special significance' of the legacy of Gallipoli: 'It was here that New Zealanders, in April 1915, first stepped onto the world stage', 'were tested in the fire of battle' and 'established a tradition that underpinned a developing sense of national unity'.[7] Such is the anticipated demand to attend the centenary commemoration at Gallipoli on 25 April 2015 that the Australian and New Zealand Governments announced that the 10,500 passes will be allocated by ballot in 2014, with 8,000 going to Australians, 2,000 to New Zealanders and 500 to Turkish representatives.

These nationally sanctioned events will be joined by a large number of new books on the First World War, although both developments are less apparent in the Middle East than elsewhere. Recent years have witnessed an upsurge in publishing on all aspects of the war and its related societal impact, spurred on by the media interest in the dwindling band of super-centenarian survivors, the last of whom have now passed away. Yet, while these include authoritative and highly readable accounts of individual campaigns such as Gallipoli[8] and Mesopotamia,[9] no single-volume history of the Middle Eastern theatre in its entirety has appeared. Instead, the military campaigns in the Middle East during the war tend to be considered in isolation from each other, thereby limiting the overall analytical value of the interconnections that can be drawn among them.

It is this gap that the present volume seeks to fill, in so doing repositioning the campaigns as pivotal to the development of the modern Middle East and rescuing them from the marginal coverage they typically receive in general histories of the war as a whole. Much more than a military history, the book adopts a multidisciplinary approach to developments across the Middle East during the First World War and in its turbulent aftermath. In addition to offering a comprehensive documentation of the actual campaigns themselves, it also explores the socio-political and economic impacts that resulted from the regional demarcation into a series of battle zones cutting across inter- and intra-regional trade routes and commercial hinterlands. Moreover, at a time of heightened interest in the effects of repeated Western military incursions into the region, the book documents how the often hasty and ad hoc decisions taken to meet wartime exigencies have left a complicated legacy that forms the contextual parameters through which much current Western policy is filtered in the Arab and Islamic world.

Such linkages were clearly delineated in the upsurge of popular interest in the apparent similarities between the British invasion of Mesopotamia in 1914 and the US-led invasion of Iraq in 2003. In addition to the aforementioned British proclamation of 'liberation', which could just as easily have been uttered by George W. Bush, Donald Rumsfeld or Tony Blair, attention swiftly focused on the nature of the backlashes that greeted the attempts to force through external state-building projects. Numerous boxes of archival material dealing with British policy towards Mesopotamia in 1919 and 1920 were withdrawn from the National Archives for government use in February 2005, much to the frustration of scholars whose access to historical materials that had been available since the 1960s was severely restricted.[10]

In addition, a raft of historical memoirs written by veterans of the Mesopotamia campaign was re-released to a modern audience. One, in particular, gained wide publicity when Sir Jeremy Greenstock contributed an Introduction that allowed him to vent his dismay at the US and British Governments' mismanagement of the post-2003 occupation of Iraq. Greenstock served briefly as a Special Representative to Iraq during the immediate aftermath of the invasion but was controversially prevented by the UK Foreign and Commonwealth Office from publishing a critical account of his experience.[11] He circumvented this by alluding to the perceived failure of American policy-makers to absorb the lessons of Britain's earlier debacle in the country. 'Is it too churlish to ask whether the leaders of a more modern administration might have profited from studying this experience?' he wrote, before adding that 'Neither the British Government in 1917 nor the Coalition in 2003 really understood what they were taking on when they assumed control of Baghdad.'[12]

Structure of the book

There are three parts to this history. Part I sets the scene in two chapters that detail the historical background and contextual parameters for the campaigns that followed. Chapter 1 examines the international political economy of empire in shaping the contours of regional development in the half-century to 1914. It focuses not only on the different trajectories of the Ottoman, British, French and Russian Empires in the Middle East in the years immediately prior to the outbreak of the First World War, but also on the varying ways in which local leaders and elites responded and adapted. Chapter 2 picks up by documenting the particular logistical, administrative and ecological challenges of campaigning in the Middle East. In the unforgiving terrain over which the majority of the fighting ranged, these factors were critical to military success or (more often) failure and had an indelible, albeit only belatedly appreciated, effect on the evolution of strategy and tactics. This overview also contains a section on the crucial role of India in supplying British imperial forces in the Middle East with manpower and resources, demonstrating the trans-regional connections that defined the region's participation in, and exposure to, the conflict.

Part II consists of four chapters that explore in depth the wartime campaigns across the region. Chapter 3 examines the struggle for supremacy in the Caucasus between the Russian and Ottoman Empires; although not strictly a part of the geographic label of the 'Middle East', these campaigns are inseparable from any study of the war on the region as a whole, as they contributed to the exhaustion of Ottoman capabilities that greatly weakened subsequent military performance in Palestine and Mesopotamia. The ethnic and religious aspect of the Caucasus campaign was also a key factor in sharpening identity politics in both the Russian and Ottoman imperial polities. As both empires were trans-national in scope and contained substantial ethnic and religious minorities, the consequences of this politicisation of identity were severe. The fate of the Armenians is the most well-known example, but numerous other instances of mass deportation and targeting of civilian populations (on both sides) also occurred.

In Chapters 4, 5 and 6, the analysis shifts towards the British-led campaigns in the Middle East. The futile attempt to force the Strait of the Dardanelles and seize the Gallipoli Peninsula is among the most evocative memories of the war, continuing to stir passionate interest and debate a century later. Chapter 4 documents the campaign waged by British and Anzac forces and describes how Gallipoli played a decisive role in the subsequent development of national identities, not only in Australia and New Zealand but also in the modern Republic of Turkey. The chapter ends by examining the little-known Salonika campaign as emblematic of the uneasy balance between British and French interests in the Mediterranean as well as mutual suspicion about each other's motives and objectives in the wider region.

Chapter 5 takes the reader into Egypt, Sinai and Palestine. The strategic importance of the Suez Canal to British imperial supply lines required the immediate formalisation of the de facto British occupation of Egypt that had existed since 1882. British and Indian troops subsequently repelled an early Ottoman thrust against the canal before pushing forward to secure control over the Sinai Peninsula as well as in the Western Desert along the Libyan frontier. With Egypt secured by mid 1916, British commanders pushed into Ottoman Palestine, suffering two major military setbacks at Gaza in 1917 before breaking through to capture Jerusalem in December. Subsequent military operations in the final months of the war culminated in the British occupation of Syria, setting the seeds of the triangular British–French–Arab struggle for control that greatly embittered and complicated post-war ties.

British and Indian forces were also involved in large numbers in Mesopotamia. Chapter 6 details the ebbs and flows of the campaign that started with an assault on Basra in November 1914 and ended with the capture of Mosul eleven days after the Ottoman war formally came to an end in November 1918. The Mesopotamia campaign was one of great contrast, as a series of initial 'easy victories' for British and Indian troops came to a shuddering halt with the surrender of their garrison at Kut in April 1916. Until the fall of Singapore in 1942, this was considered the greatest imperial humiliation yet suffered, and it triggered a damning governmental inquiry that (unlike its twenty-first-century successors) claimed ministerial scalps. Following a thorough reorganisation which also made enormous demands on local resources, Baghdad was captured in March 1917 and offensive operations continued up until the very end of the war.

Part III consists of two chapters that provide cross-cutting analysis of the major themes and controversies of the wartime experience in the Middle East, still felt today. Chapter 7 explores the struggle for political control of the 'new' Middle East as old certainties disappeared and new possibilities opened up. In addition to bringing long-standing imperial rivalries to a head, the chapter focuses on the complex and contradictory set of secret wartime agreements that have been bitterly contested ever since. These include the pledges of British support to the Hashemite dynasty for the Arab Revolt (while simultaneously backing rival Saudi rulers in the Arabian Peninsula), the Sykes–Picot Agreement which carved out spheres of British and French influence across the region, and the Balfour Declaration of support for the establishment of a Jewish national home in Palestine. The chapter also covers the evolution of wartime rhetoric that gradually converged in support of the principle of national self-determination as made in the US Fourteen Points and the Anglo-French Declaration of 1918. Such sentiments also laid the seeds of much of the contestation and bitterness that characterised the immediate post-conflict aftermath, as national groups across the region jockeyed for position and power while the war came to an end.

The book ends with Chapter 8 describing the tortuous nature of the post-war settlements that ultimately shaped the emergence of the modern state-system in the Middle East. Controversy over who would be represented at the Paris Peace Conference in 1919 set the immediate tone as it triggered a backlash among disaffected nationalists in Egypt and Mesopotamia, while tensions soared in Syria between Arab nationalists who had taken control of Damascus and French officials who asserted their influence as per the wartime agreements. A series of sharp clashes between enraged coalitions of local groups and British and French forces laid bare the scale of the nationalist backlash against the Anglo-French attempt to reorganise the Middle East in their interest. At the same time as the status quo rapidly became unsustainable, revolutionary developments in Turkey heralded the final demise of the Ottoman Empire and the rise of Mustapha Kemal 'Atatürk'. The creation of the League of Nations' mandate system and the signing of the Treaty of Lausanne meant that by 1922-3 the lengthy period of uncertainty finally came to an uneasy settlement.

Far from being tangential 'sideshows' to the main theatre of the First World War in Europe, the military campaigns in the Middle East played the decisive role in reshaping the regional political economy. The fighting involved nearly every socio-economic grouping either directly or indirectly, whether through the experience of famine, widespread hardships, or economic dislocation and population displacement. These ensured that its impact on local (often unwilling) participants was close to the conditions nearing total warfare that only belatedly developed in parts of Europe in 1917-18. It is the aim of this book to anchor the history and legacy of the multiple conflicts in the Middle East firmly at the core of First World War studies and to draw out their full and lasting ramifications for a region that remains, a century later, in a state of flux.

PART I

PRELUDE

1

THE POLITICAL ECONOMY OF THE EMPIRES
IN 1914

This opening chapter examines the international political economy of empire in 1914. It covers the differing trajectories of the British (and Indian), French, Ottoman and Russian Empires and how their policies towards the Middle East interacted with one another. Significantly, it focuses on the impact of imperialism in delineating the course of state–society relations throughout the Middle East before 1914. This is important as the pre-war patterns of colonial penetration determined the initial extractive capabilities and methods of waging war of the various machines when war broke out. Moreover, the different intellectual conceptions of colonial control inflected both the contours of policy toward the Middle East emanating from the centre, and the impact of the early campaigns on the ground.

Two broad themes run through this study of the patterns of colonial penetration of, and control over, the Middle East to 1914. The first is the converging agreement on the region's commercial and strategic value in the international political economy of the early twentieth century. The struggle for influence in the Middle East straddled overlapping and competing influences for Western-based hegemony at the local, national, regional and international levels. Nevertheless, the chapter emphasises the longer-term continuities in the extra-European links of settlement, trade and exchange that integrated the Middle East firmly into a much larger (and non-Western) world. During the First World War, many of these links revived and solidified, and particularly those between the Middle East and India, albeit under British direction. It thus positions these later developments within the wider framework of an Indian Oceanic/Western Asian community. This corrects some of the Western-centricity of much of the literature that addresses the course of the war in the Middle East.

This is closely related to the second major thread, which is the need to give voice to the local agents of change that populated the Middle East in 1914. Many of these agents were already prominent advocates of change and reform, and contributed to a vibrant socio-political atmosphere throughout the region. Although scholarly and public attention has focused overwhelmingly on T. E. Lawrence 'of Arabia', a multitude of such personalities made their mark on the region before and during the war. These included local participants, such as the Emir of Kuwait, Mubarak the Great (Mubarak bin Sabah Al-Sabah), who skilfully manipulated foreign rivalries and concerns to maximise his own position, as well as foreign actors, such as Wilhelm Wassmuss 'of Persia'. Other prominent personalities spanned the political and intellectual horizons and contributed to a dynamic environment that was far from passive when faced with the imposition of external structures and forms of control.

With the onset of war in 1914 the trajectories of these local agents varied widely. Some were eliminated under the cover of the fighting and replaced with more pliable collaborators. Other individuals and groups actively sought co-optation into the wartime hierarchies with a view either to bettering their own interests or building up political capital in return for greater self-rule and eventual autonomy afterwards. Increasingly nationalistic platforms in Egypt and incipient national identities thus developed elsewhere as local officials, businessmen, private citizens and the massed ranks of the dispossessed and landless peasantry reached their own accommodations with the greater levels of external and state intrusion into their daily lives. These disparate socio-economic groupings also reached conclusions on the meaning and purpose of the war, and the ways that participation could be turned to their advantage, diverging significantly from colonial narratives. Hence this first chapter sets up what follows in the main body of the book by laying down the contextual parameters for the outbreaks of unrest that began to emerge in 1917-18 and peaked in 1919 as the hasty initial decisions taken for short-term gain began to fragment as the war drew to a close.

Before focusing on the meso- and micro-level features of the political economy of imperial control in the Middle East in 1914, this chapter addresses the powerful macro-processes that shaped the region in the half-century beforehand. These were the extension of formal and informal forms of colonial penetration, the reformulation of socio-economic structures and patterns of trade and commercial activity as the region was incorporated into the global economy. Their interlocking nature meant that each fed off the other and resulted in a period of transition as state capacities expanded in reach and developed extractive capabilities designed to organise and mobilise their societies in profoundly new ways. The chapter ends by examining the emergence of national and increasingly pan-Arab identities and notions of belonging, and the ways that local actors came to accommodate and shape the outbreak of war in 1914. First, though, it begins with a look at the international political economy within which these issues subsequently took shape.

POLITICAL ECONOMY OF DIFFERENT EMPIRES IN 1914

A trans-regional system of settlement and exchange

The land and peoples of the Middle East have been at the forefront of human civilisation since prehistoric times. Well before the rise of Islam and its irruption from the Arabian Peninsula in the seventh century of the Common Era, the region that today constitutes the Middle East featured great cities home to centres of culture and learning and at the hub of international trade routes.[1] As the birthplace of the great religions and the crossroads of three continents, the Middle East experienced a cosmopolitan intermixing of peoples and cultures throughout recorded history. Patterns of cross-cultural settlement and exchange with surrounding regions in the Mediterranean, north and east Africa and west Asia extend back into antiquity, imparting a pluralistic diversity to the forces and flows influencing human development in the area.

Hellenistic remains dating back to the period of Alexander the Great have been found in modern-day Kuwait (Ikaros), Bahrain (Tylos) and locations in the Eastern Province of Saudi Arabia, in addition to the better-known programmes of colonisation and settlement in Babylon, Alexandria and the Levant.[2] Less propitiously, and reflecting its geographical position astride the major land route between Europe and Asia, the city of Adrianople (modern Edirne in Turkey) holds the unfortunate distinction of being the most besieged site in history. Between 323 and 1913, control of the city and the three river valleys linking Turkey with Macedonia and Bulgaria was contested on no fewer than fifteen occasions.[3] The Strait of the Dardanelles, the site in 1915 of the Battle of Gallipoli that has entered political and popular folklore on two continents as a foundational nation-forging event, is another example of enduring military significance, with struggles for local and regional primacy going back to the wars between the Hittites and Achaeans.[4]

In the Arab world, as elsewhere, patterns of political and socio-economic organisation gradually became more complex both in their relationship to the territorially-bounded polities they covered and to each other. From the spread of Islam to the experience of Western military intervention during the Crusades and the Ottomans' replacement of the Byzantine Empire and subsequent expansion into Europe, identities and boundaries were constantly subjected to supra- and international influences and diverse cultural contacts. Thus the Middle East became both highly penetrated by external forces and closely integrated into the transcontinental system operating around it. Long pre-dating the imperial penetration in the nineteenth century, travel and trade, and new modern forms of economic and social mobilisation, produced a certain confluence of ideas in the Levant and North Africa with trends in Europe.[5] Major recent works, notably by C. A. Bayly, have focused precisely on the myriad strategic, commercial and ideational linkages that interconnected the political economies of the Indian Ocean and Eurasian worlds. They emphasise the interdependence of political and social changes across the world and bring together the hitherto separate regional or national histories and narratives into a distinct form of 'global history'.[6]

The influence of India has also come to the forefront of recent research on the broader maritime world that stretched in an arc from the subcontinent to the Persian Gulf and Arabian Peninsula and East Africa. Thomas Metcalf has emphasised the trans-colonial interactions and extension of influence through settlement and trade that linked the peoples of the Indian Ocean since at least the fifteenth century.[7] Patricia Risso and William Beeman have documented the multifaceted encounters between India and the Arabian and Persian coastlines of the Persian Gulf, and described a commercial sphere of influence that influenced a distinctive outward-looking identity throughout the Indian Ocean region.[8] This built on earlier pioneering research by B. R. Tomlinson into the political economy of India, which documented the flourishing intra-Asian foreign trade linkages binding India into a non-Western trading system.[9]

Work by James Onley has drawn attention to the crucial role of influential local intermediaries, many from leading merchant families – see, for instance, his study of the class of native agents that represented the Government of India in the Persian Gulf.[10] Meanwhile, John Willis brought together the overarching themes of European–Asian interdependencies as he argued persuasively that 'many important aspects of European–Asian interaction in maritime Asia cannot be understood if we maintain an analytic separation of European intrusion and Asian response; they emerged in highly contingent and specific ways from the interaction, the congruences and mutual adaptations, of specific facets of the European and various Asian civilizations'.[11] Sugata Bose extended this line of inquiry with a detailed analysis of the Indian Ocean as 'an interregional arena of political, economic and cultural interaction' that interlinked regions as geographically diverse as southern Africa, India, the East Indies and western Australia. Bose argued that the trans-oceanic littoral shared a 'common historical destiny' that survived the imposition of European political and economic domination during the nineteenth century.[12]

A case study of the fluidity of notions of identity and boundaries in Oman captures the dynamics at play throughout the wider region. Its geographical and cultural boundaries have been heavily influenced by patterns of migration and periods of territorial expansion. During the eighteenth and nineteenth centuries the Sultanate of Muscat exercised sovereignty over Gwadar and the Makran coastline in present-day Pakistan as well as the island of Zanzibar off the coast of East Africa, as part of an arc of influence across the north-western littoral of the Indian Ocean stretching from Mozambique to Baluchistan.[13] This had a significant human dimension, as waves of inward migration of Baluch tribes from the Makran provided the backbone for Omani military recruitment, while two sizeable communities of Indian origin, the Lawatiyya and the Banyan, established networks of traders and financiers who exerted considerable economic influence and facilitated the Omani expansion into Africa.[14]

These non-Western patterns of human interaction gradually became enmeshed within the colonial penetration of the Middle East. During the half-century before 1914, the opening of the Suez Canal and the introduction of railways and steamships created a multilateral, global trading network based on the principle of comparative advantage. This superseded the hitherto predominantly bilateral trading links between regions that were largely under the control of the European chartered companies. Although the more formalised European imperialisms wrought extensive damage to indigenous socio-economic structures, local networks survived and even flourished well into the twentieth century. A prime example is the intricate trading routes that connected the ports of the western coast of India with those in the Persian Gulf and Aden and along the coastline of east Africa in a trans-regional maritime community. Each year, *booms* and *dhows* made lengthy round-voyages with their cargoes of silks and cotton textiles from India, dates and cooking oils from Basra and the Gulf ports, rice and salt from Aden bound for Mombasa and Somaliland.[15]

During the First World War these physical and ideational links again came to the surface, in a variety of ways. The relation of the extra-European military campaigns to each other has traditionally been viewed through the prism of grand strategy or via the individual examination of a particular empire's engagement in the war.[16] More recently, work has begun to focus on the way in which the different campaigns – both in the Middle East and beyond – became interconnected logistically and administratively as well.[17] This occurred as decision-makers both in the imperial metropolis and on the ground filtered policy-making through their individual and collective experience of colonial governance elsewhere. Specific policies and imperial civil servants were often transplanted from one to region to another, leading to the reproduction of hierarchies of power and structures of control regardless of local conditions. For their part, the localised backlashes against the closer imposition of colonial control that emerged during the war and peaked between 1919 and 1922 were themselves interlinked through the cross-border exchange of ideas and inspiration.

Ottoman weakness and decline

In 1914 the Ottoman Empire held sway in much of the Middle East, as it had done for much of the previous 400 years. Nevertheless its power had been declining throughout the nineteenth century and its reach over the more distant parts of its empire, particularly in Mesopotamia and the Arabian Peninsula, was never great. In these peripheral regions, Ottoman administrative control was fragmented and often nominal, and largely confined to urban neighbourhoods and functions of security and justice. As late as 1908, it took fourteen days to travel the 2,400 kilometres from Istanbul to the port of Basra at the head of the Persian Gulf, and implementation of Ottoman legal codes and administrative decrees beyond these urban outposts was sporadic at best.[18] Closer to its core, the loss of its Libyan territories in 1911 and its European provinces in Greece, Serbia, Montenegro, Bulgaria and Romania in the two Balkan Wars of 1912 and 1913 amounted to a political and military disaster that appeared to signal the withdrawal of the Ottoman Empire as a regional power and its vulnerability to the predatory designs of its European rivals.[19]

Yet this pessimistic outlook was tempered somewhat by the partial modernisation of the Ottoman Empire during the nineteenth century, and particularly during the *Tanzimat* (reorganisation) that began in 1839 and lasted until 1876. During this period a limited transformation of state and military structures took place amid a process of recentralisation of Ottoman control over its far-flung inhabitants and large agrarian resources.[20] Simultaneous administrative reforms and improvements to means of communication and transportation assisted in the reincorporation of outlying territories into the Empire, following the Mamluk Interregnum of 1704-1831.[21] Although unevenly implemented and never quite successful, these reforms did create an environment in which business with the wider world could be facilitated. A case in point was the rapid expansion of provincial branches of corporate banks after 1889, accompanying and enabling a prolonged period of sustained economic growth that drew hitherto remote outposts into the orbit of the commercialised economy.[22]

These reforms notwithstanding, their partial and incomplete nature had significant implications for the eventual capacity of the empire to mobilise in periods of major conflict. Attempts to broaden the narrow social base of the Ottoman regime, in part through the politicisation of Islam as a tool of legitimacy, were offset by the rigid political–bureaucratic structure of the imperial system and the delicate balance between its Muslim and non-Muslim (yet culturally and economically influential) inhabitants.[23] Moreover, the increased visibility of bureaucratic structures and their deeper penetration of Ottoman society were similarly undermined by rampant levels of corruption, personalised and uneven access to services and government favours, and a growing sense of bottom-up alienation among the very bureaucrats who were supposed to implement the reforms handed down from above.[24] Additional obstacles to coherent development included centre–periphery tensions that manifested themselves in institutional and personal cleavages between the different bureaucratic players both in Istanbul and in the outlying regions.[25] The empire's extractive capacity was further limited by the failure to overcome the military–fiscal shortcomings that delayed the implementation of an empire-wide conscription regulation until 1909 and masked great inequities and inefficiencies in the system of tax farming and its collection at provincial levels.[26] These resulted in a legacy of limited extractive capabilities that undermined Ottoman attempts to mobilise local resources during the First World War. They also exacerbated socio-economic tensions arising from multiple years of poor harvests and poor agricultural returns in Mesopotamia and the Levant.

The Ottoman Empire also became drawn into the world economy as global improvements to transport and infrastructure facilitated the rise of an expanding international economy. In 1838 the signing of the Anglo-Ottoman Commercial Treaty opened the doors to significant inflows of investment, trade and foreign loans, which in turn shaped the direction of economic and social change in the empire. Long-standing patterns of social organisation and commercial exchange were disrupted and channelled into productive capital formation geared towards the production for export (rather than local consumption) of highly specific commodities.[27] European investment in the Ottoman railway network was especially significant in integrating the empire into global markets by linking agricultural production centres to harbours. The empire developed into an exporter of raw materials and agricultural goods to Western markets while importing its manufactured products.[28] Trade with Europe surged again after the opening of the Suez Canal in 1869 while commercial ties with India, chiefly through the Persian Gulf seaport of Basra and the coastal sheikhdoms of the Arabian Peninsula, accelerated after 1900.[29]

Alongside the shift in economic patterns towards commercialised international markets was the political penetration of the Middle East by European powers. These two arms of imperialism framed the region's incorporation into the international system, both formally and informally, and were themselves the outcome of myriad political, economic and strategic forces. In the Ottoman context, they converged in the tumultuous decades preceding the start of the First World War. A combination of fiscal and revenue-raising difficulties and unsustainable levels of borrowing ushered in foreign intervention in Egypt in 1876, following the bankruptcy of the Khedivial state, and the creation of the Ottoman Public Debt Administration under French and British auspices in 1881.[30] Both developments severely curtailed Ottoman sovereignty and capacity to act autonomously of external interests, and, in the case of Egypt, was followed by British military intervention and subsequent occupation from 1882.

The final years prior to 1914 marked the culmination of the Ottomans' interconnected challenges, encompassing near-continuous political, economic and military crisis, as well as revolution and counter-revolution that transformed the apex of the imperial system in Istanbul. This cathartic period began with the coup mounted by the Committee of Union and Progress (CUP) in 1908, and oversaw the loss of Libya to the Italians in 1911 and nearly all of the empire's remaining territories in Europe before and during the Balkan Wars of 1912-13. The Ottomans' failure to mount more than a token resistance in Libya stood in stark contrast to the localised resistance organised by the Sanusi in Cyrenaica that rapidly gathered momentum, and tied down 60,000 Italian troops at its height in 1914.[31] It also reflected the mixed legacy of decades of Ottoman administration in Libya since 1835, which had generated little in the way of consensual mobilisation for its continuation. This was, in large part, attributable to the Ottomans' inability to create a common identity among the peoples they governed, to construct a viable economic alternative to the gradual erosion of traditional caravan-based trading systems, or to reformulate notions of regional political authority, which remained stubbornly tribal and local.[32]

Military defeat in Libya occurred contemporaneously with the contraction of the empire's final remaining territory in Europe and the final withdrawal of Ottoman forces from the Tihamah and central Yemeni highlands, following substantial losses of men, material and expenditure in combating local Zaydi resistance, in 1911.[33] The newly appointed CUP was immediately challenged by the Bulgarian declaration of independence and Austria–Hungary's annexation of Bosnia and Herzegovina in 1908. In Albania, a series of major uprisings began in 1910 in reaction to the CUP government's attempts to increase central control and raise taxes. The Albanian Revolt lasted until the country's declaration of independence in 1912 and the 50,000 Ottoman troops sent to (unsuccessfully) quell it significantly lessened the empire's capacity to respond militarily to the Italian invasion of Libya.[34] This was followed by the rapid and decisive military defeat of the Ottoman armies in the First Balkan War, exposing its administrative mismanagement, operational un-readiness, poor leadership and dysfunctional political–military policy-making – all of which would subsequently colour European observers' assessments of the Ottoman capacity for war in 1914.[35] Nevertheless, as Hew Strachan has adroitly demonstrated, the military defeats in the Balkans proved the catalyst for a thoroughgoing reform and restructuring of the Ottoman armed forces. This actually began in 1909 under Mahmud Sevket Pasha (commander of the 3rd Army and subsequently Minister of War and then Grand Vizier in 1913) and accelerated with the arrival of a German military mission headed by Otto Liman von Sanders in 1913, although the reforms were incomplete when war broke out in 1914.[36]

Between 1908 and 1912 the Ottoman Empire shed almost 40 per cent of its territorial landmass and a sixth of its population. The succession of losses was particularly damaging to its human and intellectual capital, as the European territories had been by some distance the most productive and advanced regions in the Ottoman Empire. They had provided much of its wealth and military and bureaucratic recruits, and after 1913 the centre of gravity in the empire shifted eastwards to Anatolia. The steady 'Turkification' of the empire, instigated by the Committee of Union and Progress as the self-appointed agents of modernisation on its own Turkic terms, had profound significances for the future direction of the Ottoman (as opposed to Turkish) polity, and for its non-Turkish inhabitants throughout the Middle East. Thus, the years immediately preceding the war were ones in which the empire underwent a radical transformation politically, socially and economically, all with consequences for its military performance and posture during the war that followed in 1914.[37]

Colonial penetration of the Middle East and North Africa

Ottoman decline during the second half of the nineteenth century (and accelerating rapidly after 1908) was matched by the rise in European colonial penetration throughout the Middle East. These two meta-processes were intermixed, to a degree, although the European Powers came to an uneasy agreement to respect Ottoman territorial integrity in the 1856 Treaty of Paris. British and French trading interests opened up Ottoman markets to the world economic system and in so doing created commercial and overlapping strategic interests, particularly in the contest for territory in Africa and influence over trade routes.[38] Nevertheless, the roots of imperialism were complex, and the projection of external influence into the region took a variety of forms, with outright colonial annexation only occurring in rare cases – notably the British in Aden, the French in Algeria and the Italians in Libya. Elsewhere, the 'colonial state' was a multifaceted organism projecting power in numerous direct and indirect ways; through different types of alliances with notable sheikhs and landowners in some cases, or working with existing bureaucratic tools in others. But in each instance the extension of colonial influence led to new political dynamics and methods of organisation, and powerful external pressures over the direction and pace of change, with political authority refracted through the colonial state and its multiple interactions with society.[39]

These complexities were clearly evident in France's expansion to become an imperial power in the Middle East. This was an outcome of converging feelings of national prestige and resentment at the continuing expansion of the British and (after 1880) German Empires, as well as a reaction to the crushing defeat in the 1870-1871 Franco-Prussian War. It also represented the result of concerted lobbying from economic pressure groups and French nationalist societies with close connections to the political elite, as well as the army and navy, which all called for colonial acquisitions and exploited the newly controlled territories.[40] Varying combinations of political and economic factors led to periods of expansionary dynamics and the acquisition of Algeria (1830) and Tunisia (1881), together with a Franco-Spanish agreement in 1907 regarding the division of North Africa. French strategic concerns for Algeria's boundaries also played a role in the latter two cases, as did geopolitical rivalries with Britain and Spain in North Africa and the Mediterranean.[41]

The differing political economies of colonial control were important in structuring the extractive and mobilising capacities that came to the surface in 1914. France's colonial rule in Algeria was direct and intrusive, in contrast to Britain's more indirect style of governing in its colonies. A policy of assimilation gradually drew the colony into the metropolitan political orbit, with the three departments being granted parliamentary representation in Paris and more than 660,000 Europeans, mainly agriculturalists, establishing settler communities.[42] Meanwhile, Tunisia and other French colonies in Africa were administered as protectorates, maintaining an appearance of local sovereignty but devising mechanisms to reshape and take over real administrative power and control of society. Although Tunisia escaped outright annexation, as in Algeria the implantation of a class of settlers acted as a powerful transmission belt of imperialist interests onto the French political scene. Indeed, as Gary Wilders' highly original history of French colonial history makes clear, by 1914 the socio-political system had been reconfigured into an 'imperial nation-state' that encompassed a single political formation with a dual character consisting of structurally interrelated parliamentary republican and authoritarian colonial dimensions.[43]

French strategic and commercial interest in the Levant was longer standing than in North Africa, but took a very different form. It dated to Napoleon's invasion of Syria (from Egypt) in 1799 although his advance was halted by the Ottomans at Acre. France later extended support to the Egyptian ruler Muhammad Ali during his own invasion of Syria in 1831-2, but this renewed attempt to gain influence again proved short-lived as Egyptian forces withdrew from Syria in 1840. A third effort to embed French influence in the region occurred following the Druze massacre of the

Maronite community of Mount Lebanon in 1860, whereupon France dispatched 6,000 troops ostensibly to act as the protector of the Christian population. Once again, success was transient, as the Ottoman Government reasserted control, and French influence remained informal until the opportunity for renewed forward action presented itself with the outbreak of the First World War.[44] Instead, French interests advanced through cultural and religious emphasis on cultivating the French language and its 'mission civilisatrice', as well as responsibility for the protection of Catholics in Palestine, and the Maronites in Lebanon.[45]

Patterns of external penetration therefore took multiple forms, both within and across regions. The nature and extent of colonial influence determined the structures of governance and extractive institutions that developed. French incorporation of its imperial possessions into metropolitan structures paved the way for direct transfers of military and labour resources from the colonies to France during the war, both for fighting and factory work.[46] Between 1914 and 1918, some 450,000 soldiers and an additional 135,000 factory workers, mostly from French North Africa, were sent to France.[47] Tunisia alone sent 80,000 to the French Army and suffered upwards of 20,000 casualties on the Western Front, while a further 30,000 Tunisians worked in mines, factories and farms in France, thereby releasing French workers for the military.[48] This direct involvement in the war was strikingly different from the mobilisation of Britain's extra-European colonial resources, as spatial and hierarchical divisions remained far more rigid.

French interests in the Levant also primed officials to take advantage of the outbreak of war with the Ottoman Empire, and stake territorial claims that would make generations of French efforts to establish themselves a reality. Great Power rivalries – both real and imagined, and in the case of the 1911 Moroccan (Agadir) crisis a mixture of both – thus proved important pivots of policy-making in the Middle East. In Britain's case, a combination of strategic and commercial considerations, intimately bound up with the protection of the route to India, exerted critical influence over the spread of predominantly indirect imperial control in the Middle East, although strategic and commercial rivalries with France (and latterly Germany) were other drivers of policy. India became the 'jewel in the crown of the British Empire', and required strategic planning to defend its eastern and western flanks in an arc stretching from East Africa to the Arabian Peninsula and as far as South East Asia.[49] Indian human and military resources were pivotal to the development of the British Empire, in part through the provision of indentured labour and small traders. Nevertheless it was the Indian Army that represented the basis for the security of India and guaranteed the stability of imperial trade and investment.[50]

During the nineteenth century the dynamics of imperial security interlinked the political economy of India to strategic developments in the Middle East and Africa, as well as Asia. An Anglo-Indian 'sub-imperial system' developed over the course of a 'century of commerce and diplomacy' that locked India into a vast protective region of pro-British states and polities, initially mindful of a potential threat from a southwards Russian move through Afghanistan or to the Persian Gulf. Most often this was achieved through military intervention to secure British and Indian objectives, and the Indian Army proved an effective tool in the context of nineteenth-century limited-liability colonial campaigning. Thus, the Indian Army intervened in China (1860), Abyssinia (1868), Perak (1875-6), Baluchistan (1876-9), Malta and Cyprus (1878), Afghanistan (1878), Egypt (1882), Burma (1886), Nyasa (1893), Mombasa and Uganda (1896) and the Sudan (1885 and 1896-8).[51] Its role in ensuring the security of the Anglo-Indian periphery was an important development that foreshadowed the Indian Army's experience in the two world wars in the twentieth century.

Following the operational and logistical shortcomings exposed by the year-long effort to quell the frontier uprising at Tirah in 1897-8, the Indian Army underwent a gradual programme of modernisation under Lord Kitchener and Douglas Haig. This culminated in Haig's secret drawing-up of plans in 1911 to dispatch an Indian Expeditionary Force to Europe in the event of a general war on the continent. Nevertheless, the political economy of laissez-faire and light taxation represented powerful political and financial constraints that held back the development of a military–industrial complex in India and its concomitant ability to regulate and extract resources in times of war.[52] So, too, did British memories of the backlash against a previous attempt to penetrate more deeply into rural society in 1857-8, and the legacy of the Great Rebellion was a conservative approach to governance and an emphasis on collaboration with carefully identified groups within Indian society. These shackles proved significant limiting factors in the opening phase of the First World War as the Indian Army resumed its long-standing role as an 'imperial fire brigade' by sending forces to Mesopotamia, East Africa and Aden, in addition to Egypt, yet wary officials failed to take steps to press Indian society too deeply to mobilise for the war effort, with catastrophic results in Mesopotamia in 1916.[53]

India was one centre of gravity for the British Empire's policy in the Middle East. The other was Egypt, and the security of the route through the Mediterranean and Suez Canal to the Red Sea and India. Here, too, a specific political economy of colonial control developed in the decades prior to the war that directly influenced the nature of the campaigning during it. As in other parts of the Ottoman Empire, the partial modernisation and its gradual incorporation into a global trading system during the nineteenth century left a legacy of flawed industrialisation and heavy indebtedness that culminated in national bankruptcy in 1875-6. This was followed by external intervention, initially in the form of an Anglo-French system of Dual Control to reach a financial settlement and manage Egyptian debt repayment.[54] Local resentment at the imposition of tighter external control escalated into anti-European feelings and culminated in the 'Urabi rebellion in 1881. The military uprising was led by four Egyptian colonels and featured the slogan 'Egypt for the Egyptians' in a proto-nationalist display of anger at foreign incursion. It managed to gather broad cross-class support from rural and urban groups alike, before being defeated by the Khedive's forces working with British support following anti-European riots in Alexandria in June 1882 and fears that a nationalist Egypt might end its debt repayments to European bondholders.[55]

THE FIRST WORLD WAR IN THE MIDDLE EAST

The decades that followed the (temporary) dispatch of British warships to Alexandria saw the evolution of a particular 'Anglo-Egyptian' mode of colonial governance. This was based on the three principles of free trade, low taxation and limited government. British officials also maintained an increasingly fictitious line that the occupation was only temporary, but after 1892 the Foreign Office in London accepted that withdrawal was unlikely, and British influence began to spread more widely.[56] By 1914, British advisers and sub-inspectors permeated the upper reaches of the Egyptian Government, armed with mandates to modernise what one leading imperialist, Alfred Milner (who also coined the notion of the 'veiled protectorate'), labelled the frightful misgovernment of Khedivial rule.[57] Between 1882 and 1914, British policy in Egypt aimed to uphold London's commercial and strategic interests and secure sufficient local political cooperation to avoid having to impose direct rule. This required a delicate yet awkward balance as reforms taken to restore Egypt's political and fiscal stability paradoxically solidified British influence through the further influx of officials who gradually supplanted the layer of Egyptian bureaucrats.[58]

Yet the fundamental feature of the political economy of the British Empire, in India as well as in Egypt, lay in its small official size and reliance on networks of local collaborative agents. British influence in both places remained tiny, in Egypt numbering between 300 and 400 civil servants and 4,000 to 5,000 soldiers alongside a small commercial community of agriculturalists and businessmen. Their presence was largely limited to urban areas and did not extend to rural Egypt, where 68 per cent of the population remained in agricultural employment. To the extent that rural Egypt came (indirectly) into contact with the occupation, it was through its agricultural policies. These continued the Khedives' pre-1882 policy of integrating Egypt into the international economy through the production of cotton as an export-based cash crop.[59] Irrigation engineers were brought in from India and transformed Egyptian agriculture into a year-round activity. Cotton became so lucrative that the cultivation of foodstuffs declined to the point that Egypt was close to becoming a single-crop economy reliant on imported food to meet shortfalls in local supplies.[60]

The political economy of British imperialism in Egypt and India structured what followed the outbreak of fighting in the Middle East in the autumn of 1914. The commercialised economies and light-touch governance in both countries initially proved ill-suited to regulating and extracting the resources of man- and animal-power, with logistical support, necessary to sustain large-scale military campaigns. In both cases, it required the cathartic experience of military shocks to galvanise political support for a far more direct and authoritarian reach into local socio-economic patterns to divert resources to the war. This led to an abrupt and disruptive (yet ultimately temporary) juncture in imperial policy-making, which later reverted to its preference for indirect rule through collaborative elites after 1922. Nevertheless, the course of the campaigns did underscore the durable value of Britain's extra-European networks constructed to support the Indian Raj before 1914. These linkages oversaw the transfer of human and material resources both to and from Britain and between the different zones of conflict in the Middle East. They were made possible by, and based upon, the strategic value of the Suez Canal as the pivotal 'artery of empire' and protection of the route to India and the southern Dominions.[61]

This system took its most pronounced form in the Arabian Peninsula and Persian Gulf. Civil and military planners in India considered the region to be a vital flank on the sea route to India, and maintained a close watch for signs of Russian and German competition for influence. In 1903, concerns for British pre-eminence led the British Foreign Secretary, Lord Lansdowne, to proclaim 'a sort of Monroe Doctrine for the Persian Gulf' and warn that Britain would regard the establishment by any other power of a naval base or fortified port as a 'grave menace' to its interests.[62] This reflected Britain's careful construction of a sub-imperial system in the Persian Gulf over the previous century, beginning with a General Treaty outlawing maritime piracy in 1820 and maturing into the agreement of protective treaty relations between the Government of India and the small Arab sheikhdoms of the Trucial States (1835), Bahrain (1861), Kuwait (1899 and 1914) and Qatar (1916).[63]

To the north, British and Indian interests expanded steadily throughout the second half of the nineteenth century, albeit more informally. British and Indian companies took advantage of the Ottomans' administrative reforms and improvements to transport and communication outlined above. British shipping interests acquired the right to navigation on the rivers of the Ottoman provinces in Mesopotamia in 1846, and by 1911 Britain and (British) India were Basra's principal trading partners.[64] Another means of expanding British influence in Mesopotamia was through participation in large-scale irrigation and agricultural projects, while the discovery of oil in neighbouring Persia in 1908 heightened still further the perceived strategic and commercial value of the region. British officials suspected that substantial oil reserves existed around Mosul, although no firm discoveries would be made until 1927.[65] In 1914, the British Government acquired a majority shareholding in the Anglo-Persian Oil Company (APOC) and thus secured for the Admiralty a steady supply of oil for its ships. This reduced Britain's dependence upon non-imperial sources of oil in the United States, Russia, Mexico and Rumania, but introduced a powerful new dynamic into Mesopotamian policy-making considerations on the eve of war.[66]

Assertions of greater British influence in the Persian Gulf were driven in part by a desire to counteract perceived German or Russian forward moves, in the same way that British policy in Africa and the Mediterranean was acutely tuned to supposed French machinations. The perception of a Russian threat to British interests faded after the signing of the Anglo-Russian Convention in 1907, whereupon Germany became the primary object of concern. British suspicions were initially alerted by German railway and trading moves. In 1903, the Ottoman Government granted a railway concession to the German Anatolian Company, for a line stretching from Konya in Anatolia to the Persian Gulf, and the Foreign Office anxiously followed its progress eastwards. After 1910, the imminent prospect of the line's extension to the shores of the Persian Gulf prompted anxious speculation as to where it might terminate, alongside a heightened awareness of the strategic importance of Mesopotamia and the northern Gulf. This provided opportunities for local Arab leaders, particularly Sheikh Mubarak bin Sabah Al-Sabah of Kuwait, to exploit these uncertainties by skilfully playing off the European powers in order to maximise local advantage and negotiating power.[67]

Additional British concern at German objectives related to the increasing volume of its trade with the Arabian Peninsula and the activities of some of its agents in the Persian Gulf. In 1912-13 the number of packages transported on the (German) Hamburg–Amerika Line from Europe to Basra exceeded, for the first time, the combined total of all its British rivals. Further unease arose from the work of Wilhelm Wassmuss, the German Consul at the important Persian city of Bushehr (also the seat of the British Persian Gulf Residency). In a dispatch to Berlin in December 1913, Wassmuss claimed that the outgoing British Political Resident at Bushehr, Sir Percy Cox, had 'feared every economic influence that Germany might obtain in the Gulf'. He added that Cox 'saw his ambition of making the Gulf an exclusively British sea endangered by every shipload of barley and every ton of oxide exported by Germans.'[68] Another prominent German to attract British concern was Baron Max von Oppenheim, whose travels in the Arabian Peninsula and extensive reports on Arab politics to the German Foreign Office caused considerable alarm in London at his anti-British tone and advocacy of Islamic rebellion in Britain's Muslim possessions, especially in the event of any war with the Ottoman Empire.[69]

For their part, both Cox's replacement as (Acting) Political Resident, John Lorimer, and the acting Consul-General in Fars, Stuart Knox, believed that German commercial policy was indeed underpinned and influenced by political motives aimed at challenging Britain's regional supremacy, which 'it is considered essential in the interests of India to preserve'. Official British unease at the direction of German policy in the Persian Gulf subsequently was made clear in April 1914, when the Foreign Office refused a German request to lay a cable in the Persian Gulf as part of a direct telegraphic link between Germany and China.[70] Thus, by the time of the outbreak of conflict in 1914, the supposed German 'threat' to Britain's Middle Eastern interests had firmly replaced the earlier perceived Russian challenge to imperial security, which had been dominant in the official mindset prior to the signing of the 1907 Anglo-Russian Convention.

British officials were clearly aware and increasingly uneasy about Germany's growing rivalry in the Middle East and beyond. Germany's global outlook after the 1890s manifested itself in the acquisition of formal colonies in east, west and south-west Africa and the Pacific, as well as the projection of a near-controlling influence over the Ottoman military machine. German ties with the Ottoman Army extended back multiple generations to Helmut von Moltke (the Elder's) appointment to modernise the army, which he subsequently led in the Anatolian campaign against Muhammad Ali of Egypt in 1838. In the 1880s the Ottoman rulers again turned to German help in military reorganisation, with Baron Colmar von der Goltz spending twelve years (1883-95) in Constantinople. Their legacy of practical and intellectual influence on the Ottoman Army meant that Liman von Sanders' appointment as head of the German Military Mission in 1913 represented an organic continuation of a long-standing relationship. Germany's informal influence also spread through the attachment of senior Ottoman officers (including Sevket Pasha) to the German Army early in their careers.[71]

The awarding of the Baghdad railway concession to Germany in 1903 and the subsequent (halting) construction captured the imagination and anxieties of Germany's competitors for regional influence in the Middle East. It has also been the subject of a major recent work entitled *The Berlin–Baghdad Express: The Ottoman Empire and Germany's Bid for World Power*. In part it became conflated with the concept of *Drang nach Osten* (Drive to the East) although British officials, in particular, feared it posed a direct threat to their commercial and strategic interests in the Persian Gulf, the newly discovered oilfields of Persia, and the route to India.[72] The line remained incomplete by 1914 with the Taurus mountain range in south-eastern Turkey an insurmountable obstacle, and when war broke out the railhead was nearly 500 kilometres short of Baghdad. Moreover, it caused friction between German and Ottoman officials for whom the line did not meet their military needs, thereby reflecting its primarily economic and financial (rather than geo-strategic) basis.[73] This notwithstanding, its significance lay in its impact on British sceptics of German motivations and objectives towards the Ottoman Empire, though British attempts to wean the Sublime Porte away from German influence were notably weak and unsuccessful.

German influence in the Ottoman Empire was also manifested in other less tangible, yet arguably more significant forms. Kaiser Wilhelm II visited Constantinople in 1889 and again in 1898, on which occasion he also visited Jerusalem, Damascus and Beirut in displays of considerable ceremonial pomp. Moreover, in a speech in Damascus in November 1898, he saluted the Ottoman Sultan Abdul Hamid II as leader of Muslims across the world, in a direct affront to the British, French and Russian Empires' own Muslim communities in India and Egypt, North Africa, the Caucasus and beyond.[74] With British (in particular) colonial control dependent more upon the projection of power than the sizeable deployment of the tools of coercion, any attempt to undermine the collaborative pillars of imperial rule constituted serious challenges to British interests. This threat eventually culminated in the formation of an alliance between the Ottoman Empire and Germany on 2 August 1914, and with Austria–Hungary three days later, and the Porte's declaration of Islamic holy war, exhorting Muslims across the world to fight against Britain, France and their allies, on 14 November 1914.[75]

The emergence of national identities by 1914

The projection and intensification of European control over large parts of the Middle East did not occur in a vacuum. Rather, it took place alongside powerful ideational currents that began to reshape notions of belonging and cast them into proto-national identities. These occurred synchronously and fed off each other in a dialectical process of interaction between competing ideas, ideals and the emerging realities of external power. C. A. Bayly has documented how the emergence of national feelings was a global phenomenon rather than a European export, and that affinities of nationality began to occur contemporaneously in the late-nineteenth century in large areas of Asia, Africa and the Americas. In part, this reflects what he labels the 'paradox of globalisation' as the solidifying of boundaries of nation-states and empires after 1860 caused new methods of social organisation and communication that often drew upon indigenous histories and memories for appeal.[76]

Numerous processes lay behind the rise of new forms of identity, in the Middle East as elsewhere. These included the growth of print capitalism and the emergence of a new class of intelligentsia, partially as a result of French educational initiatives in North Africa and (particularly) the Levant. American missionary activity was also important in the expansion of education in the Levant, and was instrumental in establishing the Syrian Protestant College, later the American University of Beirut, in 1866. By the 1870s French became the language of trade and of the urban elites, while Cairo and Beirut became regional centres of publishing, with newspapers and periodicals disseminating modern knowledge and new ideas. An important corollary of this was the appearance of political journalism and the linking of political education with social development, particularly in Egypt both before and after the British occupation in 1882.[77]

The expanding intelligentsia and vernacular printing presses in turn spearheaded the spread of an Arabic national consciousness and intellectual renaissance. This was a broad movement that encompassed both Islamic modernist thinkers and proponents of a more narrowly defined national identity. Among the former, Jamal al-Din al-Afghani and Mohammed Abduh emerged as the leading 'Islamic modernists' intent on re-interpreting Islam to make it compatible with modern ways of organising society and the state while remaining true to their faith.[78] Their writings had an enduring impact in the Arab world, but starting in the late-nineteenth century more particularistic nationalisms also began to put forward a different form of socio-political mobilisation. In Egypt, Western penetration produced a forceful response, ranging from the 1882 'Urabi rebellion's slogan of 'Egypt for the Egyptians' to local outrage at the Dinshawai incident in 1906, which marked the turning point in Egyptian attitudes towards Britain's military occupation, and the rise to prominence of the Egyptian nationalist Mustafa Kamil, founder of the National Party (*al-Hizb al-Watani*) shortly before his death in 1909.[79] In neighbouring Libya, a young Egyptian nationalist, Abd al-Rahman Azzam (later the first Secretary General of the Arab League between 1945 and 1952), played an important role in articulating and spreading Arab nationalist ideals within the Libyan resistance to Italian occupation, culminating in the formation of the short-lived Tripolitanian Republic in 1918.[80]

Azzam's long career – from Egyptian nationalist to pioneering advocate of pan-Arab ideals – demonstrated the fluidity of early notions of identity and multiple belongings. The rise of pan-Islamic and Arab national feelings in the lands of the Ottoman Empire was on occasion compatible with a residual attachment to Ottoman nationalism. As Bayly points out, Egyptian nationalists could remain Ottoman patriots similar to many in Britain's White Dominions who remained loyal to the British connection even as distinct regional identities emerged in Australia, New Zealand and Canada.[81] In this regard, the breakdown of the Ottoman polity following the loss of many of its Christian European communities, and the subsequent introspective turn of the Young Turks after the 1908 revolution, created the conditions for the growth of the idea of a Turkish nation and facilitated the emergence of an Arab nationalist response in its Arabian provinces. The appearance of Turkish nationalism and pan-Arab affinity fundamentally altered the traditional loci of political loyalty in the Ottoman Empire, in ways that became fully apparent during the course of the regional conflicts during and immediately after the First World War.[82]

Shifting focus to the granular level of society, this brings out the varying methods and choices by which individuals and communities accommodated and shaped the macro-processes of change described above. Much recent literature has focused on the role of Western – chiefly British and American – officials in determining the shape of the region as it exists today. One such book, provocatively entitled *Kingmakers: The Invention of the Modern Middle East* and published in 2008, focused exclusively on ten British and three American figures who 'were instrumental in building nations, defining borders, and selecting or helping to select local rulers'. The list included familiar figures such as T. E. Lawrence, Gertrude Bell and Sir Mark Sykes, in addition to later meddlers Kermit Roosevelt and Paul Wolfowitz.[83] These officials did have important parts to play in the creation of the colonial states and post-colonial structures that continue to reverberate today. But, they must not obscure the equally important role of local agents in shaping the realities on the ground, often far from the gaze of the 'official mind' of empire.

Shifting Great Power rivalries did allow local leaders a degree of manoeuvrability in turning these concerns for the balance of power to their own advantage, although most of the key decisions that affected local politics, economics and society in the Middle East continued to be taken by external, colonial actors. Yet within this overarching rubric, opportunities existed for local agents to make themselves felt. Particularly on the imperial peripheries, as in the Arabian Peninsula, several of the sheikhly rulers proved quite adept at playing off Ottoman and British fears about the other's presence. This pragmatic realpolitik was practised most successfully by the rulers of Kuwait (Sheikh Mubarak Al-Sabah, 1896-1915) and Qatar (Sheikh Jassim Al-Thani, 1878-1913), as well as Abdul-Aziz bin Saud in his gradual conquest of central Arabia after 1902.[84] Here, the invocation of external (British) support, motivated in part by the outbreak of the war and the desire to obtain a local ally in the war against the Ottomans in 1915, played a critical role in enabling Saudi expansion at the expense of the rival Rashidi dynasty, which supported the Ottomans.[85]

To the immediate north of the Arabian Peninsula, in Basra in 1913, the powerful local notable, Sayyid Talib, led a movement agitating for greater local autonomy from Ottoman rule and the retention of all taxes collected in the vilayet for local use. Descended from the most important family in Basra, the extent of Talib's influence and freedom of action was detailed by the American vice consul in Baghdad, who noted in 1914 that:

Talib…continues to exert an almost undisputed sway over those regions, and the Official Ottoman Government Authorities are practically powerless and condemned to an absolute and shameful inactivity in view of his overbearing personal position…

In March 1914 a partial reconciliation occurred between Talib and the Ottoman vali (governor) of Basra, to the extent that by July Taleb was able to persuade the Ottoman authorities in Basra to take up arms against his most significant local rival, the sheikhs of the Muntafik tribal confederation, on his behalf.[86] The transient nature of Talib's coalition with external (later British, temporarily) actors presaged the fluidity of tribal alliances that unfolded once hostilities broke out in November 1914. During the war, tribal leaders in Mesopotamia displayed an acute sensitivity to changes in local power relations and the source of economic and political influence, and often switched sides with the shifting fortunes of battle.[87] Considerations of personal and tribal gain, rather than awareness of a nationalist political consciousness, were initially more significant in shaping choices made. This began to change after 1917 with the appearance of a nationalist discourse in response to external events, namely the British declaration of intent to remain in Mesopotamia and the enunciation of the Fourteen Points, including the principle of national self-determination, by President Woodrow Wilson in January 1918.[88]

Elsewhere, in regions where centralised power was more entrenched, local accommodations took different forms. Egyptian politicians acquiesced in a military proclamation issued by the British in November 1914 pledging that no Egyptian would be asked to participate in the defence of Egypt, and provided collaborative support following London's declaration of Protectorate status in December. These decisions transformed the Anglo-Egyptian political relationship and planted the seeds of bitterness and unrest that erupted into violence in 1919. The terms of the Protectorate and the proclamation were ambiguous and susceptible to misinterpretation by the British community in Egypt, who welcomed the measures, and Egyptians, who regarded them as emergency wartime measures pending the final settlement of Egypt's future status. Indeed, Percival Elgood, who served in the Ministries of War, Interior and Finance during a long career in Egypt, observed retrospectively (in the 1920s) that the Protectorate 'inferred much and promised little' and that the proclamation 'should never have been given' since 'no human intelligence in November 1914 could foretell the development of the War, or whether Egyptian assistance would not become necessary to the success of military operations'.[89]

Nationalists in Lebanon and Syria drew upon nineteenth-century cultural and educational developments to create a vibrant literary and political landscape during the final years of Ottoman rule. Many of them had participated in the first Arab Congress that met in Paris in June 1913 and adopted resolutions demanding greater autonomy within the Ottoman Empire as well as making Arabic an official language in the Arab provinces of the empire. They formed the vanguard of a proto-Arab nationalist movement seeking to establish a Greater Syria in what is today Syria and Lebanon. Following the discovery of their plans in documents confiscated from the French consulates in Beirut and Damascus, two large groups of activists were hanged in the cities in August 1915 and May 1916. Their deaths are commemorated to this day by a national holiday on the anniversary of the hangings (Martyrs' Day on 6 May) and in the naming of Martyrs' Squares in each city.[90]

The Middle East on the cusp of war

The Ottoman Empire did not immediately become involved in the European war following the outbreak of conflict in August 1914. It did, however, establish a binding alliance with Germany on 2 August, the day after the German invasion of Russia and the day before its declaration of war with France. The agreement largely resulted from Austrian pressures to tie the Porte into the Triple Alliance in order to control Ottoman ambitions in the Balkans. Although a majority of the Ottoman Government initially favoured remaining neutral, the triumvirate of Prime Minister Said Halim, Interior Minister Talaat Bey and War Minister Enver Pasha won the argument in favour of alliance with Germany, arguing that this offered some protection against the Russian threat and the potential to make territorial gains in North Africa and the Caucasus. The decision was swiftly followed by the assumption of German control over the Ottoman Navy on 15 August.[91]

Although the Porte did not enter the European war until late October, relations with the Entente powers (Britain, France and Russia) soured rapidly after two German cruisers, the *Goeben* and the *Breslau*, were granted refuge in Constantinople from their British pursuers in the Mediterranean. Hostility between the Ottomans and Britain was further inflamed by an Admiralty decision to seize two battleships under construction for the Ottoman Navy in British shipyards. On 1 October the Ottomans raised the stakes in the as yet undeclared conflict by closing the Strait of the Dardanelles to British and imperial shipping, wiping out more than half of Russia's entire export trade in the process. The trigger for the declaration of war was the Ottomans' launch of pre-emptive naval strikes against the Russian Black Sea ports of Odessa and Sevastopol on 29 October. Russia declared war with the Ottoman Empire on 2 November, followed by Britain and France on 5 November, and the proclamation of Holy War on 14 November.[92]

The course of the campaigns in the Middle East will be examined at length in the chapters that follow. The changing military fortunes of the combatants created opportunities for the reshaping of political boundaries and commercial spheres. Russia re-entered the Middle East as much of the Ottomans' offensive military thrust was north-eastwards, motivated by the Young Turks' pan-Turanian sentiments and a desire to make gains in Transcaucasia. Although the focus of many Anglophonic military histories of the regional campaigns has been directed towards the fighting at Gallipoli, Mesopotamia and Palestine, the Ottoman military machine was largely bled dry on the Russian front.[93] This wearing down was accentuated by rekindled expansionist designs in the Caucasus following Russia's exit from the war later in 1917, severely weakening Ottoman resistance to rapid British (and French) moves through Mesopotamia and the Levant in 1918.[94]

Moreover, the multinational nature of the imperial belligerents complicated the conduct of the campaigns and set the context for the massacres and enforced displacements of entire communities in the years that followed. This was especially apparent in the Russo-Ottoman theatre, where Muslims formed the largest minority in Russia and Christians the largest minority in the Ottoman Empire; this 'mirror image' was the cause of untold suffering and easy scapegoating among populations on both sides of the imperial–religious divide. Recruitment in both the Russian and Ottoman Armies prior to and during the war had to navigate this ethnic landscape. Non-Muslims in the Ottoman Empire remained exempt from serving in the military throughout the nineteenth-century modernisation of governing (and military) structures. This changed only after the 'Young Turks' came to power and began to overhaul the military by reducing the number of exemptions in order to broaden the base of recruitment. Hence, the military conscription law was changed in July 1909: extended to include students in religious colleges, as well as Jews and Christians. Leaders of the Greek, Bulgarian, Syrian and Armenian communities agreed in principle but argued that they should serve in separate units and, in the case of Bulgarians, be deployed only in the empire's European provinces. Ottoman commanders resisted this and many young Christian men either procured foreign passports or emigrated in order to avoid military service, while those from communities whose 'loyalty' was suspect (primarily Greeks and Armenians) were channelled towards the labour units.[95] The Russian Army was also multi-ethnic and was a mass conscript army 'famous for its inefficiency and for its lack of a professional NCO corps'. Similar to the Ottoman rank and file, the majority of soldiers were peasants recruited from villages across the empire, many of them speaking little or no Russian at all.[96]

Beginning in 1914, the meta-processes of the end of colonisation and competition for regional influence came together to frame the parameters of the military campaigns that followed. Pre-war trajectories of formal and informal imperialism and patterns of external penetration created distinct models of political organisation that influenced the initial conduct of the campaigns and methods of mobilisation. These differed substantially between British, French and Ottoman colonies, but in all three the war years witnessed an unprecedented expansion of the breadth and depth of state control and the sharpening of its extractive institutions. Steven Heydemann has noted how exposure to, and participation in, large-scale warfare reconfigured institutional structures and state capacities while profoundly affecting state–society relations and modes of governance.[97] The remaining chapters in this book investigate the multiple dimensions of the conflicts in the Middle East during the war, beginning with a detailed examination of the campaigns themselves.

2

MILITARY CAMPAIGNING IN THE MIDDLE EAST

The First World War was a global conflict. The fighting that originated in south-eastern Europe at the end of July 1914 rapidly internationalised and spread to all corners of the globe. Networks of military and diplomatic agreements drew in non-European regional powers such as Japan and (after April 1917) the United States. Meanwhile, the European belligerents' imperial possessions became zones of major conflict and sites of contestation for control of strategic resources and access routes across the globe. Although the extra-European campaigns were smaller in scale than the giant offensives on the Western and Eastern Fronts, they nevertheless had a momentous impact on the host societies involved. This occurred as the logistical demands of industrialised warfare clashed with the largely pre-industrial terrain in which the fighting took place.

This chapter sets out some of the contextual parameters that influenced military campaigning in the Middle East during the First World War. It leads into the following section of four chapters that provide a detailed narrative of the military campaigns in the Middle East. These encompass the campaigns in the Dardanelles, Egypt and Palestine, and Mesopotamia, in addition to the succession of battles between Ottoman and Russian armies in the Caucasus, and the smaller yet still significant fighting in Persia. Campaigning in these diverse theatres continued for the entire duration of the war and even outlasted – by one day in Mesopotamia – the declaration of the Armistice in November 1918. It goes beyond a narrow focus on military history to contextualise the campaigns in the broader course of the First World War and its strategic direction, and integrate them with the processes of political change, economic transformation and social upheaval that afflicted each belligerent in different ways.

In this contextual chapter, the focus is on the myriad logistical, administrative and ecological challenges of campaigning in the Middle East, where the majority of resources had to be brought in and manhandled across large distances usually devoid of existing transportation or infrastructural links. It leads into Part II of this book, which contains four chapters that chart the course of the campaigns in detail and demonstrate the near-total impact of modern warfare on host societies and local communities. Together, they set the scene for the chapters in Part III, which investigate the domestic political, economic and societal implications as well as the impact of the campaigns on host communities and societies. Furthermore, this chapter also describes how the role of India became integrated into the Middle East campaigns, as the administrative and logistical hub for the British war effort in the Middle East, paving the way for the Raj to become the security guarantor for the region after 1919.

The military campaigns in the Middle East tend to be examined in isolation from each other and from area-studies and disciplines such as comparative politics or international relations. Yet the fighting involved enormous quantities of man- and animal-power on all sides, and greatly distorted existing patterns of political organisation and social and economic activity. With the exception of the Palestine campaign, they happened to take place in the geographically peripheral regions of the Ottoman Empire, where existing infrastructural and transportation links were at their weakest. This placed great additional strains on all warring participants, and the societies over which the campaigns were fought, to organise and extract the resources necessary to conduct and sustain the fighting.

The results of these campaigns also had profound geopolitical implications for the five empires involved, as well as for the regional system that emerged from the post-war settlement. This notwithstanding, existing literature lacks a general history of the Middle East during the First World War that emphasises the many interconnections – military, logistical, socio-political and economic, among other more intangible ideational linkages – that bound the different zones of fighting together. (In a short history of the First World War published in the *Seminar Studies in History* series and intended to provide a 'concise and reliable introduction to complex events and debates', the campaigns outside Europe were ignored altogether, with three pages on Gallipoli the sole indication that fighting of any sort occurred beyond the European fronts.)[1]

Thus, the account of the campaigns presented in this section focuses on the administrative and logistical factors critical to their outcome as much as on the evolution of strategy and tactics. It explores the linkages between the campaigns in the Middle East and broader strategic developments, and assesses how central (or peripheral) were the campaigns to policy-makers in the imperial metropolises. Meeting the logistical requirements of the campaigns greatly strained scarce shipping capacities, and a network of extra-European sources of supply developed to meet them. No less important were the ecological dimensions of conflict, particularly in the harsh terrain over which much of the fighting took place. Here, the relative absence of roads or railways magnified the difficulties of supplying, transporting and sustaining the military forces, and underscored the logistical challenges of mobilising and extracting local resources from already impoverished host communities.

MILITARY CAMPAIGNING IN THE MIDDLE EAST

Societal exposure to – and participation in – the military campaigns in the Middle East further intersected with two powerful external forces. These were the weakening of the Ottoman and Russian Empires and the intensifying rivalry between competing British, French and local nationalists' visions for the future organisation of the region. As these processes of change interacted with each other, they created the macro-parameters that ultimately reshaped the political structure of the Middle East. Moreover, the contours of the wartime necessities of mobilisation deepened and widened the reach of the state and its extractive demands. That the states involved were primarily colonial implantations added a further complicating layer to the impact of the war on society. Although this is explored in much greater detail in subsequent chapters, it nevertheless must be borne in mind when considering the impact – and legacies – of the military campaigning.

Beginning with a general overview of the physical and logistical difficulties of campaigning in the diverse theatres in the Middle East, this chapter explores the challenges of conducting complex military operations in a forbidding host environment. Individual sub-sections focus on the ecological aspects of war, its logistical and administrative dimensions, and the strain they placed on local resources of man- and animal-power. It ends with a section detailing the role of India in acting as an organisational and resources base for the major British military incursions into Mesopotamia and Palestine. These set the context for the following chapter's examination of each conflict in the Middle East during the war: the Caucasus, Egypt and the Western Desert, the Dardanelles, Palestine, Mesopotamia and Persia. A number of important cross-cutting themes emerge from the foregoing analysis. These include the importance of utilising local resources to resolve the supply constraints posed by shortages of shipping, the creation of more authoritarian forms of state control necessary to mobilise and extract these resources, and the ways that the experience of conflict began to reformulate relations between states and societies throughout the region.

The challenges of campaigning in the Middle East

The conduct of warfare in the Middle Eastern theatres was complicated by multiple challenges. Chief among them was the gap between the voracious demands of modern armies and the low levels of existing resources available to military – and civilian – planners. This meant that in the initial stages of the campaigns all stores and supplies had to be brought in as very little was procurable locally.[2] It also meant that an uneasy balance needed to be struck between civilian and military demands for scarce local resources, particularly as the division of the Middle East into war zones cut across and disrupted existing trade routes and economic hinterlands. These factors greatly magnified the strain on the logistical networks that connected the military units to their base depots, often over vulnerable lines of communications extending over hundreds of miles. So did the relative paucity of roads and railways in the Middle East and the concentration of the Ottoman Empire's limited industrial resources in Istanbul and its vicinity, hundreds of kilometres away from the battlefronts to its east and south-east. Similar constraints faced the Russian and British armies operating far from their logistical bases which, in the case of the latter, were located more than 2,500 kilometres distant in India until substantial utilisation of local resources could be developed in the areas that came under occupation in Palestine and Mesopotamia.[3]

Emphasising the interlocking logistical and operational dimensions of conflict makes it possible to see the frequency with which this crucial link in the chain broke down. In his *War Memoirs,* wartime British Prime Minister David Lloyd George vividly recalled how Douglas Haig, commander of the British Expeditionary Force on the Western Front between 1915 and 1918, presented an update on the plans to attack the Germans at Ypres to a meeting of the War Policy Committee in June 1917: making 'a dramatic use of both his hands to demonstrate how he proposed to sweep up the enemy – first the right hand brushing along the surface irresistibly, and then came the left, his outer finger ultimately touching the German frontier with the nail across'.[4] Although embellished retrospectively to suit Lloyd George's self-serving objectives, the description does illustrate the temptation for politicians and generals to underestimate, or, still worse, ignore, the on-the-ground challenges and realities of military campaigning, especially in the more difficult and varied terrain of the Middle East. Civilian and military planners additionally faced a steep learning curve as they struggled to adapt the new – and often unfamiliar – requirements of large-scale warfare to the specific settings of the Middle Eastern campaigns.

Climate and ecology

Climatic and ecological factors played a critical role in determining the success or failure of military operations in the Middle East. The low margin of subsistence and limited amount of physical infrastructure such as roads, railways or industrial capacity meant that they became symbiotically connected to logistical and operational capabilities. This notwithstanding, these factors were regularly disregarded in the planning and execution of the campaigns, and their significance has often been overlooked in subsequent studies. An early case in point was a book published in November 1917 entitled *Topography and Strategy in War.* In it, the author set out to explain 'the interesting relationship between inanimate Nature and the science of war' as 'the role played by land forms in plans of campaign and movement of armies is no less important today than in the past'. It nevertheless focused solely on the European fronts to the total exclusion of the Middle East and all other non-European theatres.[5]

In the Caucasus, the region around Sarikamis, where much of the initial fighting in 1914-15 took place, exemplified both the ecological challenges involved, as well as the failure to take them into account adequately when planning military operations. Topographically situated in a valley between two high mountain ranges, the zone of operations was remote from road and railway connections and other lines of communication. Moreover, it was subject to extremely harsh winter conditions, with heavy snows and temperatures plunging to minus 30 degrees centigrade. Yet large-scale fighting between the Russian and Ottoman armies commenced in late November 1914 and lasted through to early January 1915, during which period advancing Russian forces found 30,000 frozen bodies in and around Sarikamis alone. The leading British military historian of the First World War, Hew Strachan, rightly observes that 'it was the terrain and the weather, and the failure to plan for these, not fighting the Russians that broke the Turkish 3rd army'.[6]

Elsewhere, similar issues manifested themselves in different ways. In the largely desert terrain of Mesopotamia and Egypt, climatic difficulties arose primarily from the extreme heat, rather than cold, although freezing conditions proved a hindrance in the Judean hills in the advance through Palestine to Jerusalem in December 1917. In Mesopotamia, the advance of British and imperial forces northwards from Basra towards Baghdad began in April 1915 and continued throughout the summer heat. Similarly in Egypt, their advance eastwards from the Suez Canal through Sinai to Palestine in 1916 only began in earnest in June, with a major skirmish with Ottoman forces occurring at Romani in August. A letter written home from a British officer in the Camel Transport Corps vividly described the effects of a march undertaken during the heat of the day in Sinai in July 1916: 'nearly every Englishman and scores of natives got sunstroke and many died, both men and camels…It was a pitiful sight, the poor devils fainting with thirst, heat and wariness, falling out or plodding on blindly.'[7] These difficulties later assumed a new form, as operational setbacks in both campaigns for a time dictated the place and timing of further operations. This was most evident in the three British-led attempts to relieve its besieged garrison in Kut (in Mesopotamia) between January and April 1916.

Problems of terrain were a further complicating factor in the Egyptian and Mesopotamian campaigns owing to the near-total lack of infrastructure in the desert. In Egypt, the advance across the Sinai Peninsula took the Egyptian Expeditionary Force away from the Suez Canal and its associated communications and supply lines. The soft and sandy desert soil presented a particular challenge as it initially proved impassable for wheeled transport unless fitted with special wooden blocks called pedrails.[8] Prior to the completion of the desert railway from the Canal base at Qantara to the border town of El Arish in February 1917, this created a dependency on camel transport for supplying and maintaining the advanced positions in the Sinai Peninsula. Reliance on camels extended to water supplies, as local water sources were virtually non-existent east of the post at Katia only 28 miles from the Suez Canal, and completely inadequate for a large force of any kind.[9]

By contrast, in Mesopotamia the line of advance followed the route of the Euphrates and Tigris rivers, as they provided the sole route of penetration for invading British-led forces. However, the early operations conducted by the Mesopotamian Expeditionary Force were severely constrained by the paucity of information available in India (the operational and administrative base for the campaign until 1916) on the hydrological and navigable condition of the rivers. British–Indian planners were taken by surprise when the Euphrates proved too shallow to be navigable by military craft. Meanwhile on the Tigris, they only belatedly realised that 'the method of navigation and type of craft required are quite unique and unlike anything employed on the inland waterways of India'.[10]

Climate and terrain intersected on numerous occasions during the campaigns. The Mesopotamian rivers experienced strong seasonal variations in depth and strength of current. Melting snows upriver caused widespread spring flooding, yet the summer heat led the rivers to fall to a depth of only 4-5 feet in the autumn. These placed important constraints on strategic, tactical and operational movements throughout 1915 and early 1916. A British official stationed in Basra graphically captured the scale of the problem as he described how the annual spring flood transformed the alluvial soil into 'a particularly glutinous kind of mud…in which cars and carts stick fast, and horses and camels slide in every direction'.[11]

Conversely, the advance upriver towards Baghdad in 1915 occurred between September and November, when the Tigris was at its lowest, and most unsuited to the river craft that provided the primary logistical line to the supply bases in Basra. In early 1916, adverse weather played a direct role in all three operations to relieve the besieged British–Indian garrison at Kut al-Amara. The urgency of the situation dictated that operations take place without regard for climatic or ecological conditions. Consequently, the relief operations took place during the height of the spring floods, and were further hampered by heavy rain. The official British eyewitness to the Mesopotamia campaign, Edmund Candler, wrote that after the failure of the first attempt in January 1916, 'there was a freezing wind and the wounded lay in pools of rain and flooded marsh all night; some were drowned; others died of exposure'. Later, in April 1916, the third attempt occurred in conditions in which 'the water was clean across our front six inches deep, with another six inches of mud…the second-line of trenches was knee-deep in water; behind it there was a network of dugouts and pits into which we foundered deeply'.[12]

British forces made similar errors of judgement with regard to climatic and ecological factors in Palestine in 1917-18. Logistical and administrative reorganisation meant that the advance northwards from Gaza towards Jerusalem did not begin until 31 October 1917. The late season meant that the troops, their support personnel and animal transport suffered greatly from freezing rain and wintry conditions as they passed through the Judean hills in November and December. Appalling weather nearly derailed the advance as tracks and roads became impassable, and many men and animals fell victim to exposure and frostbite. Conditions were exacerbated by the fact that the soldiers and labourers lacked appropriate cover or winter clothing, and a contemporary observer marvelled that the Egyptian labour units 'did not desert in a body to the enemy. They could hardly have been worse off in Turkish captivity.'[13]

At Gallipoli, the failure of the initial Anglo-French naval attempt to force its way through the narrow Strait of the Dardanelles and make its triumphant way to Istanbul meant that a land attack had hurriedly to be prepared. Between April 1915 and January 1916, a patchwork of isolated beachheads served as the jumping-off points for successive British and Anzac (Australian and New Zealand Army Corps) offensives against Ottoman positions on the high ground overlooking the beaches. One such landing (X beach in Cape Helles), for example, consisted of a strip of sand 200 metres long and 10 metres wide. Lacking land-borne communications and mutually supporting lines of supply, the small beachheads rapidly became clogged with jetties, encampments, makeshift field hospitals, improvised forward headquarters and supply depots. Furthermore, the steep cliffs offered the Ottomans a vantage-point from which to pour down fire on the beachheads from up to three sides.[14] Ellis Ashmead-Bartlett, the outspoken war correspondent attached to the campaign, later wrote that 'No army has ever found itself dumped in a more impossible or ludicrous position, shut in on all sides by hills, and having no point from which it can debouch for an attack, except by climbing up them.'[15] Forced by necessity to campaign in this inhospitable terrain, and worn out by military fatigue that affected the Ottoman forces just as much as the British and Anzac troops, the campaign ended with a violent thunderstorm in late November that flooded both sides' trenches and positions, and an intense blizzard that inflicted thousands of casualties through frostbite and exposure. The ferocity of the wintry weather played a significant role in forcing the issue of evacuation in the minds of senior British civilian and military leaders, and led to the remarkably successful pullback in December 1915 and January 1916.[16]

Campaigning in hostile terrain was not, of course, unique to the Middle Eastern zones of combat. The fighting that took place in East Africa imposed physical and medical hardships on combatants and non-combatants that arguably exceeded those in any other theatre of war.[17] In Europe, the British offensives in Flanders in the autumn of 1917 provide a particularly vivid example of the ecological and climatic challenges in other sectors. Nevertheless, the fighting on the Western Front took place in an industrialised context. This existing infrastructure facilitated the mass production of goods that supplied and transported the military machinery up to the battlefront, which (instead) is where problems began to mount. In the Middle East, the difficulties of conducting an industrialised war, in which motorised transport, heavy artillery and aircraft gradually assumed greater prominence, magnified many times the logistical and administrative complexities. These challenges hampered operational fluidity and held back the possibilities for speed and tactical manoeuvre offered by the otherwise more open terrain.[18]

Logistics and administration

The challenges described above magnified the already immense logistical challenges posed by the scale and complexity of mass, industrialised warfare. Works by John Lynn and Martin van Creveld have added important detail to the logistical dimensions of industrialised conflict. Lynn examined the rapid technological changes brought about by the industrial revolution in Europe and North America in the nineteenth century. These, he argued, transformed 'both the means of transport and the items consumed' and 'redefined modern logistics' and, with it, the nature of modern warfare.[19] Meanwhile, van Creveld suggested that the First World War revolutionised the concept of logistics as machine-produced goods replaced food and fodder as the main items of consumption. This created new dependencies on factories and rail- and road-based lines of supply and transportation, effectively tying the armies to their logistical networks.[20]

Numerous factors complicated and magnified the logistical and administrative difficulties facing belligerents in the Middle Eastern theatres of war. On a 'human resources' level, the campaigns in the Middle East were very much secondary to the central focus of the war in Europe. This was as true of the Ottoman Empire, for whom developments in Palestine and Mesopotamia did not pose the same regime threat as the fighting in the south-eastern Balkans, as it was for the French, British and Russians. For this reason, the military personnel despatched to the Middle East were frequently inferior in quality to the elite resources sent to the main fronts. In 1917-18, for example, the Ottoman high command starved the Palestine and Mesopotamia fronts of resources as their attention turned to the opportunities for pan-Turanian expansion in the Caucasus and Persia following Russia's exit from the war.[21] This extended to the non-combatant and administrative support as well. For their part, British officials regarded the Indian Expeditionary Force which arrived in Basra in November 1914 as containing units unfit for European service, as well as being devoid of any forms of land transport.[22]

These problems were compounded by the ecological and climatic issues described in the previous section. The scarce availability of local resources at the onset of military operations placed great strain on logistical machines to supply and transport the military forces. So, too, did the tools of industrialised warfare, which greatly increased the demands on the cadres of local man- and animal-power, and food and fodder initially required to construct the lines of communication and supply. In addition to the relative absence of roads or railways (which meant that the majority of supplies initially had to be carried into theatre), the creation of transportation networks added greatly to demands on local resources, as the construction material also had to be manhandled into place over long distances and harsh terrain.

An example of the difficulties facing combatants might be found in Ottoman attempts to supply their forces operating in the Caucasus and Mesopotamia. Both regions were as far from Istanbul and the industrial centre of the empire as possible. Their peripheral status was further complicated by the underdeveloped railway network which barely extended beyond modern-day Turkey (with branch lines to Damascus and northern Palestine, and the famous Medina narrow-gauge railway). This meant that the Ottoman troops fighting the British–Indian armies in Mesopotamia and the Russians in the Caucasus were separated by up to 400 miles of desert and mountain respectively from their nearest railhead. As with other combatants in the Middle East, the Ottoman forces therefore relied on local man- and animal-power and – on the rivers of Mesopotamia – on primitive river craft constructed, as they had been for centuries, from animal hides.[23]

British logistics were complicated by the need to meet the burgeoning demands of simultaneous campaigning in Gallipoli, Salonika, Mesopotamia and (from 1916) Palestine. Egypt and India developed into the primary supply and administrative hubs for the campaigns. These multiple requirements stretched the limited existing resources of the Force in Egypt and the Army of India to their limits as they assumed responsibility for maintaining the maritime security of the British Empire. The Government of India raised and dispatched four Indian Expeditionary Forces to France, East Africa, Egypt and Basra between August and December 1914. This exhausted its pre-war reserves of officers, transport cadres and other non-combatant branches such as medical personnel, and British civil and military leaders in India feared that the Indian Army's organisational and logistical capacity was nearing breaking-point. Indeed, in March 1915 the Viceroy of India, Lord Hardinge, felt that his military resources had been denuded to the extent that 'India was left with practically no margin to meet unforeseen circumstances'. He thus informed London that India had done its duty to the empire and added that 'it is quite impossible... to do more'.[24]

In Egypt, the rapid build-up of British, Indian and Anzac forces in late 1914 and early 1915 similarly threatened to overwhelm existing resources. The haphazard arrival of military units played havoc with the small British garrison and its modest network of logistical and administrative facilities, while in 1915 the planning for the campaigns at Gallipoli and (subsequently) Salonika further increased the sense of looming chaos. Personnel acting on behalf of the Mediterranean Expeditionary Force (fighting at Gallipoli) and the Force in Egypt competed against each other for resources on the open market.[25] This confusion impacted the conduct of operations at Gallipoli as the lack of suitable deep-water ports in the eastern Aegean meant that Alexandria became its main supply base. An advanced base was established at the port of Mudros on the Aegean island of Lemnos and 120 transport ships maintained the force of 75,000 men in rations, ammunition and reinforcements of troops and pack animals.[26]

Matters reached a head as the Anglo-French failure to break through the Strait led to a stalemate at Gallipoli (discussed further in Chapter 4). A major new history of the campaign published in 2011 by the Imperial War Museum's oral historian, Peter Hart, noted how it consisted of 'troops from all over the world, thrown together with no planning or forethought...with the various units broken up on different ships and their equipment randomly intertwined below decks'.[27] Considerable difficulties confronted commanders in supplying the five beachheads with personnel, ammunition, foodstuffs and water stocks. By July 1915, the commander of the Mediterranean Expeditionary Force, General Sir Ian Hamilton, was 'in despair' at the lack of labour and insufficient lighters to unload the transport ships from Egypt. This, he wrote, meant that 'ships arrive carrying things urgently required, and then, before they can be unloaded, sail away again...with all the stuff on board'. He added that 'there are ships containing engineering plant that have been five times out here and five times have gone away again without anyone being able to unload them owing to want of lighters'.[28] Hamilton confessed to Sir John Cowans, Quartermaster-General at the War Office in London, that 'I worry just as much over things behind me as I do over the enemy in front of me'.[29]

The conduct of large-scale industrial warfare across the large open spaces of sea, desert and mountainous terrain of the Middle East and Caucasus underscore the uneasy relationship between the logistical requirements of modern conflict and the more 'traditional' and primitive means of supplying them. This adds an important qualification to van Creveld's assertion of a logistical revolution that took place during the First World War. On the contrary, the campaigns in the Middle East remained highly reliant on local resources – of food and fodder as well as manpower and animals – until very late in the war. Notably, the belated introduction of mechanised transport and substantial road- and railway networks in 1917-18 did not lessen dependence on these items. Instead, they required significant additional labour to construct and maintain them, thereby demonstrating how industrial requirements actually augmented (rather than replaced) demands on traditional resources.

Logistical requirements were interlinked with military demands on locally produced resources necessary to sustain the war effort of each belligerent. The logistics of industrialised warfare as it evolved required combatant states to out-produce as well as out-fight their enemy. During the war, the penetrative power of the wartime state expanded (at different paces) as grand strategy gradually encompassed the mobilisation of national economic, commercial and human (non-combatant) resources. In the European powers this built upon existing bureaucratic and institutional structures that provided the framework for moves towards forms of 'total war'. A different challenge faced civil and military planners away from the consolidated structures of European states. Both political constraints and industrial limitations significantly restricted the organisational capabilities of the Ottoman and Russian states as well as the Anglo-Indian imperial system as it evolved after the Great Rebellion of 1857.

Important contextual factors inhibited the preparedness for – and conduct of – military operations in the Middle East, although Erickson has emphasised how Ottoman soldiers (if not their support services) were of a very high calibre and demonstrated their resilience throughout the war, often in appalling conditions.[30] Ottoman, Russian and British–Indian policy-makers all faced shortcomings in their ability to organise and extract societal resources, a difficulty made more pronounced by the location of the campaigns in the most peripheral regions of the Ottoman Empire. A small local manufacturing base hampered Ottoman production of war materials such as pig iron, steel, chemicals and refined petroleum products. Moreover, the Empire's sole gunpowder factory, shell and cartridge factory, and cannon and small arms foundry were all located in the vicinity of Istanbul. Consequently, the war material needed to be transported across hundreds of kilometres of poor roads and incomplete railway networks to the battlefronts in the east.[31] In addition, the more immediate danger to the empire posed by the campaigns at the Dardanelles and in Macedonia meant they took priority over Mesopotamia and Palestine in 1915-16;

while, following the Russian withdrawal from the war in 1917, official attention turned to the possibility of making territorial gains in the Caucasus.[32] Nevertheless, in spite of all these constraints, the Ottoman Empire managed to sustain an albeit-faltering war effort for four long years, repel the Gallipoli attacks in 1915, and tie up very large numbers of Russian and British forces in the Caucasus, Palestine and Mesopotamia. As the Turkish economic historian Sevket Pamuk has noted, 'despite all these shortcomings, it is remarkable that the Ottoman war effort did not experience a total collapse' as 'the Ottoman side managed to stay in the war and continue to hold its own on most fronts until the end in 1918'.[33]

The Russian war effort was also focused elsewhere. Battles on an enormous scale took place in East Prussia against the Germans and in Galicia against the Austro-Hungarian Empire. By early 1915, Russia had lost more than one million soldiers and much of its industrial and agricultural heartland, as well as 20 million inhabitants, lay under enemy occupation. Further battles in the summer and autumn meant that one and a half million soldiers were in enemy captivity, to say nothing of those killed and wounded, with 90,000 surrendering on one day in August 1915 alone.[34] It was against this backdrop of an existential threat to its very survival that the Russian war effort in the Middle East and Caucasus unfolded. These areas had been considered secondary in Russian pre-war military planning and were viewed through the prism of internal security rather than conflict with the Ottoman Empire or Persia. A major local complication was simmering: a centre–periphery tension which escalated into a violent backlash in 1916 by Muslim communities in Central Asia against conscription into the Russian Army.[35]

Mobilisation in India was held back by a set of political constraints imposed by the British authorities and reinforced in the years after the 1857 rebellion. The mutineers' attempt to capture the Ferozepore arsenal alerted British officials to the dangers of creating a military–industrial complex in India. Furthermore, the Peel Committee established after 1857 to examine measures to prevent another mutiny breaking out recommended that the post-mutiny Indian Army be confined to internal security duties requiring small quantities of low-grade weaponry.[36] These decisions considerably hampered the expansion of the arms industry in India for the next half-century. British policy prioritised Indian de-industrialisation and conspicuously under-utilised its abundant natural resources and manpower. This ensured that India lacked skilled labourers, technicians, supervisors and managers, in addition to engineering and metallurgy factories and machine-building facilities, as virtually all plant, equipment, stores and skilled personnel had been brought in from abroad before 1914.[37]

British insecurity about its position in India therefore translated into a fear of training an indigenous pool of military and technological expertise among Indians. Armament factories were particularly affected and consequently their output remained tiny, and the Indian Army remained reliant on Britain for technical expertise and machinery. In its year of peak production in 1908-9, the Ferozepore arsenal, the largest in India, produced a mere 12 artillery pieces and 22,000 shells.[38]

This introduced an additional layer of complexity into the logistical machinery as many items required for Mesopotamia simply could not be obtained in India but had to be ordered (and shipped) from the United Kingdom first. In the case of river craft desperately needed for Basra in 1915-16, the resulting delay in delivery had dire consequences for the Indian Expeditionary Force as it struggled (and failed) to relieve the besieged garrison at Kut al-Amara.[39]

Local resources and the war at sea

The shortcomings in industrial resources and extractive capabilities listed above took on greater significance as the fighting dragged on. Any early aspirations that the war might be short were quickly disabused, as early as September 1914 in the case of the belligerents on the Western Front. By the time the Ottoman Empire entered the war on 2 November, the First Battle of Ypres was well under way, signalling the end of mobile operations and the solidifying of entrenched positions in France and Flanders, while the battles on the Eastern Front assumed a still greater order of magnitude. Thereafter, the launching of submarine warfare and economic blockade preyed on vulnerabilities in the lengthening lines of communications and supply as the war spread to the Middle East and Africa. This placed a premium on sourcing locally-produced resources and mobilisation of man- and animal-power in order to alleviate the strain on overstretched shipping and land-borne transportation networks.

A major recent volume on the economics of the First World War emphasised the significance of economic factors to the outcome of the conflict. Stephen Broadberry and Mark Harrison argued that 'the outcome of global war was primarily a matter of the levels of economic development of each side and the scale of resources that they wielded'.[40] This built on earlier pioneering research by Avner Offer and Christopher Wrigley into the economic dimension of the war. Offer highlighted the existential aspect of maintaining shipping routes and sea lanes for the imperial powers, particularly Britain, for whom 'the transport and supply of land forces, even across the Channel, to say nothing of the long hauls across the Atlantic and Indian oceans, depended on the Royal Navy's capacity to secure them'.[41] This was a logical extension of developments in the international trading system before 1914 that internationalised the production and distribution of commodities such as foodstuffs (particularly grain) according to the principle of comparative advantage. Thus, Wrigley noted how the war disrupted the relationship between the European industrialised 'centre' of the international economic system and the comparatively underdeveloped 'peripheral' areas.[42]

Economic dislocation had local and regional, as well as international, repercussions, and its impacts were magnified considerably in areas where the margin of subsistence was already thin. These included the cutting off of intra- and inter-regional trade routes as the Ottoman Empire and the Caucasus became divided into warring spheres of influence, the effect of economic blockade and imposition of massive demands on local resources arising from the presence of thousands of additional military mouths to feed, and competition between overlapping campaigning and agricultural calendars for labourers and animals. An uneasy balance thus developed between civilian and military demands for resources. This did not leave much room for error and the fragile equilibrium broke down on numerous occasions during the war, as will be discussed in detail in later chapters. The famine that struck Syria, Lebanon and parts of Palestine in 1915-16 was the most pronounced example of the economic dislocation caused by the war. However, by 1918 people throughout the region, from North Africa to Persia and India, were facing conditions of real hardship and acute starvation.

Destabilising combinations of these factors interacted in different ways to hit individuals and communities throughout the region. Their impact was compounded by the difficulties of transporting supplies to (and between) the battlefronts throughout the war. As the previous sections made clear, the relative absence of transport infrastructure or industrial resources in the Middle Eastern battlefronts meant that almost all supplies and reinforcements initially had to be brought into position over long lines of communication. British supplies for the campaigns in Mesopotamia and Palestine had to navigate either the Mediterranean (for supplies coming from the United Kingdom) or Arabian Sea routes (for supplies from India). Ships transiting the Mediterranean were vulnerable to enemy U-boats (leading in mid-1916 to the temporary re-routing of transports to the much longer Cape route), while shipping from India for Mesopotamia was complicated by the seasonal Arabian Sea monsoon as well as wholly inadequate port facilities in Basra until 1917.[43] The Ottomans also depended greatly on seaborne supplies as major shortcomings in road and rail-based infrastructure meant that the bulk of internal and external transportation and trade had been carried by sea before 1914.[44]

The early stages of the campaigns suffered from bottlenecks created by insufficient port facilities to receive and send on all the logistical requirements of modern warfare. Previous sections alluded to the difficulties of landing stores at the Gallipoli beachheads. Elsewhere, a major base, supply depot and trans-shipment hub was constructed at Qantara, on the Suez Canal, to service the British forces in Sinai and Palestine, while in Mesopotamia, a visiting British delegation to Basra found, as late as 1916, that harbour installations were 'very remarkably absent' from the major base for the British–Indian struggles at Kut al-Amara.[45] The initial absence of wharves and jetties meant that transports lined the Shatt al-Arab awaiting their turn while stores were first unloaded onto lighters and then a second time onto the shore, and – in many cases – further loading onto scarce river craft for transport upriver. This labour-intensive and time-consuming process was made more difficult by the innumerable creeks punctuating the shoreline and hindering lateral onshore communications. Annual flooding each spring constituted a further obstacle to port development, leading one contemporary chronicler to describe 'the familiar Mesopotamian conditions...while there was too much water for the Army there was not enough for the Navy'.[46]

As the war continued and the campaigns expanded in scope, the nature of the shipping problem evolved. From an issue of initial physical constraint it developed into one of insufficient capacity. This occurred as requirements for manpower, materiel and other resources continued to increase while conditions for international shipping worsened. These intersecting challenges reflected the rapid 'mission creep' in the extra-European campaigns as they expanded from initial 'sideshows' into major military commitments. By 1916, all belligerents felt the impact of these diverging trends, with routes through the Mediterranean especially hard-hit. German and Austro-Hungarian U-boats operating from seven bases along the Adriatic coastline wrought havoc on Entente merchant and naval vessels plying between Marseilles and Taranto (in Italy) and Egypt. During the last quarter of 1915, a mere four U-boats sank 21,000 tons of shipping, but poor liaison among British, French and Italian naval commands, and a lack of available convoy escort destroyers, complicated effective responsive measures.[47] In December 1915, the Chief of the Imperial General Staff in London, General Archibald Murray (and soon to be Commander-in-Chief of the Egyptian Expeditionary Force), drew the attention of Secretary of State for War Lord Kitchener to the submarine menace in the Mediterranean. In bemoaning the lack of coordination between the British, French and Italian navies in the Mediterranean, Murray quipped that 'all I know is that there are more Naval Commanders-in-Chief knocking around here than there are submarines!!!'[48]

Shipping difficulties worsened considerably from 1916 onwards. British, French and Italian shipping losses in the Mediterranean escalated in 1916 to a peak of 113 ships and 248,018 tons of cargo between October and December as inter-allied cooperation remained slack.[49] In December 1916, the British General Staff submitted a memorandum which baldly acknowledged that in Egypt 'we are faced with a situation which amounts practically to a break-down in our shipping arrangements… we have, in fact, reached a stage where the available shipping is inadequate to meet requirements'.[50] At an Anglo-French conference in London later in the month, Britain's First Sea Lord, Admiral John Jellicoe, then warned of great difficulties in finding sufficient merchant shipping to supply the forces in Salonika and Egypt. He added that it was even harder to provide escorts for transport and troop ships, and that these difficulties made it nearly impossible to consider any increase of force in either theatre.[51]

In January 1917 the German Chancellor, Theobald von Bethmann Hollweg, announced the beginning of a strategy of unrestricted submarine warfare. This built on earlier developments in the war at sea. German U-boats had targeted commercial shipping entering and leaving British waters with increasing intensity since early in 1915. The sinking of the RMS *Lusitania* off the Irish coastline on 7 May 1915 was the highest profile early casualty, though it raised questions as to what constituted a legitimate target as the liner was carrying substantial quantities of small arms ammunition destined for the British war economy, in addition to its 1,959 passengers and crew. Among the 1,198 deaths were 128 Americans and the sinking caused outrage in the United States and a severe deterioration of relations with Germany, although not to the point of a declaration of war.[52] German military pressure for a policy of unrestricted submarine activity increased throughout 1916 owing to the impact of the British blockade of German ports and the outcome of the Battle of Jutland on 31 May. Jutland demonstrated that the German High Seas Fleet was not strong enough to defeat the Royal Navy in a conventional battle, and that alternative methods would be required to attack the lines of supply to the British Isles.[53]

Although the implications of the German decision to launch unrestricted submarine warfare were felt most directly when the United States declared war on Germany in April 1917, it had important consequences for the campaigns in the Middle East. Entente shipping losses from the German–Austrian Mediterranean U-boat flotilla operating out of Pula (in modern-day Croatia) escalated in the first quarter of 1917. The amount of tonnage lost to the Mediterranean flotilla and submarine-laid mines rose from 78,541 tons in January to 105,670 tons in February before falling back to 61,917 tons in March and climbing steeply to peak at 254,911 tons in April 1917. Although losses subsequently fell back from this high-point owing to the emergence of countermeasures, the figures for May and June (170,626 and 164,299) remained two to three times higher than those of January to March.[54]

Specific countermeasures were identified at the four-power (British, French, Italian and Japanese) conference that took place in Corfu in late April 1917. These included recommendations that navigation occur at night along patrolled coastal routes wherever possible, along with greater protection for shipping through the belated deployment of convoys and escorts. Protective cover for merchant shipping and naval transports was especially important on the non-coastal routes that took ships into open water, most notably from Malta to Crete, Crete to Egypt, Malta to Egypt and Marseilles to Algiers.[55] Nonetheless, these took time to implement and came too late for the significant expansion in the Palestine and Mesopotamia campaigns, which also occurred in the spring of 1917. The increase in the combatant size and territorial scope of military operations in both theatres created new difficulties of supply and transportation already stretched to the limit. They hastened British moves towards maximising the use of local resources (both in the supply centres of Egypt and India and in the areas under occupation) to alleviate demands on shipping wherever possible.

In this context, the maximal development of resources available locally became a strategic objective. This was especially the case for the British (and Indian) war effort as the strain of supporting geographically disparate campaigns increased sharply. In addition to meeting the logistical requirements of the campaigns in Palestine and Mesopotamia, Britain and India also had to supply the forces in Salonika and East Africa as well. These burgeoning demands led the Quartermaster General at the War Office in London, Sir John Cowans, to urge in the summer of 1916 that local resources be utilised as much as possible.[56] The War Office also decided that India would become the supply base for all British and imperial forces east of Suez, and that Indian resources be utilised to meet Mesopotamian demands as far as possible.[57] Near simultaneously, officials in Britain urged their counterparts in Egypt to maximise their own resources of fodder to reduce demands for shipment of this bulky commodity to Sinai, Palestine and Mesopotamia.[58]

Nevertheless, the escalating demands for food and fodder and the imposition of large numbers of additional mouths to feed stretched resources to their limits. In Mesopotamia, Basra and its hinterland were hit hard by poor local harvests in 1912 and 1913. Substantial imports of rice and wheat from India averted a crisis but these ceased with the onset of war in 1914.[59] Elsewhere in the Ottoman Empire, successive poor harvests between 1914 and 1916 and a plague of locusts in 1915 led to conditions of severe famine afflicting the vilayets of Syria, Lebanon and Palestine. Their impact was magnified by the impact of predatory wartime demands for resources. Repressive Ottoman measures restricted the flow of food supplies to the region for fear that they would fall into enemy hands. Moreover, the extractive impact of Ottoman requisitioning of labour, draft animals, cattle and agricultural appliances for military use imposed further strains on the local civilian population, as did the internal displacement of peoples and the disruption to trading routes and patterns.[60]

The uneasy balance between civilian and military access to resources gradually broke down in the face of rising demand and faltering supply. A major complicating factor was the timing of the campaigning seasons each spring, which coincided with the spring harvest and peak demands for labour. Military demands for labour and draft animals thus interfered with rural labour markets and the agricultural cycle. Furthermore, in areas such as Egypt which had been drawn into international markets and commercialised agriculture, improvements to irrigation ensured that agriculture had become a year-round activity by 1914. Unlike in nineteenth-century demands for labour (such as the corvée), an agricultural 'off-season' no longer existed, while the opportunity cost of enlistment rose sharply in 1917 and 1918 as emerging shortages in rural labourers also drove up agricultural wage rates.[61]

In Russia, the strain posed by the campaigns against the Ottomans led to a much heavier regional imprint as the military authorities searched for new sources of manpower and local resources. This provoked a fierce backlash from the populations of Central Asia which had enjoyed a relatively high level of autonomy from centralised demands before 1914. In June 1916, a decree introducing conscription for military service coincided with the labour-intensive demands of the cotton harvest. This proved the tipping-point for an uprising of Kazakh, Uzbek and Kyrgyz rebels that built upon existing sources of wartime hardship and grievance. These included local peasant communities' discontent at shortages of manufactured goods and foodstuffs as well as military purchasing of horses at prices below market levels. Against this backdrop of escalating anger at local scarcities, the drafting of Muslims for military service against their co-religionists in the Ottoman Empire provided the spark that lit the tinderbox. The resulting uprising was brutally put down with between 250,000 and 500,000 people forcibly displaced and deported from their homes in 1916.[62]

The military footprint became more distinct in all theatres of war in 1917 and 1918, not only in the Middle East. A form of 'remobilisation' occurred in the United

Kingdom as the strategy evolved towards a form of 'total warfare' characterised by more directly interventionist state activity.[63] In France and Russia, rising social tensions led to mutiny and revolution respectively in 1917, while the impact of the blockade on German towns and cities tightened.[64] The political, economic and social costs of the fighting took an increasing toll on war-weary populations in every belligerent nation. Escalating food demonstrations occurred in Paris in May and June 1917 while food riots in the Italian city of Turin killed more than 500 people in August as the linkages between food and resource supplies and civilian morale became acutely clear to policy-makers. [65] Even in these European states, which enjoyed a degree of legitimate political authority that allowed them to make heavier demands on their citizenry, popular acquiescence was begin to reach breaking-point by 1917. In the very different circumstances of the colonial constructions in the Middle East, no such legitimacy existed to buttress these new extractive pressures. Instead, more predatory (and external) institutional structures were imposed to manage and regulate the mobilisation of resources.[66] Lacking social roots or the local legitimacy to reach down into society, a new dialectical narrative of resistance to power began to emerge, which will be discussed in detail in Chapter 8.

The role of India

Britain's campaigns in the Middle East reflected the strategic importance of maintaining its Indian Empire and the arteries of maritime routes and naval stations that sustained it. Chapter 1 described the wide range of military, economic and political connections that developed during the nineteenth century as the political economy of British India increasingly became linked to strategic developments in the Middle East. By 1914, therefore, an array of ideational and also institutional linkages imparted a degree of cohesion to Britain's imperial periphery, and constituted a reservoir of ties that facilitated and regulated the diffusion of ideas between the dispersed sites of empire. The career of Sir Evelyn Baring (later Lord Cromer) is a notable example of this trans-national network of governing mentalities, as his formative career experiences in India profoundly shaped his vision of rule in Egypt as Agent General from 1883 to 1907.[67] Another was Richard Meinertzhagen, who joined the Staff College at Quetta in 1913 and spent Christmas that year travelling through Mesopotamia. In a diary he published in 1960, he recalled how 'the Government of India asked me to collect information about road and river transport, what boats and animal transport are available, roads etc.'. He later gained some fame as an intelligence officer in the Palestine campaign in 1917.[68] Such connections became significant during the Great War as officials and officers from the imperial civil service and military in India (and Egypt) played key roles in conducting and administering the campaigns in Mesopotamia and Palestine respectively.

In the absence of any meaningful threat to India during the months following Britain's declaration of war on Germany on 4 August 1914, defence planners and strategists in London decreed that imperial interests could best be defended through restoring the balance of power in Europe. This would remove the threat to imperial lines of communications posed by German control over the Channel ports in the Low Countries. The decision underscored how the British Empire depended above all on the maintenance of its maritime supremacy and ability to project its naval power.[69] Accordingly, two Indian infantry divisions (the 3rd Meerut and 7th Lahore Divisions) were dispatched to France (via Egypt) in August 1914, where they played a vital role in stemming the German advance through France at the First Battle of Ypres in November.[70]

Between August and December 1914 the Government of India also assumed responsibility for raising and dispatching four Indian Expeditionary Forces. These sailed to East Africa, Egypt and Mesopotamia in addition to France. Their mobilisation was a response to emerging threats to Britain's maritime security as German cruisers interfered with the flow of men and munitions from the Dominions to Britain. In September 1914, three cruisers – the *Emden*, *Konigsberg* and *Karlsruhe* – played havoc with shipping in the Bay of Bengal, East Africa and Caribbean respectively, and delayed the transportation of troops from Australia and New Zealand as naval escorts had to be organised at short notice. Thus, the elimination of the network of German coaling and wireless stations in East and West Africa and the Atlantic became a short-term priority. By December 1914 this had been achieved through the hunting and sinking of the cruisers in the Indian Ocean and the defeat of the German Asiatic Squadron at the Battle of the Falkland Islands.[71]

India supplied the bulk of the troops and food supplies for these extra-European contingents. This represented a continuation of the Indian Army's pre-1914 function as a strategic imperial reserve.[72] Its new function became necessary in the autumn of 1914 for two reasons. The most urgent was Britain's reliance on imported foodstuffs, as detailed in the previous section, which rested on making the sea lanes safe from the threat of disruption. This was related to the second reason, which was to smooth the passage of troops, munitions and supplies from the empire to Britain and the European theatre of war. Crucial to this was safeguarding the security of the Suez Canal following the declaration of war with the Ottoman Empire in November 1914. In this context, the continued control of the Persian Gulf sheikhdoms to safeguard the strategic approaches to India meant that the maintenance of British supremacy in the broader Indian Ocean region became an important imperial objective.[73]

Nevertheless, India's capacity to contribute to the war effort was constrained in two significant ways. The first was that the Government of India remained responsible for funding the expansion of the Indian Army and the maintenance of its armies deployed overseas. While this spared the British exchequer of additional strain, it meant that military financing was held back by powerful assumptions among British governing elites concerning the need for a light-touch state in India. Tax revenues were kept at a very low rate (accounting for a mere 5-7 per cent of national income) and public expenditure also was subjected to the prevailing policy of fiscal conservatism.[74] Importantly, these policies continued into the first two years of the war even as military (and administrative) requirements on India grew exponentially, creating bottlenecks and a diverging gap between policy intent and capability that culminated in the debacle in Mesopotamia in 1916 (see Chapter 6).

This meshed with the second impediment that held back the mobilisation of Indian resources for the British campaigns in the Middle East, which was the legacy of decades of British policies to de-industrialise India before 1914. During this period, India was transformed gradually from being an exporter of manufactured goods, primarily textiles, to being a supplier of primary commodities and an import market for finished consumer goods. Partially done for reasons of 'national security' after the 1857 rebellion shook British rule in India to its core, and partially to protect British commercial enterprise, the net result was that India was denuded of indigenous skilled expertise and industrial capacity, both of which remained almost entirely reliant on British skilled workers for what amounted to the small 'military–industrial' complex that did exist in India in 1914.[75] It was only later in the war, in 1917 and 1918, that military exigency finally led to a sharp change in the structure of taxation and public expenditure in India, belatedly enabling the Government of India to raise and equip the mass armies of soldiers and labourers that formed the backbone of the Egyptian and Mesopotamian Expeditionary Forces and made possible the rapid advances of late 1918.

For these reasons India became interlinked with the British campaigns in the Middle East at multiple levels. Its wartime experience is therefore a part of this book, as decisions and events in India had immediate and serious implications for the conduct of the campaign in Mesopotamia, as well as for British military and civilian planners in Egypt and the territory that came under British control in Palestine. As with the contours of British influence in Egypt, the wartime processes of mobilisation and extraction of man- and animal-power and local resources required the colonial state hastily to expand its political footprint and penetrate much deeper into society. A re-working of state–society relations gradually occurred (in both India and Egypt) as the British civil and military authorities embedded themselves within local social organisation and interfered with existing structures and hierarchies of power. This took different forms in each case, reflecting the uneven exposure to centralised control – both British and Ottoman – prior to 1914, as well as the differing ways that British power and influence were structured and projected.

Overview of campaigning in Middle Eastern theatres

This chapter has provided an overview of the major contextual factors that framed the military campaigns in the Middle East during the First World War. Issues of climate and ecology, logistics and administration, and local resources and the war at sea interacted with each other to magnify the impact of the fighting on the local populations involved. So, too, did the mismatch between the voracious demands of modern industrialised warfare and the largely pre-industrial terrain in which the campaigns were fought. Moreover, the location of the fighting often at great distance from population centres meant that militaries were reliant on long and vulnerable lines of communication and supply. This increased their dependence upon locally produced resources yet also necessitated the mobilisation of large amounts of non-combatant man- and animal-power to maintain the military machines during the initial lack of motorised transport.

Part II of this book turns to the military campaigns themselves. It contains four chapters focusing on the regional experience during the war. The first (Chapter 3) examines the fighting between the Ottoman and Russian Empires, as the battles between 1914 and 1917 inflicted the great majority of all Ottoman casualties sustained during the entire war. Ottoman attention then shifted towards making pan-Turanian gains in the Caucasus following the Russian decision to withdraw from the war and the Treaty of Brest-Litovsk in March 1918. Chapter 4 explores the British-led campaign at the Dardanelles in 1915 and the decision to divert British and French forces to Salonika in October that year, where they remained until the break-out towards Istanbul in September 1918. The final two chapters in this section (5 and 6) focus on the two major British campaigns against the Ottoman Empire, in the Sinai Desert/Palestine and in Mesopotamia respectively. Both campaigns tied up Expeditionary Forces with ration strengths that exceeded 400,000 each, and had important ramifications for the contours of the post-war geopolitical settlement. As major military efforts, all the campaigns involved huge strains both on the imperial powers and, not least, on the host societies involved, where the experience of war-making became intertwined with that of state-making and the radical reconfiguring of patterns of local socio-political organisation and economic activity.

PART II

MILITARY OPERATIONS

3

THE CAUCASUS CAMPAIGNS

In the voluminous English-language literature on the First World War, comparatively little attention has been paid to the succession of large-scale battles between the Ottoman and Russian armies in the Caucasus. An otherwise excellent volume on 'new directions in First World War studies' published in 2011 does not, for instance, contain a single reference to the region or the campaign.[1] In part a reflection of the Anglophonic centricity of much of the historiography, the campaigns in the Caucasus additionally lacked the allure of fighting over holy and historic battlegrounds that fired the public imagination, then and ever since. Yet, the fighting in the Caucasus constituted the major drain on Ottoman military resources during the Great War and contributed to the 'grinding down' of its operational and manpower capabilities. Indeed, Malcolm Yapp has estimated that between November 1915 and February 1917, three-quarters of all Ottoman casualties were sustained in the Caucasus, leaving the Ottoman military machine much weakened when the British campaigns in Palestine and Mesopotamia increased in intensity in 1917-18.[2]

The Caucasus campaigns represented the clash of two empires which would not survive the Great War. It was magnified by historical animosity and competing claims for territory that spanned the Crimean War of 1853-6 and the Russo–Turkish War of 1877-8. Both in St Petersburg and in Istanbul, the imperial machinery mobilised and channelled immense resources to the renewal of the campaign against a familiar foe. The resulting battles were fought on an epic – and tragic – scale along a front more than 700 miles in length and pocked by high mountain ranges blanketed in snow and sub-freezing temperatures. Individual battles such as that at and around Sarikamis (22 December 1914 – 4 January 1915) have been described as 'one of the greatest military disasters of the twentieth century' as IX Corps of the Ottoman Third Army was utterly destroyed.[3]

Moreover, the significance of the struggle between the Russian and Ottoman Empires had consequences which transcended regional boundaries. It knitted together the fighting in the Balkans and the Middle East and also encompassed such profound issues as the Armenian genocide and the competing Russian, British, French and Ottoman visions for regional organisation. Towards the end of the war, with the Russian Empire in collapse and the Ottoman Empire in retreat, newly found petroleum considerations came to the fore in London. These motivated the extraordinary (in view of the diversion of increasingly scarce military resources) British drive to Baku and the Caspian Sea in September 1918. Thus, a campaign that started as a contest for regional hegemony between two imperial powers, and was characterised by battles that appeared to belong to a bygone era, eventually came to anticipate the oil-based reconfiguration of geopolitical interests that marked the subsequent evolution of policy in the Caucasus in the twentieth century.

Empires at war

The region extending from the Caucasus to Central Asia had long been a battleground between the Russian and Ottoman Empires. During the nineteenth century, the 'Eastern Question' was bound up with Russian designs on parts of the Ottoman Empire and its desire to exert control over its Christian communities and its religious sites in the Holy Land. The prospect of Russian intervention in Ottoman affairs threatened to upset the uneasy balance of European power as established by the Congress of Vienna in 1815. The tenuous equilibrium had been reaffirmed in June 1841 by the London Straits Convention, signed by the United Kingdom, France, Austria, Prussia and Russia, which closed the Bosporus and the Dardanelles to international warships, thereby blocking Russian access to the Mediterranean from its Black Sea ports. However, with the Ottoman Empire seemingly in terminal decline and known as 'the sick man of Europe', it soon became a flashpoint between the European powers, and led directly to the outbreak of the Crimean War in 1853. The conflict lasted three years as Britain and France sided with the Ottoman Empire to defend it against Russian encroachment. Especially heavy fighting occurred in the Caucasus as both the Russians and the Ottomans went on the offensive and sought to extend and entrench their influence in the region at the expense of the other

In the 1870s and continuing up until the outbreak of the Great War, the question of Ottoman weakness once again dominated European agendas. This occurred as rising nationalist tendencies among the empire's many ethnic minorities seemed to portend its political fragmentation and eventual collapse. Triggered by the Serbian and Greek revolutions in the first two decades of the nineteenth century, the era of national awakening rapidly spread beyond the Balkans. It included Mohamed Ali's pioneering modernisation and reforms in Egypt in the 1830s and 1840s, which created a specifically Egyptian consciousness in place of affinity with Ottoman norms and ideals. By the time of European intervention in Egypt after 1876, this new 'sub-Ottoman' Egyptian national feeling was palpable. The British occupation of 1882 stimulated further the emergence of a new sense of identity in what was still nominally a part of the Ottoman Empire. Contemporaneous awakenings also occurred in the

Levant and elsewhere in the empire's Arab territories as political ideologies interacted with the growth of an educated class and the emergence of a print culture.[4]

Rising national aspirations clashed with the Ottoman programme of reforms and modernisation. As described in Chapter 1, the *Tanzimat* (reorganisation) that began in 1839 and lasted until 1876 included an attempted recentralisation of Ottoman control over its outlying territories amid a more general overhaul of state and military structures. Simultaneous administrative reforms and improvements to methods of communication and transportation took place alongside efforts to broaden the narrow social base of the Ottoman regime. However, the reforms also had the effect of disrupting the uneasy balance between the Empire's Muslim and non-Muslim communities. Moreover, they were undermined by rampant levels of corruption and growing feelings of alienation as the realities of Ottoman control became more direct and visible.[5]

The combustible intersection of ethnic nationalism and imperial control accelerated in the 1870s. It centred on the Balkans and among the Slavic communities which possessed strong religious ties with Russia. Serbs living in the Ottoman provinces of Herzegovina and Bosnia rebelled in 1875-6 and were followed by Christian populations in the other Ottoman provinces in the Balkans. Most notable was the Bulgarian insurrection which began in April 1876 before being brutally suppressed by regular and irregular Ottoman military units. The accompanying reprisals and massacres galvanised political and public attention in Europe, with the veteran British politician William Gladstone denouncing 'the Bulgarian Horrors' and urging the British Government to withdraw its support for the empire. This had immediate political and diplomatic consequences as Britain refused to side with Istanbul in the resulting Russo-Turkish war that began in April 1877.

During the eleven-month conflict, which lasted until March 1878, the Russian armies succeeded in regaining territories in the Caucasus lost in the Crimean War. A two-pronged attack in the Balkans and the Caucasus led the Russian forces to the outskirts of Istanbul itself while retaking the provinces of Batum and Kars in eastern Turkey. Moreover, the Ottoman position in Europe crumbled and fragmented, with the resulting Treaty of San Stefano signed on 3 March 1878 recognising the independence of Serbia, Montenegro and Romania, and creating a pro-Russian Greater Bulgarian state. However, these radical changes to the configuration of power in the Balkans so upset the balance of equilibrium in the post-1815 European settlement that the German Chancellor Otto von Bismarck convened the Congress of Berlin in June and July 1878 to adjudicate the final frontiers. This notably revised the plans for a Greater Bulgaria by returning Macedonia to Ottoman control and assigning parts of Kosovo to Serbia and Montenegro rather than Bulgaria. The Kosovo issue was especially momentous, as described by Noel Malcolm, the foremost historian of the Balkans:

…the hand-over of an Albanian-inhabited area to a Slav state…was the spark that lit a movement of resistance in Kosovo, first to the Treaty of Berlin and eventually to Ottoman rule itself; and within thirty-four years the conflagration it caused would be one of the principal reasons for the downfall of the Ottoman Empire.[6]

The Treaty of Berlin additionally assigned to the Austro-Hungarian Empire special administrative and occupation rights in the Ottoman provinces of Bosnia and Herzegovina. Over the three decades to 1908, the Austrian grip tightened even though Bosnia and Herzegovina remained nominally a part of the Ottoman Empire. This increasingly fictitious state of affairs was resolved by Austria's unilateral annexation of the provinces on 6 October 1908 and their formal incorporation into the empire. This triggered serious and long-lasting tension with Serbian and other Slavic nationalists who wished to create a unified south Slavic state in the Balkans. On 28 June 1914, the practical manifestation of these escalating political and nationalist tensions became clear when the young Serbian nationalist, Gavrilo Princip, assassinated Archduke Franz Ferdinand, the heir to the Austrian–Hungarian throne, and set off the train of events that ultimately led to the start of the Great War exactly one month later, on 28 July.

In the Caucasus, a similar sharpening of identities followed the turbulent upheaval of the 1870s. In the 1880s and 1890s, the Russian authorities responded to the absorption of a multi-lingual collection of ethnic groups with a concerted campaign of 'Russification'. This targeted the significant populations of Armenians, Georgians and Tatars, which collectively accounted for nearly half the population of the newly assimilated Caucasian territories. It also involved the forced displacement of some 75,000 Turks and a general decline in the Muslim population of the region. Simultaneously, the economic value of the Caucasus to the Russian Empire increased rapidly; as noted by Hew Strachan, 'in 1913, the value of the goods passing through Baku exceeded that of all other Russian ports, and 85 percent of them were petroleum products'. Their value to Russia's emerging industrial (and, after 1914, war) economies were augmented by the substantial quantities of commodities such as gold, zinc, iron, copper and cobalt.[7]

By 1914, the condition of the ethnic minorities subsumed within the Ottoman and Russian Empires therefore resembled a tinderbox awaiting a spark. Nationalism combined symbiotically with the rise of an intellectual middle class among the Armenian, Azerbaijani and Georgian communities in the Caucasus. In the Azerbaijani case, it fused with pan-Islamic fervour through a secret organisation (*Musavat*) which aimed at achieving equality for, and eventually the unification of, all Muslims, in Russia and beyond.[8] All of these resurgent nationalisms clashed with the reorganisation of identity underway at the apex of the Committee of Union and Progress after it came to power in Istanbul in 1908. Amid the general backdrop of the military and financial weakening of the Ottoman Empire following its defeat in the Russo-Turkish War and the stringent imposition of European economic controls, feelings of latent and actual hostility among the empire's multi-ethnic groups became sharper and easier to mobilise. This reached its grim denouement with the genocide of the Armenians in 1915, but its roots are traceable to the clash of identities and national awakenings of the nineteenth century.

The winter campaign, 1914-15

The Ottoman war began in the Russian theatre. It involved a surprise naval bombardment of Russian Black Sea ports on 29 October 1914 by ships belonging to the Germans' Mediterranean Squadron. This was under the control of the Rear Admiral Wilhelm Souchon, who had escaped Allied pursuit in the Mediterranean in August 1914 and successfully sought refuge in Istanbul. They included the *Goeben* and the *Breslau*, respectively a battle cruiser and light cruiser that were reflagged as ships of the Ottoman Navy following their arrival in the Bosporus. At this point, the potent legacy of German military influence in Istanbul made itself felt, as Souchon and the influential German Ambassador Hans von Wangenheim worked with the pro-German Enver Pasha to guide the Ottomans into the war. This occurred through a series of confrontational naval manoeuvres undertaken by Souchon in September and October 1914, culminating in the shelling of the Russian ports of Sevastopol, Odessa and Yalta on 29 October.[9]

Once Ottoman entry into the Great War was secured, the focus of its military objectives centred on the recapture of the Caucasian territories lost in the Russo-Turkish War. Launching an offensive in the Armenian highlands in the area between eastern Turkey and the Caspian Sea would serve two purposes in Istanbul. The first was to retake the provinces of Kars and Batum and the Russian railhead in the small city of Sarikamis, while the second was the diversion of Russian forces from the Eastern Front developing on the Polish and Galician fronts. This would additionally cut off Russian access to the oil-bearing Caspian Sea region, and it found favour among the German military personnel who held positions of influence in the Ottoman Army. The Ottoman Third Army faced a Russian Caucasus Army heavily depleted by having to deploy half its strength to the Eastern Front following the destruction of its First and Second Armies at the epic battles of Tannenberg and the Masurian Lakes in August and September. For both the Ottoman and Russian high commands struggling to balance between competing demands for force deployments across multiple theatres of war, the logistical and administrative difficulties of campaigning in the Caucasus contributed significantly to the enormous loss of life on each side.

The Ottoman move towards Sarikamis that began on 22 December 1914 was their first major offensive of the war. It took place at the height of winter across a battlefield consisting of a highland plateau nearly 2,000 metres above sea level, reachable only by marching across high mountain passes. Heavy snowstorms and hypothermic temperatures added to the formidable logistical challenges facing the Ottoman and Russian Armies gathered at their respective forts in Erzurum and Kars. The Ottoman campaign aimed to encircle the over-extended Russian Army and force its collapse by cutting through the lines of communication at Sarikamis. Enver and his generals in the Third Army were emboldened by German military reports of a rapid breakdown in command and control in Russian units during the battle of Tannenberg. However, the Ottoman operational plan depended heavily on mobility and was closely modelled on Napoleonic tactics of fixing, enveloping and destroying the enemy force. The trouble was that the severe winter conditions meant that the required level of speed was simply impossible to achieve.[10]

The Third Army launched its attack on 22 December: 118,000 Ottoman forces faced a total of 65,000 Russian troops, but Enver's numerical majority was severely eroded by the fact that his army possessed little more than 200 artillery pieces and 75 machine guns. Nevertheless, the Third Army's IX and X Corps initially made steady progress along the front that stretched up to 930 miles in places. This was enough to sow initial panic among Russian military commanders, who prematurely ordered the evacuation of the entire region, but soon the momentum began to slow. Many of the Ottoman troops lacked winter clothing and sufficient rations, while a snowstorm that began on 25 December increased further their exhaustion as frostbite and hypothermia set in. Conditions worsened the following day and several thousand Ottoman soldiers perished from the cold as temperatures plunged to minus 26 centigrade. By the time the Third Army finally reached Sarikamis on 29 December its men were nearing the end of their physical endurance. Its IX and XI Corps made two frontal attacks on Sarikamis on 29 December and 1 January 1915 but were beaten back with heavy casualties. With the Ottoman offensive losing momentum, the Russian forces themselves encircled the Third Army and completely destroyed IX Corps. On 4 January, the Ottomans began to retreat back to Erzurum, where they arrived, bedraggled and defeated, on 11 January.[11]

The human cost in life and suffering at Sarikamis was colossal. Up to 47,000 Ottoman and 28,000 Russian soldiers died, nearly one in two of the total men deployed. An estimated 15,000 and 12,000, respectively, succumbed as a result of the adverse weather conditions rather than enemy action, with tens of thousands of frozen bodies being recovered after fighting finally came to end. One Ottoman division, alone, lost 4,000 of its 8,000 men to frostbite in just four days of campaigning.[12] The lack of roads or railways meant that material deprivations compounded the hardships caused by the freezing weather and lack of adequate supplies. Accounting for the decimation of IX Corps, as well as a typhus epidemic that swept through the exhausted Third Army, less than one-fifth of the Ottoman troops that had set out on the campaign returned to Erzurum.[13] The terrible toll of suspected disloyalties and retributive actions added further to the immense human cost of the battle. Strachan notes how the (Muslim) community of Adzharis was ruthlessly repressed by the Russian Empire after the battle ended, with its population falling from 52,000 to just 7,000 between February and April 1915, in a precursor of what was to befall other minority groups in the Caucasian patchwork of nations and ethnicities.[14]

Even more momentous was the legacy of the Ottoman reverse for the Armenian communities of the empire, as Enver blamed his chaotic defeat on their alleged disloyalty. Between 1.5 and 2 million Armenians lived in the Ottoman Empire.

Nearly half of these lived in eastern Anatolia but large numbers also lived across the Russian boundary, particularly in the Caucasian towns taken from Istanbul in 1878. The fact that their communities straddled both sides of the Ottoman–Russian border rendered the Armenians uniquely vulnerable after the outbreak of war. So, too, did the fact that they represented a Christian minority in a campaign against their co-religionists in Russia. Although Armenian leaders pledged loyalty to Istanbul in November 1914 and more than 100,000 obeyed the mobilisation orders, they refused to call on those Armenians living on the Russian side of the border to rise up.[15] Instead, many thousands of Armenians materially assisted the Russian forces and harassed the Ottoman Third Army as it retreated from Sarikamis, while Armenians living in Russia called for popular resistance to the Ottoman invasion and mobilised groups of local volunteers. The decisions of Armenians both in the Ottoman Empire and in Russia to do so reflected decades of persecution at the hands of pan-Turkic nationalists, with earlier massacres in the 1890s and, more recently, mass expulsions of Armenians as well as Greeks early in 1914. With the Ottomans now pitched in an existential clash with Orthodox Russia, the empire's suspicion of its Christian minorities redoubled and took on a virulently aggressive form.[16]

The Armenian genocide

The Armenian genocide started in earnest on 24 April 1915 with the arrest and deportation of thousands of Armenian political leaders and intellectuals. This act triggered widespread massacres that subsequently killed an estimated 1 million Armenians. The combination of the outright killings and the forced marches through the Syrian Desert constituted one of the earliest examples of a 'crime against humanity', although the term 'genocide' only came into usage in 1944.[17] However, it did not occur in a vacuum; rather, it took place within the context of the increasingly bitter confrontation between the imperial Ottoman elite and the sharpening national identities of its many minority groups. An Armenian Revolutionary Movement had emerged in the late nineteenth century to defend Armenian communities and villages from Ottoman oppression and attacks. Along with the launch of the Armenian Democratic Liberal Party in the city of Van in 1885, it developed the burgeoning Armenian national movement, and deepened its consciousness, which spread rapidly among the intelligentsia and among the Armenian diaspora.[18] The revolutionary upheaval also affected Armenians living in the Russian territories in the Caucasus. It culminated in an uprising against oppressive Russian rule in 1905 as thousands of Armenians were killed in Baku, Tbilisi (Tiflis) and Erevan.[19]

Between 1894 and 1896, the tense relations between Armenians and Ottomans culminated in a series of massacres that killed up to 100,000 Armenians. Known as the Hamidian massacres, they took place against the backdrop of a greater assertion of Islamic identity under the rule of Sultan Abdul Hamid II (reigned 1876-1909). The economic and financial decline of the Ottoman Empire further increased the vulnerability of relatively wealthy religious minorities to incited attacks. Thus, the

Armenian communities within the empire came to be viewed with suspicion as their loyalties to the Porte were called into question. A destabilising and deadly cycle of killing and retaliation swept through Istanbul and towns and cities in central and eastern Turkey with large Armenian populations. It also stimulated counter-responses, such as the audacious storming of the Imperial Ottoman Bank in Istanbul by Armenian revolutionaries demanding European protection in August 1896. In other areas, the attacks targeted other minorities, too, such as Greeks. Once again, as with the Bulgarian killings of the 1870s, the plight of a Christian minority mobilised international opinion, particularly in Europe and the United States, both home to large communities of expatriate Armenians.[20]

The successive loss of Ottoman territories in Libya, Bosnia and the Balkans in the decade prior to 1914 heightened the anxieties felt by the new Committee of Union and Progress that came to power in Istanbul in 1908. This resulted in a recalibration of 'imperial identity' that took somewhat diverging directions. On the one hand, the emphasis on Islam, mentioned above, attempted to bind the many provinces together through the unifying glue of religion. On the other hand, however, a more narrow, ethnocentric nationalism developed in the Turkish Anatolian heartland of the empire and, specifically, among the energetic new generation of 'Young Turks' in power in Istanbul.[21] Leading Turkish historian and sociologist Taner Akçam has argued that 'the Unionists simply used Ottomanism as a screen for their policy of Turkifying the country around the axis of Islam'.[22]

Caught in between were the Armenians and the Greeks, the two most visible and influential minorities in the empire, vulnerable to accusations of sympathy towards foreign interests. This increased after Armenian groups in Turkey had, in 1912, appealed to Russia for support in carving out an autonomous entity within the Ottoman Empire under great-power protection.[23] Moreover, during the Balkan Wars, one of the most famous Armenian commanders moved to Bulgaria and organised volunteer units against Ottoman forces. This act escalated still further the tensions between Turks and Armenians immediately prior to the outbreak of the First World War.[24]

In February 1914, multinational negotiations to reach an Armenian Reform Agreement were launched in Europe. They involved a specially appointed commission of French, German, Russian, British, Italian and Austro-Hungarian representatives to consider a Russian plan for a single Armenian province in eastern Turkey under the auspices of an Ottoman Christian or European governor. The Russians were anxious to prevent any spill-over of tension in eastern Anatolia to its own volatile patchwork of ethnic and religious communities in the Caucasus. It initially failed, in part due to German and Austro-Hungarian opposition, but conditions on the ground continued to deteriorate, and a compromise agreement was eventually signed on 8 February 1914. The final draft was heavily watered down, reflecting the strenuous efforts of the German Ambassador to Istanbul, Wangenheim. This notwithstanding, the Russian Foreign Minister, Sergei Sazonov, did warn the Ottoman Ambassador in St Petersburg that Russia would intervene if any further mass killings of Armenians occurred.[25]

THE CAUCASUS CAMPAIGNS

In August 1914, the Armenian Revolutionary Federation publicly declared its support for the Ottoman Empire in the event of any war with Russia. Delegations travelled to the Caucasus to dissuade Armenians from volunteering for the Russian Army. Nevertheless, there was enormous pro-Russian sympathy among Armenian communities living in Ottoman territories. Most notably, up to 50,000 mostly Armenian soldiers deserted from the Ottoman garrison at Erzurum and crossed to Russian lines between August and November 1914 alone. Bands of guerrillas organised themselves along the Ottoman frontier in the Caucasus and started to receive supplies of Russian arms and ammunition. These were smuggled across the porous boundary zone, further increasing Ottoman suspicions of cross-border fraternisation.[26] Then, in late February, the Ministry of War ordered that all Armenian conscripts serving with the Ottoman Army be transferred from active to passive duties in labour battalions. Enver intended the segregation of Armenians within the military to reduce the likelihood of further mass desertions to Russian units, signalling also the complete lack of trust in Istanbul for Armenian loyalty.[27]

Mass killings of Armenians began in April 1915 when residents in the town of Zeitan violently resisted attempts to conscript them. The Ottoman governor of the province of Van, Djevdet Bey, had replaced a more conciliatory governor shortly after the outbreak of war in November 1914. Djevdet was the brother-in-law of Enver Pasha, and he advocated a harsh policy towards the Armenians. Henry Morgenthau, the American Ambassador to Istanbul whose contemporary account of the massacres galvanised international opinion when it was published in 1918, asserted that Djevdet 'hated the Armenians'. Moreover, Morgenthau added that 'There is little question that he came to Van with definite instructions to exterminate all Armenians in this province, but, for the first few months, conditions did not facilitate such operations.'[28]

On 19 April, Ottoman forces launched a siege of the city of Van and fought against armed Armenian civilians for four weeks before withdrawing. Five days later, on 24 April, Armenian notables and intellectuals in Istanbul and other Ottoman centres were rounded up and arrested. This followed an order issued by the Minister of Interior, Talaat Bey, and the date is now commemorated as Genocide Memorial Day in Armenia. By the end of April, some 50,000 Armenians had been killed in the province of Van in an intensifying orgy of violence coordinated by 'Special Organisations' operating under the Ottoman Ministry of War. More than 30,000 prisoners were released from Ottoman jails to form the nucleus of the *chetes*, or killer bands, although they were augmented by military and provincial police in a systematic organisation of mass murder.[29] These militia groups faced increasing resistance by local Armenian communities, but desperate appeals for protection to their Christian co-religionists in Germany were unsuccessful. German officials in Berlin had little desire to embarrass their Ottoman ally, and consequently made no official protest, although the Vice Consul at Erzurum did make a half-hearted attempt to restrain Ottoman activities.[30] Instead, the priority of the influential German contingent in Istanbul was to keep the Ottomans in the war and ensure that they did not leave the Triple Alliance, as Italy had done in 1914. Thus, they consistently failed to apply sufficient pressure on their Ottoman ally to stop the killings or to attempt to improve conditions for surviving Armenian deportees.[31]

The large-scale deportations of Armenians commenced in earnest in May 1915. The Ottoman authorities responded to the events in Van by authorising a series of measures that called for removing Armenians from the sensitive zones of military operations in the Caucasus. Accordingly, a Temporary Law of Deportation was approved by the Committee of Union and Progress (CUP) Central Committee in Istanbul on 30 May 1915. This allowed the Ottoman Government and military to deport anybody it deemed a threat to national security, and it led to the establishment of a series of concentration camps in the Syrian desert to receive the deportees. Although the law did not explicitly name the Armenians as intended targets, and in fact affected Christian communities as well, they were the primary victims of the mass displacements that subsequently took place. Peter Balakian notes that the definition of who represented a threat to security was so loose that it gave 'total license for the administrative network and the killing squads to round up, deport, and massacre Armenians'. On 13 September 1915, a further law was passed by the Ottoman parliament, enabling the expropriation and confiscation of properties and livestock belonging to Armenians.[32]

During the summer of 1915, the unfolding massacres began to generate enormous media coverage, particularly in the United States. Attention focused on the notorious 'death marches' as hundreds of thousands of Armenians were forced to walk from Anatolia through the desert to the Syrian town of Deir ez-Zor. In addition to the unforgiving desert terrain and the harsh summer climate, the majority of the refugees were destitute and succumbed in huge numbers along the march. Many of them, including women and children, were robbed, raped and killed by Ottoman soldiers along the way. Survivor accounts collected by Donald and Lorna Miller for their oral history of the genocide paint a horrifying picture of mass and very public deprivation along the roads from Anatolia to Deir ez-Zor:

At the first station, we saw a lot of Armenians who had gotten there much earlier than us, and they had turned into skeletons. We were surrounded with skeletons so much that it felt like we were in hell.[33]

When we were going to the village, the road on both sides was filled with dead bodies. I have seen with my own eyes thousands of dead bodies. I did not see how they got killed, but I saw the dead bodies...It was summer, you know, so the fat from the body would be melted around the body...It was so bad that it began to stink everywhere, so that they [the Turks] gathered up all the corpses and burned them by pouring kerosene on them.[34]

While being deported, Aghavni observed hundreds of young women commit suicide by drowning themselves in the Euphrates. She said the rivers were awash with bodies of people who had been killed by the Turks, as well as those who had drowned themselves.[35]

Another eyewitness account, collected by Guenter Lewy, of conditions at a transit camp at Meskene, 70 miles east of Aleppo in Syria, described 'the camp as a place at which thousands arrive, but which most do not leave alive':

These are but living phantoms. Their superintendents distribute to them sparingly and very irregularly a piece of bread. Sometimes three or four days pass when these famished people who have nothing to eat but this piece of bread, receive absolutely nothing. A dreadful dysentery makes numerous victims among them, especially among the children. These latter fall ravenously upon all that come under their hands, they eat herbs, earth and even their excrement.[36]

In his book *Armenia: The Survival of a Nation*, Christopher Walker grimly notes that '"Deportation" was just a euphemism for mass murder. No provision was made for their journey or exile, and unless they could bribe their guards, they were forbidden in almost all cases food and water.' Furthermore, those who survived the march ended up in primitive open-air concentration camps, where many more were killed by their prison guards.[37] By August 1915, the *New York Times* carried an explosive account of the Armenians' plight, in which an anonymous eyewitness described how 'the roads and the Euphrates are strewn with corpses of exiles, and those who survive are doomed to certain death'.[38]

As the atrocities mounted, many Armenians fought back to defend themselves and their livelihood. This caused further bloodshed as in response the Ottomans mobilised irregular militias among the local Christian and Kurdish communities. Heavy fighting in areas of eastern Anatolia resulted in more massacres and, by the end of 1915, culminated in the forced removal of almost all Armenians from the region. The series of mass killings and death marches killed hundreds of thousands of people and caused several hundred thousand more to flee to Russian-controlled territory in the Caucasus. Regrettably, there is no consensus regarding the total number of deaths that occurred during the Armenian genocide, and the issue is fiercely contested by contemporary Turkish and Armenian governments, with estimates ranging from 500,000 to well over 1 million.[39] Martin Gilbert, for his part, notes the overwhelming scale of individual massacres, such as the mass killing of nearly all the 17,000 Armenian inhabitants of Trabzon (Trebizond) over two weeks in 1915, and another 15,000 killed in Bitlis in just eight days. Gilbert also provides figures of 600,000 Armenian deaths during the massacres in Anatolia, a further 400,000 during the expulsion and forced marches into the Syrian desert, together with the forced conversion of up to 200,000 Armenians to Islam.[40]

The numerous eyewitness accounts galvanised international opinion, particularly in the United States, whose neutrality until 1917 enabled it to maintain a network of consulates and officials in Ottoman provinces. In September 1916, a Committee on Armenian Atrocities was formed and subsequently grew into 'one of the most remarkable international philanthropic agencies in American history', raising an incredible $116 million between 1916 and its closure in 1929.[41] Of additional special note is the memoir of Henry Morgenthau, America's Ambassador in Istanbul between 1913 and 1916. Since its publication in 1918, *Ambassador Morgenthau's Diary* has served as an important reference point and primary source for tracking the Ottoman atrocities against the Armenians. Another significant contemporary work, partly released for British wartime propaganda reasons, was *The Treatment of Armenians in the Ottoman Empire*. Written by the former British Ambassador to the United States, Viscount Bryce, and the influential historian Arnold Toynbee, the book compiled eyewitness accounts and statements from survivors of the massacres. Although it has since come under fire as constituting part of a wartime propaganda drive against the Ottoman Empire, its lengthy testimonies played a significant role in mobilising international opinion upon its publication in 1916.

Persia and Erzurum, 1915-16

For the remainder of 1915, the main focus of the Ottoman war effort lay in repelling the Allies' attempts to seize the Gallipoli Peninsula. The resources poured into the ultimately successful campaign reflected the grave implications that a strategic defeat at the Dardanelles would have on the empire's very existence. More than 60,000 soldiers had died and almost a quarter of a million had become casualties during the eleven-month campaign. These were massive numbers that could barely be replaced. Russia, too, was engaged in a series of massive battles on its western (European) front against the German and Austro-Hungarian Empires. During 1915, Austro-Hungarian forces had driven the Russians back and recaptured the Habsburg frontier cities of Czernowitz and Brody, and an attempted Russian counter-attack in mid December failed with heavy losses. More serious still was the news that the German Army had swept through Russian Poland and the Lithuanian provinces in the Russian Empire. The general Austro-German advance had started after their overwhelming success in the Gorlice-Tarnów offensive in May 1915, resulting in the complete collapse of the Russian lines and the beginning of a strategic retreat far into Russia itself. Meanwhile, rising war-weariness in Russia began to manifest itself in a growing anti-war movement and an escalating series of strikes, including two in January 1916 – among port workers at the naval bases in Nikolayev and St Petersburg – at the time of the resumption of operations in the Caucasus.[42]

Both the Ottoman and Russian high commands therefore were militarily exhausted by the battles of 1915. These had resulted in a striking and morale-boosting success for the Ottomans, in sharp contrast to the series of military setbacks for the Russian forces. In addition, both militaries were affected by the difficulties of maintaining large armies in the distant Caucasus, particularly when faced with such direct threats to the imperial heartland. The physical distance along the battlefront presented further difficulties to mounting an effective campaign in the Caucasus, and meant that activity on the front in the summer and autumn of 1915 consisted largely of isolated attacks and counter-attacks as the Russians made repeated attempts to capture the Ottoman city of Erzurum. These produced heavy casualties on both sides but failed to achieve strategic breakthrough for either party. The result was a pause in military operations as the front stabilised while the Ottoman and Russian forces attempted to regroup and recover their battle strength.[43]

The ending of major military operations at Gallipoli in December 1915 transformed the situation. Large numbers of Ottoman infantry divisions now became available for operations elsewhere, although there was considerable disagreement about where and how to deploy them. Enver wished to maintain offensive operations whereas Mustapha Kemal, the hero of Gallipoli, favoured a defensive posture. In accordance with Enver's wishes, he dispersed the Ottoman troops to far-flung provinces rather than concentrating them in a strategic reserve around Istanbul and Anatolia. As 1915 drew to a close, Ottoman troops in the Caucasian theatre of the war were being reorganised into two expeditionary forces and the Third Army, which had gradually been reassembled following its crushing reversal at Sarikamis in January.[44] Between November 1915 and February 1917, fully three-quarters of all Ottoman casualties would be sustained on the Russian battlefronts, weakening the empire's military capability ahead of the final British successes in Palestine and Mesopotamia in 1918.[45]

For their part, the Russian military overstretch was exacerbated by the decision to send a sizeable force into Persia in November 1915 in order to forestall rumours that the country might enter the war on the Germans' and Ottomans' side. Long-standing British concerns, dating back to the nineteenth century, about forward Russian designs on Persia and Central Asia, suddenly were set aside for the sake of wartime expediency. Starting in December 1915, a Caucasian expeditionary force under Major General Nikolai Baratov advanced rapidly into Persia, taking the cities of Qom, Kangavar, Kermanshah and Isfahan by March 1916. The succession of victories placed Russian forces little more than 100 miles away from the Persian boundary with Ottoman Mesopotamia. Ironically, this placed Baratov relatively close to the beleaguered British garrison that was desperately attempting to stave off a humiliating surrender at the town of Kut. However, despite receiving orders from the regional Russian command in Tbilisi to advance into Mesopotamia to relieve General Townshend's 6th Indian Division, Baratov was unable and unwilling to do so, and was still inside Persian territory when the British garrison surrendered on 29 April.[46]

The commander of Russian forces in the Caucasus at this time was Lieutenant General Nikolai Yudenich (working alongside Grand Duke Nicholas). Yudenich began preparing for a winter offensive in the belief that this would catch the Turks by surprise following their own disastrous experience of winter campaigning in 1914. The gamble paid off at the Battle of Koprukoy in early January 1916 when Yudenich caught the Ottoman XI Corps completely by surprise. Attacking on 10 January, the Russian Caucasus Army enjoyed a substantial numerical advantage that enabled it to overpower XI Corps and send the Third Army into full retreat. Just as at Sarikamis, one year previously, the Third Army withdrew in disarray towards Erzurum after having suffered exceptionally heavy losses concentrated in the beleaguered XI Corps. The difference in January 1916 was that this time the Russian advance continued all the way into Erzurum itself, culminating in the capture of the third most powerful fortress in the Ottoman Empire, on 16 February. The fall of Erzurum represented an exceptional strategic triumph for the Russians and a disaster for the Ottomans, as the entire defence of eastern Anatolia had depended on the city.[47]

The taking of Erzurum immediately became popularised as the setting for the dramatic ending of John Buchan's novel, *Greenmantle*. Published in October 1916, shortly after the actual battle of Erzurum, and written while Buchan worked at the War Propaganda Bureau in London (prior to becoming Director of Intelligence in the Ministry of Information), the thriller's plot revolved around a supposed German plan to use religion to inspire an anti-British uprising in the Muslim world. Its main character, Sandy Arbuthnot ('Greenmantle'), was modelled both on Lawrence of Arabia and the prominent British diplomat and intelligence officer, Aubrey Herbert. In the climactic final scene, Sandy leads the cavalry charge into Erzurum that successfully thwarts the German plot:

In the very front, now nearing the city ramparts, was one man. He was like the point of the steel spear soon to be driven home…As he rode it seemed that the fleeing Turks were stricken still, and sank by the roadside with eyes strained after his unheeding figure…Then I knew that the prophecy had been true and that the prophecy had not failed them. The long-looked for revelation had come. Greenmantle had appeared at last to a waiting people.[48]

Heavy fighting continued around Erzurum for the rest of the year. The Russian forces initially maintained the offensive momentum and captured the city of Bitlis on 2 March and the strategically important Black Sea port city of Trabzon in April 1916. The Caucasus Army was now deep inside Anatolia and appeared poised to make further sweeping advances either in the direction of central Anatolia or into Mesopotamia. Moreover, the capture of Trabzon opened up the maritime lines of communication across the Black Sea to Russian logistical and supply arrangements. In order to forestall this, the Ottoman Third Army attempted to recapture Trabzon in June 1916, but was beaten back on 2 July – one day after the launch of the momentous Battle of the Somme on the Western Front. Worse still for the Ottomans, Yudenich immediately launched a counter-attack of his own, resulting in the Russian capture of the Ottomans' communication centre at Erzincan on 25 July.[49]

These successes in the Caucasus campaign came at a propitious time for the wider Russian military effort. On 4 June 1916, the Brusilov Offensive had been launched against the Central Powers on the Eastern Front (in modern-day Ukraine), and broke through the Austro-Hungarian lines across a wide front, taking more than 70,000 prisoners in the first five days alone. This was a startling success that left the Austrians reeling. However, the advance soon slowed owing to a combination of delays and poor operational planning by General Alexei Evert, the commander of the Russian Western Army Group; an overextended front line; and the rushing of German reinforcements to the front. Although offensive operations continued throughout the summer, they became bogged down and the troops were exhausted. Thousands of Russian soldiers also began to desert as conditions along the Russian front lines deteriorated and morale plummeted.[50]

The Russians therefore appeared to be in the ascendancy by the mid-point of 1916, having made significant progress on the Austrian and Ottoman fronts, and with little inclination of the transformative upheaval that was about to unfold. Furthermore, the Russian war effort was producing striking results as industrial mobilisation expanded rapidly, with shell production more than doubling from 1915 to 1916, and making a significant contribution to the early success of the 1916 offensives.[51] Yet, the eventual petering out of the Brusilov offensive decisively cracked the veneer of success and exposed an intensifying domestic opposition to the continuation of the war. Moreover, by late 1916 the combination of economic dislocation and mass internal displacement within Russia was creating fertile ground for new expressions of political, even revolutionary, opposition to the Tsarist regime. The additional influx of between 200,000 and 300,000 Armenian refugees strained further an economic system close to collapse, as the majority of the newcomers were destitute, malnourished, and required urgent medical and humanitarian assistance.[52]

Revolution in Russia

By the winter of 1916-17, Tsarist authority was coming under unprecedented attack. Notwithstanding an intensified campaign of state surveillance and the creation of special councils to mobilise and manage Russia's war economy, popular discontent in the key urban and industrial centres soared during the autumn months of 1916. In the imperial periphery, large areas of Central Asia rose in revolt in mid-1916 as local communities reacted to wartime hardships, specifically the growing shortages of food and basic commodities, the influx of large numbers of refugees, and the imposition of onerous demands for conscription into military and labour units. Put simply, Russia, in common with other agrarian-dominated economies, 'ran short of food long before they ran short of guns and shells'. This reflected the profound difficulties of organising peasant economies for war as industrial mobilisation diverted resources from farming, particularly men and horse-power.[53] As will be analysed in the later chapters on the impact of labour requirements on Egypt and Mesopotamia, the call-up of manpower interfered with local labour-intensive patterns of agriculture as they coincided with the cotton harvest (as British demands for Egyptian manpower in 1917 and 1918 would coincide with the wheat harvest).[54] The revolt expanded to include well-organised bands of rebels in Kazakhstan, Kyrgyzstan and Uzbekistan, before being mercilessly crushed by the end of 1916, with up to half a million Kazakhs fleeing or being deported across the border into China.[55]

More troublingly for the Tsar, this growing unrest at the periphery of empire was matched by escalating unrest at the heart of the imperial core. Episodes of economic and social unrest rose markedly during the autumn of 1916 as the frequency and size of strikes increased. Popular frustration with the authorities' perceived mishandling of the war effort intersected with deep discontent at the direction of domestic policy. This left the Tsar dangerously exposed as the lightning-rod of anger following his decision in 1915 to anoint himself Commander-in-Chief and leave responsibility for governing Russia to his German-born (and unpopular) wife, the Tsarina Alexandra. Her German background aroused much comment and anger, as did the unmistakable influence of the mystic and healer Grigori Rasputin on imperial policy-making. Rasputin's assassination in December 1916 provided an indication of the surging levels of anger at Tsarist rule. The combination of military setbacks and growing discontent at authoritarian misrule therefore converged on the Imperial family. Moreover, they coincided with rising food prices and general inflationary pressures that cut into the meagre incomes of families struggling to survive in the conditions of wartime hardship.[56]

By late 1916 and early 1917 the escalating popular anger manifested itself in waves of strikes that targeted Russia's industrial and military mobilisation. The fact that thousands of workers and soldiers were grouped together in factories or billets both facilitated and magnified the potency of these gatherings. Matters came to a dramatic head in February 1917 when a series of massive strikes began at key industrial plants in St Petersburg and within days between 200,000 and 300,000 factory workers were on strike. The 'February Revolution' that swept the Tsar out of power started with a mass mobilisation of industrial workers at the Putilov machine factory, gathered momentum with rallies, political gatherings and demonstrations to mark International Women's Day, and led to the near-total shutdown of industrial and commercial activity in the city by 25 February. Students and workers joined forces to demand the removal of the Tsar and an end to Russian involvement in the war. Tsar Nicholas responded by ordering the army to quell the unrest by force on 26 February, but thousands of troops mutinied as they rejected their commander's order.[57]

As the authority of the Tsarist regime quickly ebbed away and symbols of government control were attacked and destroyed, opposition political groups moved in to fill the void. The Duma established a Temporary Committee in an effort to restore law and order while socialist organisations launched the Petrograd Soviet to represent workers and soldiers. The intersection of mutinying soldiers with the mass industrial unrest tipped the balance towards a revolutionary upheaval. The final vestiges of imperial authority crumbled with the failure of last-ditch plans to transfer power first to the Tsar's son Alexei, and then to his brother, the Grand Duke Michael. These did not find any political support as governmental authority in the major cities collapsed. The Tsar himself was detained by disloyal troops on 1 March and finally announced his abdication the following day, 2 March 1917, thereby bringing to an end three centuries of Romanov rule in Russia.[58]

The Tsar was replaced by a Provisional Government formed by members of the Duma. It was headed first by Prince Georgy Lvov and then by Alexander Kerensky of the Socialist Revolutionary party. The choice of these two prime ministers encapsulated the diverging trends within the post-imperial revolutionary struggle. Although the Provisional Government nominally exercised power and control, it did not monopolise legitimate political authority in Russia. Its rule was contested on the ground by the network of *soviets* (workers' councils) controlled by more radical socialist factions. Strikes and mutinies continued during the volatile aftermath of the February

Revolution, allowing militant organisations such as the Bolshevik party to make inroads among the *soviets*. Differences climaxed over the Provisional Government's controversial decision to continue Russian participation in the war and reaffirm the Tsar's war aims. Kerensky launched a major new offensive on the Austro-Hungarian front in June 1917, partly under heavy Allied pressure following the large-scale mutinies in the French Army and escalating signs of war-weariness in Britain.[59] Once again, early success quickly gave way to eventual failure, as the enemy mounted a strong counter-attack and the Russian units suffered heavy losses. Many soldiers refused to follow orders to return to the battlefield and a new revolutionary situation rapidly developed during the July Days crisis. Although its immediate overthrow was averted, the Provisional Government was left in disarray, and fell to the eventual Bolshevik takeover during the October Revolution on 25 October 1917.[60]

During this tumultuous period, the Caucasus front remained quiet, despite the Provisional Government's 4 April 1917 reaffirmation of its war aim of seizing control of the Strait of the Dardanelles as well as of Istanbul itself. Notably, this statement of intent by the new Foreign Minister, Pavel Milyukov, was immediately and publicly repudiated by the Petrograd Soviet and denounced by the aspiring Bolshevik leader, Vladimir Lenin, as 'thoroughly imperialist'.[61] Milyukov's strong support for continuing the war left him bereft of political allies and he resigned in May, while the Russian armies in the Caucasus and in Persia had to digest and absorb the Order No. 1 issued immediately after the February Revolution, which replaced most of the officer ranks with 'soldier soviets'. This notwithstanding, recent research has indicated that the Russian armies in the Middle East remained operationally ready to resume the offensive, following their successes in 1916, with Baratov's force in Persia not only holding its foothold in the north of Mesopotamia throughout 1917 but even mounting a small attack as late as January 1918 against Kara-Tepe in north-eastern Mesopotamia.[62]

Imperial hubris

Although the Ottoman Empire outlasted the Russian Empire, it did not do so unscathed. The campaigns in the Caucasus inflicted unparalleled damage on the Ottoman military machine. During the fifteen months that elapsed between the ending of major British operations at Gallipoli in November 1915 and the start of the Russian withdrawal from the Middle Eastern war in February 1917, wholly two-thirds of all Ottoman casualties were sustained in the Russian campaign. As Malcolm Yapp has noted, this figure constituted a grinding down of Ottoman resources of manpower and materiel and significantly weakened the military position of the empire as the British campaigns in Palestine and Mesopotamia prepared to expand in scope and scale.[63] Flush from the successful defence of the Dardanelles against Anglo-French attack, the fighting in the Caucasus did much to blunt the Ottomans' offensive thrust as momentum slowed to a halt. The Ottoman Third Army effectively ceased to exist as a fighting force by summer 1916, and the continuing operations in the Caucasus decimated the Ottoman Second Army during the winter of 1916-17 even as Russia lurched towards revolution. Indeed, the total number of Ottoman combatants dropped precipitously from its peak of 800,000 in 1915 to 400,000 in March 1917 before halving again to 200,000 in March 1918.[64]

As Chapters 5 and 6 will show, military fatigue manifested itself in 1917-18 as the Ottoman forces in Palestine and Mesopotamia grew weaker. Thus, while the Ottoman war effort was able to inflict important defeats on British and Indian forces in Mesopotamia in April 1916 and in Palestine early in 1917, it was little able to withstand the subsequent build-up of enemy forces in each area. The problems of supply and transportation in the vast and difficult terrain of the Caucasus and Central Asia added immeasurably to the difficulties facing the Ottoman forces in 1918. It has been estimated that Ottoman soldiers in the Caucasus, Palestine and Mesopotamia only received between a half and a third of their nominal rations, largely because of the disruption to traditional methods of seaborne transportation of foodstuffs. These were hard-hit by the strangulating British blockade of the Ottoman coastline in the Mediterranean and the Red Sea, and completely overburdened the limited Ottoman railway network. Most of the system was single-track and the critical tunnels through the Taurus mountain range connecting the Anatolian and Arabian provinces remained unfinished until September 1918. This meant that severe bottlenecks developed, and there never was any railway communication between Ankara and any of the Ottoman positions on the Russian front. Widespread corruption and a lack of transport animals (primarily camels) magnified still further the supply failures that threatened to overwhelm the Ottoman military machine in the Middle East by 1918.[65]

Nevertheless, significant developments continued in the Caucasian theatre during the last year of the war, the Treaty of Brest-Litovsk notwithstanding. This peace treaty between post-revolutionary Russia and the Central Powers was signed in modern-day Belarus on 3 March 1918. It marked the formal exit of Russia from the First World War as the Bolsheviks made large territorial concessions in Finland, the Baltic States, Poland, Ukraine, as well as the return to the Ottoman Empire of the Caucasian provinces seized in 1878. The scale of the Russians' territorial loss at Brest-Litovsk had the secondary effect of fuelling the latent pan-Turkic ambitions of the Ottoman elite in Istanbul. Irredentist dreams in the Caucasus and in Central Asia suddenly opened up as the 'peace of Brest-Litovsk had opened wide fields for pan-Turanian dreams of empire'. Consequently, during the final year of the First World War, the Caucasus, Caspian region and even Persia once again became prime Ottoman targets.[66]

Reports of a possible Ottoman drive towards Central Asia and Persia alarmed the British civil and military authorities in London and Delhi. The 'Great Game' between the British and Russian Empires for influence in Persia and Afghanistan may have ended with the Anglo-Russian Convention of 1907, but its strategic legacy remained alive. Accordingly, the Ministry of Information in London prepared a 'Report on the Pan-Turanian Movement' in October 1917. Written before the Russian exit from the war and the Treaty of Brest-Litovsk, it argued that any Russian collapse would negatively impact British imperial security. Rather ambitiously, the report suggested that the road lay open for an Ottoman advance into the heart of Central Asia. If Ottoman – and, by extension, German – troops ever reached Afghanistan, they could pose a direct threat to the security of India. By May 1918, an alarmist report prepared by the Political Intelligence Department of the Foreign Office in London claimed that the 'rapid advance of the Germans eastwards through the Ukraine serves to draw attention once again to their evident designs upon the Caucasus'. However, by early 1918, the Ottoman military machine was incapable of supporting such a lengthy extension of military operations. Nor was it supported by Istanbul's German allies, which did not favour diverting Ottoman troops from tying down hundreds of thousands of British troops in Palestine and Mesopotamia.[67]

This notwithstanding, the Russians' withdrawal and the signing of the Treaty of Brest-Litovsk caused great alarm in London. As befitted a former Viceroy of India, Lord Curzon led the current of alarmist opinion in the War Cabinet. On 25 June 1918 he went so far as to state that 'the pendulum of the war, swinging so fiercely in the West, is also swinging…increasingly toward the East'.[68] This was a remarkable statement to make in light of the successive German offensives that so nearly broke through the British and French lines on the Western Front between March and May 1918. However, as an influential imperial spokesman and a political heavyweight both in the Conservative party and within the coalition government led by David Lloyd George, Curzon's view carried considerable weight. For Curzon, the real danger lay to Britain's imperial security arising from the potential German gains in Russia and Ottoman gains in Central Asia. Thus, developments in Russia in 1917-18 reawakened the older fears of a German thrust towards India – something that had much exercised Curzon's mind in the early 1900s while he was still Viceroy in Delhi.[69]

Benjamin Schwarz has noted how, for some of the imperial strategists such as Curzon who occupied positions of influence in London, 'Russia's collapse marked a turning-point in the war by highlighting the imperial aspect of the conflict and therefore necessitating a change in Britain's priorities from the west to the east.'[70] The (British) Government of India began to panic following the signing of the Treaty of Brest-Litovsk and also the Treaty of Bucharest that imposed a punitive peace on Romania in May 1918. German forces reached Odessa on the Russian coastline of the Black Sea, and British military leaders in India expressed their alarm at the possibility of an imminent Turkish–German invasion of Afghanistan.[71] For doomsayers in London and Delhi, it appeared that a renewed 'drive to the east' (*Drang nach Osten*) was about to take place. As a result, the Government of India began to divert a large amount of military supplies sorely needed by the British–Indian forces in Mesopotamia to meet the imagined threat emanating from Persia.[72]

Such fears among imperial officials in London and Delhi that Persia and Afghanistan lay ready for the taking shifted the centre of gravity of the campaign from the Caucasus to Central Asia in 1918. They tapped into the growing recognition among British policy-makers of the importance of the oil deposits that had been discovered in Persia in 1908 and were widely believed to exist around Mosul in northern Mesopotamia. The rapid rise of Mesopotamian and Persian oil to the top of the agenda of Britain's War Cabinet is examined in full in Chapter 6, as is the hastily organised campaign to the Azerbaijani oil town of Baku led by General Lionel Dunsterville in August 1918. Here, it is sufficient to note that the injection of perceived new German and Turkish pressures forced British policy-makers to reassess their imperial motivations in the Middle East. As one historian has written, 'the fine calculations and cynicism which underpinned British War Imperialism in the Middle East was swept along by a tide of hysteria' during the spring and summer of 1918, even as the situation on the Western Front deteriorated alarmingly. This set in motion a process that would have significant consequences for both the post-war political settlement across the region as well the growing confrontation between national movements and advocates of continuing Western intervention.[73]

Neither the Russian nor the Ottoman empires recovered from the high cost of their participation in the First World War. Although the Caucasus campaign represented one part of a much longer battle for influence in the region, the fighting between late 1914 and early 1917 hastened the ultimate exhaustion of the two imperial polities. For the scale of individual and collective suffering in the Caucasus campaign was immense. By early 1917, there were an estimated 6 million refugees living in the Caucasus and the Russian interior. Following the battles of winter 1914-15, the Tsarist authorities expelled tens of thousands of Muslims from the provinces of Kars and Batum that had been seized from the Ottoman Empire back in 1878. Other non-Russian minorities in the Caucasus, such as the Crimean Tatars, whose loyalty was also suspected, were deported as well, while more than 1 million Russians, White Russians and Ukrainians living in what became the war zone were displaced. In addition to justifying the deportations on grounds of suspected loyalties to the Ottoman enemy, they also served to make land and properties available to Armenian refugees and survivors of the genocide across the border.[74]

Unlike its Russian counterpart, the Ottoman Empire (barely) survived the campaign. It nevertheless caused enormous loss of life and material destruction in north-eastern Turkey. Importantly, too, the campaign contributed to the fragmentation of the empire as the lure of recovering lost provinces and expanding pan-Turanian influence into Central Asia fanned the flames of a narrower, less inclusive Turkish nationalism. Coupled with the gradual alienation of the Arab portions of the empire (see Chapters 5 and 6), formalised in 1916 in the Arab Revolt (discussed in Chapter 7), the effect of the events of 1917-18 was to accelerate the drawing in of the empire around its Anatolian heartland. This hastened the fragmentation of the Ottoman Empire even before the withdrawal from the war in October 1918, and the subsequent peace treaties signed between 1919 and 1923, confirmed the final break-up of the imperial system. Like Mustafa Kemal's heroic actions at the Dardanelles in 1915 (see Chapter 4), which propelled him to national prominence, the ending of the Caucasus campaign accelerated the reformulation of identity from Ottoman to Turkish.

THE CAUCASUS CAMPAIGNS

Nevertheless, the impact of the campaign had a lasting legacy that continues to reverberate today. The memory of the Armenian genocide and post-war republican Turkey's reluctance to acknowledge the magnitude of the killings have been defining features in each country's historical narrative of the First World War, made more potent after Armenia's independence from the Soviet Union in 1991. Turkish writers, such as the Nobel Prize-winning novelist Orhan Pamuk, who have recently broached the issue of Ottoman responsibility for the atrocities are subjected to harassment, vilification and, in the case of Hrant Dink in 2007, assassination. Countries that move to recognise the Armenian genocide as such face campaigns organised by Turkish lobby groups and overt threats to break commercial and trading relations. Nor is the legacy of conflict much less tangled in the post-Soviet sphere in the Caucasus, where relations between Russia and its Muslim minorities in Chechnya and surrounding territories have sparked some of the bloodiest conflicts in the post-Cold War period. Here, memories of the First World War battles are interwoven into longer patterns of civil conflict and political repression that have been a recurring feature of the regional landscape. Yet, for all sides, the common experience of the Caucasus campaign was one of unprecedented hardship as two faltering empires battled each other while inflicting massive displacement on communities that sought to challenge the weakening of imperial controls.

4

GALLIPOLI AND SALONIKA

Of all the military campaigns undertaken away from the Western Front during the Great War, the Gallipoli operations are the most famous and well-remembered today. They parallel the battles of Verdun, the Somme and Ypres (Passchendaele) in their collective imprint in modern historical memory. For the Australian and New Zealand Army Corps (Anzac) troops involved, the campaign has become a 'foundational myth' of modern nation-building. It has come to symbolise the rise of a national consciousness in both countries, and the memory and bravery of those who took part continue to reverberate a century on, although a burgeoning wave of 'revisionist' histories have questioned both the utility of the campaign and the role it played in the nation-building process, provoking furious debate in Australia, in particular. Recent books such as *Gallipoli: The End of the Myth* and *Blood Brothers: The Anzac Genesis*, both published in 2009, argue respectively that 'The campaign was fought in vain. It did not shorten the war by a single day, nor in reality did it ever offer that prospect';[1] and that 'the true birthplace of Anzac is…not to be found on the sandy, bloody beaches of Gallipoli but 50 years earlier' in the frontier campaigns by colonial forces with the indigenous peoples of Australasia.[2]

For the Ottomans, the operations at the Dardanelles hold equal historical importance, as the Ottoman military fought with bravery and with distinction, and inflicted a resounding reverse on the Allied armies. No less significantly, Mustapha Kemal emerged from relative obscurity to begin his transition into 'Atatürk', the Father of the (Turkish) Nation. The Turkish war memorial at Cape Helles with Atatürk's inscription paying tribute to the fallen of all nations remains one of the most moving memorials to the Great War.[3] For the British, who made up the majority of the invading forces, there is no heroic mythologising to hide what was a protracted operational fiasco; had Winston Churchill not achieved greatness between 1940 and 1945, he would probably be remembered today with anger as the instigator and architect of military failure.

THE FIRST WORLD WAR IN THE MIDDLE EAST

This chapter assesses the origins and course of the Anglo-French attempt to seize control of the strategically important Strait of the Dardanelles, before moving on to examine briefly the three-year-long campaign at Salonika, as this was a derivative of the failure to break through at Gallipoli and ultimately had profound consequences for ending the wars in the Middle East in 1918. Pressure to open up a new front in the Mediterranean had been building up since the Ottoman entry into the Great War in November 1914. It was magnified by the solidifying stalemate on the Western Front as the initial battlefield fluidity gave way to the lines of trenches that stretched from the English Channel to the Swiss border. Led by Churchill and British officials such as Sir Maurice Hankey, the influential Secretary to the War Council in London, pressure grew for a way of overcoming the bloody stasis and lengthening lists of casualties on the Western Front. Moreover, the need to open up the Dardanelles to Russian shipping, and the Tsarist regime's long-standing interest in the city of Istanbul, added a potent Russian dimension to the campaign. For these reasons, the battles to gain control of the Gallipoli Peninsula drew in a wide array of actors with different visions for the regional reordering.[4]

The road to war

Gallipoli represented the intersection of Russian expansionist objectives in the Middle East with British attempts to construct a wartime alliance of convenience against the Ottoman Empire. During the Crimean War six decades earlier, the fundamentally different Russian and British visions for the future of the Ottoman Empire and the city of Istanbul were a *casus belli*. Russia's long-held desire to control Istanbul (Constantinople) resonated with its pan-Slavic ambitions and the importance of the city for the Russian Orthodox Church. Less evocative, but more materially important, the narrow Strait of the Dardanelles was also a chokepoint through which all seaborne trade entering and leaving Russia's only warm-water ports on the Black Sea had to pass. The Commander of the Russian Black Sea Fleet, M. N. Girs (himself a former Ambassador to the Sublime Porte), spoke for many in Russia when he declared, in October 1914, that 'We need a strong boss ruling over Constantinople, and since we cannot let any other power assume this role, we must take her for ourselves.'[5]

For the British part, policy-making towards the Ottoman Empire combined respect for its territorial integrity intermixed with awareness of its growing weaknesses. The possibility of Ottoman fragmentation took on important strategic considerations in light of its provinces along the vital sea route to India in the Eastern Mediterranean and the Arabian Peninsula. Officials in London and Delhi thus viewed any potential break-up of the empire with deep misgivings lest it encourage rival powers such as Russia or Germany with eastwards designs. The signing of the 1907 Anglo-Russian Convention blunted the competitive rivalry that existed between London and Moscow in Central Asia, though vestiges of it remained. Its place in the conspiratorial mindset of British officialdom was taken by Germany and its burgeoning commercial and seemingly strategic ties with the Sublime Porte. The granting of the concession to the Deutsche Bank-owned Anatolian Railway Company to construct a rail route from Berlin to Baghdad and the Kaiser's promotion of pan-Islamic fervour coalesced with the activities (real and imagined) of German civilian and military personnel (described in Chapter 1) such as Wassmuss and von Sanders. The result was fanciful talk among British policy-makers of a German *Drang nach Osten* or 'drive to the east'.[6]

Three months elapsed between Britain's entry into the First World War on 4 August 1914 and its declaration of war against the Ottoman Empire on 5 November. During this period, the formulation of Britain's imperial strategy was greatly complicated by Istanbul's adoption of hostile neutrality. Relations between London and the Sublime Porte deteriorated rapidly as the countdown to war began. On 29 July, Britain impounded two Turkish Dreadnought battleships (the *Sultan Osman* and the *Reshadieh*) which were being constructed in British yards. Funds for these had been raised by public subscription and their seizure caused uproar in Constantinople. Four days later, on 2 August, the Ottomans signed a treaty of alliance with Germany, followed by a similar treaty with Austria–Hungary on 5 August. The presence in Turkey of a substantial and influential German military mission under the command of General Liman von Sanders, and the assumption of German control over the Ottoman Navy on 15 August, contributed further to the breakdown in Anglo-Ottoman relations. So, too, did Istanbul's decision to permit two German cruisers, the *Goeben* and the *Breslau*, to escape their British pursuers in the Mediterranean by passing through the Dardanelles before reaching Istanbul, where they were symbolically transferred to the Ottoman Navy.[7]

This caused two particular difficulties for British policy-makers, acutely conscious of the religious dimension to any conflict with the Ottoman Empire. This was especially the case in the 'arc of empire' that ran from East Africa through Egypt and the Persian Gulf sheikhdoms to India. First, the Ottoman rulers' claim of caliphal authority resonated deeply among Muslims in India and Egypt, as elsewhere in the Islamic world. Any declaration of war with the Ottoman Empire would thus require the British to persuade their Muslim subjects to join, or at least acquiesce in, a Christian campaign directed against their co-religionists and source of spiritual leadership. This became more pressing as Ottoman nationalism had increasingly acquired an Islamic tinge, culminating in the Sultan's declaration of Islamic holy war on 14 November 1914.[8] For this reason, British officials felt strongly that Istanbul be seen to make the first aggressive move towards war. Their concerns about the loyalty of Indian Muslim soldiers sent to Egypt in 1914 subsequently proved unfounded, owing to the substantive ethnic and linguistic differences that prevented any serious degree of communication or collaboration with local Egyptians.[9]

The second factor influencing British policy formulation in the autumn of 1914 was its long-standing commitment to upholding the integrity of the Ottoman Empire. This had been a core component of Britain's Eastern policy ever since 1815. Initially it reflected the strategic imperative of keeping Russia away from Istanbul and the approaches to India. Latterly, as detailed in Chapter 1, the focus had shifted to preventing Germany from establishing a foothold in the Persian Gulf.[10] It also reflected the fact that rival Great Power interests in the Ottoman Empire conversely resulted in a shared commitment to its political survival in the nineteenth century. Russia and France wished to prevent Britain from becoming too powerful in the Middle East, while German influence in the Ottoman Empire increased in visibility towards the century's end.[11] European encroachment on Ottoman territories in the decade prior to 1914 strained this arrangement, while the signing of the Ottoman–German treaty on 2 August turned Britain's policy of support for the empire on its head.

These two factors initially coexisted in an uneasy balance from August to October 1914. British anxiety to avoid appearing the aggressor against the Caliphate led its Foreign Secretary, Sir Edward Grey, to reaffirm London's commitment to Ottoman territorial integrity. This decision frustrated British advocates of constructing a Balkan alliance to contain and counter the Ottoman Empire, as sensitivities relating to the empire's substantial Muslim populations in India and Egypt prompted the Cabinet to affirm on 17 August 1914 that 'She [Istanbul] ought to be compelled to strike the first blow.' This frustrated the advocates of a more aggressive posture, which included the newly appointed Secretary of State for War, Herbert Horatio Kitchener, and the combative First Lord of the Admiralty, Winston Churchill, who wished to create a 'Balkan bloc' of Romania, Greece and Bulgaria against the Ottomans.[12] Yet, during this period, British policy was in a state of drift and lacked direction. This was symbolised by the absence of the Ambassador in Constantinople (Sir Louis Mallet) on a holiday that lasted more than a month, encompassing the signing of the Ottoman–German treaty, seizure of the Turkish Dreadnoughts, and pursuit of the *Goeben* and *Breslau*, until his belated return to work on 16 August.[13]

However, on 1 October, the Ottomans raised the stakes in the as yet undeclared hostilities by closing the Dardanelles to British and Allied shipping. This wiped out more than half of Russia's entire export trade and exposed Britain's vulnerability to imported food supplies. Uniquely among major belligerents in 1914, Britain had not made an arrangement to safeguard its food security. The President of the Board of Agriculture, Lord Lucas, remarked insouciantly, 'why trouble growing it [wheat] when you could import any amount you wanted?'[14] Now, with all wheat imports from Russia ended, Britain's patience with Istanbul rapidly dwindled. The actual trigger for the outbreak of war came when the Ottoman Navy launched pre-emptive naval strikes targeting the Russian Black Sea ports of Odessa, Sevastopol, Yalta, Novorossiysk and Feodosia on 29 October. Britain severed diplomatic relations with the Ottomans the next day and declared war on 5 November, three days after the Russian declaration of war with Istanbul.[15]

Notably for the campaign that followed, immediately prior to the declaration of war the Royal Navy had undertaken a preliminary and speculative bombardment of the Ottoman fortifications at the Dardanelles. This was ordered by Churchill and took place on 3 November 1914. Two British battlecruisers and two French battleships conducted a short bombardment that lasted approximately twenty minutes. They succeeded in severely damaging one Ottoman fort, at Sedd el-Bahr on the tip of the Gallipoli Peninsula east of Cape Helles, killing some eighty-six Ottoman and around forty German soldiers. The comparative success of this short operation raised British expectations and encouraged an ultimately dangerous belief that the Strait was there for the taking. By contrast, the Ottomans immediately began to improve and strengthen their fortifications, having been placed on notice that this strategic chokepoint was an intended target for attack.[16]

The declaration of war with the Ottoman Empire removed the geopolitical restrictions that hitherto had held back British policy formulation in the Middle East. It intersected with rising voices of concern within the British Government at the onset of trench warfare and the emerging stalemate on the Western Front, amid unmistakable signs that the war would be lengthy and not 'over by Christmas'. After the 'race to the Channel' culminated with the (First) Battle of Ypres in early November 1914, the solidifying front lines separating the British and German forces in northern France and Flanders set in motion the search for potential alternative approaches. Churchill, the combative First Lord of the Admiralty anxious to deploy and maximise the dominance available to the world's greatest maritime power, emerged as the leading advocate of the decisive use of British superiority on a peripheral front, rather than sending additional troops to the Western Front. On 29 December 1914, Churchill famously wrote to Prime Minister Herbert Henry Asquith asking (rhetorically) 'how ought we to apply our growing military power? Are there not other alternatives than sending our armies to chew barbed wire in Flanders?'[17]

In the immediate aftermath of the Ottomans' entry into the war, Churchill began to develop an audacious naval plan to force a passage through the Strait of the Dardanelles as a prelude to laying anchor off the shore of Istanbul. This, he hoped, would compel the Ottomans to sue for peace, and would open the Strait as a supply route from the Allies to Russia, while (at the very least) forcing the diversion of Ottoman troops to relieve pressure on the Russian Front described in the previous chapter.[18] Churchill additionally shared the view of many British officials that Ottoman military capabilities had been severely weakened by the two Balkan Wars in 1912 and 1913, as well as the deceptive results of the 3 November bombardment of the forts. Consequently, in the words of military historian David French, when war broke out in November 1914 the British Cabinet believed the Ottomans could be defeated quickly, and therefore 'the political dangers of pitting Britain against the Caliph could be contained'.[19]

Genesis of the campaign

Momentum for a diversionary strategy gathered pace over the winter of 1914-15. The idea for a naval assault on the Dardanelles was first put forward to the British War Council by Churchill on 13 January 1915. It originated in a request from the Russian Commander-in-Chief for a British diversionary attack to relieve the pressure of the Ottoman advance against Russian forces in Anatolia. Churchill's support for a campaign against the Ottomans also reflected his waning enthusiasm for another of his ideas to open a new naval front against the enemy, by attacking the north German coastline. His advocacy of the Dardanelles front won the support of influential members of the British Government with direct responsibility for the war effort, including Kitchener at the War Office and the Chancellor of the Exchequer, David Lloyd George, although not, notably, the veteran First Sea Lord, Admiral John Fisher, who expressed misgivings about a strategy that he did not believe had much chance of succeeding.[20] The result was an extremely vague operational objective, as the War Council mandated the Royal Navy to 'prepare for a naval expedition in February, to bombard and take the Gallipoli Peninsula, with Constantinople [Istanbul] as its objective'.[21]

Yet, as the plan moved towards becoming operational, it suffered from a mismatch between aims and objectives from the beginning. A number of key questions notably remained unresolved right up to the commencement of operations on 19 February 1915. Could a naval operation by itself force its way through the network of onshore fortifications and defences that protected the Strait? How, indeed, could ships 'take' a heavily fortified land-based target? Kitchener felt that the Ottoman garrison on the Gallipoli Peninsula would flee or surrender without requiring the landing of British forces, but was this likely? If the force succeeded in pushing through the Strait, would its presence at Istanbul precipitate an Ottoman withdrawal from the war, given the substantial military direction and assistance rendered by its German military missions? And if it did not, could military planners in London find sufficient troops and draw up an operational plan quickly enough to regain the initiative without sacrificing the element of surprise in the campaign?[22]

The initial decision to utilise naval force (through a combination of minesweepers, submarines and battleships) alone began to unravel almost immediately. Early in February 1915, the British commanders decided that an infantry division would after all be needed, in addition to the small contingents of Royal Marines. One final regular division remained available, the 29th Division. This had been created at the start of the year by amalgamating disparate units of infantry that had been scattered across various garrison posts throughout the British Empire. Accordingly, it was dispatched to Egypt, where it joined the infantry forces that had been arriving from Australia and New Zealand for onward transit to the war zones in Europe and, now, the Dardanelles. Thus, the Anzac soldiers undergoing training in Egypt were grouped into the Australian 1st Division and the composite New Zealand and Australian Division. Together, they made up the now-legendary Anzac Corps. It was joined by the Royal Naval Division, a 'strange combination of barely trained troops with next to no artillery provision' but including the acclaimed English poet, Sub-Lieutenant Rupert Brooke.[23]

A French contingent grouped around the 1st Division of the Corps Expéditionnaire d'Orient rounded out the hastily assembled force, ostensibly with a view to keeping a close watch on British operations in the Middle East. Incidentally, the British lead-role in the Dardanelles campaign actually contravened an understanding reached on

6 August 1914 between the sometimes wary allies over the demarcation of naval responsibilities in the theatres of war. This had stipulated that the British Navy would direct naval operations in the Atlantic and the North Sea, while the French would take responsibility for the Mediterranean. As such, the French Navy did not react well when presented by what they saw as a British *fait accompli* in the form of the detailed operational plan on 19 January 1915. Nevertheless, their contribution throughout the campaign was important, and they suffered over 27,000 casualties, yet have been almost entirely written out of the historiography of the campaign.[24]

Together, the British and French assembled a naval force one Dreadnought-class battleship, one battlecruiser, 16 pre-Dreadnought battleships, 20 destroyers and 35 minesweepers. Facing the force (which became known as the Mediterranean Expeditionary Force) at the 1,600-yard-wide passage through the Strait was the Ottoman Fifth Army under the command of the German General Liman von Sanders.[25] The Ottoman force of some 84,000 men was divided into III Corps and XV Corps, and consisted of five infantry divisions, with a sixth in reserve alongside a brigade of cavalry. Importantly, they enjoyed numerical strength against the 75,000 invading troops, and had the great advantage of holding the high ground overlooking all potential landing-points. In addition, the Fifth Army's troops were far more resilient and better trained than was acknowledged by the British, and prepared a robust system of eleven field fortifications and lines of defence around potential landing-sites. In part, they built on defensive works that had been constructed to counter possible Greek or Bulgarian attacks on the Strait during the Balkan Wars.[26]

Opening shots

Hostilities commenced on 19 February 1915, when two British destroyers and two British battleships bombarded the Ottoman forts on the Gallipoli Peninsula. However, this, and further engagements later in February and in March, made little progress in clearing the Ottoman minefields that had been meticulously laid across the Strait. Insufficient minesweepers meant that these could not be cleared in order to allow the larger and more powerful battleships to close in on the fortifications. Largely for this reason, the successive bombardments did little to silence the enemy artillery pieces or put them out of action, with particularly heavy and effective Ottoman resistance being recorded on 10-11 March. Hence, the difficulty of forcing a passage by naval means alone was becoming increasingly evident, but Churchill's patience was growing thin. On 11 March, he telegraphed the naval commander of Britain's East Mediterranean Force at Gallipoli, Admiral Sir Sackville Carden, to press for an immediate attack, while noting that 'We do not wish to hurry you or urge you beyond your judgement...' Three days later, Churchill telegraphed again to state that 'Two or three hundred casualties would be a moderate price to pay for [mine-] sweeping up as far as the Narrows.'[27]

The day after this missive, Carden resigned as naval commander of British forces. He had been suffering from ill health and increasing stress, and was on the brink of a nervous breakdown. Accordingly, just three days before the eventual launch of the main attack on 18 March, the force leadership was shaken up, with his second-in-command, Vice Admiral John de Robeck, hastily taking charge. Equally abruptly, General Sir Ian Hamilton was summoned to Kitchener's War Office on 12 March and placed in charge of the Mediterranean Expeditionary Force. This came two days after the decision to dispatch the 29th Division to form the cornerstone of the fighting force, as British political and military planners began the transition from a purely naval to an amphibious plan of attack.[28] With the Ottoman minefields largely uncut, and the howitzers still largely in place, the stage was set for the major Allied effort to break through the Dardanelles and make its thrust toward Istanbul.

On 18 March, the Anglo-French naval force assembled in three lines of attack. Six British battleships would attack first and would be followed by four French ships, with a flotilla of six more British ships acting as a relief force to replace damaged vessels. That sunny morning saw the failure of Churchill's grandiose and overly ambitious scheme as three battleships were sunk and three more critically damaged. Heavy Ottoman shelling of the beleaguered minesweepers – essentially converted fishing trawlers manned by inexperienced and terrified civilians – meant the minefields could not be cut, while a freshly laid stretch of mines went fatally undetected. One French warship, the *Bouvet*, struck a mine while attempting to withdraw after being hit by a heavy shell. This deadly combination caused it to sink in little more than three minutes with the loss of 639 lives, leaving only 66 survivors. The French flagship boat, the *Suffren*, was also hit by a heavy shell that caused heavy fatalities, in a scene evocatively described by Rear Admiral Emile Gueprette:

The scene was tragically macabre: the image of desolation, the flames spared nothing. As for our young men, a few minutes ago, so alert, so self-confident, all now lying dead on the bare deck, blackened burnt skeletons, twisted in all directions, no trace of any clothing, the fire having devoured all.[29]

By the end of the day, the plan to force the Dardanelles lay in tatters, and the operational vision for the campaign needed to be recast. Accordingly at a hastily convened conference aboard the HMS *Queen Elizabeth* on 22 March, de Robeck took the decision to combine military operations with the infantry force. This went against Churchill's desire to resume the attack, and command was vested in Hamilton's Mediterranean Expeditionary Force (MEF). Hamilton had arrived in theatre on 17 March in time to witness the failed naval attack, and it was agreed that the Royal Navy should only resume its action *after* the infantry had seized control of the Kilid Bahr plateau on the Gallipoli Peninsula.[30]

Plans were therefore hurriedly drawn up for a landing on the Gallipoli Peninsula itself. However, they had to await the actual arrival of troop reinforcements from Britain. This gave the Ottomans much-needed time to regroup and reorganise their defences at the potential landing-sites, as they too had taken substantial losses in the March fighting. In particular, their gunners had come close to running out of ammunition on 18 March prior to the decision to withdraw the British fleet. The

Ottoman command also had to address a division of opinion between von Sanders and Mustapha Kemal over the optimal placing of defensive positions and reinforcements. Kemal believed the British would attack at the southernmost tip of the peninsula at Cape Helles and at its narrowest point at Gaba Tepe. This clashed with von Sanders, who decided to concentrate the majority of his force in the interior of the peninsula as a strategic reserve, and spread the remainder over three positions at Helles, Bulair (at the northern end of the peninsula) and Besika Bay, on the Asiatic coast of the Dardanelles.

Hamilton's preparations for the landings at Gallipoli were therefore beset by problems. The Anzac Corps was inexperienced and lacked suitable training, yet its objectives were formidable: in the words of the most recent history of the campaign, 'to make a night landing on a hostile shore, overcome an ill-defined opposition, take control of the high ground surrounding the landing beaches and then push across the Peninsula...'[31] Hamilton chose to make simultaneous landings at six beachheads spread between Anzac Cove, on the western flank of the peninsula, and Cape Helles, at its southernmost tip. Cape Helles offered the advantage that naval firepower could be provided from three sides, but it was remote from the other major operational objectives and separated from them by difficult, hilly terrain.

On 25 April 1915, Australian and New Zealand forces landed at Anzac Cove while British and French troops assaulted Cape Helles. Lacking the element of surprise, they met intense resistance from the Ottoman defenders on the high ground surrounding all the beachheads. At the site of the main landing at V Beach at Cape Helles, the British and Irish troops leading the attack suffered appalling casualties as they were picked off by the Ottoman machine guns and barbed wire. The scale of the slaughter was such that a mere 21 out of the first 200 soldiers who tried to get ashore made it alive.[32] Up the coast at Anzac Cove, the bulk of the Australian and New Zealand force managed to establish a foothold on the peninsula and advance inland. For a time, the Anzacs appeared to be on the verge of taking the critically important high ground that offered a vantage point over the entire peninsula. However, Kemal responded by personally leading the Ottoman counter-attack and famously leading the 57th Infantry Regiment into battle with the cry 'I do not expect you to attack, I order you to die!'[33]

This act of heroism seized the momentum from the attacking forces just as it appeared to hang in the balance. In addition, it laid the foundations for the mythologising of Atatürk as the great national figure he later became. By the end of the first day of the land attack, the Ottomans had managed to contain the British and Anzac landings to the beachheads, and deploy the reserves to reinforce their defensive lines. A separate French attack on the Asian coastline (at Kum Kale) had similarly been contained without meeting any of its objectives. Von Sanders also benefited from the arrival of reinforcements which he was able to send into battle on the second and subsequent days. These fresh troops proved instrumental in halting the waves of attacks from an enemy that was becoming increasingly fatigued and weakened by persistently heavy casualties. On April 28, they broke up the first major attempted sortie from the beachheads (at Cape Helles) that aimed to capture the strategically important village of Krithia. A second British attack on Krithia on 6 May also failed, as did a third battle on 4 June with heavy casualties, ending any lingering hopes of a breakthrough, and bringing to an end the opening phase of the Gallipoli campaign.[34]

Preparations for a summer landing

Both sides then began a process of reorganisation and reinforcement that lasted from May through to the resumption of the Allied attack on 6 August. The Ottoman 2nd Division arrived in mid-May while the British received one Territorial Army Division (the 52nd) in June. Hamilton also began to develop his lines of communication and supply between his advanced bases on the Aegean island of Limnos and the supply depots in Egypt. In the absence of suitable deep-water ports in the eastern Aegean, Alexandria was designated the main base for the Mediterranean Expeditionary Force. An advanced base was established at Mudros (on Limnos), and up to 120 transport ships sailed between them to maintain the troops in rations, ammunition and reinforcements of troops and pack animals. However, the advanced base initially was little more than a natural harbour, and lacked piers, jetties and transportation networks, which all had to be built with material and labour from Egypt.[35]

As the Allied landings became bogged down and spread over five separate beachheads, it became a complex logistical challenge for Hamilton. This was compounded by the lack of easily available fresh water on the Gallipoli Peninsula as the troops were unable to secure sufficient supplies. This, too, had to be hastily arranged from Mudros. Meanwhile, the heavy stream of casualties needing evacuation back to Egypt imposed a further burden on the maritime lines of communication. The medical situation also threatened to damage British prestige in Egypt should they be visibly perceived to be faltering at the Dardanelles; in May 1915 the powerful British adviser to the Egyptian Government, Sir Ronald Graham, informed the Viceroy of India (Sir Charles Hardinge) that 'The wounded are pouring in here, every hospital is overflowing, every available hotel and school has been commandeered and fitted out as well as possible to take them.'[36] In another letter received by the Viceroy the following month, the British High Commissioner in Cairo, Sir Henry McMahon, acknowledged that 'The war and our losses are brought very closely home to this country [Egypt], because Egypt is one large hospital of wounded. Not only Cairo and Alexandria, but every Provincial Capital is full of our wounded…in every available public building, hotel, and school.'[37]

By July, Hamilton was in despair at the deteriorating logistical situation, noting how the lack of sufficient labour and lighters (for unloading the transport ships) meant that 'ships arrive carrying things urgently required, and then, before they can be unloaded, sail away again…' He added grimly that 'there are ships containing engineering plant which have been five times out here and five times have gone away again without anyone being able to unload them owing to want of lighters'.[38] Hamilton went so far as to confess to the British Quartermaster General at the War Office in London, Sir John Cowans, that 'I worry just as much over things behind me as I do over the enemy in front of me.'[39]

To counter this growing deployment and in an attempt to interdict its vulnerable sea-lines, the Germans dispatched a small U-boat squadron to the Dardanelles in late April. They included U-21, one of the most famous and highly decorated U-boats in the Imperial German Navy. Having left Germany on 25 April, the day of the Anzac landings, it arrived at Cape Helles on 25 May. In short order, it torpedoed and sank two British battleships, the HMS *Triumph* that day, and the HMS *Majestic* two days later. The U-boats' arrival did much to alter the balance of power at Cape Helles as they restricted the activities of Allied battleships in support of the troops on the beach by preying on the 'tenuous supply chain open to disruption and disaster every link of the way'.[40] Most dramatically of all, some three months later, another German U-boat sank a British transport ferrying troops from Alexandria to the Dardanelles, drowning nearly 1,000 men. The stunning efficacy of these attacks led the Admiralty in London, shorn since 25 May of its First Lord, Winston Churchill, the campaign's progenitor, to withdraw two of its largest battleships, HMS *Queen Elizabeth* and HMS *Inflexible*, to the comparative safety of the North Sea.[41]

Small-scale actions continued throughout June and early July, primarily on the southern tip of the peninsula around Helles, as first the Allies and then the Ottomans attempted to seize the upper hand on the peninsula. These caused high casualties but failed to alter the balance of forces materially. Some, such as the Battle of Gully Ravine, fought at Cape Helles between 28 June and 5 July, largely achieved their (limited) objectives, albeit at heavy cost for both sides, including an incredible 16,000 Ottoman casualties alone. Others were efforts in futility when little obvious advantage could be gained from attacks which nevertheless went ahead. Kenneth Best, the chaplain to the 42nd East Lancashire Division, recalled the aftermath of one such attack at Krithia in early June:

All along trench, am stepping over dead bodies. Some men shot clean through heart or head, looked quite natural and peaceful, except for yellow-green hue of skin. Most with looks of agony or horror on their faces – if faces were not blown away – nearly all mangled in ghastly fashion…In some places one has to tread on corpses. In middle of a heap of bodies, one moves. It is the most gruesome ghastly experience I can imagine…Our poor boys behaved like heroes, but are sadly cut up. No clear orders. Told to make for unidentified objective. They went over trench after trench till they had a mere handful of men left and could get no further…[42]

Similarly, two brigades of 52nd Division which mounted a final attack on 12 July sustained a 30 per cent casualty rate without yielding any significant progress. This disastrous battle was made during the heat of a scorching summer day and with insufficient water for the advancing troops. It ended with 'hundreds of men wandering about in the captured trench system in the burning sun, with corpses blackened and stinking…'[43] Yet the Allies remained stuck in their beachheads while the strategically vital high ground remained in Ottoman hands, and constant sniper fire and rising temperatures caused further grievances among the troops. By July:

> …the heat was becoming almost unbearable. The trenches were like ovens; the grass had long since withered and vanished, and the hot wind stirred up the dust, which drifted across the Peninsula, covering everything, and horribly pungent with the stench of war and death… Ashore, the bloated loathsome green flies – 'corpse flies' the men called them – were becoming literally pestilential. Feasting on the corpses in No Man's Land, swarming hideously in the latrines, filling every trench and dug-out and covering the food…[44]

With conditions on the peninsula beachheads deteriorating as the heat and the flies spread diseases such as dysentery and diarrhoea, and criticism of General Headquarters (GHQ) and the logistical arrangements mounting, the deadlock led Hamilton to consider alternative approaches that might unlock the stalemate.

As Allied forces were hemmed in both at Anzac Cove and Cape Helles, a new landing was proposed. This would take place 5 miles to the north of Anzac Cove, as part of an assault on the Sari Bair ridge. The initial plan was relatively small in scale and had limited objectives that matched the force capabilities at Hamilton's command. However, War Office notification that three further infantry divisions were being dispatched to join the Mediterranean Expeditionary Force led to a commensurate expansion in the scope of the operations. Hamilton now envisaged breaking out of the Suvla Bay landing zone, and seizing the summit at Chunuk Bair, a six-hour climb away. This was to be achieved in the face of constant enemy fire from surrounding hills on three sides, using a combination of inexperienced New Army troops untried in battle and fatigued Anzac troops, both lacking the stamina to undertake the strenuous uphill march in the summer heat and carrying the weight of their packs and equipment.[45]

The August offensive

The offensive was set for 6 August 1915. The three New Army Divisions (10th, 11th and 13th) were grouped into IX Corps. Controversially, it was placed under the command of Lieutenant General Sir Frederick Stopford, a 61-year-old retired general closely associated with the military disasters that had marked the start of the Boer War in 1899. IX Corps was entrusted with the initial landings at Suvla Bay in spite of the hesitancy and indecision displayed by Stopford in key meetings during the run-up to the battle. To the south, the Anzac forces and the British 13th Division were to attempt to break out from Anzac Cove, seize the high ground and link up with the operations further north. Their joint goal was to seize the Sari Bair ridge that ran down the centre of the peninsula from north to south. However, they faced a reorganised and considerably reinforced Ottoman Fifth Army that now consisted of sixteen divisions all holding the higher ground around the landing zones.[46]

Writing on 25 July, eleven days before the launch of the offensive, the British war correspondent attached to the Mediterranean Expeditionary Force, Ellis Ashmead-Bartlett, expressed his misgivings at the sight of the New Army troops arriving from Britain. After describing them somewhat uncharitably as 'a weedy-looking lot', Ashmead-Bartlett wondered, more seriously:

How can these newcomers, who have never been out of England before, resist the prevailing conditions? They are landed on a Sahara of sand where their tents are pitched, the heat of the sun is terrific, water is very scarce, and they are tormented all day by millions of flies, which for weeks have been feasting at Helles and Anzac on the bodies of the slain.[47]

Moreover, transport difficulties delayed the arrival of the three New Army divisions, meaning that only the 13th Division arrived on time to acclimatise (partially) and gain some battlefield experience. By contrast, the 10th and 11th Divisions went into battle without having seen any action whatsoever, and performed noticeably worse than 13th Division as a result. Poor staff work, an obsession with secrecy at Hamilton's GHQ, and the general substandard leadership from Stopford down the chain of command all contributed to the eventual failure of the offensive.[48]

The August offensive began on 6 August with attacks at Cape Helles and Anzac Cove prior to the main assault on Suvla Bay. At Helles, three British battalions belonging to the 29th and 42nd Divisions mounted what was intended to be a minor diversionary action but instead turned into a series of bloody battles. Hampered by a shortage of artillery and yet another change of leadership, the British brigades met determined and effective opposition from four Ottoman divisions. Repeated Ottoman counter-attacks between 7 and 9 August swung the momentum firmly in favour of the defenders, and the fighting continued until 13 August with heavy casualties on both sides. The second attack at Anzac Cove featured the Australian force's 1st Infantry Brigade as it sought to break out of its salient by capturing the ridge at Lone Pine. This attack was more successful as the Australians captured the main Ottoman defensive line and held their ground against enemy counters, but crucially it failed in its broader objective of tying down significant numbers of Ottoman troops away from the main offensive thrust at Suvla Bay.

More galling still was the experience of troops from the Wellington Battalion of the New Zealand Brigade belonging to the New Zealand and Australian Division who briefly broke out of the Anzac sector and reached the summit of the Chunuk Bair ridge early on the morning of 8 August. The ridge was exposed to enemy fire and difficult to defend or reinforce, particularly as attempts to capture crucial flanking positions did not succeed. Liman von Sanders hurriedly appointed Mustafa Kemal to lead the Ottoman counter-attack, consisting of three divisions with two more on their way, which he did with a degree of bravery that earned him legendary status within the post-war Turkish Republic, and on 10 August he led an overwhelming counter-attack that recaptured the most tangible (albeit temporary) Allied success during the campaign.

Over the course of the four-day battle at Anzac, the Anzac Corps suffered extraordinarily high rates of casualties. It lost 12,500 men – fully 33 per cent of its total. The 1st Australian Division and the New Zealand and Australian Division between them lost 5,800 men, while the British 13th Division lost 5,500 men alone. Most shockingly, 711 of the 760 men of the Wellington Battalion who reached the summit of Chunuk Bair on 8 August became casualties. In Hart's withering summary of the battle, 'The planning, the secrecy, the courageous attacks, the heroic resistance – in the end the attack from Anzac had been for nothing.'[49] Yet it left a lasting legacy on both the Ottoman and Anzac sides, as Kemal's heroic resistance cemented his rapidly rising position within the Ottoman hierarchy. Meanwhile, the courage and bravery of the thousands of Australians and New Zealanders in the face of overwhelming odds fed into potent national narratives that developed during and after the war, and continue to be memorialised and commemorated a century later.

Away from these unfolding attacks, the 10th and 11th British Divisions of IX Corps landed at Suvla Bay on the night of 6-7 August 1915. They had a numerical advantage over the three Ottoman battalions opposing them, but the landings were marred by general confusion, mismanagement and muddled objectives. As a result, little progress was made beyond securing the beachhead, as Ottoman reinforcements arrived on 9 August and pushed the British forces back. IX Corps suffered 1,700 casualties on the first day of action alone, and made little attempt to assault the higher ground from which the Ottoman snipers and defenders inflicted such deadly results. In mounting desperation, Stopford ordered the 53rd and 54th Divisions into action on 9-10 August, but they, too, failed to seize the advantage against a much strengthened opposition now led by Kemal. Stopford was sacked on 15 August and blamed by his superiors at the War Office for the complete failure of the Suvla landing. His temporary successor as head of IX Corps was the commander of 29th Division, Major General Beauvoir de Lisle, who made one final attempt on 21 August to connect the landings at Suvla Bay and Anzac Cove.

The unrelenting failure of the August offensive had a severe impact on the morale of the Allied soldiers at Gallipoli. Their commanders had gambled on one final throw of the dice but had been let down by the poor quality of leadership they exercised. The effect on the morale of the men who had fought – and died – in their thousands was crushing. Ashmead-Bartlett vividly captured the desolate mood as he returned from the Dardanelles to the advanced base at Imbros on 17 August:

On my way home I could not help reflecting on the change that has come over Anzac and the Dominion troops since I last visited their camps before the great offensive. Then Anzac was like a gay, heavily-populated city full of life and hope, with confidence in itself and in its ability to carry through any task it might be called up on to perform…Nearly half Birdwood's army has now melted away from death, wounds, and disease. The men who return stand outside the dug-outs and think of the comrades who will know them no more…They have the air of men resigned to their fate, but who are determined to see the matter through. There is still the grim decision, but the look of hope and expectancy has altogether vanished. No illusions as to the real position remain. Every officer and every man realises only too well that there is nothing more to be done.[50]

End of the campaign

Although the campaign at the Dardanelles continued for four more months before finally petering out, the failure of the Allied forces to break out of their beachheads in August signalled the end of any lingering hopes of operational or strategic success. Yet, admitting defeat and ordering the evacuation of the peninsula was no easy matter as it became intertwined in the minds of British policy-makers with the issue of imperial prestige. Officials in London, Delhi and Cairo all feared for the consequences of British rule were they seen to have been defeated by an 'Asiatic' enemy. This was compounded by the slender pillars of imperial rule in their colonial possessions. Comparatively small clusters of British soldiers and civil servants were buttressed by much greater numbers of local collaborators, who determined the scope and penetrative depth of imperialism.[51] In the words of military historian David French, prestige was 'the "cement" which supported the foundations of their rule and their ideology which they used to explain their superiority over the masses they ruled'.[52]

As the fighting at Gallipoli wound down, it coincided with the expansion of the British campaigns elsewhere in the Middle East, in Egypt and Palestine and in Mesopotamia. This was not coincidental, as the following two chapters make clear. Uppermost in the minds of British and imperial policy-makers was the need to minimise the damage and potential contagion from their setback at the Dardanelles. In part, this was achieved by rigorous censorship and firm and rapid action against potential and actual agitators in Egypt and India.[53] However, it also spurred officials to advocate, or at least acquiesce in, military actions against the Ottomans in other theatres that might otherwise not have gone ahead. Thus, as early as May 1915, the Viceroy of India, Sir Charles Hardinge, warned that 'defeat, or the necessity of cutting our losses in the Dardanelles, would be absolutely fatal in this country', adding that the boost it would give to opponents of British rule would mean that 'Pan-Islamism would become a very serious danger'.[54] By October, as the gravity of their position at Gallipoli became clear, the Foreign Secretary, Sir Edward Grey, told the Cabinet despairingly that 'At present we are practically bankrupt of prestige in the East, and our position could hardly be worse…'[55] This had direct (and, as it turned out, disastrous) implications for the British and Indian force encamped halfway between Basra and Baghdad in Mesopotamia (see Chapter 6). On 21 October, the Secretary of State for India, Sir Austen Chamberlain, called for 'a striking success in the East' to offset the debacle at Gallipoli, setting in motion the hasty, ill-prepared and ultimately catastrophic attempt to capture Baghdad in November 1915.[56] The Political Secretary at the India Office in London, Sir Arthur Hirtzel, agreed, telling the subsequent commission of inquiry into the Mesopotamia disaster that British prestige in the Middle East in October 1915 'stood at a lower ebb than at any period during the past 50 years' – since the Indian Rebellion of 1857. Accordingly, he advocated 'the desirability of striking some signal blow' in Mesopotamia in recompense.[57]

On the peninsula itself, the change in the seasons caused new problems as the searing summer heat gave way to bitterly cold winter weather. While the politicians and the generals pondered and prevaricated over how and when to wind down the campaign, localised fighting continued throughout the autumn. Moreover, the Ottomans' control of the high ground ringing each of the Allied beachheads resulted in a steady stream of casualties from sniper fire. Further adding to the misery on the beaches, contagious and deficiency diseases spread rapidly in the insanitary and overcrowded camps. By the autumn of 1915, Hart estimates that up to half of the 100,000 or so Allied forces on the peninsula were unfit for action.[58] Conditions gradually worsened as the bad weather set in, with a three-day rainstorm in late November flooding trenches and washing unburied corpses into them. On 28 November, the rain turned to snow as the temperature dropped well below freezing and high winds accelerated the wind chill factor. This combination wrought havoc on the forces on both sides still equipped with their light summer kit and over-exposed to hypothermia and frostbite. Moreover, for many of the Indian and Australian troops, it was the first time they had ever experienced snow and freezing conditions. The great snowstorm caused more than 200 deaths and over 5,000 cases of hypothermia at Suvla Bay alone, in addition to 3,000 at Anzac Cove and 1,000 at Cape Helles, although it did afford the opportunity for some British soldiers to shoot dead groups of Ottomans who left the safety of their trenches in a desperate attempt to collect firewood.[59]

The prospect of Allied evacuation was first raised on 11 October 1915 when the British Secretary of State for War, Lord Kitchener, asked Hamilton to predict the likely human cost of any potential evacuation. When Hamilton truculently refused to contemplate the possibility, he was removed from his command three days later and replaced by General Sir Charles Monro. Since the start of the war, Monro had commanded units on the Western Front. Beginning with the 2nd Infantry Division of Douglas Haig's I Corps, he replaced Haig as Corps Commander in December 1914 when Haig was promoted to Commander-in-Chief of the British Expeditionary Force, and his upward trajectory continued in July 1915, when he took charge of the newly created (British) Third Army. Monro was a committed 'Westerner' in the sense that he firmly believed that the Great War could only be won by defeating the primary enemy (Germany) on the main field of battle in France and Flanders. In sending him to command the Mediterranean Expeditionary Force, his remit from Kitchener was to assess whether it would be better to evacuate the Gallipoli Peninsula rather than launching a new attempt to take it.[60]

Monro reached the Dardanelles on 27 October and immediately embarked on a three-day tour of the battle sites. While his visit and staff consultations were in progress, on 29 October Kitchener demanded an immediate response to the question of whether Monro advocated 'staying or leaving'. Accordingly, Monro replied on 31

October with a memorandum advising evacuation, but warning that it might come at the cost of unprecedented casualties amounting to one-third of the Mediterranean Expeditionary Force.[61] The assessment of the military situation that he sent to Kitchener was a withering indictment of Hamilton's folly:

The position occupied by our troops presented a military situation unique in history. The mere fringe of the coast line had been secured. The beaches and piers upon which they depended for all requirements in personnel and material were exposed to registered and observed artillery fire. Our entrenchments were dominated almost throughout by the Turks... The force, in short, held a line possessing almost every military defect. The position was without depth, the communications were insecure and dependent on the weather.[62]

Accordingly, Monro came out unequivocally in favour of evacuation, 'since we could not hope to achieve any purpose by remaining on the Peninsula, the appalling cost to the nation involved in consequence of embarking on an overseas expedition with no base available for the rapid transit of stores, supplies and personnel...'[63] This drew a furious response from the campaign's progenitor, Winston Churchill, who commented in his post-war *The World Crisis* how 'General Monro was a man of swift decision. He came, he saw, he capitulated.'[64]

Immediately after transmitting these words, Monro sailed to Egypt to discuss the impact of evacuating the peninsula In London, the British Government's newly created War Committee decided to send Kitchener himself to inspect the position before taking any final decision. He arrived on 9 November and initially was keen to make one final, possibly suicidal, naval attempt to blast through the Strait, only to be firmly rebuffed by Monro and his Chief of Staff, Major General Arthur Lynden-Bell, who deemed the scheme completely impracticable. Further staff conversations and a tour of the battle front convinced him, too, that no substantial results could be gained by clinging to their footholds at Gallipoli.[65]

Instead, a conference involving the commanders-in-chief in Egypt, Gallipoli and the recent Anglo-French force dispatched to Salonika was held at Mudros in mid November 1915. At it, the generals 'went into the situation in considerable detail' and acknowledged that the military situation at Gallipoli was little short of hopeless. After considering alternative schemes to 'cope with the Turko-German menace to the East', the High Commissioner of Egypt, Sir Henry McMahon, ruefully recorded how a suggested attack on the Ottoman's Mediterranean port of Alexandretta (today's Iskenderun near the modern-day Turkish–Syrian border) was blocked. Hence, he gloomily informed the Viceroy in India that 'we are reduced to the policy of awaiting attack in Mesopotamia and Egypt with all the political dangers of an approaching menace and its attendant circumstances of loss of prestige and local unrest'.[66]

The decision to evacuate the Mediterranean Expeditionary Force was taken on 22 November 1915. Although Kitchener proposed that only the forces at Suvla Bay and Anzac Cove be pulled out, leaving the troops in place at Cape Helles, the War Committee in London overruled him in favour of a complete withdrawal. This came as a meeting of the Joint [Anglo-French] Staff Conference in France on 8 December recommended the immediate evacuation of Gallipoli and the organisation and strengthening of the recently opened front at Salonika in northern Greece. Suvla Bay and Anzac Cove were successfully evacuated on the night of 19-20 December 1915, followed by Cape Helles on 8 January 1916. Remarkably, both evacuations occurred without losses in men, although considerable quantities of war materiel had to be left behind. Unintentionally, but ironically, they represented the two most striking successes of a campaign that claimed 230,000 Allied casualties (including more than 27,000 of the less heralded French Expeditionary Corps) and up to 300,000 Ottoman casualties.[67]

Writing in *The World Crisis* in 1931, Churchill argued that 'The campaign of the Dardanelles had been starved and crippled at every stage by the continued opposition of the French and British High Commands in France to the withdrawal of troops and munitions from the main theatre of the war.' He also blamed the withdrawal for reinvigorating the Ottoman war effort and claimed that, as a result, the subsequent resistance encountered in the Salonika, Egypt and Palestine, and Mesopotamia campaigns meant that all three 'grew rapidly into very great undertakings, and all continued until the last day of the war to make enormous drains upon the British resources...'[68] A very different account was given by the official 'war correspondent' at Gallipoli, Ellis Ashmead-Bartlett, following a meeting with Churchill on 14 October 1915. He described a narcissistic man in complete self-denial about the military disaster he had instigated, finding that:

...to my amazement that his views had undergone but little modification, even since the final disasters. He had apparently profited but little from the lessons of the last few months and still possessed the same exaggerated optimism on the possibilities of eventual success. He continued to reiterate his opinion that the fleet could have forced the Narrows, if it had only been allowed to make another effort after the reverse of March 18th. He even suggested that another attempt could yet succeed. This idea had become a regular obsession – a fetish which had gained possession of his mind, blinding him to facts and filling his brain with illusions.[69]

Instead, the fact is that the Allied forces faced a formidable foe at Gallipoli. The Ottoman forces at Gallipoli performed with great combat effectiveness. In the words of the pre-eminent historian of the Ottoman Army during the First World War, Edward Erickson, 'the Turks won the Gallipoli campaign because, in many ways, their army was more combat effective than the allied armies in 1915...the Turks fielded a very well-trained, well-led and highly-motivated army on the Gallipoli Peninsula that met the Australians, British and French man-to-man on very even terms'.[70] Moreover, the Ottoman command and control structures, high mobility in difficult terrain, and control over central positions on the peninsula, all presented operational advantages, as did the close cooperation and interoperability with the German units and advisers interspersed through the force. Importantly, it also reinvigorated the Ottoman war effort and, coupled with the victories over the British and Indian forces in Mesopotamia at Ctesiphon in November 1915 and Kut in April

GALLIPOLI AND SALONIKA

1916 and the two victories at the First and Second Battles of Gaza in March and April 1917, shifted the momentum in the Middle East campaigns.[71]

Sideshow at Salonika

As the campaign at Gallipoli drew to a close, the focus of British and French attention shifted 180 miles westwards to the northern Greek port city of Salonika. There, in early October 1915, a curious sideshow began that tied down considerable numbers of Allied forces for almost three years before precipitously breaking out to enforce Bulgaria's withdrawal from the war and setting the stage for the final collapse of the Ottoman front in October 1918. The genesis of the Salonika campaign had more to do with internal French political manoeuvring and the state of Anglo-French military relations than any grand strategic or even operational rationale. As a reflection of the requirements of alliance politics, rather than military strategy, British support for the campaign survived the Gallipoli debacle as a result of French pressure and desire to maintain the uneasy internal political consensus underpinning French politics.

This was the *union sacrée* (sacred union) by which the powerful French left wing agreed not to oppose government policy or undermine the war effort through industrial action. Although it eventually broke down acrimoniously in 1917, in its early stages it did influence British policy-makers anxious to prevent the former prime minister, Joseph Caillaux, from returning to power and, so they feared, making a compromise peace with Germany. For their part, French interests in opening a front at Salonika centred on their suspicion of British post-war intentions, and anxiety that they might find themselves at a disadvantage in the Middle East. Thus, as the pre-eminent scholar of the campaign, David Dutton, has observed, building up a stronger French position in the Balkans was designed to counteract Britain's position further east. Hence, the course and conduct of the Salonika campaign demonstrates the uneasy interplay between political and military considerations between the two most important Allied powers.

In addition, the genesis of the Salonika campaign also marked the temporary intersection of the Balkan and Ottoman fronts. This began as the Austro-Hungarian and German armies invaded Serbia on 7 October 1915 and rapidly captured its capital, Belgrade. One week later, Bulgaria ended its policy of prevaricating between the Allied and Central Powers and entered the war on the side of the latter as well as breaking through and smashing the remaining Serbian resistance in Macedonia. This triggered British intervention as Foreign Secretary Grey had pledged in the House of Commons to support Serbia in the event of a Bulgarian attack. Consequently, an Allied Expeditionary Force of 13,000 men was hastily mobilised and diverted from Gallipoli in mid-October, to be followed soon after by 18,000 French troops. However, after moving north from Salonika they failed to break through the Bulgarian lines on the River Vardar, still less enter Serbia itself. Instead, the Serbian army embarked on a desperate retreat through the mountains to the

93

Adriatic port of Durazzo, from where they were transferred to the Greek island of Corfu. Up to 20,000 soldiers out of the 300,000 who set out died during the retreat, and several thousand more perished from contagious diseases at the camps set up to receive them in Greece.[72]

Although any hope of saving Serbia was lost by the end of 1915, the campaign at Salonika continued for the duration of the war, and it eventually expanded to include more than 300,000 men. Deeply enmeshed in domestic French politics, the troops encamped at Salonika faced heavy hardships in the malarial plains of northern Greece and southern Macedonia. They also became entangled in a long-standing Greek political struggle between the pro-Allied government of Prime Minister Eleftherios Venizelos and the pro-German King, Constantine I. The latter had his power base in Athens, and tensions between the two escalated in August 1916 when followers of Venizelos established a provisional state in northern Greece, based in Salonika itself. This effectively divided the country into two halves, which were only reunited in May 1917, following the King's abdication the previous November, whereupon Venizelos returned to Athens and Greece officially joined the war on the side of the Allies. Britain and France had already, since the August 1916 coup, recognised the provisional state in northern Greece, and cooperated with Venizelos in instituting a naval blockade around royalist forces in the Peloponnese in southern Greece, in a remarkable act of occupation in a country they were supposed to be allied with.[73]

For the most part, the front at Salonika was primarily static. A major exception was the Monastir offensive between September and December 1916, which succeeded in recapturing the town from the Bulgarians but at the cost of exceptionally heavy casualties. These included more than 80,000 casualties from disease, which outnumbered the 50,000 battle casualties suffered by the Allies. Moreover, even this localised success was immediately overshadowed by the far greater reverse in Romania, which surrendered to the German onslaught on 6 December 1916, less than four months after entering the war on the Allied side. After that, the front stabilised once again, until very close to the end of the war in September 1918, when the Anglo-French forces finally made a decisive breakthrough.[74]

Yet throughout 1917, at a time when war-weariness in France and Britain peaked and the slow attritional battles on the Western Front showed little sign of bringing an end to the war any closer, six French and seven British infantry divisions remained tied down in Salonika as the 'Army of the Orient'. They were labelled more colloquially as the 'Gardeners of Salonika' as they systematically developed and diverted civil resources to military use. In particular, the Salonika Mixed Supply Commission oversaw the cultivation of large areas of land, both to boost the local production of vegetables, straw and hay, and to counter the malarial threat. Other services worked on improving local wells to improve the supply of drinking water, and reopened six lignite mines to make the force as self-sufficient in coal as possible.[75] The campaign against malaria was especially urgent as the estuarial marshlands and swamps ensured that the disease spread rapidly among the troops and labourers associated with the force. At one point, 20 per cent of the British force was hospitalised, before an intensive programme of medical research and widespread distribution of quinine in 1917 and 1918 brought the numbers of casualties down.[76]

Set against the strategic and operational limitations listed above, it is all the more remarkable that, when the campaign finally burst into life in September 1918, it triggered the chain of events that led to the end of the war in the Middle East. The decisive advance began on 15 September 1918 at the Battle of Dobro Pole. A force of 36,000 French, Italian and Serbian troops attacked 12,000 Bulgarian and German soldiers and captured the strategically vital mountain passes that had provided Bulgaria's natural defence against invasion. This gave the Allied forces control of the valleys leading northwards and eastwards, and a British attack on the right flank at Lake Doiran prevented Bulgarian reinforcements from rushing to repair the breach in the lines, albeit at extremely high British casualty rates of up to 30 per cent. Vastly outnumbered and quickly encircled, the hitherto static defensive lines rapidly collapsed and, when two Bulgarian regiments mutinied, a large-scale retreat commenced.[77]

The Royal Air Force successfully harassed the Bulgarian troops and turned a retreat into a rout. British, French and Greek troops entered Bulgarian territory on 25 September. The same day, the Central Powers' edifice began to crumble as the Bulgarian Government asked for an armistice. Meanwhile, French colonial forces made a lightning 60-mile advance which carried them around enemy lines into the city of Skopje on 29 September. Its capture secured the critical railhead that linked the Central Powers to the front lines, and sealed Bulgaria's withdrawal from the war the following day.[78] The Allied forces then diverged as French and Serbian troops began a grand advance northwards to liberate Serbia and cross the Danube to threaten the Austro-Hungarian Empire itself, while British forces swept eastwards through Thrace towards Turkey-in-Europe. This directly threatened the heart of the Ottoman Empire, Constantinople, in a way that advances in distant Palestine and Mesopotamia simply could not do.[79] Moreover, by October 1918, the German forces on the Western Front were in full retreat, and Bulgaria's exit merely confirmed to the leaderships in Vienna and Constantinople the hopelessness of their position.

5

EGYPT AND PALESTINE

The next two chapters analyse the two major campaigns conducted by British (and imperial, primarily Indian) forces that took place in Palestine and Mesopotamia. Although each campaign forms the basis for an individual chapter, there are a number of commonalities to consider. For this reason, a brief introductory section will briefly examine these common themes before the chapter continues with the campaign undertaken by British-led forces in Egypt and Palestine. Chapter 6 picks up with the campaign initiated primarily by British–Indian troops in Mesopotamia (at its outset). Together, the two campaigns represented the major focus of the British Empire's war-making in the Middle East during the Great War, and had repercussions that still reverberate today.

Both began with small Indian Army detachments that were despatched from India to Egypt and Mesopotamia in the autumn of 1914. The forces expanded during 1915 and made steady initial gains in the desert terrain of the Sinai Peninsula and southern Mesopotamia. Each then suffered a major pair of reverses during the middle years of the war – at Ctesiphon and Kut al-Amara in Mesopotamia between November 1915 and April 1916, and at the First and Second Battles of Gaza in March and April 1917. In both cases, the shock of defeat spurred a thorough military reorganisation and a renewal of the offensive. This resulted in the capture of the cities of Baghdad on 11 March 1917 and Jerusalem on 10 December 1917. Both were hailed in Britain as successes that lifted a war-weary population in an otherwise bleak year filled with stories of military stalemate and growing socio-economic discontent elsewhere.

Chapter 4 noted how Egypt served as the primary base for the Dardanelles campaign in 1915. The Mediterranean Expeditionary Force returned to Egypt in January 1916 and was reorganised into the Egyptian Expeditionary Force (EEF) before commencing its advance through the Sinai Peninsula towards the border with Ottoman Palestine. In Mesopotamia, advances along the Tigris and Euphrates rivers in 1915 left detachments of the Indian Expeditionary Force (IEF) D holding isolated and mutually unsupportable positions and reliant on an overstretched system of river transport for its supplies. Although the trajectory of the two campaigns was broadly synchronous (initial advance, military check, subsequent offensives), they differed significantly in operational and logistical timelines. British officials attempted too much too soon in Mesopotamia, whereas the offensive in Sinai and Palestine was characterised by a more careful build-up of force and logistical resources.

The campaigns made enormous demands on local resources and host societies. By the end of the war, the ration strength of the EEF was 458,246 combatants and non-combatants while that of the Mesopotamian Expeditionary Force (MEF) was only slightly smaller at 408,138. These strained their principal supply bases in Egypt and India to breaking-point by 1917, as well as the resources of man- and animal-power, food and fodder, in the territory that came under British occupation in Palestine and Mesopotamia. In addition, the EEF and MEF relied upon 'armies' of local labourers and animal transport columns for their logistical needs, as well as local resources of food and fodder. Recruitment and patterns of appropriation interfered with local labour markets and rural economies, and caused significant dislocation as requirements intensified in 1917-18. Furthermore, the division between British and Ottoman spheres of control cut across trading routes and agricultural hinterlands, and greatly exacerbated hardships resulting from poor harvests and crop failures between 1913 and 1916. The intrusion of substantial military forces thus eroded the delicate balance between civil and military requirements for often scarce resources.

Exposure to the lengthy fighting therefore made a heavy footprint on the communities caught up in the fighting. Its intensity required belligerents (on both the Ottoman and British sides) to deepen their penetration of local political and economic patterns. Levels of resource extraction and state interference became more demanding as the demands of the 'war economy' increased in complexity. The regulation and management of mobilising and extracting resources in turn led to a process of intensifying the reach of state control. This unfolded at varying speeds across both campaigns owing to the different interplay between domestic political factors and the regional and international requirements of the military situation. They also reflected diverging patterns of integration into the international (and colonial) system before 1914 and the different rates of absorption into new spheres of influence during the war itself. In addition, the ebb and flow of the fighting provided new opportunities for individuals and communities seeking to maximise their interests within the changing local order.

For the British, the evolution of the fighting led to a pronounced (if gradual) shift in attitudes towards extra-European military campaigning. They represented a decisive shift away from the limited 'frontier campaigns' that had predominated before 1914. Lingering mentalities of frontier warfare were gradually superseded by recognition of the need to expand strategy to include the mobilisation of local man- and animal-power and agricultural resources. Yet old habits died hard, particularly in British India, and a combination of institutional and intellectual constraints initially caused great damage to the war effort and the allocation of resources to the forces in

Mesopotamia. A prime example of the extent of shifting attitudes may be found in a statement made to the Mesopotamia Commission of Inquiry in October 1916 by the British officer responsible for all water transport arrangements for the Indian Army detachment that captured Basra in November 1914: the campaign 'was going to be some sort of expedition on the beach in the Persian Gulf...I had no conception, no idea whatsoever, that it was going to be up the Shatt al-Arab.'[1]

The campaigns in Palestine and Mesopotamia constituted the major thrust of Britain's offensives in the Middle East following the withdrawal from the Dardanelles in December 1915. By contrast, the Ottoman focus after Gallipoli was very much on the Russian front, with the loss of Erzurum in February 1916 followed by heavy fighting that summer. As mentioned in Chapter 3, the fighting against the Russians inflicted three-quarters of all Ottoman casualties between November 1915 and the time of the February Revolution in Russia in 1917.[2] During that year of revolutions, Russian weakening and eventual withdrawal opened up the possibility of Ottoman gains in Central Asia and the Caucasus, and attention shifted towards the 'pan-Turanian' option. Thus, by the time of the big British pushes towards Baghdad and Jerusalem, a combination of military overstretch and expansionary aims elsewhere severely weakened the Ottoman armies facing them in Mesopotamia and Palestine.[3] Moreover, the geographical distance and relative isolation of the battlefronts from the Ottoman heartland meant they did not threaten Istanbul to anything like the same extent as the campaigns at the Dardanelles or, in September 1918, the break-out from Salonika, which brought about the final collapse of the Ottoman war effort.[4]

Britain's campaigns also provided the context for the controversial wartime agreements reached with the Sharif of Mecca, the French and Zionist advocates of a Jewish 'national home' in Palestine. They occurred as British and French officials sought to exploit internal tensions within the Ottoman Empire by manipulating rivalries and encouraging proto-nationalist sentiments.[5] Yet they also committed Britain to following what Jukka Nevakivi has aptly labelled 'flagrantly clashing lines of policy'. These contradictory wartime decisions created a legacy of great bitterness and feelings of betrayal.[6] The genesis and detail of the Hussein–McMahon correspondence of 1915, the Sykes–Picot of May 1916 and the Balfour Declaration of November 1917 will be analysed in Chapter 7. In addition to these three major 'agreements', other declaratory statements of support for local self-governing aspirations, such as the Declaration to the Seven in Syria and the Anglo-French Declaration in 1918, added to the hopes and expectations for meaningful political change once the war was over.

The campaign in Egypt and Palestine

British rule in Egypt in the three decades between the 1882 occupation and the outbreak of war with Istanbul in 1914 rested on a small official presence. Governance was facilitated by, indeed dependent upon, layers of local collaborative groups such as civil servants, provincial and municipal officials, and military personnel. These acted as crucial intermediaries between the 'light-touch' colonial edifice and societal demands for social and economic betterment and a functioning rule of law. As in other instances of colonial occupation, the political, economic and social inequalities inherent in foreign rule generated a nationalist movement and spirit of resistance in Egypt. This emerged in part as a response to the negative economic effects of the British occupation, which displaced Egyptian artisans in favour of southern European immigrants, inhibited the industrialisation of Egypt through reforms to the legal and taxation systems, encouraged the commercialisation of agriculture which squeezed small landholders off their land and forced many peasants into bondage, and entrenched a new 'business oligarchy' of large landowners and foreign investors who monopolised income-generating possibilities in Egypt before 1914. Nationalist opinion was also galvanised by specific incidents such as the Dinshawai massacre of 1906 and the resulting exoneration of its British perpetrators.[7]

Egyptian exposure to, and enforced participation in, the Great War placed great strain on the collaborative networks that underpinned British power and projected its influence. Military demands for resources, manpower and animals required the British authorities to broaden and deepen substantively their penetration of local social and economic patterns. Moreover, the extension of operations into Palestine in 1917 and the subsequent takeover of enemy territory involved taking responsibility for an impoverished and war-ravaged region stricken by famine. Emergency transfers of foodstuffs and scarce manpower from Egypt to Palestine occurred just as localised scarcities began to appear and spread more widely in Egypt itself. This squeezed Britain's ability to maintain control by indirect and 'cheap' means – in its empire more widely as well as in Egypt – as the workload on officials increased (and their numbers reduced through diversion to military positions), while collaborators and groups affected by military requirements began to demand a tangible return on their wartime assistance. Thus, in the words of British historian Anthony Stockwell, 'War sapped the Empire, and cracks opened up on the surface.'[8]

The decisions taken between November 1914 and November 1918 therefore had important ramifications that extended into the post-war era. The pressures of sustaining major military campaigns led to a significant enhancement of state powers of mobilisation and extractive capabilities. A more authoritarian form of colonial control developed as the British authorities asked more of their local collaborative elites. This in turn reconfigured local power relations and generated local backlashes against the more onerous and visible demands for resources and manpower. These issues will be covered in detail in Part III of this book, while the following sections in this chapter describe how the military effort provided the context for the profound changes that followed. To begin with, British officials had to regularise the position of Egypt within the empire.

EGYPT AND PALESTINE

Resolving Egypt's anomalous status

Following the declaration of war with the Ottoman Empire on 5 November 1914, British policy focused on resolving the anomalous political and military status of Egypt within the British Empire. Egypt had been under 'temporary' British occupation since 1882 and hosted a small British garrison of between 4,000 and 5,000 soldiers.[9] In 1914, the British general in charge was John Maxwell, a veteran of more than thirty years' experience of Egypt. He worked alongside the networks of British government and commercial advisers, civil servants and inspectors that were spread throughout every branch of the Egyptian administration.[10] A. P. G. Elgood described them as 'advisers in name, controllers in fact' who operated behind the facade of the Egyptian Government in a theoretical separation of powers.[11] Their shadowy influence persuaded the leading British imperialist and colonial administrator, Alfred Milner, to coin the term the 'Veiled Protectorate'.

Egypt remained nominally part of the Ottoman Empire in November 1914. The outbreak of the war with Istanbul naturally focused attention on this fact. Grey initially proposed the outright annexation of Egypt but was opposed by the acting Consul General in Cairo, Sir Milne Cheetham. Cheetham defended the cooperative tradition of the 'temporary' occupation and argued that annexation would contradict the British Government's declared aim of upholding the rights of small nations.[12] The religious dimension (covered in Chapter 4) was a further complicating factor that led the Residency in Cairo to advocate a cautious approach in 1914. They did this because officials regarded Egyptians as 'potential if latent enemies whose neutrality and quiescence it was advisable to purchase at a price'.[13] Cheetham also foreshadowed later British attempts to act as the protector and promoter of Arab national sentiment, as he suggested that British leverage over Arab and Muslim feeling might better be projected through the 'creation of a Mahommedan [*sic*] nation under our protection'.[14]

In August 1914, British defence planners decided that imperial interests could best be defended by restoring the balance of power in Europe. In this respect, Britain entered the war in order to preserve the status quo rather than to make territorial acquisitions in the Middle East or elsewhere. Nevertheless, Britain's imperial position was based on maintaining control of the 'strategic artery' of the empire, the Suez Canal. This has aptly been described as the 'umbilical cord' of empire connecting India and the Dominions of Australia and New Zealand, and allowing the passage of men, materiel and munitions to and from the various front-lines.[15] Alongside the elimination of Germany's global network of communications and coaling stations, securing the Suez Canal and, by extension, maintaining stability in Egypt and its approaches, were critical to securing for the Royal Navy control of the oceans that would keep Britain's far-flung empire functioning.

An initial measure taken in October 1914, before the outbreak of war, saw the Residency adjourn (and subsequently suspend) the Legislative Assembly that had been established in 1911. On 2 November, with war imminent, the British military authorities issued a proclamation to the people of Egypt. This stated that Britain would assume full responsibility for its defence and that no Egyptian would be asked to participate in the fighting. A system of rigorous press censorship and counter-intelligence work added further layers of protection. Together, these measures successfully blunted Istanbul's declaration of holy war on 14 November.[16] During this period, military units from India, Australia and New Zealand all passed through Egypt on their way to the European front. In addition, two Indian divisions (the 10th and 11th Indian Infantry Divisions) arrived as the core of a new Force in Egypt, tasked with securing the Canal Zone.[17]

The 10th and 11th Indian Divisions were hastily put together in India as relations with Istanbul deteriorated. They consisted of disparate infantry brigades lumped together with insufficient staff, artillery or divisional troops. Nevertheless, Sir Ronald Storrs, Oriental Secretary at the Residency, welcomed their arrival in Egypt. He believed that the sight of the Indian troops represented a valuable corrective to Egyptian nationalist opinion, which had alleged that the British 'rode' Indians 'like asses' and that they would never fight. Maxwell also thought highly of the Indian soldiers, who he declared were 'keen as mustard and are longing for the enemy to appear'. He also wrote that the Indians were certainly better than a batch of Territorial Army men who had just arrived from England 'swarming with lice' and 'so badly vaccinated that they could hardly move'.

Maxwell placed the two Indian divisions along the Suez Canal in a line from Port Said in the north to Suez in the south. Their position benefited from excellent lateral communications in the form of a broad-gauge railway that ran along the entire length of the canal, and from the Royal Navy's command of the sea approaches to Suez and Port Said. Behind the front line, he established secure lines of communication on the west bank of the Suez Canal. These linked Alexandria (the destination for supplies arriving from the United Kingdom and the west), Suez (the destination for supplies from India and the east) and Cairo (the place of assembly for supplies purchased in Egypt). Meanwhile, the Indian troops patrolled and maintained the famous 'swept track' that ran the entire east bank of the canal. This acted as a rudimentary warning system against any enemy activity or mine-placing in the strategically vital Canal Zone. No ship was allowed to move in the canal until it had been inspected by British officers at first light each morning and reported clear of any incriminating footprint or other evidence.[18]

On 19 December 1914 Britain declared Egypt a protectorate and replaced the pro-Ottoman Khedive, Abbas Hilmi II, with his nephew, the pliant pro-British Hussein. This move settled the issue of Egyptian sovereignty while London acquired a valuable local ally. The Foreign Secretary to the Government of India, Sir Henry McMahon, became the first High Commissioner in Cairo. He succeeded the last British Agent, Lord Kitchener, who was appointed Secretary of State for War in London upon the outbreak of war. McMahon lacked prior experience of Egypt, spoke neither Arabic nor French (the language of bureaucracy in Egypt), and made little effort to liaise with his civilian and military colleagues as wartime demands grew more onerous and complex.[19] Martial law was introduced to bypass the system of Capitulations whereupon the British military effectively became the supreme legislative and executive authority in Egypt.[20] However, it initially had little impact on daily life. Maxwell was a popular figure with long experience in Egypt, and ensured that his 'tactful yet strong administration' ruled in close accord with the civil administration.[21]

Initial engagements in 1915

These initial measures proved sufficient to avoid the anti-British fervour that many officials feared after the declaration of hostilities with Istanbul. The immediate military threat to Egypt lasted until 3 February 1915, when an Ottoman force of 20,000 men and a complement of field artillery managed to cross the Sinai Desert from Palestine. They were led by the German general Friedrich Kress von Kressenstein (a member of Liman von Sanders' military mission) and consisted of two divisions (the 10th and 25th Infantry Divisions), totalling 25,000 men, of Djemal Pasha's Fourth Army. In his post-war memoirs, Djemal recalled the interlocking military and political objectives of the raid:

...I hoped that the Egyptian patriots, encouraged by the capture of Ismailia by the Turkish Army, would rise en masse, and Egypt would be freed in an unexpectedly short time by the employment of quite a small force and insignificant technical resources.[22]

The raiding force attempted to block the Suez Canal and blow up the Sweet Water Canal that ran parallel to it. However, the attempt to infiltrate the Suez Canal using inflatable pontoons and rafts was beaten back by the canal's Indian defenders with the heavy loss of more than 1,500 Ottoman lives, though not before two companies had actually managed to cross the canal and establish a small bridgehead on its western bank. Kress retreated to Palestine having performed creditably, albeit unsuccessfully, though his difficulty in procuring the 14,000 camels necessary to accompany the raid presaged the intensified requisitioning of local resources that was to follow. The engagement marked the end of the direct military threat to the canal.[23]

During 1915, Egypt served as the main base for the Dardanelles campaign. Military operations at Gallipoli occupied British attention during the spring and summer as the campaign expanded in scope and size. The Egyptian city of Alexandria became the main base for the Mediterranean Expeditionary Force, owing to the lack of suitable deep-water ports and infrastructural facilities in the eastern Aegean. A fleet of 120 transport ships plied between Alexandria and the advance base on the island of Mudros. The ships kept the troops supplied with rations and ammunitions, as well as reinforcements of troops and pack animals. Meanwhile, the main supply base at Alexandria made use of the substantial pre-existing manufacturing and repair facilities available locally. An Ordnance Base also opened, with stocks initially drawn from the pre-1914 Army of Occupation peacetime depots at Alexandria and Cairo.[24]

British military officials in Egypt also recruited an Egyptian Works Battalion of 650 men and a fledgling Egyptian Labour Corps of 1,150 men for construction work at Mudros. Both units performed valuable service constructing piers, jetties and a light railway network, often in difficult conditions under shellfire. However, the Works Battalion suffered an 'unfortunate incident' in September 1915 that left nine Egyptians dead and seven more injured after British officers opened fire on them to quell a disturbance. The unrest arose after some of the labourers claimed they had only agreed to serve for three months and that they were not to be employed under fire. Their British officers disputed both claims and tensions flared following the heavy-handed actions of one officer who flogged several of the men. British officials in Egypt criticised the 'deplorable lack of tact and self-control' of the officer involved. They also worried that the incident might reawaken memories of the Dinshawai massacre of 1906 and again enflame local opinion against them. In the event, this was diverted through strict censorship, although it did result in the Works Battalion being recalled to Egypt. Its loss was lamented by Hamilton at Gallipoli, who commented ruefully that 'the abused and troublesome Works Battalion also did magnificent work as long as it was here, and I wish very much I had another'.[25]

Outright military demands on Egypt were not at first onerous in 1915. They consisted primarily of constructing hospital accommodation for the casualties from Gallipoli, requisitioning buildings for military works, and implementing military regulations to control the twin vices of drink and prostitution. Egypt's role in sustaining Britain's military effort in the eastern Mediterranean increased significantly in October 1915 after German and Austrian forces invaded and quickly overran Serbia. The previous chapter has described how this led to the dispatch of British and French troops to the northern Greek port-city of Salonika and the opening of the protracted Bulgarian front in the campaign against the Ottomans. The beginning of operations complicated Egypt's role as logistical and administrative base as it assumed responsibility for supplying Salonika as well as Gallipoli.[26]

General Edward Altham, the Inspector General of Communications in Egypt, oversaw the rapid enlargement of the Alexandria supply bases. These were reorganised into the Levant Base and placed under direct War Office control in order to coordinate the purchase of stores and allocation of supplies to the forces in Salonika and Gallipoli, as well as those in Egypt. A Resources Board was created to make all local purchases and overcome tensions between competing demands for resources. This had occurred earlier in 1915 when the Mediterranean Expeditionary Force and the Force in Egypt found themselves competing on the open market for the same stocks.[27]

The military demands for maintaining forces at Gallipoli and Salonika meant that military policy in Egypt was relatively limited in 1915. Aside from quelling the revolt in the Western Desert (discussed in the next section), the 60,000 troops of the Force in Egypt were confined to a passive defence of the Suez Canal. This led to concerns among the military authorities in London that 'the canal seemed to be defending the troops, not the troops defending the canal'. Consequently, on 16 November 1915, Maxwell ordered that reserves of stores and materiel be built up in order to strengthen defences of the canal. This involved the construction of three lines of defence progressively further away from the canal. They were protected by a series of mutually supporting outposts covering bridgeheads and vital posts on its east bank. Egyptian labourers recruited into the Egyptian Labour Corps, following its return from Gallipoli, completed the work early in 1916.

The Sanusi Revolt in the Western Desert

British and imperial forces also conducted a military campaign to quell the Sanusi rebellion in the Western Desert between Egypt and Libya. This had its origins in Sanusi resistance to the Italian invasion of Libya in 1911. An armed uprising began in November 1914 in Tripolitania and the southern Libyan province of Fezzan before spreading west to the Sanusi heartland in Cyrenaica, at the edge of Egypt's Western Desert. Italy's decision to enter the Great War on the side of Britain and France led the Ottomans to increase their levels of material support to the Sanusi, who themselves had declared holy war (jihad) on the Italian presence in Cyrenaica as early as 1913. The Italians' hold on Libya contracted steadily and by the end of 1915 was reduced to the coastal cities of Tripoli and Benghazi. Moreover, they suffered a major reverse in April 1915 at the battle of Gardabiyya at the hands of an erstwhile local ally, Ramadan al-Suwayhli of Misurata, resulting in the virtual annihilation of the Italian force in Libya.[28] Al-Suwayhli inflicted a further defeat on an Italian garrison at Bani Walid and, helped by inflows of Ottoman and German aid, became the most powerful notable in eastern Tripolitania, where he formed a local government that managed to exert control over the region's powerful Warfalla tribe. In retaliation, the increasingly desperate Italian authorities ordered the hanging of more than 700 Libyans, but this atrocity merely added to the momentum and depth of the anti-colonial resistance movement.[29]

To the east, Ottoman pressure grew on the Grand Sanusi, Sayyid Ahmad al-Sharif, to launch an attack on British forces in Egypt from the rear. This paid off in November 1915 as a force of 5,000 combatants crossed the frontier and marched eastwards along the coast towards Alexandria. Simultaneously, a German U-boat transported Ottoman and German officers to the Egyptian coastal settlement of Sollum and overpowered a British force there. In response, the British formed a Western Frontier Force of two (infantry and mounted) brigades, a squadron of the Royal Flying Corps and units from Australia, New Zealand, South Africa and India. It established its headquarters at Mersa Matruh, midway between Alexandria and Sollum, and methodically began to roll back the Sanusi advance. This was achieved between December 1915 and March 1916 in a series of five engagements that marked the end of the Sanusi threat along the Mediterranean coastline. However, fighting flared up again in October 1916 when Sanusi forces occupied a number of strategic oases, forcing the British to divert troops from the Sinai campaign to maintain a garrison in the Western Desert. Finally, in February 1917, a British Light Armoured Car brigade defeated the Sanusi and forced their final withdrawal across the Libyan frontier.

In the subsequent peace negotiations, the British engineered the replacement of Sayyid Ahmad al-Sharif, whom they regarded as a militant pan-Islamist, with his cousin, Idris al-Sanusi (who much later became the first King of Libya in 1951 until his overthrow by Colonel Gaddafi in 1969). Idris favoured good relations with Britain and blamed Ahmad for the military defeats suffered by the Sanusi in 1916. He was drawn into the network of British patronage and he banished Ahmad and his entourage of Ottoman officers from Cyrenaica. This fulfilled Britain's strategic objective, which was to control a pliable client regime along its western flank and negate the spread of Sanusi influence to sympathisers in Egypt or elsewhere in North Africa.[30] With the threat of attack from the rear nullified, the British could focus on the advance east across the Sinai Peninsula and into Ottoman Palestine.

Into Sinai and Palestine

The Mediterranean Expeditionary Force returned to Egypt in January 1916 following its successful evacuation from Gallipoli. On 9 January, General Archibald Murray replaced Monro as its Commander-in-Chief. Murray's force initially coexisted in an uneasy partnership alongside the Force in Egypt. Murray assumed responsibility for the canal defences while Maxwell retained responsibility for internal affairs and security on Egypt's Western Frontier. Nevertheless, the presence of two army commands created a duality of command and a complexity which led Maxwell to suggest his position be abolished in March 1916. This, he told London, was because he found the dual system 'unnecessary, wasteful and inconvenient and in times of stress probably dangerous'.[31] Murray assumed sole charge of the amalgamated force, which was renamed the Egyptian Expeditionary Force. However, Maxwell's departure deprived Egypt of a respected commander with long experience of local conditions. His successor, by contrast, lacked experience of Egyptian conditions, and during his tenure (which lasted until June 1917) critics argued that general headquarters become a closed society and isolated from awareness of Egyptian issues and problems.[32]

Murray faced an immediate challenge as sole commander in Egypt, as the military situation was one of considerable chaos in the spring of 1916. Eleven British and imperial divisions returned from Gallipoli and needed to be accommodated, supplied, refitted and sent on to other fronts. This task stretched local logistical capabilities to the limit as resources available in Egypt became increasingly unable to supply the troops and animals with foodstuffs and fodder. The situation became critical when an imminent breakdown in food supplies loomed large, existing facilities becoming overwhelmed by demand. This was averted only through a massive emergency shipment of bread and hay from India in March 1916.[33] It proved an early warning of the difficulties of transplanting large military forces onto civilian societies in which no substantial margin of subsistence existed. This would become a recurring problem for host societies and belligerent forces in Egypt and Mesopotamia as the campaigns progressed and expanded, as well as for India, the 'supplier of last resort' until its own stocks approached crisis point late in 1918.

Between March and June 1916, ten infantry divisions were reorganised and re-equipped and sent to France, while one (the 13th Division) was dispatched to Mesopotamia. Four Territorial Divisions remained in Egypt as Murray began to reconsider the optimal means of securing the Suez Canal Zone. This took shape on 15 February 1916. Murray informed his successor as Chief of the Imperial General Staff (CIGS) in London, William Robertson, that Egypt could best be defended by advancing across the Sinai Peninsula to the town of El Arish, close to the border with Ottoman Palestine. Murray argued that this would deny the Sinai to the enemy by securing British control over El Arish, the only town capable of providing sustaining any raiding force with water, making impossible any repeat of the February 1915 assault. Furthermore, the capture of El Arish would place the EEF in a position to undertake rapid offensive action against any enemy concentration in southern Palestine.[34]

British plans for a methodological advance were underpinned by painstaking logistical preparation. This reflected their growing awareness of the contemporaneous breakdown in the logistical arrangements in Mesopotamia (discussed later in this chapter). In Sinai, the advance was to be accompanied by the construction of a single-track railway and a water pipeline. Both commenced at the Suez Canal port of Qantara and constituted what one contemporary observer labelled an 'umbilical cord' linking the advancing troops with their food, water and military stocks.[35] Their construction was essential because the soft sandy desert terrain made it nearly impossible for motorised transport, while the water found in many of the wells was known to be brackish and unfit for human consumption.

On 9 March the War Office in London approved the construction of the railway from Qantara to Qatia. This was 28 miles east of the canal and its strategic value lay in the many springs there, and at Romani, 5 miles away. Together, Qatia and Romani contained the last available water supplies before El Arish, some 60 miles further to the east. Besides being a vital stepping stone for the EEF as it advanced, their occupation denied to the enemy the stocks of water that would be necessary to sustain any assault on the canal. Kress von Kressenstein led a second Ottoman raiding force of nearly 4,000 men across the Sinai to mount a surprise attack on the 5th Mounted Brigade at Qatia on 23 April. As with an attempted raid on the canal the same day, and with the earlier February 1915 assault, it was beaten back, albeit with severe British casualties and following an initial retreat from their positions. The attack served further notice of the need to secure strategic depth in Sinai. The British railway reached Romani on 19 May and enabled 52nd Division to advance and hold the position with its wells.[36]

The final Ottoman threat to Egypt and the Suez Canal came on 4 August 1916 when a joint German–Ottoman expeditionary force comprising the 3rd (Anatolian)

Infantry Division and machine gun companies and trench mortar battalions from the German Pasha I group attacked British and Anzac forces at Romani. The 1st and 2nd Australian Light Horse Brigades and the New Zealand Mounted Brigade joined with the 5th Mounted Brigade to beat back the attackers in the heat of the summer's day, taking more than 4,000 prisoners and inflicting 9,000 casualties on a force of 18,000 men. On 12 August the raiders abandoned their staging post at Bir el-Abd and retreated to El Arish. Britain's victory at the Battle of Romani finally secured the Suez Canal from enemy attack. In retrospect, it marked the end of the defence of Egypt and the beginning of the transition of the Sinai campaign from a defensive manoeuvre to defend the canal into an offensive posture aimed at invading Ottoman territory in Palestine itself.[37]

The Eastern Force of the EEF captured El Arish on 21 December 1916 and pushed on to take the border town of Rafa on 9 January 1917. These two engagements marked the end of military operations in Sinai, and the gradual (though uneven) progress of the railway and a water pipeline across the desert enabled Murray to build up a significant military force on the border with Ottoman Palestine. This allowed the EEF to move forward in numbers and prepare for an advance into enemy territory. By March 1917, three infantry divisions and two cavalry divisions had moved forward to a new set of front lines directly opposite the city of Gaza. In response, the Ottoman authorities ordered the mass evacuation of the civilian population in areas of southern Palestine, including all 50,000 inhabitants of Jaffa, partially because they feared their possible co-optation by invading British forces.[38]

By December 1916, the British military authorities were responsible for maintaining a force of 200,000 combatants and non-combatants along the border with Palestine. The 1.2 million gallons of water required each day reflected the complexity and scale of the logistical operation that underpinned the advance. This consisted of units such as the Egyptian Labour Corps and the Camel Transport Corps, which both made constantly growing demands on rural Egypt for manpower and resources. As the scale of operations escalated in 1917, so the link between logistical preparedness and strategic and military success (or failure) became inseparable. Yet this required British officials to intervene much more aggressively in order to penetrate and divert agricultural and economic activity towards the war effort. It also exposed divisions between the civilian and military branches of Britain's administration of Egypt. This originated in 1916 as McMahon embarked on 'frequent and bitter disputes' with Murray. In addition, McMahon passed a great deal of control to his Financial Adviser, Edward Cecil, who was disliked by the Sultan and his Egyptian ministers, laying the seeds of future conflict over the separation of powers between British and Egyptian branches of the administration.[39]

The Gaza offensives, 1917

In March 1917, the EEF launched offensive operations in southern Palestine. The assault on the Ottoman town of Gaza on 26 March constituted the juncture at which the hitherto defensive campaign to protect the Suez Canal became a thrust into enemy territory. A combination of military–logistical and broader geopolitical factors lay behind the decision to extend the campaign into Ottoman territory. The seizure of Gaza and the town of Beersheba to its east would secure control over the two principal sources of water supply in the region.[40] Its more temperate climate and ecology of grassland, wheat and barley fields, gardens and orchards would provide a healthier summer base for the EEF than the malaria-ridden coastal plain, as well as critical supplies of food and fodder for the troops and their pack animals. One British lieutenant described the area as 'delightful country, cultivated to perfection' and expressed his 'relief of seeing such country after the miles and miles of bare sand…'[41] Control of Gaza and Beersheba would also deny the Ottomans the use of the towns to block the EEF's routes of advance. Furthermore, their capture would provide cover for the extension of the military railway into Palestine itself.[42]

These local factors interacted with macro-level geopolitical and international considerations in shaping British military policy. During the early months of 1917, the new Prime Minister, David Lloyd George, was engaging in an acrimonious struggle with General William Robertson, Chief of the Imperial General Staff. This civil–military dispute concerned the direction of military operations and the question of whether military force should be deployed primarily on the Western Front or elsewhere. Lloyd George displaced Herbert Asquith as Prime Minister in December 1916, largely due to his support for a more aggressive war effort, but he was also critical of the mounting losses in France and Flanders and sought a new approach. This rested on his determination to take a longer-term view of the war that would preserve British manpower which, he felt, was being squandered in the series of battles of attrition on the Western Front. Innovative research by Brock Millman has also suggested that the offensives in Palestine and elsewhere in the Middle East may have been intended to strengthen Britain's global position in the event of any negotiated or compromise peace with Germany.[43]

At any rate, the invasion of southern Palestine was part of a broader international strategy of exerting combined pressure on the Central Powers on all fronts. This was agreed at an Anglo-French conference in Calais on 26 February 1917, an occasion notable for Lloyd George's attempt to marginalise and bypass Robertson and General Sir Douglas Haig by creating a unified military structure under the French commander Robert Nivelle.[44] This controversy (and Robertson's threat to resign) notwithstanding, the War Cabinet in London believed that the conquest of Palestine would help restore British strategy in the east. This was particularly relevant in the aftermath of the military humiliation and defeat suffered at Kut al-Amara in Mesopotamia in April 1916, which officials worried had dealt a damaging blow to British mystique and prestige. They also hoped that a successful campaign would stimulate the Arab Revolt in the Hejaz, draw Ottoman troops away from Russian troops in Armenia and British forces in Mesopotamia, and assist in the general expulsion of the enemy from the Middle East.[45]

On 26 March 1917 the EEF made the first of what would eventually be three attempts to take Gaza. Initially the assault was successful as cavalry units quickly enveloped the town, although plans to use shells filled with poison gas did not materialise. This was in part because of a faulty British assessment that the Ottomans would fall back to a line stretching from Jerusalem to Jaffa rather than hold the position at Gaza. Hence, Murray was unwilling to 'expose his weapons of surprise too early' and chose instead to retain his chemical ammunition for a future engagement.[46] This decision, as well as the early optimism, backfired badly, as a combination of poor staff work and communication resulted in the premature order to withdraw the cavalry units as staff officers wrongly feared they would run out of water before nightfall.[47] The Australian *Official History* of the Sinai and Palestine campaign alluded to the futility of the battle as it 'affected the troops on both sides to a degree out of all proportion to the casualties suffered…'[48]

This notwithstanding, Murray sent a very misleading and optimistic account of the battle to London, and it was reported a success in press accounts of the action. In response, the War Cabinet requested that Murray continue the advance into enemy territory in Palestine.[49] This necessitated a second attempt to take Gaza on 17-19 April, featuring the (eventual) first use of poison gas in any Middle Eastern theatre of war. The two-phased operation sought to attack the main Ottoman defences along a 4-kilometre line while pinning down enemy reinforcements to its east.[50] However, the attack was beaten back by a forewarned and reinforced Ottoman garrison numbering more than 20,000 men, with no progress to show for the heavy casualties sustained.[51] This second setback left the EEF demoralised and defeated, and Murray and the commander of Eastern Force, General Charles Dobell, were both soon replaced.

Murray was succeeded by General Sir Edmund Allenby on 11 June. Allenby had commanded Britain's Third Army on the Western Front during the spring 1917 offensives, but paid the price for failing to exploit a breakthrough at the Battle of Arras in April. He also fell out with Haig over tactics amid a clash of personalities between the two taciturn men, on one occasion finding themselves alone in a room in General Headquarters (GHQ) and unable to muster a single word to each other.[52] His transfer to the Middle East therefore represented a snub as much as an opportunity to refashion a military reputation, and he arrived in Palestine despondent and under a cloud of uncertainty, though he held an intimate knowledge of the Bible (and Greek) and the geography of the Holy Land.[53] More practically, he benefited from Murray's final decision in charge, which was belatedly to take measures to integrate his logistical network into an emerging strategic vision, and thus be capable of supporting a sizeable increase in the EEF opposite Gaza.[54] During the summer and autumn of 1917, the stability imparted by the static front line at Gaza also enabled the EEF to improve its intelligence capabilities significantly. The Intelligence Bureau at Port Said operated networks of Jewish and Bedouin Arab agents who relayed large quantities of information about Ottoman positions, intentions and combat and reserve strengths. These enabled EEF commanders to build up an accurate picture of the enemy's strategic intentions and force capabilities in the run-up to the resumption of offensive operations.[55] Allenby also received the full political backing of Prime Minister David Lloyd George, who tasked him with achieving a success that would boost flagging morale and reinvigorate an increasingly war-weary British public.

In July, the War Cabinet in London approved the doubling of the railway line from Qantara to the front line. Meanwhile, the new General Officer Commanding (GOC) of Eastern Force, Lieutenant General Philip Chetwode, and his Brigadier General, General Staff, Guy Dawnay, drew up a new plan to envelop and capture the water supplies at Beersheba, before turning back towards Gaza and rolling up the Ottoman defences.[56] Their plan aimed to restore fluidity to the battlefield and relied on a thorough reorganisation of lateral railways and reserve supply dumps over the summer. This systematic preparation enabled Allenby to assemble two infantry (XX and XXI) and one mounted corps (the Desert Mounted Corps) totalling ten divisions in total. They faced the newly formed Eighth Ottoman Army under Kress von Kressenstein, consisting of nine infantry and one cavalry division. Although the Ottomans had strengthened still further their lines of defences in Gaza since the spring, their operational capability was blunted by high rates of desertion, shortages of transport, ammunition and rations, and a regional strategic focus on Mesopotamia rather than Palestine.[57]

The Third Battle of Gaza took place between 31 October and 7 November 1917. It began with the seizure of Beersheba and its water supplies by XX Corps and the Desert Mounted Corps on 31 October. Gas shells were fired by 52nd Division at Gaza, but in general were found to be largely ineffective. At the time, this was attributed to the fact that 'The sea breeze at Gaza made use of gas difficult. The air was too clear and too volatile for gas to be very effective and [we] never had enough gas for a good barrage.'[58] Instead, Third Gaza became notable for the famous Charge of the Australian 4th Light Horse Brigade that overwhelmed the Ottoman trenches and resulted in the (vital) capture of 15 of the 17 wells intact. In his dispatch to headquarters, the unit's commanding officer, Lieutenant Colonel Murray Bourchier, described how 'the morale of the enemy was greatly shaken through our troops galloping over his positions therefore causing his riflemen and machine gunners to lose all control of fire discipline'.[59] With the Ottomans' left flank secure, XXI Corps attacked Gaza on 2 November, and succeeded in breaking through the Ottoman lines on the 7th.[60] Such was the extent of the logistical reorganisation carried out since the First and Second Battles of Gaza that the Third Battle opened with the heaviest extra-European artillery bombardment in the entire war. The gun concentration was equivalent to that of 1 July 1916 on the Somme, testimony to the success of the painstaking preparatory overhaul of the networks of supply and transportation.[61]

As XX Corps subsequently advanced northwards, it then encountered stiff Ottoman resistance in the Judean Hills. The breakthrough at Gaza and Beersheba forced the former Chief of the German General Staff (and in 1917 overall commander of Ottoman forces in Palestine) General Erich von Falkenhayn to withdraw the Seventh and Eighth Armies to Jerusalem. The Seventh Army, in particular, conducted a strong rearguard action that held up the EEF advance and required much hard fighting to overcome it.[62] Three major engagements took place at Mughar Ridge (13 November), Nebi Samwil (17-24 November), as well as a series of Ottoman counter-attacks that began on 27 November. In spite of these, and also of burgeoning difficulties of supply and transport as the advancing British Imperial troops left their railheads behind and moved into the cold and exposed hills, Jerusalem surrendered on 9 December 1917. Its defenders began a disorganised retreat as most Ottoman army units in the area were in poor shape, chronically short of supplies and reinforcements, under continuous pressure from the EEF, and in very low morale. Two days later, Allenby formally entered the city on foot through the Jaffa Gate, flanked by civilian and military officers including T. E. Lawrence and François Georges-Picot, as well as representatives from the small Italian and French contingents with the EEF.[63]

On 27 December an Ottoman counter-attack attempted to retake the city. It failed in this objective, but did inflict more than 1,300 casualties on the EEF, and minor operations around the city continued until February 1918. The setbacks at Gaza and Beersheba also prompted the Ottoman high command to divert the Yilderim Army Group (also known as *Heeresgruppe F*) to Palestine. This group, whose name meant 'Thunderbolt' and was under the command of the German General Erich von Falkenhayn (and subsequently, from February 1918, Liman von Sanders), was originally intended to form the nucleus of an Ottoman counter-attack in Mesopotamia in 1917. Much depleted in strength, it consisted of three German infantry battalions and nine promised Ottoman divisions. These failed to arrive before the fall of Jerusalem and finally came in fits and starts, so weakened that one recent historian of the Palestine campaign, Matthew Hughes, described them as a 'paper formation' that was 'more nominal than real'.[64] Nevertheless, the Ottoman units halted their retreat and dug themselves into a line stretching from the coastline north of Jaffa through the Judean Hills to the Jordan River. Major military operations in Palestine then halted as the Germans nearly broke through the British Third and Fifth Armies in France in their great spring offensive (*Kaiserschlacht*) on 21 March 1918. In the rush to reinforce the Western Front, Allenby transferred two of his three British divisions to France and had to reorganise his force with units raised hastily in India. Only in September 1918, with the general momentum shifting decisively toward the Allies, did the advance resume, with devastating results.[65]

The seizure of Jerusalem in December 1917 represented a political triumph far more than a military or strategic victory. It came at the end of an especially turbulent period for the Entente and Allied powers, after a year in which the Russian revolutions and French mutinies threatened its very existence, and the bloody stalemates at Ypres and Passchendaele appeared to be wearing down the morale of the British people just as much as the strength of the enemy formations. In satisfying Lloyd George's desire for a flamboyant gesture that would deliver Jerusalem as a 'Christmas present to the British nation', its capture was celebrated by the ringing of church bells across Britain, as well as a seminal cartoon in *Punch* entitled 'The Last

Crusade' that depicted Richard the Lionheart looking down on the city and saying 'My dream comes true!'[66] Yet it did nothing to determine the outcome of the Great War or even the more limited balance in the campaign against the Ottoman Empire. Hence the Germans' assessment of its fall was rather more pragmatic and perceptive: 'This is doubtless a success for the English, though more moral than military...the conqueror of the city, of course, gains a halo.'[67]

Palestine: invasion and occupation

The extension of the military campaign into Palestine required the EEF to assume responsibility for a land ravaged by the economic impact of war. The Ottoman vilayets (provinces) of Syria, Lebanon and Palestine suffered unimaginable hardship and dislocation during the war years. They were especially badly hit by a severe famine that began in 1914 and lasted through 1916. This was partially attributable to successive poor harvests and a devastating plague of locusts in Palestine between March and October 1915, heavy Ottoman demands for local man- and animal-power, and the closure of trading routes occasioned by the division of the region into warring spheres of influence and control. The locusts stripped many areas in Syria and Palestine bare of any vegetation and decimated local food supplies, while a continuous hot wind in June 1916 badly affected wheat yields in Syria's grain-producing region around Aleppo. Supplies of foodstuffs were further limited by the trading disruption, insufficient transportation to carry crops to market, and the lack of any organisation to coordinate food supply and consumption.[68] Simultaneously, thousands of young men were conscripted into the Ottoman military machine and work brigades, while the requisitioning of labour, draft animals, cattle and agricultural produce diverted what scarce resources existed to military use. These measures imposed a very great strain on the civilian inhabitants of Syria and Lebanon as food shortages began in the cities and towns before spreading rapidly to rural areas, and close to half a million people died of famine.[69]

The impact of these extractive policies was magnified by repressive Ottoman measures that restricted the flow of supplies to the Levant for fear they would fall into enemy hands. In 1915 Djemal Pasha was appointed Military Governor of Syria with special and extensive military and civilian powers. In addition to leading the Ottoman Fourth Army, Djemal was a member of the Young Turks' triumvirate as Minister of the Navy alongside the Minister of War (Enver Pasha) and the Minister of the Interior (Talaat Pasha). His dispatch to Syria reflected the triumvirate's uncertainty about the political loyalty of the Arab populations of the empire, particularly in the vibrant urban centres that had nurtured the cultural and secretive proto-nationalist societies before 1914. In part, this atmosphere of mutual suspicion reflected the growing alienation of public and notable opinion in Syria as the CUP in Istanbul embraced a more Turkish form of nationalism.[70] Moreover, the region's Christian communities, especially in Lebanon, came under suspicion over their ties with French interests and influence. Placing the region under the direct supervision of the powerful and influential Djemal signalled Istanbul's intention to keep it under close surveillance. During the subsequent three years, Djemal's suppression of political dissidents (particularly Arab nationalists) earned him the grim sobriquet *al-Saffah* ('the blood-shedder').

Djemal's arrival in Syria in early 1915 was quickly followed by an event which sealed the emerging divisions between the Turkic centre and Arab periphery of the empire. This was the seizure of a cache of secret documents from the French consulates in Beirut and Damascus that contained extensive details concerning the activities of a network of Arab nationalists operating subversively in each city. A number of leading Arab notables were arrested and charged with treason based on the documents, and sentenced to death in military tribunals. Eleven were publicly hanged in Beirut in August 1915 and a further twenty-one in Beirut and Damascus in May 1916. The hangings shocked Arab society as they included one senator, three parliamentary deputies, members of several leading families in Syria, and others associated with activity in the Ottoman Decentralisation Party. One prominent historian, William Cleveland, described how their deaths, which took place just before the start of the Arab Revolt, 'gave the victims an aura of martyrdom...and came to be associated with the cause of Arabism'.[71]

The legacies of Djemal's harsh and increasingly repressive policies intersected with the deeper and more penetrative Ottoman mobilisation of wartime resources of manpower and agricultural resources. They were magnified by the impact of an Allied blockade of Palestinian and Syrian seaports, as well as the economic dislocation arising from the disruption to inter- and intra-tribal trade routes, particularly to Mosul. As a result, the regions the EEF moved into in 1917 and 1918 were afflicted by famine and epidemics of diseases such as typhus, made worse by malnutrition, forced population transfers and severe levels of personal indebtedness and financial ruin. These affected urban and rural residents of Palestine and Syria alike, and confronted the occupying authorities with the urgent need to recreate a semblance of state authority and take emergency relief measures. Since 1915, a measure of alleviation to the local populace had been provided by the American colony in Jerusalem through charitable works and the opening of orphanages, soup kitchens and the administration of Ottoman military hospitals.[72]

In July 1917, William Yale, an American employee of the Standard Oil Company of New York who lived in Jerusalem between March 1915 and May 1917, reported that 'three years of war have reduced Palestine to a deplorable condition, the villages depleted by military drafts, devastated by cholera, typhus and recurrent fever', and added that conditions were even worse in Lebanon.[73] Yale had been sent to the Middle East in 1913 to explore for oil and lived initially in Istanbul before moving south. He left Palestine in 1917 to take up the position of special agent in Cairo for the US Department of State, only to return in 1918 as American Military Observer with Allenby's forces. Meanwhile, the Lebanese chronicler of the emergence of Arab nationalism (and contemporary observer of the campaign), George Antonius, also documented eyewitness accounts of the suffering in Syria and Lebanon: 'The scenes were indescribable, whole families writhing in agony on the bare floor of their miserable huts, whose moans could be heard a mile away. Every piece of their household effects had been sold to buy bread…'[74]

These accounts of the deprivations and hardships facing the civilian inhabitants of the region were corroborated by British officials. Sir Mark Sykes observed in June 1916 that 'the people of Lebanon are now being systematically exterminated by starvation'.[75] Following the capture of Jerusalem in December 1917, its new Military Governor, Sir Ronald Storrs, noted how 'the most urgent problem is of course food' as 'my chief, my nightmare anxiety, was the scarcity of food amounting almost to famine'. This reflected the reality that taking the city brought 'glamour and glory such as the Great War seldom gave, but…little else'. Storrs attributed this to the fact that Jerusalem had been on 'starvation rations' for three years, cut off from its pre-war supplies of grain from Odessa and – closer to home – from grain-producing districts across the Jordan River.[76] A further problem was the high incidence of disease in the areas that came under British control during 1917. An outbreak of typhus in the spring of 1916 had killed thousands of people across southern Palestine. Meanwhile, a British study conducted shortly after the capture of Jerusalem found that 27.3 per cent of its schoolchildren had malaria parasites present in their bloodstream. The malaria was a particularly malignant form spread by a specific type of mosquito (*anopheles bifurcates*) that thrived in the many cisterns containing rainwater in the city.[77]

Stalemate and resolution in 1918

It was against this grim socio-economic backdrop that the British occupying authorities began to set up a local administrative structure in their areas of control in Palestine. As detailed above, large-scale military operations halted after the capture of Jerusalem in December 1917, aside from relatively minor initiatives to consolidate and strengthen the EEF line of defence. These included the capture of the ancient settlement of Jericho in mid-February and an extension of the line in early March to give it greater depth. The major exception to this localised activity was two failed raids across the Jordan River towards Amman in March and May 1918. These were intended to support Emir Faisal bin Hussein's Northern Arab Army (NAA) as it conducted its flanking guerrilla-style operations in the Hejaz. The first attack occurred between 21 and 30 March but was beaten back by Ottoman and German forces who successfully defended the city of Amman. It began on the same day as the great German offensive on the Western Front, which ultimately led to the thorough reorganisation of the EEF yet did not preclude a second (and more ambitious) trans-Jordan attack between 30 April and 4 May. This again failed to dislodge the Ottoman and German troops, whose counter-attack at Es-Salt led to the withdrawal of the Desert Mounted Corps from the Jordan valley.[78]

During the summer, the EEF limited its activities to small-scale raids designed to improve positions on a very local level. Quite apart from the inadvisability of undertaking large operations during the summer heat, Allenby needed to reorganise his force after losing most of his British battalions to France. This created logistical difficulties as the replacement battalions from India needed to be transported to Egypt, equipped and trained, before being sent up the line to Palestine.[79] Moreover, the broader focus of the war swung sharply to the situation on the Western Front in Europe, as the British and French armies first fought for survival after the German spring offensives, and then began to turn the tide with victory at the Battle of Amiens on 8 August. Only thereafter, with the succession of military victories in the 'Hundred Days' firmly underway, did the Allies smash the crumbling resistance of the Central Powers in southern Europe and the Middle East.

The final Battle of Megiddo began on 19 September 1918. It coincided with General Louis Franchet d'Esperey's decisive breakthrough from the Salonika front at the Battle of Dobro Pole, and thus caught the Central Powers in a state of general retreat. For their part, Allenby's force in Palestine smashed through the Ottoman lines in a joint infantry–cavalry offensive. Large numbers of aircraft and mechanised transport cut off and routed the retreating Ottoman armies in what was later recognised as a textbook example of a mobile, deep battle.[80] A disorderly Ottoman withdrawal turned into a rout that surprised and surpassed Allenby's own expectations. The destruction of the Ottoman Seventh and Eighth Armies and the retreat of the Ottoman Fourth Army from Amman paved the way for the EEF to advance northward through Syria and Lebanon.[81] This resulted in the capture of Damascus on 30 September, and T. E. Lawrence's encounter with the squalor of a local hospital, as described so vividly in *Seven Pillars of Wisdom*:

I stepped in, to meet a sickening stench: and, as my eyes grew open, a sickening sight. The stone floor was covered with dead bodies, side by side, some in full uniform some in under-clothing, some stark naked. There might be thirty there, and they crept with rats, who had gnawed wet red galleries into them. A few were corpses nearly fresh, perhaps only a day or two old: others must have been there for long.[82]

Some 75,000 Ottoman troops were taken prisoner during the offensive, which halted after the capture of Aleppo on 26 October, for the cavalry and mechanised transport had far outstripped their supply lines and railheads. Allenby's 4th Cavalry Division, for example, advanced 70 miles in little more than a day (on 20 September) and out-distanced its supply and transport services by 50 miles. The Australian Mounted Division also advanced rapidly – 11 miles in just 70 minutes on 21 September – though this had the unexpected advantage of surprising the enemy and capturing intact a great quantity of stores at Jenin. To their delight, they included 120 cases of German champagne, which were promptly issued to the grateful Australian troops.[83]

The Palestine campaign formally ended with the armistice of Mudros on 30 October, which took the Ottoman Empire out of the war. Nevertheless, the British-led invasion and occupation of Palestine in 1917-18 had far-reaching administrative and regional ramifications. Following the capture of Jerusalem in December 1917,

Allenby established an Occupied Enemy Territory Administration (OETA) in Palestine under the auspices of the Chief Political Officer with the EEF, Gilbert Clayton, and with General Ronald Storrs as Military Governor of Jerusalem. The latter appointment came as something as a surprise to Storrs, who recalled in his memoirs how 'I possessed no military competence whatever, and very little administrative experience.'[84] Their appointments reflected the urgent need to restore order and create a framework through which control could be projected over the occupied territory. Nevertheless, Clayton's advocacy for a military administration as the only way of maintaining order in the newly occupied territories ran against the tenor of the Sykes–Picot Agreement.[85]

The issue of local administration became yet more urgent in the rapid crumbling of Ottoman positions after the Battle of Megiddo in September 1918. As the EEF advanced northwards through Syria and Lebanon, it assumed responsibility for a famine-afflicted region in a state of economic collapse. The administrative vacuum caused by the retreating Ottomans at the end of the war with the Ottoman Empire focused attention in London and Paris on the possible forms that local and regional governance could take in the areas under occupation. This also required officials to reconcile the various statements and pledges made during the war itself, culminating in the Anglo-French Declaration issued on 7 November 1918 with its promise that Britain and France would 'assist in the establishment of indigenous Governments and administrations in Syria and Mesopotamia', though not, explicitly, Palestine. Official thoughts additionally turned to possibilities for realising the more grandiose schemes for territorial expansionism that were now coming into view with the collapse of the Ottoman Empire.[86]

These will be covered fully in Part III of this book, but here it is sufficient to note that on 23 November 1918 the British issued a military edict formally dividing the region into three Occupied Enemy Territories. Occupied Enemy Territory South covered Palestine and was to be under British occupation; by contrast, Occupied Enemy Territory West comprised coastal Syria and was placed under French responsibility; while Occupied Enemy Territory East included the interior of Syria from Aleppo to Aqaba, and was designated to an Arab administration under Emir Faisal bin Hussein, the son of the Sharif of Mecca and leader of the Northern Arab Army. Finally, the Occupied Enemy Territory North contained areas outside the other three zones (notably Cilicia) and was placed under French administration. Needless to say, these decisions clashed with the diverse agreements made during the war and laid the seeds for much future bitterness and divisiveness.[87]

With these decisions the campaign in Egypt and Palestine came to a formal, if messy, end. However, the legacies of wartime hardship and the implications of the political agreements made between 1916 and 1918 came to haunt the transition to post-Ottoman forms of control. They still remain issues a century later, both in terms of their enduring impact on regional dynamics and in terms of the nations and states that came into being (or, in the Kurdish case, did not) after the war. Moreover, they meshed with the mechanics of state-making to influence the nature of the patterns of political organisation, economic mobilisation and extractive institutions that subsequently developed in the formative inter-war (and also post-Second World War) decades of state-building and consolidation in the Middle East.[88]

6

MESOPOTAMIA

'I am charged with absolute and supreme control of all regions in which British troops operate; but our armies do not come into your cities and lands as conquerors or enemies, but as liberators.'[1] These words were spoken not in 2003 as British forces swept into Basra as part of George W. Bush's invasion of Saddam Hussein's Iraq. Instead, they were uttered on 19 March 1917 – coincidentally eighty-six years to the day before the launch of Operation Iraqi Freedom – by the commander of the Mesopotamian Expeditionary Force (MEF), Lieutenant General Sir Frederick Maude. Written by the arch-imperialist Sir Mark Sykes, the Proclamation of Baghdad eerily foreshadowed the sort of sentiments that nine decades later could have come from the mouths of Bush, Donald Rumsfeld or Tony Blair. The historical overtones of the latter conflict crystallised when one of the principal Iraqi resistance groups in 2003 named itself the 1920 Revolutionary Brigade in memory of the national backlash that followed the First World War.

The military campaign in Mesopotamia lasted from November 1914 to November 1918. In addition to providing an example of Western intervention that was to be emulated three times (in 1941, 1991 and 2003), it framed the way for the creation of the modern state of Iraq in 1921. It thus represented the formative politico-historical development in modern Iraqi history.[2] Yet that outcome was not the result of a coherent or consistent policy, but rather stemmed from 'a sequence of unintended consequences', as the most recent English-language campaign history notes.[3] Moreover, the legacy of political decisions made during and immediately after the First World War were instrumental in shaping the nature of the Iraqi polity that emerged from the *al-Thawra al-ʿIraqiya al-Kubra* (the Great Iraqi Revolution). Far more than British politicians drawing 'lines in the sand' (as the title of a recent book by James Barr puts it),[4] the political and inter-communal settlement reflected patterns of wartime participation by local communities and groups; in other words, local agency was just as representative as structure (Ottoman-era hierarchies of power) in determining subsequent developments.

British, Ottoman and local interests intersected in a variety of ways during the course of the campaign in Mesopotamia. This reflected the shifts in the balance of military power as it swung first one way and then the other before finally tilting back towards the British in 1917. Gradually the campaign acquired an awkward 'double aspect' as British civilian and military officials clashed over operational objectives and levels of institution-building in their zone of occupation. These diverging lines of British policy acquired momentum as the war went on. They peaked in November 1918 with the hasty advance to capture the city of Mosul ten days after the armistice of Mudros had ended the war with the Ottoman Empire. Its seizure came after the looming end to hostilities led Britain's acting Civil Commissioner in Baghdad, Arnold Wilson, to urge every effort be made 'to score as heavily as possible on the Tigris before the whistle blew'.[5]

The course of the First World War in Mesopotamia illustrated most clearly the interaction between military and civilian requirements for administrative order and resource extraction as described in Chapter 2. The campaign also demonstrated how the operations shaped the nature and depth of colonial penetration into society, and the bitter dispute between British and British–Indian conceptions of empire and imperialism. The surrender of the British garrison at Kut al-Amara in April 1916 was, at the time, the greatest military humiliation the British Empire had ever known, laying bare the breakdown of operational control among scattered authorities in London, Delhi, and on the ground in Basra. Yet military demands for local resources did more than merely determine the level of mobilisation of existing socio-economic and commercial patterns. The different responses to these demands played a critical role in determining the composition of post-war Iraqi state structures and hierarchies of power.[6]

Origins and objectives of the campaign

The three provinces (vilayets) of Basra, Baghdad and Mosul constituted the south-eastern extremity of the Ottoman Empire. During the nineteenth century, improvements to communications and infrastructure created political and economic linkages that connected the provinces in a loosely defined regional entity with Baghdad as its centre of gravity.[7] Nevertheless, its geographical remoteness from the centre of the Ottoman Empire meant that it took up to fourteen days to reach Istanbul, some 2,400 kilometres away. This forced the Ottoman administration to prioritise its tasks and effectively limit its role to administrative functions and the provision of services in the major urban areas alone.[8]

Although their distance from Istanbul complicated imperial communications, the Mesopotamian provinces benefited considerably from other factors. These included Mosul's positioning on lucrative trading routes running east–west between the Levant and Persia, control over the holy Shiite sites at Najaf and Karbala that attracted pilgrims from across the Islamic world, and Basra's location at the juncture of the Shatt al-Arab and the Persian Gulf. Basra, in particular, was strategically located astride the major land and seaborne trading routes that radiated westwards to the Arabian Peninsula, eastwards to Persia, and south to the Persian Gulf ports, India and East Africa. This fostered a cosmopolitan and externally oriented outlook in the city. Taken together, these processes integrated the Mesopotamian provinces firmly into regional and (increasingly) international networks of trade and exchange.[9]

Trade with the wider world – and British commercial interests – increased rapidly after British shipping interests acquired the navigation rights on Mesopotamia's rivers in 1846 and the Suez Canal opened in 1869. By 1914, more than two-thirds of imports and half of the exports that passed through Basra were controlled by British or British–Indian commercial interests.[10] In addition (as detailed in Chapter 1), British strategic planners were acutely, indeed overly, sensitive to concerns that Germany or Russia might expand their influence on what was seen as the flank of India. This concern was summed up by an editorial in *The Times* around 1903, which warned that:

If we lose control of the Gulf, we shall not long rule in India…The moment it became known that Russia, or Germany, or France, or any other powerful nation, had planted a post within easy reach of the shores of India, an ineffaceable impression of the impermanence of British rule would be produced throughout Hindustan.[11]

These fears were augmented by British Indian fears about the perceived threat from pan-Islamic solidarity to the 'loyalty' of their Muslim populations in India (and Egypt). Officials' memories of proto-nationalist backlashes in India in 1857 and Egypt in 1882 ran deep, as did the major uprising on the North-West Frontier of India in 1897. This had, in part, been fanned by mullahs and (in one instance in the Swat valley) a call for jihad. British sensitivities towards Indian Muslims' opinion thus entered into policy-making calculations in the Middle East, as the Ottoman Empire was seen by officials to lie at the heart of a resurgent pan-Islamism.[12]

Consequently, officials in London and Delhi needed to take a set of broader considerations in mind as they framed Mesopotamian policy. The campaign fell under the responsibility of the Government of India and its representatives in the India Office in London, and the Indian Army would conduct its initial military operations. Yet the 'Indian' outlook differed greatly from the 'Arabism' espoused by many British officials in the Foreign Office and the British Residency in Cairo. It also introduced diverging sets of domestic pressures into civil and military policy. This triangular struggle between the three poles of British Middle Eastern policy (London, Cairo and Delhi) had profound consequences for the subsequent (mis)conduct of the campaign in Mesopotamia. The conflicting opinions led to damaging gaps in policy that contributed to confusion about its overall objectives.[13]

Foothold in Basra

Although British and Indian troops were only dispatched to the Persian Gulf in October 1914, plans to raise a fourth Indian Expeditionary Force (alongside the forces sent to France, East Africa and Egypt) began shortly after the outbreak of war in Europe. On 11 August, reports reached London that the Ottoman Army had started to mobilise in Baghdad and was seizing British property in the city. In fact, the Ottoman Army had started a general mobilisation on 3 August, and three days later the authorities in Baghdad proclaimed martial law, 'as a result of objections of the local populace to being impressed into service'.[14] The mobilisation took place in a haphazard manner, with isolated detachments being sent north to Mosul and south to Basra. One eyewitness stated that 'The Vali [of Baghdad] professes to have no knowledge as to why the troops are being collected but opinion among the native population of this city attributes it to anticipated trouble with Russia.'[15] By mid-September, Ottoman troops in Basra were preparing defensive positions along the Shatt al-Arab waterway, and limited (though unsuccessful) attempts had been made to mobilise the major tribal groupings around Baghdad.[16]

Nevertheless, the news trickling out from Mesopotamia alarmed Sir Edmund Barrow, the Military Secretary at the India Office in London. His office, along with the Government of India, was responsible for the British-protected sheikhdoms of Kuwait, Bahrain and the Trucial States in the Persian Gulf. Barrow feared that the Ottomans' actions might damage British prestige in the region and sway the loyalty of the local tribal sheikhs, upon whose collaboration rested British commercial, political and strategic supremacy in the Gulf. Accordingly, he suggested sending a military force to the Shatt al-Arab at the northern head of the Gulf. This would, he argued, repair local prestige and reassure any wavering local allies of British support. Furthermore, it would demonstrate British military might to regional observers, protect the Anglo-Persian Oil Company's installations and pipeline at Abadan on the eastern (Persian) Gulf coastline, and cover the landing of any reinforcements which might subsequently be required.[17] At this stage, and in striking contrast to the importance that Mesopotamia's oil potential later assumed in 1918, British interests were primarily motivated by issues of prestige, rather than strategic control of oil-bearing areas.

The 16th Indian Brigade of the 6th Division of the Indian Army left Bombay on 16 October 1914 in a convoy headed to Egypt and then on to France to reinforce Indian Expeditionary Force A. However, the brigade was ordered to detach itself from the convoy and make its way to the British-protected Persian Gulf sheikhdom of Bahrain, where it arrived on 23 October. Once there, it encountered unexpectedly stiff local unease at its presence, which forced the 5,000 men and 1,200 animals to remain on their cramped troopships in hot and oppressive conditions.[18] They remained there until 31 October. With the declaration of war with the Ottoman Empire imminent, 16th Brigade sailed northwards to the Shatt al-Arab at the head of the Persian Gulf and prepared for an attack on the Faw Peninsula south-east of Basra. At 6 a.m. on 6

November 1914, HMS Odin fired the first shots of the campaign as it bombarded the local Ottoman fort and landed 600 men on the peninsula. The brigade proceeded to Abadan (in Persian territory) on 9 November, where it disembarked with some difficulty, owing to a lack of suitable river craft and high winds. Two days later, they beat off an Ottoman counter-attack to confirm their foothold on the peninsula.[19]

The 16th Brigade (and later the remainder of 6th Division) formed the nucleus of what became Indian Expeditionary Force D in Mesopotamia. Yet it was held in very low esteem by British military officials in London and Delhi, who considered it unfit for fighting in Europe but adequate for colonial-style operations. This reflected the prevalent belief among the top military echelons in the Indian Army and in Force D itself that the operation would amount to nothing more than a traditional exercise in 'gunboat diplomacy'. Indeed, in 1916 (and speaking with the benefit of hindsight), the Principal Maritime Transport Officer responsible for all the water transport arrangements for the force retrospectively admitted to the Mesopotamia Commission of Inquiry that he envisaged 'some sort of expedition on the beach in the Persian Gulf...I had no conception, no idea whatsoever, that it was going to be up the Shatt al-Arab'.[20] This mentality and the general assumption that Force D would undertake a limited frontier-style operation resulted in 16th Brigade leaving India without its land transport of camels and mules, as well as its river craft.[21]

The declaration of war with the Ottoman Empire led the British military authorities in India to the rapid dispatch of a second infantry brigade (the 18th) to reinforce 16th Brigade. It arrived at Abadan on 14 November with Force D's commander, General Arthur Barrett, together with a quantity of stores, artillery and camel transport units. Two days later, the Cabinet in London authorised the capture of Basra on the condition that the Arab political situation and general military conditions were favourable. A sharp engagement took place at Salih on 17 November in a downpour that turned the desert 'into a veritable sea of mud' and claimed nearly 500 British and Indian and over 1,000 Ottoman casualties.[22] This relieved the strain on already scarce river transport resources by making available to Force D a number of craft in the Persian port of Mohammerah, and paved the way for the final advance to Basra. The city was taken on 21 November, one of the first signal British successes in the Great War.[23] To the delight of the British officers with Force D, the English Club was found undisturbed by the looting that took place after the Ottoman withdrawal, allowing them to drink 'some very acceptable lager beer'.[24]

The occupation of Basra completed the initial objective of Force D. It took the Ottoman General Staff somewhat by surprise as they had not anticipated a British thrust against Mesopotamia. Moreover, the General Staff admitted that the 17,000 Ottoman forces in the three provinces were 'below establishment, ill-trained, ill-disciplined and badly equipped, with no proper organisation for supply and maintenance'.[25] These failings notwithstanding, the capture of the city secured an important strategic position at the head of the Persian Gulf, ensured the safety of the Anglo-Persian Oil Company facilities at Abadan, and obtained the loyalty of the Arab notables and paramount tribal sheikhs in and around Basra. These influential local figures acquiesced in the British takeover, while the city's mercantile community actively welcomed it. The show of support reflected the equivocal relationship between local communities and a largely distant Ottoman state, as well as the greater levels of interaction and communication between the British and Basra. These were mediated partially through local allies such as the Sheikhs of Kuwait and Mohammerah, through the commercial ties built up before 1914, and by the proximity of Basra to powerful tribal confederations such as the Muntafik, the Bani Lam and the Albu Muhammad.[26]

Expansion of initial operations

The successful capture of Basra did not lead to a halt in military operations in Mesopotamia. Instead, and largely for reasons of prestige, the campaign expanded rapidly throughout 1915. This left Force D dangerously over-exposed across mutually unsupportable positions and dependent on a supply and transport network that creaked at the seams before breaking down completely early in 1916. The constant extension of operations took place against the backdrop of a lack of adequate oversight, as it remained divided between London and Delhi. This reflected and reinforced the pre-1914 division of responsibility for military preparation and the collection of intelligence in the Ottoman sphere between the War Office in London and the Government of India.[27] The result was a fragmented policy-making process that produced gaps in command which severely and negatively impacted the conduct of military operations in Mesopotamia. It also exposed the material and conceptual failings of a Government of India simply not organised, in the words of the outgoing Viceroy, Lord Hardinge, in 1916, 'for war on the present stupendous scale... [where] what does quite well for a six-week war on the frontier will not do at all...'[28]

The politics of prestige

Particular confusion lay over the physical terrain that any advance into Mesopotamia would cross. The British Government's acquisition of significant oil interests in the Persian Gulf in 1914 was not followed by any clarity over how those interests were to be defended should that become necessary. Nor was there a cadre of political or intelligence officers in India with sufficient local knowledge of physical, tribal or social conditions either in Mesopotamia or in Persia.[29] Lack of information-sharing between London and Delhi was matched, after war was declared in November, by inadequate consultation or awareness of the type of operation being envisaged in Mesopotamia. On a practical level, this manifested itself in serious drawbacks in knowledge of the rivers that provided the only routes of penetration into the country. These differed significantly from Indian rivers in terms of their shallow draught and strong seasonal variations. Yet these differences were not understood by British military planners once they assumed operational command for the campaign. The result, as an official admitted to the Mesopotamia Inquiry in 1916, was that 'the characteristics of the

Tigris and Euphrates were little known previous to our advance up them' as there had been no plans for 'establishment for the building and upkeep of a river fleet suitable or sufficient for the requirements of operations'.[30]

Deficiencies were magnified by the continuous pressure from Delhi and (to a lesser degree) the India Office in London to extend the scope of operations beyond Basra. This flowed from the perceived need to maintain prestige and reflected the lure of a succession of 'easy' military victories that came at comparatively little cost to the attacking Force D during 1915. The combination of these factors led British officials in the India Office and the Government of India to sanction a series of military offensives which, they argued, were necessary to consolidate control over Basra and a progressively larger hinterland. Furthermore, the potential prize of Baghdad was a tempting source of much-needed prestige as the fighting in Europe became an increasingly bloody stalemate. In this vein, the Political Secretary at the India Office, Sir Arthur Hirtzel, set aside the operational limitations of Force D to argue (as early as 25 November 1914, four days after Basra was taken) that 'the eventual occupation of Baghdad is so desirable as to be practically essential'.[31]

Even at this early stage, the idea of an advance towards Baghdad was also supported by Barrow (the Military Secretary at the India Office) and by Sir Percy Cox, the Chief Political Officer with Force D.[32] The issue of prestige was raised again just three days after Hirtzel's memorandum. On 27 November, Barrow warned against 'a policy of passive inactivity' if 'we are to impress the Arab and Indian world with our ability to defeat all designs against us'. He accordingly proposed that Force D advance to Qurna, a town 50 miles north of Basra located at the confluence of the Tigris and Euphrates. Its capture would, he argued, 'secure a strong strategic point and a dominating position' covering the approaches to Basra.[33] It would enable Force D to control the entire stretch of deep water between Basra and Qurna, which was the point at which deep-draught transport ships could go no further. General Sir Beauchamp Duff, the Commander-in-Chief of the Indian Army, agreed and added (without ever visiting Basra) that Qurna was 'so obviously the advanced post of Basra that the occupation of the latter involves the occupation of the former also'.[34]

The advance to Qurna first revealed the extent of the logistical constraints that later crippled Force D. The shortage of suitable river craft was compounded by the fact that it took place when water levels were at their lowest following the long hot summer months. The first attempt to take Qurna on 4 December had to be abandoned as an absence of pack animals to transport supplies (which could not be borne upriver) forced the advancing party to return to Basra. This failure necessitated a second try which succeeded, albeit in the face of determined Ottoman resistance, in capturing the town on 9 December 1914.[35] Its seizure represented a watershed in the embryonic campaign in Mesopotamia, as from that point on the oversight of operations shifted from the India Office in London, which hitherto had sanctioned all moves, to the political authorities in India and the 'men on the spot' with Force D in Basra.[36]

Vacuums of responsibility

In large part this abdication of responsibility occurred as a result of the growing complexity of military operations in Europe and – during 1915 – at the Dardanelles. These dominated British Cabinet discussions and ensured that scant attention was paid to developments in Mesopotamia. In India, entrenched barriers between the Government of India and the Indian Army meant that they neither intervened nor concerned themselves with their respective activities. As a result of this vacuum of control and oversight, power devolved onto the military (and political) officers in Force D as a major operation emerged almost by default. Over the course of 1915 this transformed the initial holding operation in the Persian Gulf into a large-scale military campaign that its planners had neither anticipated nor prepared for.

The euphoria of the initial military successes overshadowed the logistical difficulties that had nearly derailed the advance to Qurna. Instead, they fuelled a sense of complacency as the Government of India sanctioned the dispatch of a third infantry brigade to Mesopotamia in January 1915. Intended to reinforce the newly conquered territory, it was the first of many such instances of 'mission creep' in the months that followed. This ultimately resulted in the arrival of a second infantry division that formed the backbone of the moves northwards on the Tigris and Euphrates. While London was preoccupied with the European war and the succession of battles of attrition on the Western Front in 1915, the Government of India sacrificed administrative and logistical details for victories on the cheap. However, the breakdown in communications between the two ensured that widening gaps in policy were not discovered or resolved before it became too late to avert disaster.

During 1915, Force D expanded beyond breaking-point as its operational growth far exceeded the capacity of its overstretched supply and transport network. Simultaneous advances occurred on the Tigris and Euphrates but without fitting into any strategic plan. The towns of Amara (on the Tigris) and Nasariya (on the Euphrates) were captured with relative ease in June and July, while a large-scale Ottoman counter-attack had been beaten back at Shaiba on 12 April. By July, this haphazard growth left Force D distributed over five disparate positions in southern Mesopotamia: at Basra, Qurna, Ahwaz, Amara and Nasariya. Moreover, insufficient intelligence capabilities meant that neither the commander of the new Army Corps, Lieutenant Colonel John Nixon (a 'fighting, pushing kind of general'), nor the commander-in-chief of 6th Division, Major General Charles Townshend, was aware of the arrival of significant Ottoman reinforcements as Baghdad grew inexorably closer. This was attributed to the 'inexperienced zeal' of the incoming political officers who struggled to cope with the weight of demands on:

…the cramped and ill-furnished Political Offices, staffed with Indian clerks and thronged with petitioners, [which] witnessed from morning to night the rough-and-ready disposal of land and revenue and tribal cases, criminal trials, municipal and police business, and attempts to meet ever-increasing military demands for information, billets, labour, and supplies.[37]

MESOPOTAMIA

Broader developments in the war and international considerations also contributed to the eagerness of officials in London and Delhi for military successes that would offset the ongoing stalemate at the Dardanelles. With prestige playing an integral part in the 'imperial bluff' that enabled small contingents of civil servants and soldiers to rule vast territories in India (and now Egypt), they became anxious for good news that would overcome the failure to break through and decisively defeat the Ottoman forces at Gallipoli.[38] Their concerns were further heightened by the sensitivities of operating against an enemy whose Caliph was the spiritual head of Sunni Islam, and the fact that campaigning in Mesopotamia occurred close to the Shiite holy shrine cities of Najaf and Karbala. While the Sunni aspect most closely concerned British authorities in (Sunni-majority) Egypt, its Shiite dimension reared its head early in 1915 when the Viceroy of India, Lord Hardinge, refused to send the 136th Regiment to Mesopotamia because he felt he could not trust the loyalty of two of its (Shiite) Hazara companies.[39]

In this complex atmosphere of hope, expectation, but also trepidation, the (eventually) successful taking of Basra and Qurna camouflaged the logistical, administrative and operational shortcomings of Force D. As the two brigades expanded into a full infantry division (6th Division under Townshend) it remained chronically short of river-borne and land-based transport. As with the abortive first attempt to take Qurna in December 1914, this rapidly became an issue during the spring flooding in February 1915. This transformed the permeable clay soil around Basra and Qurna into a quagmire that paralysed all forms of land (pack animal and motor) transport. Its devastating impact was vividly described by Major Hubert Young following his transfer to Mesopotamia from the North-West Frontier of India:

It is difficult for anyone who has not seen the effect of rain upon the flat alluvial desert of the Basra delta to form any idea of the resulting abomination. A particularly glutinous kind of mud is evolved in which it is almost impossible to stand upright, and in which cars and carts stick fast, and horses and camels slide in every direction.[40]

Young recalled how during the 1915 flooding 'our troops at Basra found themselves upon an island, with the Shatt al-Arab on the east and a flooded area ten miles wide on the west…' He also noted how Force D lacked any personnel 'who had any knowledge of local conditions or of the effect of wind, tide, and rain on the water and soil of the Tigris–Euphrates basin'.[41]

As the operational scope of Force D expanded steadily throughout 1915, its lack of sufficient land transport effectively tied the zone of military operations to the rivers. This increased the troops' reliance on the already over-stretched river craft for almost all of their supply and transportation. Furthermore, Force D's growth placed a very great strain on the 'practically non-existent' port facilities at Basra, the only point of entry for the supplies that were necessary to maintain the campaign in the near-absence of locally procurable alternatives. When Basra was occupied in 1914 it was only capable of receiving two transports every three weeks, but the Government of India parsimoniously refused to sanction additional expenditure to increase its capacity. As a result, when George MacMunn arrived in the spring of 1916 as Inspector-General of Communications he found absolutely 'no conception of what modern transportation required' as nobody 'seemed to grasp what would be required if the force increased or moved up river'.[42]

Overstretch without oversight

Set against this disparity between force strength and logistical capabilities, the arrival of additional troops merely increased the logistical requirements. They compounded the congestion and disorganisation in Basra and the lengthening lines of communication and supply. Two factors made the position inexorably worse. One was the stringent financial constraints imposed on Lieutenant Colonel Nixon and Force D by the Government of India. Officials in Delhi, led by the powerful Finance Member, Sir William Meyer, consistently refused to sanction expenditure on the port facilities or other infrastructural works, such as a proposed railway from Basra to Nasariya to take the strain off the river, unless and until it was decided to make the occupation of Mesopotamia permanent. Moreover, the Government of India simply did not comprehend the scale of state intervention and mobilisation required to manage and conduct industrialised warfare against a modern enemy. From the beginning of the war until mid-1916 (when its shortcomings in Mesopotamia could no longer be ignored), Delhi pursued a 'business as usual' strategy that did not depart from the cherished tenets of 'Indian administration': notably low taxation and laissez faire economic policy. Remarkably, the military budget adopted in March 1915 for the 1915-16 fiscal year remained on an essentially peacetime basis, and the conduct of military operations involving the Indian Army (in Egypt, East Africa and Mesopotamia) was not discussed in the Viceroy's Council before 1916.[43] The impact of this policy continually hindered attempts to expand the scope of the Indian war effort until 1916, even as operational requirements grew rapidly. The Adjutant General of the Indian Army, Sir Fenton Aylmer, even referred to 'the terrorism created by the Finance Officer' [Meyer]. He concluded pessimistically that 'trying to get anything through at Simla is like a man trying to struggle through quicksand or a bog. He becomes exhausted by opposition on all sides and sinks.'[44]

This policy placed the Government of India in stark contrast to the incremental process of strategic mobilisation underway in London in 1914-15. Financial parsimony was magnified by a crippling failure to oversee the escalating operations in Mesopotamia. This reflected the widening gaps in responsibility between the Government of India, the India Office in London, and the political and military officers with Force D in Basra. At the Mesopotamia Inquiry in 1916, Sir Robert Carlyle, the member of the Viceroy's Council in charge of Revenue and Agriculture (and in a position to have made an important contribution to the mobilisation of Indian resources) acknowledged that 'the war was not treated as a thing beside which everything else becomes of no importance'.[45] Sir Beauchamp Duff, the Commander-in-Chief of the Indian Army, refused to visit Mesopotamia during his tenure and obstinately blocked all requests for logistical assistance. Both the political and military leadership in Delhi remained largely unaware of the progressive breakdown in the administrative services in Mesopotamia.[46]

Their myopic attitude was also evident in the second factor that contributed to the eventual catastrophic overstretch of Force D. This was the failure of staff in Delhi and London to recognise or act upon the urgent requests for additional river craft to meet the force's burgeoning supply and transportation requirements. As mentioned above, the specific characteristics of the Tigris and Euphrates differed substantively from river conditions in India. This rendered the motley collection of boats collected from the Irrawaddy Flotilla Company and other suppliers in India unsuitable for service upriver from Qurna, and the difficulty of procuring such craft was further magnified when the Government of India informed Force D that it would not be possible to construct boats in India itself. This reflected the distorted and narrow base of British pre-1914 industrial development in India, which prevented the build-up of an indigenous 'military–industrial complex' with local skill sets on the spurious grounds of 'national security'.[47]

As a result, orders for the river craft had to be placed in England instead. However, the bureaucratic inertia that gripped the Government of India and the India Office, as well as their lack of mutual cooperation or communication, caused long delays in their construction. Most notably, a major order placed on 3 August 1915 for 9 steamers, 8 tugs and 43 barges remained largely unfulfilled as late as August 1916. By that time, only 1 steamer, the 8 tugs and 20 barges had actually been delivered to Mesopotamia, arriving long after the succession of military disasters that befell Force D between November 1915 and April 1916. In these circumstances, Force D became heavily reliant on river craft procurable locally. Large numbers of bellums (dugouts) and mahelas (sailing boats) accompanied Townshend's advance towards Kut, and the ragtag collection became known as 'Townshend's Regatta'.[48]

Even with this additional capacity, the river fleet failed to keep pace with the rapid rises in troop numbers and the lengthening lines of transport and supply as Force D simultaneously advanced along the Euphrates to Nasariya and the Tigris to Kut. Among the administrative staff in Basra there was growing recognition of its shortcomings, prompting a senior member of staff (Major Kemball) to warn in July 1915 that 'if steps [are] not taken in good time to meet these requirements we are running great risks of a breakdown at possibly a serious moment'. However, the response from India was as emphatic as it was dismissive, as Duff warned the commanders of Force D not to bother him with 'any more querulous and petulant demands for shipping'.[49] His reaction was mirrored by the lackadaisical attitude within the India Office in London, where the Military Secretary, Barrow, was on holiday when Kemball's memorandum warning of a breakdown was received. Barrow subsequently admitted to the Mesopotamia Commission that the first he heard of it was when it was produced by the commissioners during the course of his interview (in 1916). This picture of institutional ignorance – both in Delhi and London – was further corroborated by the Secretary of State for India, as Lord Crewe informed the Commission that throughout his time in charge (lasting until May 1915) he had 'no hint or warning that transport was deficient' in Basra.[50]

Local responses to the British advance

This opening phase of the campaign elicited a range of varying responses from local and regional actors, were mediated through an array of political, economic and socio-cultural factors. In addition, the fact that the Basra vilayet was the scene of fighting from the outset forced the local tribes (and larger tribal confederations) to adopt strategies of self-preservation and/or take sides in the nascent conflict. Thair Karim identifies three dominant criteria in shaping tribal decisions: their history of prior engagement with centralised political authority, the 'politico-economic' benefits they might expect to derive from alignment with either of the competing forces, and considerations of expediency relating to the existing balance of forces. He suggests that 'maximum personal advantages sought by various sheikhs were the ultimate consideration that determined the actual positions taken by various tribes'. Importantly, these interests were neither static nor rigid. They shifted with the changing momentum of military operations, as several tribal sheikhs who had cooperated with British forces during the advances of 1915 switched back to the Ottoman fold following the Battle of Ctesiphon in November.[51]

A case in point was the very differing attitudes towards, and experiences of, the projection of Ottoman political authority. Contrary to British (and British–Indian) official thinking, the myriad tribal groupings and confederations in Mesopotamia certainly did not constitute a monolithic bloc. Quite the opposite, they exhibited wide variations in tribal structure and in their relationship to centralised government. These reflected the unevenness with which Ottoman control had been projected before 1914. The tribes along the Tigris were larger and more homogenous, with a longer history of exposure to centralised power by virtue of their location astride the trading artery of Ottoman Mesopotamia.[52] Their condition differed sharply from the tribes of the middle and lower Euphrates region, which generally had a much looser organisation and were fragmented into multiple sub-tribal units. These tribes also had long records of rebellion against the projection of governmental authority. This reflected a fiercely protective attitude towards their agricultural land from a state whose neglect they blamed for the silting up of land and the blighting of agricultural productivity.[53]

An additional factor mediating local responses was the sectarian composition of the Ottoman polity. While not wishing to overplay this divide, and agreeing fully with Fanar Haddad's observation that 'sectarian relations defy formulaic generalisations' and are linked to 'wider socio-economic and political conditions',[54] it was nevertheless the case that Shiites had been outsiders in the Ottoman Empire and not treated equally with its Sunni majority.[55] In the cities of Mesopotamia, the urban notables tended to be Sunni, and they held the levers of administrative power, supported by a merchant class that included many members of the Jewish and Christian communities. The British invasion made the latter group particularly vulnerable to Ottoman targeting. In April 1915, the American Consul in Baghdad described how 'at the moment there is considerable excitement in Baghdad against the Christians' after three were publicly hanged following accusations of espionage.

Hanna Batatu vividly described the diversity of Mesopotamian society in his classic work, *The Old Social Classes and the Revolutionary Movements of Iraq*. In addition to listing the many religious and ethnic minorities – 'Kurds, Turkomans, Persians, Assyrians, Armenians, Chaldeans, Jews, Yazidis, Sabeans, and others' who formed 'congeries of distinct, discordant, self-involved societies', Batatu also identified wide social, political, economic and cultural divisions between urban and rural communities.[56] Further differences reflected the diverging patterns of trade and economic orientation, whereby the predominant ties in Mosul were westwards with Syria and Turkey; those of Baghdad and the Shiite holy cities of Najaf and Karbala were eastwards with Persia; while Basrawis looked south to the Arabian Peninsula and, further away, India.[57]

Atiyyah observed in his seminal socio-political study of Iraq that the Great War 'became a test of the political loyalty of the various social groups within the Ottoman Empire'.[58] The complex ethnic, sectarian and social composition of Mesopotamian society created fissures that could be exploited by the invading armies. However, the same complexity also represented a profound conceptual challenge to British political (and military) officers as they assumed responsibility for local administration. These officials were drawn overwhelmingly from the British administration in India, and were heavily influenced by 'Indian models' of imperial rule. Their prior experiences provided the frames of reference as they drew up administrative codes for the newly acquired zones of control in Mesopotamia. Thus, the Tribal Criminal and Civil Disputes Regulations drawn up and implemented in February 1916 were lifted, virtually unchanged, from the colonial code used on the North-West Frontier of India.

Shortcomings in local knowledge were therefore magnified by inappropriate responses to rectify the resulting gaps. Toby Dodge has noted how the new codes were based upon a deeply flawed misunderstanding of an apparently binary division in society between the 'corrupt' towns and the 'noble' tribes. This perception led to British officials misidentifying the tribal sheikhs as 'linchpins of rural society', through whom they could rule and transmit their authority downwards.[59] As a result, British policy aimed to reverse the Ottomans' practice of encouraging tribal fragmentation. Officers divided the areas that came under occupation into political divisions, each under a political officer who compiled tribal lists and identified local sheikhs around whom authority could be reconstituted.[60] Tribal loyalty was buttressed by generous subsidies of gold and, beginning in 1917, by the threat of swift airborne retaliation against recalcitrant tribes.[61]

THE FIRST WORLD WAR IN THE MIDDLE EAST

Kut al-Amara and Ctesiphon

By the summer of 1915, Indian Expeditionary Force D had successfully captured the pre-1914 vilayet of Basra, although physical control remained limited to the major towns and military outposts, and administrative initiatives remained in their infancy. Caught between the scent of military success and an increasingly unsustainable logistical situation, Force D then lurched towards disaster in the autumn of 1915. Following the capture of Amara in July, the remorseless logic of 'mission creep' led its political and military planners to identify the next upriver town of Kut al-Amara as vital to controlling the newly occupied territory. This was immediately made very clear, in a telegram from the Viceroy to the Secretary of State for India, when Hardinge stated that the occupation of Kut al-Amara was now 'a strategic necessity, since it commands the lower reaches of both the Tigris and Euphrates' and was necessary 'in order to ensure future tranquillity both at Amara and Nasariya'.[62] The vacuum of responsibility between Basra, Delhi and London meant that this view was insufficiently challenged, even in the face of emerging evidence that Force D was becoming dangerously overstretched.

In addition to local concerns about maintaining momentum and projecting control over the powerful tribes of southern Mesopotamia, such as the Muntafiq based around Nasariya and the Bani Lam around Kut al-Amara, the impending military failure at the Dardanelles introduced a powerful external dimension to British policy-making in the Middle East. Throughout the summer and autumn of 1915, the diverging fortunes of the 'terribly severe' fighting at Gallipoli and the apparently easy seizure of outposts in Mesopotamia, where 'General Nixon has done splendidly and has given the Turks a real good knock' became ever more apparent.[63] Politicians and military leaders in Britain and India thus became anxious for a glittering success – such as the capture of Baghdad – to offset the perceived damage to imperial prestige at Gallipoli.[64] These local and regional trajectories intersected with ultimately disastrous consequences for Force D between September and December 1915.

In particular, the shortage of river transport significantly drained the operational capability of Townshend's 6th Division even before it was finally halted at the Battle of Ctesiphon on 22 November. High rates of scurvy and other deficiency-diseases impaired the fighting efficiency of the troops. In part, this was due to the near-absence of any form of fresh produce (meat or vegetable) in their rations. Yet it was worsened by the refusal of Muslim contingents to eat tinned meat or horse flesh in the absence of an authoritative clerical ruling declaring them permissible to consume. The dietary shortcomings – which related back to the inability to transfer sufficient stores into Basra and on upriver – contributed to the appallingly high invalidity rate through disease. The full extent of its impact became fully evident in figures compiled by the War Office in London which listed 207,000 casualties from sickness in 1916 against a 'mere' 23,300 from enemy action.[65]

MESOPOTAMIA

As 6th Division moved north towards Kut al-Amara in September 1915, its commanders also lacked land transport to take the strain of the river and facilitate the movement of supplies and men. Motorised transport was virtually non-existent before 1916 and was limited to a handful of cars and six ambulances. In its absence, commanders planned to rely on the Indian Army's traditional use of animal transport during the crucial operations between September and November 1915. However, this created its own difficulties, as a contingent of bullocks sent from India to haul the heavy artillery required more forage than was obtainable from local supplies. By February 1916 the unit had to be withdrawn (and orders given not to send any more from India), as the animals simply could not be fed at the front.[66] As a result, the troops remained heavily over-reliant on the river for their provisions.

The insufficiency of all forms of river and land transport had immediate consequences for Townshend's march northwards. The advance took place in mid September, when the Tigris was at its lowest following the long summer drought, and unsuited to most types of river craft. As a result, Force D was unable to supply sufficient quantities of food and forage to the men and animals of the infantry and cavalry divisions at the front. This meant that they could not take advantage of the open spaces of the desert, or conduct operations that required self-sufficiency in food or water. These weaknesses prevented the cavalry from pursuing and destroying the retreating Ottoman units after the first (successful) battle of Kut al-Amara in September 1915. In addition, they necessitated a six-week pause in military operations in order to bring up sufficient supplies to the advanced staging-post at Aziziya. This gave the Ottomans time to regroup and reorganise with significant reinforcements arriving from Baghdad.[67]

Although the success at Kut-al-Amara had revealed alarming shortcomings in Force D's logistical capabilities, it further reinforced the forward momentum propelling Townshend to disaster. The aforementioned perceptions that British prestige would be harmed or damaged should the advance come to a halt led policy-makers to urge – once again – that it continue. This was made very clear in a dispatch sent by the Viceroy in Delhi to the Secretary of State for India in London on 6 October, eleven days after the battle. Hardinge neatly encapsulated the 'politics of prestige' viewpoint and contextualised it within the wider contours of the Great War:

On the other hand, from a political point of view, the capture of Baghdad would create an immense impression in the Middle East, especially in Persia, Afghanistan, and on our frontier, and would counteract the unfortunate impression created by the want of success in the Dardanelles. It would also isolate the German parties in Persia, and frustrate the German plans of raising Afghanistan and the tribes, while the impression throughout Arabia would be striking. The effect in India would undoubtedly be good. These are considerations to which I attach great importance.[68]

This cri de cœur paid immediate dividends as Austen Chamberlain responded two days later to the effect that 'The Cabinet are so impressed with great political and military advantages of occupation of Baghdad that every effort should be made by us to supply the force that is necessary.' Significantly, however, the Secretary of State for India added that 'We do not wish to attempt it with insufficient forces' and asked Hardinge whether he thought that one infantry division would suffice.[69] Yet, that same day, Nixon telegraphed that 'No additions are necessary to my present force to beat Nur-ud-din [sic] and occupy Baghdad, of this I am confident.'[70] As the autumn of 1915 went on, and the news from the Dardanelles continually worsened, the perceived need for what Chamberlain on 21 October called a 'striking success in the East' intensified.[71]

Yet, the pause in operations necessitated by the need to reorganise and bring up supplies meant that nearly two months elapsed between the engagement at Kut al-Amara on 25 September and the commencement of the battle of Ctesiphon on 22 November. During this period, the Ottoman field commander Nurredin Pasha had ample time to prepare a set of strong and mutually supportable defensive positions. His four infantry divisions, totalling about 18,000 men, faced Townshend's weary 6th Division, which, by this point, had been on the march for over two months, and was now beset by a combination of poor weather and wet terrain. Furthermore, 2,000 transport mules and a large quantity of carts that had been collected in Basra failed to arrive at Aziziya in time for the renewal of the advance northwards on 11 November. This was due to the fact that more than half of the river craft were required to transport the bulky comestible items, such as grain, firewood and fodder, necessary to sustain the front-line troops on a daily basis.[72]

Townshend consequently was prevented from building up a reserve either of troops or of transport. These shortcomings became critical following 6th Division's failure to break through the Ottoman defences at Ctesiphon between 22 and 24 November. Both sides suffered very heavy casualties and became exhausted by the intense yet inconclusive fighting. The lack of a strategic reserve, and the additional strain placed on the existing transport units by the 3,500 battle casualties, gave Townshend little option but to retreat to Kut al-Amara and await reinforcements. The 6th Division arrived there on 3 December, and Townshend took the fateful decision to halt there as the town contained ample reserves of stores and supplies. Originally, these had been stockpiled as a reserve to support the advance upriver, but Townshend now lacked the river transport to send them back to Basra. Moreover, his troops were exhausted by weeks of continuous hard fighting. On 4 December, therefore, Townshend decided to stand his ground at Kut al-Amara and turn it into an armed camp while he awaited reinforcements from Basra. Accordingly, he informed Nixon that he had one month's supply of rations for his British troops and fifty-five days' supplies for the Indian soldiers that made up the majority of 6th Division.[73]

This communication of Townshend's estimate had serious consequences for the subsequent operations to relieve him. Although he did not know it at the time, his men ultimately survived for more than four months on the reserves it had available. Townshend's under-estimation imparted a (false) sense of urgency to British Headquarters in Basra, and contributed to the hasty and disorganised relief operations that were put together without adequate planning or preparation. Indeed, as the two Indian infantry divisions based in France (the 3rd and 7th) rushed to Basra alongside a British division (the 13th), which diverted from the Dardanelles, the haphazard arrival of units and stores brutally exposed Basra's limitations as a port and as a base. As a result of the Government of India's above-described refusal to sanction any expenditure above the bare essential minimum, the port still did not have any modern facilities for berthing and unloading ships, or for allocating storage for supplies. Consequently, the average discharge rate was two steamers every three weeks, as men and cargoes were unloaded from ocean-going transports onto lighters belonging to local firms, and then re-loaded onto river craft for conveyance upriver.[74]

The arrival of the three additional infantry divisions with auxiliary units between January and April 1916 thus overwhelmed the makeshift facilities at Basra. This formed one of the major reasons for the progressive breakdown in military operations that culminated in the surrender of Townshend and his 6th Division on 29 April. Basra and its port became heavily congested and disastrously over-extended as reinforcements of men and supplies arrived at a quicker rate than they could be discharged and sent upstream. Neither the base nor its surrounding facilities proved capable of handling the increased traffic in the absence of wharves, insufficient numbers of port lighters and tugs, and lack of labour and dry-land availability on the riverfront itself. All of these factors became critical to the backlog that accumulated, and fed off each other in an interlocking manner that created a mutually reinforcing sense of confusion and chaos at the base.[75]

These logistical shortcomings were greatly magnified by Townshend's ill-judged estimate of supplies. The British Official History of the campaign dryly described how this effectively forced General Fenton Aylmer to conduct the three relief operations with 'an improvised staff, makeshift organisation, and inadequate transport'.[76] More damagingly, the perceived need for haste meant that the operations were launched at precisely the worst time of the year climatically and ecologically. The results became clear on 21 January 1916, when an attack on Ottoman positions at Hanna failed after heavy rain turned the battlefield into a muddy quagmire that paralysed all movement and communication.[77]

Back in Basra, Nixon's health had broken down and he was replaced as commander of Force D by Sir Percy Lake, who took command on 19 January 1916. He immediately advocated an advance owing to 'the uncertainty as to date of arrival of reinforcements and of sufficient river craft for maintaining and supporting them at the front'.[78] At this point, Duff in India and Robertson in London reversed their enthusiasm for earlier military advances by cautioning against a premature offensive and urging Aylmer to await the arrival of further reinforcements.[79] However, by this point, the congestion within Basra itself and the strain on its port facilities was so great that even this cautious proposal was deemed unsuitable in practice. By 15 February the situation reached breaking-point as Lake informed London that the shortage of transport had become so acute that it would not be possible to transport the 13th Division to the front. He also acknowledged that 'the number of my river craft limits the number of men and animals that can be maintained at the front', and informed

Duff that the dispatch of further numbers up-river would reduce by 40 per cent the amount of supplies which could be transported in the scarce river craft. In short, Force D could either transport supplies, or men, but not both at the same time.[80]

A second attempt by Aylmer to relieve Townshend failed on 8 March as the Ottomans repulsed an attack on the Dujaila Redoubt and inflicted severe casualties. Following this setback, Aylmer was himself replaced by Lieutenant General George ('Blood Orange') Gorringe as commander-in-chief of Tigris Corps. Once again, Lake informed Indian Army Headquarters in India, on 13 March, that the operations on the Tigris were paralysed owing to the incomplete and late arrival of river craft.[81] Lack of transport meant that the 13th Division had to trek to the front and take part in the third attempt to relieve Kut al-Amara, between 5 and 9 April, without any rest or their complement of land transport. As with the aborted first attempt in January, so too on this occasion heavy rain and severe flooding wrought havoc with the operation, as the battlefield became a 'veritable bog'. In these conditions, the Ottomans managed to stall an exhausted division and repel it from reaching its objective.[82]

A final, desperate attempt to move forward to relieve the 6th Division also ended in failure on 25 April. At this point, Gorringe felt compelled to inform India that the Tigris Corps had reached the absolute limit of its offensive capability. He added that it could go no further without a pause in operations, as his men had been engaged almost continuously since 5 April and had suffered some 9,700 casualties. This constituted roughly one-quarter of its fighting force, yet it remained more than 12 miles away from Kut al-Amara.[83] The besieged garrison was also reaching the limit of its endurance as Townshend's men were close to starvation and afflicted by ever-rising daily incidence of disease. On 24 April, a desperate last-ditch attempt to re-supply Townshend was made by attempting to float a ship loaded with a month's worth of supplies upriver. This, too, was unsuccessful, leaving the Secretary of State for War in London, Lord Kitchener, reluctantly sanctioning Duff to open negotiations for the surrender of Townshend and 6th Division. Their capitulation on 29 April was seen at the time as one of the greatest military humiliations ever suffered by a British army, perhaps equalled only by the fall of Singapore in December 1941. Kitchener himself was in no doubt of the magnitude of the psychological damage that the surrender inflicted on British prestige in its extra-European colonies. Privately, he wrote to Duff shortly before Townshend's surrender to state that 'I sincerely hope that it is fully realised by you and all General Officers under your command that it would forever be a disgrace to our country if Townshend should surrender.'[84]

The surrender of Kut al-Amara was the outcome of a chaotic interplay of factors that each built upon and magnified the impact of the others. Individual commanders on the ground and in Delhi were disgraced: Duff committed suicide in January 1918, Nixon was found by the Mesopotamia Commission to be principally responsible for the disaster, while Townshend never overcame the shame of his capture and the differential treatment he received under house arrest in Istanbul while thousands of his soldiers endured terrible privations on forced marches through the Syrian desert; he died in disgrace in 1924. The Mesopotamia Commission of

Inquiry launched by the British Government produced a report so damaging in its exposure of what went wrong that the government agonised for two months over whether to publish it. When it did see the light of day, it claimed the political scalp of the Secretary of State for India, Austen Chamberlain, as it shed devastating light on the administrative misconduct of the Government of India and its inability to comprehend or undertake modern military operations. However, the report also blamed the duality of control between the India Office in London and the Government of India in Delhi, which contributed to the sense of drift and failure to oversee the campaign as it faltered.[85] While no one factor was decisive in compromising the first attempt to capture Baghdad, together they overwhelmed the rudimentary military capabilities of Force D. The cathartic shock of the accumulation of failures triggered a widespread reorganisation of operational, administrative and logistical responsibility and paved the way for the resumption of the advance after months of soul-searching.

Reorganisation and renewal, 1916-17

Eleven months separated Townshend's humiliation at Kut al-Amara from Lieutenant General Maude's triumphal entry into Baghdad on 11 March 1917. During this period, Indian Expeditionary Force D was transformed into the Mesopotamian Expeditionary Force (MEF), re-equipped and reorganised. British politicians in London embarked upon a comprehensive inquiry into the scope and scale of their wartime objectives in the region. This greater clarity imparted a degree of purpose to the operations in Mesopotamia and, crucially, unlocked India's considerable materiel and manpower resources for the war effort. Meanwhile, the Ottoman gains from repelling Townshend and inflicting a signature defeat on the British military effort soon dissipated in the face of continuing heavy losses on the Russian front. By early 1917 these trends came together, as the MEF resumed its advance at roughly the same time as the Egyptian Expeditionary Force began the first of its assaults on Gaza. Although, as made clear in the previous chapter, Murray's first two attacks on Gaza failed to break through, they contributed to the general intensification of the multi-front war facing an increasingly war-weary Ottoman Empire. Later in 1917, this synchronicity made an important difference as it prevented Ottoman attempts to switch forces between theatres to match their most urgent needs.

The campaign in Mesopotamia ground to a temporary halt following the cathartic surrender of Townshend's garrison at Kut al-Amara. Over the next few months, the force underwent a thorough overhaul that tied in with a similar reorganisation of India's contribution to the war. It took the shock of what had happened to Townshend to bring home the scale of the disorganisation of Force D and the mismanagement of the wider aspects of the campaign in Mesopotamia. A Commission of Inquiry was set up in London to examine the failures in Mesopotamia and at the Dardanelles. During the summer and autumn of 1916 and the early months of 1917, its members received a stream of damning indictments about the lack of strategic overseeing and operational planning, and the logistical breakdowns that culminated in the shambolic attempts to relieve Kut-al-Amara. The final report of the Mesopotamia Commission was released in May 1917, after the capture of Baghdad had gone some way to restoring British prestige and pride, but the severity of its contents (as described) prompted the resignation of the Secretary of State for India, Austen Chamberlain, and the public shaming of Duff, which later accounted for his suicide on 20 January 1918.[86]

Thus, the administrative and logistical machines that functioned as necessary supports for the campaign were also transformed in late 1916 and early 1917. The War Office in London assumed administrative responsibility for the campaign in July 1916, having already taken over responsibility for its operational side in February. Belatedly, the campaign was integrated into the overall British military effort and brought under a centralised framework for the first time. This ended the uncertain relationship between military planners in Britain and India, which had resulted in such disastrous gaps in policy and supervision. The importance of India to the campaign now shifted from one of operational control to the primary provider of manpower and material resources to sustain the MEF. This tapped the civilian as well as military resources available to the Government of India rather better, as it tardily launched the strategic mobilisation of resources that the belligerents in Europe had done in 1915.[87]

A major factor in the transformation of India's role was the replacement of the discredited and desk-bound Duff by a War Office appointee, General Charles Carmichael Monro, on 1 October 1916. Monro had long experience of field command and, as earlier described, commanded the Mediterranean Expeditionary Force at Gallipoli. He gathered around him a group of talented administrative officers with recent military experience in Egypt and at the Dardanelles, in a prime example of cross-campaign absorption of lessons learned.[88] Another example of this trajectory at work was the appointment of General Maude as commander-in-chief of the newly renamed Mesopotamian Expeditionary Force, on 28 August. Unlike his elderly predecessor, Lake, Maude had recently commanded 13th Division at Gallipoli, and his methodological approach had gained him the nickname of 'Systematic Joe'. Both Maude and Monro appreciated the complexities of modern industrialised warfare and the importance of placing military requirements for manpower within a deeper framework of strategic mobilisation of all forms of resources.[89]

Over the course of the summer and autumn of 1916, the port facilities at Basra were rapidly expanded and two subsidiary anchorages created at Magil and Nahr Umar to further relieve congestion. These measures increased the rate of tonnage discharged from 38,916 in July 1916 to more than 100,000 tons by mid-1917, whereupon fourteen ships could be berthed at a time and cleared within three days. Improvements to the organisational and administrative apparatus also proceeded apace and created a streamlined process for receiving stores and transferring them upriver. Together, they transformed Basra into a major regional east-of-Suez port, and reflected one dimension of the general overhaul of the Mesopotamia campaign. The other, no less important, dimension was the reorganisation of the transport services into a coherent body that was responsible for general transport policy.[90]

Newly formed Directorates of Railways and Works began to recast the lines of communication that connected Basra to the forward units and defensive positions, while quantities of armoured cars and aircraft transformed the operational mobility of the MEF. Crucially, this freed the force from its near-total dependence on the rivers, and enabled Maude to establish a chain of advanced supply posts, depots and military hospitals along the Tigris in preparation for the resumption of the advance. During 1917, the network of railways expanded particularly quickly as lines radiated outwards from Basra and – after its capture in March – Baghdad. The expansion nevertheless occurred in a haphazard and piecemeal fashion and resulted in the growth of three disconnected clusters of railways of different gauges, and still dependent on India for the dispatch of often substandard locomotives and rolling stock.[91]

The thorough overhaul of the administrative services of the MEF was an essential precursor to the eventual renewal of operations in December 1916. It occurred against the backdrop of the arrival in Mesopotamia of the full panoply of industrialised campaigning with all its enormous logistical requirements. As elsewhere, this created a powerful new dependence on machine-produced goods as considerable quantities of heavy and light artillery and ammunition, and motorised, rail and air transport all arrived. The voracious demands of modern warfare necessitated the mobilisation and extraction of local resources of manpower and agricultural produce as a heavier footprint developed to penetrate local patterns of economic activity.[92] This will be examined in detail in Chapter 8, but it is necessary here to note that the period between December 1916 and March 1917 marked a decisive watershed in Mesopotamia. From that point on, the military campaign gradually gave way to the intensification of British political and economic control over tribes and communities hitherto little accustomed to the projection of state power and fiercely protective of their scarce resources.

Assertion of regional control

These processes of consolidation also acquired a regional dimension as British policies shored up their position in the strategically important Persian Gulf sheikhdoms and in the Arabian Peninsula itself. Although Kuwait, Bahrain and the Trucial States had been knitted into the patchwork of imperial possessions during the nineteenth century, the blow to prestige occasioned by the loss of Townshend's force required a countermeasure to reassert British prestige. Kuwait was particularly important by virtue of its geographical contiguity and close tribal and economic interconnections with Basra. Its ruler, Sheikh Mubarak bin Sabah Al-Sabah, had cooperated closely with the invading British force, contributing thousands of rupees to the British Red Cross, providing logistical support to Force D, and allowing British hospital ships to anchor in Kuwait City's deep-water harbour. But Mubarak – who had signed the

Anglo-Kuwaiti agreement of 1899 – died on 28 November 1915, and was succeeded by his son, Sheikh Jabir bin Mubarak Al-Sabah.[93]

In contrast to his father's staunch support for the British Empire, Sheikh Jabir was much more independent-minded. Although his short reign lasted only fifteen months until his death in February 1917, he moved towards support for the Ottomans, in part by facilitating the movement of camel caravans between Kuwait and Syria. The trade that resulted broke the British blockade of the eastern Mediterranean, and enabled vital provisions to reach the Ottoman military forces in Damascus.[94] Intensifying British protests culminated in a meeting on 23 November 1916 in Kuwait City between Sir Percy Cox and the leading Kuwaiti notables. Cox, the Chief Political Officer with the MEF, attempted to reaffirm local support for British regional objectives, but the gathering ended inconclusively. After his brother, Sheikh Salim bin Mubarak Al-Sabah, became ruler in February 1917, trade with the Ottomans increased to the point that the Royal Navy actually blockaded Kuwait to interdict and end the flows of supplies, which an aggrieved Salim attributed to illegal smuggling.[95]

Further south, the British had greater success in integrating Qatar, the only Persian Gulf sheikhdom with which it did not have protectorate relations, into its fold. The ruling Al-Thani family had moved closer to the Ottomans in the 1870s, but Qatari and British interests gradually drew closer together during the war. This occurred as the Qatari rulers sought to preserve their control over their small sheikhdom from Abdul-Aziz Al-Saud's projection of greater influence over the Arabian Peninsula. In order to safeguard their local autonomy and acquire a sought-after external guarantor of their security, the Anglo-Qatar Treaty was signed on 3 November 1916. Although it was not ratified by the British until 23 March 1918, it accorded a vital measure of support for the Qatari leadership and was a means of rebalancing the greater weight of the proto-Saudi forces.[96]

As indicated above, the nervousness of the Al-Thani in Qatar reflected the reconfiguration of the balance of power within the Arabian Peninsula itself. This pre-dated the Great War as Abdul-Aziz Al-Saud had wrested control of Riyadh and the central Nejdi region from the rival Al-Rashid dynasty in 1902. The Ottoman Empire responded to this local challenge to the status quo by siding with the Al-Rashid, with whom they had a history of cooperation, and dispatched troops into the Arabian Peninsula. Although they initially defeated the Al-Saud in 1904, this success proved to be short-lived, and Abdul-Aziz regained the Nejd and pushed eastwards to reach the coastline of the Persian Gulf by 1912. This success empowered his local position vis-à-vis the British-protected coastal sheikhdoms, as did his tentative moves to settle the local Bedouin tribes and mobilise them into the feared Ikhwan (brotherhood) religious militia. The first such agricultural settlement took place in 1913.[97]

British officials established an agreement with the Al-Saud shortly after the war began, as part of their search for supportive regional allies. They built upon the connection established by the erstwhile British Political Agent in Kuwait, Captain William Shakespear. He had made initial contact with Abdul-Aziz during the course of his journeys across Arabia, and subsequently became his Military Adviser. In November 1914, the Government of India asked Shakespear to secure Abdul Aziz's support for the operations undertaken by Force D in Basra. Two months later, however, he was killed during a battle against remnants of the Al-Rashid and, much later, replaced (in November 1917) by the noted Arabist St John Philby, father of Kim, who would become a notorious spy. In the meantime, however, the emerging relationship between the Al-Saud and the British was formalised in the 1915 'Uqayr Treaty, which recognised Abdul Aziz as the governor of Nejd, Hasa, Qatif and Jubayl. As the first international agreement signed by Abdul Aziz, it bolstered his position and allowed him to consolidate his control over the peninsula and counteract Ottoman objectives there.[98]

The impact of these alliances would only become fully apparent in the regional reordering in the aftermath of the war. Not for the first time, the short-term pursuit of local collaborators entangled the belligerents in networks of alliances that ultimately proved unsustainable and contradictory. These will be examined in full in Chapter 8. In the specific case of the Arabian Peninsula, Britain's wartime contacts with the Al-Saud created a clashing overlap with their support of the Sharif of Mecca in the Arab Revolt as the two vied for supremacy on the peninsula. It also threatened the stability and security of the much smaller and more vulnerable British-protected sheikhdoms on the Persian Gulf.

Advance to Baghdad

With their local reorganisation nearing completion and the regional position more assured, the British advance on Baghdad resumed on 14 December 1916 when the MEF attacked the Ottoman positions at Hai. They established a foothold across the Hai tributary, but heavy rains then delayed any further operation until 19 January 1917 when the town of Hai itself was captured. On 25 January the MEF attacked the strategically important Hai Salient. This was a highly professional assault that featured the preliminary registration of artillery, a creeping barrage and intense preliminary bombardment of Ottoman positions, and a coordinated infantry attack in four waves assisted by bombing raids and enfilade machine gun fire. It revealed the MEF to be in command of the most up-to-date training manuals then being disseminated to British troops on the Western Front in Europe. Despite taking heavy casualties, the MEF cleared the salient by 4 February 1917.[99]

Maude immediately followed up this success by capturing Sannaiyaat on 23 February. This unlocked the strategic position and enabled the MEF to cross the Tigris and retake Kut al-Amara on 25 February, ten months after its loss had marked the nadir of the British war effort. The aftermath of the battle demonstrated the new prowess at Maude's disposal as the retreating Ottoman units came under concerted fire from the Royal Flying Corps, while armoured cars chased and harassed the withdrawing units. Following this, the advance halted temporarily to allow a succession of temporary riverheads and intermediate supply dumps to be established.

On 4 March, the Chief of the Imperial General Staff in London and the Commander-in-Chief of the Indian Army sanctioned the final push to Baghdad. This commenced on 5 March, and culminated six days later when the 35th Infantry Brigade marched into Baghdad to restore order and halt the looting that had started after the Ottoman evacuation the previous day.[100]

The capture of Baghdad represented a dazzling political triumph and the first big British success of the war. It went a considerable way to repairing the damage inflicted to notions of imperial prestige in 1916. Maude himself delivered his proclamation to the inhabitants of Baghdad, pledging that his army did not come as a conqueror but as a liberator, on 19 March. However, for all his bombast, the seizure of Baghdad neither ended the campaign in Mesopotamia nor brought any closer a military victory over the Ottoman Empire and the Central Powers. This reflected the campaign's peripheral status in the broader geostrategic balance of forces, as a growing mismatch developed between its continuation and wider military considerations. Yet the MEF kept up its operational tempo until the end of the war in November 1918, and continually increased its responsibilities, as a growing rift developed between the British civilian and military officials in Mesopotamia over the direction of the campaign and the scope of its objectives.

Initial operations after the capture of Baghdad consolidated British control over the approaches to the city and its regional hinterland. Thus, the MEF took steps to secure the river routes into Baghdad, occupying Baquba (on the Diyala river) on 18 March, Falluja (on the Euphrates) on 19 March, and the Ottoman railhead at Samarra (on the Tigris) on 23 March.[101] Later in the year, in the autumn of 1917, further advances extended the sphere of British control over the remainder of the Baghdad vilayet by seizing the towns of Ramadi, Kifl and Tikrit. These gains were significant, as they denied to the Ottomans the three major lines of approach for any converging counter-attack on Baghdad.[102] In addition, the MEF tightened its economic blockade of the remaining Ottoman positions, attempting to close the loopholes created by Kuwaiti trade with local and regional actors. Lieutenant Colonel Gerard Leachman (nicknamed 'O[fficer] C[ommanding] Desert') was responsible for this, and he carried it out in a ruthless manner that earned him great local enmity. He described one such mission 'to correct a contrary Kurdish tribe' as 'very wonderful but very unpleasant'. Perhaps unsurprisingly in view of his aggressive tactics, he was murdered by members of the Zoba tribe near Falluja during the general uprising in August 1920.[103]

Dilution of force: Persia and agricultural development

Maude died unexpectedly on 18 November 1917 from cholera. He was succeeded as commander of MEF by Lieutenant General Sir William Marshall. With the consolidation of the Baghdad vilayet completed, this juncture represented a logical point at which military operations in Mesopotamia might have halted. Nevertheless, they resumed once more over the winter of 1917 and early months of 1918, after the

MESOPOTAMIA

Russian exit from the war prompted British politicians in London and in Delhi to conjure fanciful fears of a combined Turco-German advance through the Caucasus and Persia towards India.[104] In retrospect, these concerns seem unrealistic and far-fetched when taking into account logistical considerations and the state of exhaustion in the Ottoman (and German) militaries in early 1918. They nevertheless resulted in the dispatch of a British military mission of around 1,000 elite British, Canadian, Australian and New Zealand troops to Persia, under the command of General Lionel Dunsterville. This complicated and greatly over-extended the lines of communication facing Marshall, especially after the great German offensive on the Western Front on 21 March 1918. Similar to the pressures on Allenby in Palestine, the need to transfer British units to France imposed a hasty reorganisation on the MEF as it replaced them with units drawn up at short notice in India.[105]

'Dunsterforce' and its contingent of 750 armoured cars advanced more than 500 kilometres in 1918 and eventually reached the Azerbaijani city of Baku on the Caspian Sea in August. However, this strategic show of strength threatened to overwhelm Marshall's logistical capabilities, as he complained that he was forced to divert all possible transport to it. In May 1918, the results of this overstretch became clear when Marshall was unable to garrison the northern Mesopotamian town of Kirkuk following its capture by the MEF. Marshall reacted angrily to the limitations imposed on the MEF, reflecting a general frustration among many British officers in Mesopotamia that military operations now appeared to be restricted to 'chasing Turkish rearguards to the end of our supply tether'.[106]

These moves had absolutely no bearing whatsoever on the final outcome of the war between the British and Ottoman Empire. Neither did the other major diversion of the MEF in late 1917 and most of 1918, when it embarked on a haphazard process of incipient 'state-building' in Mesopotamia. On one level, the development of major agricultural development schemes represented a practical response to the shortages in shipping to import foodstuffs and essential items for the campaign from India.[107] Moreover, the rapid extension of the territory under MEF occupation after the capture of Baghdad created severe difficulties in meeting both civilian and military requirements for resources, notably food. These tapped into an earlier decision made by the War Office in London in July 1916 that the Government of India utilise locally procured resources as much as possible to meet the needs of the MEF. Accordingly, in the autumn of 1917, the British authorities in Baghdad sanctioned a large-scale Agricultural Development Scheme as part of an ambitious project to gain self-sufficiency in wheat, barley and straw.[108]

The intensification of local resource extraction therefore took place alongside the military conquest of Baghdad and its surrounding vilayet. Maude had stated as early as 3 March 1917 that he expected that the city's capture would enable him to 'exploit the neighbourhood considerably for purposes of supply, especially food and fodder'. These bulky items used up considerable transit space. With the occupation of Falluja on 19 March, the MEF seized control of the fertile grain-producing regions in the Euphrates valley that fed Baghdad and its hinterland. The new Oriental Secretary at the British High Commission in Baghdad, Gertrude Bell, reckoned the Ottomans' loss of this rich food-producing region to be 'one of the most disastrous consequences of the fall of Baghdad'.[109]

As British control spread across Mesopotamia, the quantities of supplies demanded and local resources extracted escalated sharply. Political officers fanned out across the occupied territories and were assisted by military columns that added a potent coercive spine to their efforts to win tribal loyalty by consensual means. An important exception was the Shiite holy shrine towns of Najaf and Karbala, which were administered indirectly through local sheikhs. The extension of direct (and indirect) control was facilitated by the establishment of a Directorate of Local Resources and by networks of supply and transport officers who accompanied the political officers as they pacified local tribes. Systematic labour recruitment into the logistical units of the MEF also accelerated sharply following the capture of Baghdad. These developments formed the backbone of the extractive institutions that now began to regulate the full mobilisation of local economic and societal resources for the war effort. They involved what the British euphemistically termed the 'submission by political means' of local tribes largely unaccustomed to the projection of centralised control over their affairs.[110]

These measures nevertheless provided the backdrop to an acrimonious dispute over the demarcation of civil and military control that developed between Maude and Cox. As commander-in-chief of the MEF and charged with responsibility over military affairs in Mesopotamia, Maude opposed the creation of a civilian administration and wished to concentrate all energy on the conduct of the war. In July 1917, he warned the British military authorities in London and Delhi that 'if we attempt…[the] development of the country…we shall be attempting too much and we shall fail'.[111] This drew Cox's ire, and he responded by labelling Maude 'purely a soldier and without any previous experience of the East', and consequently 'unsympathetic and somewhat intolerant in regard to political problems'.[112] A compromise was eventually reached as Cox was appointed Civil Commissioner in Baghdad while Maude retained the ultimate power of authority in Mesopotamia. However, Ghassan Atiyyah has observed that this arrangement 'did little to deflect Cox from his policy of building up the civil administration', and that this accelerated after Maude's death in November.[113]

Oil and Mosul

The interaction between military policy and political manoeuvring reared its head once more in the final months of the Great War, and resulted in the hasty dash to occupy Mosul before the ending of hostilities in the Ottoman theatres of war. This arose after the War Cabinet in London belatedly grasped the value of gaining control of the vilayet of Mosul as a potential source of oil supplies for the British Empire. Although oil had been discovered in neighbouring Persia in 1908, and one of the justifications for sending British and Indian troops to Basra in 1914 had been to safeguard the Anglo-Persian Oil Company installations in the region, oil did not form an important element of British 'war aims' in Mesopotamia until very late in the war. Only on 30 July 1918 did the influential secretary of the War Cabinet, Sir Maurice Hankey, describe the control of Mesopotamia's (presumed) oil supplies as a 'first-class British War Aim'.[114] In a now-famous letter to the First Lord of the Admiralty (Sir Eric Geddes), Hankey stated that 'it would appear desirable [that] before we came to discuss peace, we should obtain possession of all the oil-bearing regions in Mesopotamia and Southern Persia, wherever they may be'. Further, he added, '[T]he acquisition of further oil-bearing country…might make it worthwhile for us to push on in Mesopotamia, notwithstanding its comparatively minor importance from a purely strategical [sic] point of view.'[115]

Hankey's conversion to the value of extending British control in Mesopotamia built on an equally influential memorandum written by Admiral Sir Edmond Slade entitled 'The Petroleum Situation in the British Empire'. He argued that the control of sources (and sites) of bunker fuel was absolutely critical to 'our life as an Empire' and that as oil was expected to gradually replace coal in maritime transportation, it was 'of paramount importance to us to obtain the undisputed control of the greatest amount of Petroleum that we can'. In an early example of 'resource nationalism', he stated that 'control must be absolute and there must be no foreign interests involved' and that 'only then will the strategic position be secured and we shall be able to look forward with confidence to maintaining our hold over the sea communications of the world in the event of another war breaking out'.[116] Slade had a powerful vested interest as a director of the Anglo-Persian Oil Company and had been an advocate of the British Government's purchase of a controlling share in it in 1914. His memorandum laid out a seductive case for securing British power and influence in a post-war world at a time when the balance of the Great War was just beginning to swing the Allies' way.

This view rapidly won the wholehearted support of the Chief of Air Staff responsible for the newly created Royal Air Force (RAF), who added that 'the whole future of air power is dependent upon adequate supplies of liquid fuel' and that 'the areas in which it is contained must be safeguarded by a very wide belt of territory between it and potential enemies'.[117] The accumulation of support for Britain's acquisition of wide swathes of Mesopotamia and Persia led Hankey to write to the Foreign Secretary (and former Prime Minister), Sir Arthur Balfour, to urge him to support the new proposals. Notwithstanding Balfour's initial reluctance at what he labelled 'a purely Imperialist War Aim', Hankey persisted, writing that 'it is almost unavoidable that we should acquire the Northern regions of Mesopotamia'. To add weight to his argument, and dilute the role of oil interests in it, he added a concern to secure upstream control over the watercourses of the Tigris and Euphrates in order to prevent them falling into unfriendly hands which might then dam the rivers for irrigation and so reduce the flow of water downstream. For this reason, Hankey requested that Balfour sanction a renewed advance in northern Mesopotamia 'as far as is necessary to secure a proper supply of water. Incidentally, this would give us most of the oil-bearing regions.'[118]

These efforts to sway top-level British decision-makers ultimately paid dividends. Late in October 1918, I Army Corps of the MEF dashed to Mosul after the looming ending of hostilities with the Ottoman Empire led the acting Civil Commission (in Cox's absence in London), Sir Arnold Wilson, to urge 'every effort…to score as heavily as possible on the Tigris before the whistle blew'. The advance imposed great additional strain on a military force already severely overstretched by its operations in Persia and in Baku, underscoring how it was a geostrategic decision devoid of military objectives. Indeed, Mosul was not finally captured until 10 November 1918. This, notably, was the day before the end of the war in Europe, but, remarkably, was eleven days after the Armistice of Mudros had ended the Ottoman conflict.[119]

The (belated) capture of Mosul brought to an end the military campaign in Mesopotamia. The small-scale operation envisaged by British planners in India in October 1914 morphed into one of the most protracted military campaigns outside the European theatre of the Great War. On the British side, it combined gross initial mismanagement and eventual humiliation with later successes and concerted attempts at state-building. For the Ottomans, the major success of the campaign lay in its locking up a large amount of British and Indian forces in a faraway theatre where they could little damage the imperial heartland. Meanwhile, the local tribal groupings in Mesopotamia and the Persian Gulf sought to take advantage of the fluctuating fortunes of the two belligerents in order to maximise their own localised positions and power.

As will be documented in full later in this study, the incipient state-building efforts undertaken by British officials in Mesopotamia in 1917 and 1918 had important and long-lasting consequences. Their designs on the occupied territories were reflected in policies that thinly disguised their post-war design. Chapter 8 will describe how this resulted in the creation of a centralised state apparatus that differed sharply from its Ottoman precursor in its extension of state control and depth of penetration of society. Yet, the unevenness with which British and British–Indian control was projected, as well as the very differing reactions this provoked, also influenced the contours of the revolt that broke out in 1920 and, with it, the Iraqi polity that developed thereafter.

PART III

POLITICS AND DIPLOMACY

7

THE STRUGGLE FOR POLITICAL CONTROL IN THE MIDDLE EAST

Chapters 3-6 described the major military campaigns that took place in the Middle East and North Africa between August 1914 and November 1918. The entire region became a theatre of conflict between the pre-war hegemonic power, the Ottoman Empire, and the ascendant imperial interests of Britain and France. An early variant of the 'revolution in military affairs' occasioned by the conduct of industrialised warfare in largely pre-industrial terrain added to the impact of the military operations on local conditions. In addition to exposing the host states and societies to the above-mentioned economic dislocation and multiplying wartime hardships, the war also precipitated radical plans to reshape the regional system in the Middle East and redraw its relationship with a world order itself in a state of flux. A slew of vague wartime promises and hastily made agreements between 1915 and 1917 planted the bitter seeds of resentment and conflict once their full extent – and their blatantly imperialist and contradictory nature – became known in 1918. Moreover, they clashed, during the final year of the war, with the appearance of US President Wilson's Fourteen Points based upon the empowering notion of 'self-determination', despite the attempts – in vain – by British censors to prevent their terms being made public in Egypt, Palestine and Mesopotamia.

The final two chapters of this book explore the political dimensions of the struggle to remake the Middle East in light of the opportunities that the First World War opened up for imperial officials and local nationalists alike. This chapter tells the story of the efforts by British and French administrators to project their influence across the region and maximise their gains in any eventual post-war settlement. It is also an account of the disparities in intelligence and knowledge that resulted in the concentration of knowledge and policy-making in the imperial centres in the hands of a few self-proclaimed experts. With officials facing more imminent pressures of prosecuting the European war, this disparity of information afforded regional experts a greater degree of freedom to shape policy in their own image; nowhere was this more visible than in the policies followed by A. T. Wilson in Mesopotamia in 1918 and early 1919. Some of this group, notably T. E. Lawrence 'of Arabia' and the pair of Sir Mark Sykes and François Georges-Picot, continue to reverberate throughout the region a century later, as does mention of Britain's Foreign Secretary in 1917, Sir Arthur Balfour, whose declaration that November remains the subject of bitter dispute and contested legacy.

The present chapter further describes how oil – and other geo-commercial and geo-strategic reasons – interacted with the changing international political economy (as represented by President Wilson's Fourteen Points) to necessitate a new justification for imperial control of the Middle East. This required the external powers to move away from nakedly imperial designs, and construct new arguments for their presence. Nevertheless, the changed climate in international politics percolated through to the Middle East in spite of Anglo-French efforts to control the flow of information reaching the region. Hence the next and final chapter documents the rise of nationalist and other resistance movements in the Middle East and the rounds of bargaining that raised the hopes of local actors that they would be part of any post-war reordering of the region. These hopes were subsequently dashed during the Paris Peace Conference, and Chapter 8 ends by examining how nationalist unease at the imperial powers' attempts to legitimise and formally extend their wartime powers into the post-war era converged with the myriad socio-economic hardships and grievances arising from the war and afflicting virtually every grouping in the region. The result was a toxic alignment of shifting coalitions grouped around a vague platform of protecting local resources from further predatory demands and securing the political dividends from their wartime choices and accommodations.

Jockeying for position

Almost as soon as the Ottoman Empire entered the war, its opponents sensed an opportunity to partition and seize control of long sought after territories in the Middle East. Throughout the nineteenth century, Istanbul had been labelled 'the sick man of Europe'; now, it appeared to eager officials in London, Paris and Moscow, as well as their representatives overseas, that the demise and dismemberment of the empire might become imminent. As early as 5 December 1914, two weeks after British and Indian forces had occupied the town of Ottoman Basra in Mesopotamia, the Viceroy of India, Lord Hardinge, cabled to London to 'strongly recommend [the] permanent occupation of Basra'.[1] This, he added, would seal 'our supremacy in the Persian Gulf and this happy chance of consolidating our position there may never occur again'. However, the British Government overruled this first attempt at imperial conquest, noting instead that the annexation of Basra would be 'contrary to principle that occupation of territories by allies is provisional pending final settlement at close of war'.[2] Yet, in an example of the haste with which policy was being made in 1914, the British Foreign Secretary, Sir Edward Grey, simultaneously advocated the annexation of Egypt, only to be rebuffed by the acting British Resident in Cairo, Milne Cheetham, who argued that this would undermine Britain's declared aim of upholding the rights of small nations.[3]

Great Power rivalry began to emerge as soon as serious military operations commenced, and quickly fragmented the veneer of alliance politics. An immediate case in point was the prospect of British naval operations at the Dardanelles and the implications of any such action for Anglo-French interests in the Mediterranean. Britain and France signed an agreement on 6 August 1914, just two days after Britain entered the war, envisioning that the British Royal Navy take the lead in directing naval operations in the Atlantic, the North Sea and the Straits of Dover, while the French Navy would assume general responsibility for the Mediterranean and the western section of the English Channel. The demarcation of control reflected British planners' belief that the North Sea would be the decisive naval theatre of war and thus the concentration of British force there was deemed paramount.[4] However, French control in the Mediterranean was always nominal and never existed in practice, as the importance of Egypt to British imperial interests meant that London swiftly took measures in the eastern Mediterranean to safeguard Egypt's security. This nevertheless caused alarm in Paris at Britain's apparent encroachment on the terms of the agreement, and the French Minister of Marine urged the Admiralty in Paris to insist upon the proper division of the spheres of interest agreed in August. However, the Lord of the Admiralty in London, Winston Churchill, declined to do so, and in January 1915 his advocacy of a British assault on the Ottoman port of Alexandretta in support of the planned operations at the Dardanelles caused great French embitterment and suspicion of Britain's supposedly expansionist tactics. This culminated in the French Minister of Marine instructing Churchill that:

The Minister persists in claiming the execution of the conventions of August 6, and the entire direction of the operations in the Mediterranean for the French Command. Under these conditions any operation must be planned and directed by us.[5]

Relations between Britain and France, both imperial powers with territorial designs on the Middle East, remained tense throughout the war, as each kept a watchful and wary eye on the other. As David Dutton has noted, 'Neither side felt it could turn a blind eye to advantages gained by its wartime partner', leading to fears that unilateral military gains could or would translate into the ability to dominate any post-war political settlement.[6]

The Russians were the first to make an actual, formal claim on Ottoman territory. Benefiting from an impressive intelligence apparatus that forewarned Russian officials of the Ottoman preparations for a surprise attack on Russia, the Russian Ambassador to Istanbul, M. N. Girs, submitted a report to St Petersburg as early as 11 October 1914. Writing after the Ottomans' closure of the Strait of the Dardanelles to international shipping had disrupted Russian maritime and trading flows, Girs stated that 'We need a strong boss ruling over Constantinople and since we cannot let any other power assume this role, we must take her for ourselves.' The Ambassador added that the looming conflict with the Ottomans offered Russia an opportunity to 'liquidate the Straits question once and for all'.[7] In March 1915, Foreign Minister Sergei Sazonov reiterated Moscow's long-standing intention to annex Istanbul and seize control of the Bosporus and the Strait of the Dardanelles, without which the security of maritime access between Russia's Black Sea ports and the Mediterranean would remain vulnerable to disruption and closure.[8]

France accepted Russia's claim and began to formulate demands of its own in the Levant and along the south-eastern coastline of Turkey. This amounted to a claim on Greater Syria (encompassing modern-day Syria, Lebanon, Palestine and Jordan) as well as the Ottoman cities of Alexandretta (now Iskenderun) and Adana.[9] In response, Britain's Secretary of State for War, Lord Kitchener, declared that the aforementioned contested prize of Alexandretta should fall under British control in the event of any partition of Ottoman territory, in order to counterbalance Russia's emergence as a Mediterranean power and France's foothold in the Levant. Although it won the support of Churchill as an adjunct to the plans to assault and take the Gallipoli peninsula, Kitchener's plan was opposed by Grey and Prime Minister Herbert Asquith, as British attention was focused on the Dardanelles. However, in addition to solidifying French concerns over London's objectives in the Mediterranean and the Middle East more widely, Kitchener's intervention did concentrate British officials' minds on the need to identify 'British desiderata in Turkey-in-Asia in the event of a successful conclusion of the War'.[10]

The interdepartmental De Bunsen Committee was appointed in April 1915 and issued its report on 30 June. Its chairman, Sir Maurice de Bunsen, was the Assistant Undersecretary of State in the Foreign Office in London and membership was drawn from the Admiralty, the War Office, the Colonial Office and the India Office. The final report carefully analysed a range of four possibilities with regard to British interests in Turkey and the Middle East, recognising that these were necessarily circumscribed by the interests of Allied powers. The options the committee examined ranged from partitioning the Ottoman Empire to preserving it as an independent state in Asia. The 30 June report recommended that British interests could best be secured by maintaining the Ottoman Empire as an independent, albeit decentralised, entity, thereby indicating that partition, at this early stage of the war, was neither inevitable nor even seen as desirable among British policy-makers.[11]

Britain's initially cautious and broadly anti-annexationist stance inexorably gave way to more ambitious and sweepingly imperialist visions as the campaigns in the Middle East expanded. This occurred as men like Kitchener and Sir Mark Sykes became vastly influential in shaping policy in London, and as British officials in Cairo and Delhi exerted greater weight in swaying policy-makers increasingly distracted by the weight of wartime responsibilities in France and Flanders. During the early phase of the war in 1914 and 1915, Kitchener exerted a powerful influence over British policy-making, reflecting his decorated background both as a military commander and imperial statesman. A war hero in Britain for his service in Sudan (reflected in his title, Earl Kitchener of Khartoum) and the Boer War, Kitchener also had served as Commander-in-Chief of the Army in India between 1902 and 1909, and British Agent and Consul General in Egypt between 1911 and 1914. Upon the outbreak of the war in August 1914, Kitchener correctly foresaw that hostilities would not be 'over by Christmas', and set about organising the mass mobilisation of the 'New Armies' that formed the backbone of the British war effort.[12]

Kitchener's opinion thus carried considerable weight among his civilian Cabinet counterparts in London. Moreover, his record of service set him apart from the majority of his colleagues, whose direct experience of the Middle East and the Islamic world was extremely limited.[13] Back in London as Secretary of State for War, Kitchener emerged as a vocal advocate of the creation of an Arab state that would be closely aligned with British interests in the Middle East. Writing in a private letter to Grey on 11 November 1914, Kitchener asked the Foreign Secretary to imagine that 'Supposing that the Arabs took up arms against the Turks, I think it would be our policy to recognise a new Khalif [sic] of Mecca or Medina of the proper race and guarantee the Holy Places from foreign aggression as well as from all foreign interference.'[14] In this, he reflected the concern among British officials in Cairo and Delhi for Britain's standing in Arab notable opinion, in large part to offset the potentially awkward ramifications of involving the Empire's Muslim subjects in a war against their Ottoman Caliph.

Although British officials subsequently took the lead in the bitterly controversial secret negotiations and deals in 1915-16, they did not represent a monolithic point of view. Responsibility for Middle Eastern policy-making instead was divided across multiple organisations and locations. These included the Government of India in Delhi; the British Residency and the newly created Arab Bureau in Cairo as a regional centre for the collection of intelligence on and liaison with Arab allies; and the Foreign Office and War Office in London itself. The divisions between the British sub-imperial centres in Cairo and Delhi were particularly sharp and antagonistic, both on a personal and an institutional level.[15] The Government of India, with its hierarchically segmented methods of control and responsibility for governing a significant Muslim population in India, did not welcome the Cairo High Commission's 'pro-Arab' policy. Moreover, during the decades preceding the war, officials in Delhi had painstakingly constructed a network of collaborative Arab sheikhdoms in the Persian Gulf to ensure basic commercial and strategic interests, rather than what it saw as Kitchener's (and the Arab Revolt's eventual) grandiose scheme for a pan-Arab entity. Over the course of the war, this led to what Jukka Nevakivi aptly described as 'flagrantly clashing lines of policy' as the plurality of decision-makers in each of the three poles of gravity – London, Cairo and Delhi – all followed their own, frequently competing, agendas.[16]

Policy-making in Britain also was filtered through layers of ostensible 'experts'. Kitchener himself died on 5 June 1916 en route to a diplomatic mission to Russia when the HMS *Hampshire* struck a mine and sank near the Orkney Islands in

Scotland. He had begun to lose influence in the months before his death owing to increasing criticism of his handling of the war effort and his erratic working habits that earned him the sobriquet 'K of Chaos'. After his death, some of the more outspoken statements of support for the Arab cause were gradually toned down in favour of a more conservative approach, but the fundamental differences between Cairo and Delhi remained, as did the reliance on a new set of intermediaries. In Kitchener's stead came the Conservative MP and instigator of the Arab Bureau, Sir Mark Sykes, and the former Viceroy of India and close confidant of the incoming Prime Minister David Lloyd George, George Curzon. In 1918, the Minister of Blockade, Sir Robert Cecil, quipped that the succession of interdepartmental committees that were established to shape and formulate British Middle East policy existed 'mainly to enable George Curzon and Mark Sykes to explain to each other how very little they know about the subject'.[17]

The wartime agreements

The first contacts between British and Arab officials actually pre-dated the outbreak of the First World War. Early in 1914, Abdullah bin Hussein, the son of the Sharif of Mecca, visited Cairo and met with the Oriental Secretary at the British Agency, Sir Ronald Storrs, who was standing in for the Resident, Kitchener. That meeting was inconclusive as Storrs declined Abdullah's request for military supplies in the event that the Sharif rose in revolt against Istanbul. Although the Sharif, Hussein bin Ali, was traditionally a figure of great importance in the Islamic world as the protector of the holy cities of Mecca and Medina, and was in contact with nationalist secret societies that had formed among Arab army officers in Syria, British policy toward his Hashemite dynasty existed uneasily alongside similar support for Abdul-Aziz bin Saud, a rival claimant for power in Arabia and, ultimately, between 1924 and 1932 the victor in the struggle to unify the Hejaz with the central heartland of Najd and the eastern coastline as modern-day Saudi Arabia. As Secretary of State for War, however, Kitchener authorised Storrs on 24 September 1914 to renew contact with Abdullah to find out 'whether he and his father and the Arabs of the Hejaz would be with us or against us'.[18] Five weeks later, on 31 October and with the declaration of war with the Ottoman Empire just five days away, a new telegram from Kitchener instructed Storrs to inform Sharif Hussein that:

If the Arab nation assists England…England will guarantee that no internal intervention takes place in Arabia, and will give Arabs every assistance against external aggression. It may be that an Arab of true race will assume the Khalifate [sic] at Mecca and Medina.

This pledge was followed by a British proclamation issued on 5 December 1914 that offered to recognise the 'perfect independence' of the Arabs if they drove out the Turks. These escalating promises, some of which were embellished by Storrs in Cairo from the original texts sent out by London, culminated in a British pledge in April 1915 that 'The Arabian Peninsula and its Mahommedan [sic] holy places should remain independent. We shall not annex one foot of land in it, nor suffer any other Power to do so.'[19]

It was against this backdrop that Hussein exchanged a series of letters with Sir Henry McMahon, who succeeded Kitchener in Egypt late in 1914 as High Commissioner (as opposed to Resident). The Hussein–McMahon correspondence eventually consisted of eight letters between 14 July 1915 and 30 January 1916 concerning the future political status of the Ottoman Empire's Arabian territories. They amounted essentially to a negotiation over the terms under which Hussein would encourage and lead the Arabs in revolt against the Ottomans. Notably, on 24 October 1915, McMahon offered Hussein the option of Arab independence within the specified boundaries with the exception of the Ottoman provinces of Basra and Baghdad. With British and Indian forces then advancing rapidly towards Baghdad, officials in London and Cairo stated that the Mesopotamian territories should be governed as a special administrative unit under direct British assistance. This optimistic scenario was soon overtaken by events as the Indian Expeditionary Force was defeated at Ctesiphon and forced into humiliating surrender at Kut in April 1916, by which time the correspondence between Hussein and McMahon had lapsed. And ever since, the nature of the letters and the meaning of their contents have been chronicled and fought over at great length by all parties, as both Hussein and McMahon worked through intermediaries, and problems of interpretation and translation meant that even the letters' original meaning was often imprecise and unclear.[20]

Even at this early stage, issues of duplicity among the different centres of gravity in British decision-making processes began to occur. McMahon's 24 October 1915 offer of territory (however sincere or not it may have been) was almost immediately superseded by the signing of a treaty of independence between Sir Percy Cox, the chief political officer in Basra, and Abdul-Aziz Al-Saud in Najd. The treaty was concluded on 26 December 1915 following negotiations facilitated by the British agent in Kuwait, a part of the Government of India's zone of control. It assured Abdul-Aziz of British assistance against foreign aggression and effectively granted the future Saudi leader recognition of international independent status. Both the British agency in Kuwait and Cox himself, as a former Political Resident in the Gulf and now seconded to the Indian Expeditionary Force in Basra, reflected the 'Indian' approach to the Middle East, and their treaty rode roughshod over the promises made to Hussein, whose support originated in the British High Commission in Cairo and in the Arab Bureau. The competing support for Abdul-Aziz in central Arabia (Najd) and Hussein on the western coastline of the Arabian Peninsula (Hejaz) marked the formalisation of the battle for regional supremacy between the Saudi and Hashemite family lines that continued long after the end of the war in 1918.[21]

The Hussein–McMahon correspondence overlapped partially with the early negotiations of what became the Sykes–Picot Agreement. This took place between the French diplomat François-Georges Picot, scion of a famous colonialist dynasty and the former consul general in Beirut whose laxity in destroying documents led to the rounding-up and execution of fourteen Arab nationalist activists in Beirut in May

1916, and Sykes, a British Conservative politician close to Kitchener, who placed him on the De Bunsen Committee in 1915.[22] Sykes's influence in London rose rapidly as he gained significant influence over the formulation of British policy in the Middle East. Sykes was a leading progenitor of the Arab Bureau, which was created in Cairo in December 1915 under Gilbert Clayton. However, Sykes did not always see eye to eye with the Bureau and its 'all-star' staff, including such notable figures as T. E. Lawrence, Aubrey Herbert and Gertrude Bell, and did not involve the organisation in his negotiations with Picot.[23]

The Sykes–Picot Agreement was reached in October 1916, although its negotiations lasted many months. It began late in 1915, while McMahon was still exchanging letters with Hussein, as the British and French governments decided to conclude a formal agreement on the post-war division of Ottoman territory. The final agreement, to which Russia also consented providing that its own territorial claims be accepted by Britain and France, carved up the Arab provinces of the Ottoman Empire into British and French spheres of influence. It was ratified in June 1916, just ten days after the start of the Arab Revolt. Under its terms, Britain was allocated formal control of the provinces of Baghdad and Basra in Mesopotamia and an area of informal responsibility stretching from Gaza across northern Arabia to Kirkuk. France assumed formal control over the Syrian coastal region and Cilicia in the Levant and informal responsibility over a large area from Damascus and Aleppo east to Mosul. The agreement also fixed the boundaries of the territories claimed by Russia in the Caucasus, and left Palestine's status to be determined at a later date under 'an international administration'. As Eugene Rogan has aptly noted, with only a hint of understatement, 'The Sykes–Picot Agreement created more problems than it resolved' while it also 'respected neither the spirit nor the letter' of the Hussein–McMahon correspondence.[24]

When the war ended with the British forces in Mesopotamia and Palestine in possession of significant territorial gains following the capture of Baghdad and Jerusalem in March and December 1917 respectively, British officials regretted having made their commitments to Hussein and to the French. In June 1919 Chief of the Imperial General Staff, Sir Henry Wilson, told General Allenby (by this time effectively the Military Governor of Egypt) that 'We have made so many promises to everybody in a contradictory sense that I cannot for the life of me see how we can get out of our present mess without breaking our word to somebody.'[25] Curzon was even more trenchant, telling a meeting of the Eastern Committee of the British War Cabinet in November 1918 that 'we have been a good deal embarrassed' by McMahon's pledges to Hussein, adding that the Sykes–Picot Agreement 'has been hanging like a millstone round our necks...In May 1916 we were bound hard and fast by this deplorable Agreement, to which, as we know, the French seem disposed to adhere most tenaciously.'[26]

British misgivings about their secret agreements reflected the changed position they found themselves in at the end of the war. Put simply, during 1915 and 1916 Britain needed local and international allies to offset their military weakness in the

Middle East after the failure at Gallipoli and the humiliating surrender of Kut. By 1918, the position had changed to one of military domination, but so, too, had the international situation. This reflected two major developments: the public disclosure of the wartime agreements by the new Soviet regime, and the addition of a new commitment to a Jewish national home in Palestine. Both developments occurred late in 1917 and were followed by a third important development, which was the declaration of the Fourteen Points by US President Woodrow Wilson on 8 January 1918 and the emergence of the principle of self-determination in regional and international affairs.

Shortly after the second (and final) Russian Revolution in October 1917, and in an effort to discredit the secret diplomacy of its Tsarist predecessor, the new Bolshevik regime started to publish confidential documents they had located in the foreign ministry archives in St Petersburg. Among the documents made public was the text of the Sykes–Picot Agreement, first in *Pravda* on 23 November 1917 and then in the *Manchester Guardian* three days later. The content of the agreement created great difficulties for British and French officials throughout the Middle East, even as tensions between the two wartime partners escalated over the 'interpretation and implementation' of the Sykes–Picot Agreement.[27] Moreover, it was a propaganda coup for their Ottoman counterparts, who promptly attempted to turn the Arab Revolt to their advantage by seizing on the growing distrust between the Arabs and their British and French allies. Yet, by that time, the agreement was already out of date after little more than a year as developments (and promises) in Palestine and in the Hejaz profoundly altered the trajectory of policy toward the region, with far-reaching consequences that still resonate today.

The Arab Revolt and the Balfour Declaration

In the midst of these contradictory and conflicting pledges, Sharif Hussein and his sons launched the Arab Revolt in June 1916. Much has been written about the uprising, and not least about the (embellished) role of T. E. Lawrence in it, with his *Seven Pillars of Wisdom* remaining in print nine decades later, and the 1962 film *Lawrence of Arabia*, starring Peter O'Toole and Omar Sharif, regarded as one of the cinematic classics. Yet, the reality of the Arab Revolt was rather more mundane, as the small-scale and largely uncoordinated series of attacks on Ottoman forces failed to make any serious impression on the balance of forces in the Middle East, and still less to the outcome of military operations against the Ottoman Empire more generally. Instead, the Arab Revolt has passed into legend as the embodiment of Arab attempts to seize the initiative away from occupying and external powers, and to restore agency to the local peoples and communities that had borne the brunt of the socio-economic dislocation caused by the military campaigns; its continuing salience is reflected in the use by some commentators of the phrase 'the Second Arab Revolt' to describe the outbreak of the Arab Spring in 2011.

The political and economic genesis of the Arab Revolt lay in multiple factors that intersected in early and mid-1916. As seen above, albeit insincere British declarations of support were made by McMahon to Sharif Hussein in October 1915 and later. They were augmented by tools of coercion such as the Allied blockade of Arabia, which interrupted trading and pilgrimage routes and cut off food supplies, but which were subsequently relaxed as an inducement to the Hashemite ruler. Djemal Pasha's brutal repression of Arab groups and leaders in Ottoman-controlled Beirut and Damascus also caused great anger among the Arab nationalists in the Hejaz, and gave the incipient revolt its first martyrs.[28] These factors culminated in the start of the Arab Revolt on 5 June 1916. Sharif Hussein wished to extend his control throughout the Arabian Peninsula and the Levant, and saw an opportunity to achieve this with British support. In October 1916, he declared himself 'King of the Arab Countries' in an attempt, in part, to sideline his major rival claimant for regional power, Abdul-Aziz Al-Saud, who also was receiving British assistance, albeit channelled through the Government of India's network of sheikhdoms and political agents in the Persian Gulf.[29]

Set against Hussein's grandiose ambition was the limited strength that he and his sons could project and the fact that their influence was contested within the Arabian Peninsula itself, most notably by Abdul-Aziz. Moreover, individual Arab tribes made their own choices over whom to back and often changed sides or loyalties as the tide of battle ebbed and flowed; one recent analysis of tribes in Mesopotamia during the war concluded that 'maximum personal advantages sought by various sheikhs were the ultimate consideration that determined the actual positions taken by various tribes'.[30] Thus, up to 5,000 tribesmen of the powerful Muntafiq federation in central Mesopotamia joined the Ottoman forces who were blocking the British attempt to relieve Kut in January 1916, and they only switched their support to the British in February 1917, by which time the momentum had shifted decisively.[31] Thus, the scale of belated British military successes both in Mesopotamia and in Palestine in 1917-18 arguably had greater impact on tribal and community choices than Hussein's call for revolt.

Hussein exercised control over only a small area of Arabia (the Hejaz) and the uprising involved a relatively small number of between 10,000 and 15,000 poorly-armed tribesmen. These were divided into regular units and bands of irregular guerrilla fighters who later gained fame with their opportunistic raids on the Ottoman rail network in the Hejaz. Although they were able to secure the Hejaz and ports on the Red Sea such as Jeddah and Yanbu, and strikingly captured Aqaba on 6 July 1917, they faced only weak enemy resistance, remained reliant on British supplies of money, arms and offshore naval assistance, and failed to spread their call for rebellion among other Arab provinces or units in the Ottoman military. Especially disappointing for the Sharif was the lack of anticipated adherents to his call for revolt, neither among Arab officers serving in the Ottoman Army nor among Arab tribes. Instead, the revolt quickly became contained within a fairly narrow area of the Hejaz running up the western coast of the Arabian Peninsula to the Red Sea, from whose ports Britain could resupply the men in arms and money ferried across from the Sudan.[32]

Even Lawrence, whose role as charismatic go-between propelled him to fame after the end of the war, acknowledged in October 1916 that 'They [the Arab leaders] are weak in material resources and always will be, for their world is agricultural and pastoral and can never be very rich or very strong'; although he added that this weakness afforded Britain considerable opportunities to make post-war gains 'immeasurably greater than the money, arms and ammunition we are now called upon to spare'.[33] This notwithstanding, as he landed in the Hejazi port of Rabigh on 16 October 1916, Lawrence felt that 'The conditions were ideal for an Arab movement', although he based this assessment on a wildly optimistic view that Najaf and Karbala were in revolt in Mesopotamia and that 'the surviving Arabs in Halil's army were, on his own confession, openly disloyal to Turkey'.[34] However, his civilian and military colleagues in Cairo were less impressed by the faltering progress of the revolt as Hussein's tribal forces were ill-matched against regular Ottoman infantry and incapable of matching them in open battle without significant external assistance.[35] One of T. E. Lawrence's biographers, the British military historian Lawrence James, described in detail the full extent of British and other aid to the Arab Revolt:

Until the end of the war the Arabs would depend upon endless transfusions of Allied arms and ammunition as well as British gold to keep their forces in the field. In combat they were sustained by British, French, Egyptian, and Indian specialists such as engineers, gunners, signallers, and supply officers as well as artillery, armoured cars, and aircraft. Their bases at Jiddah, Rabigh, Yanbu al Bahr, and later al Wajh and Aqaba would be protected by British and French men-of-war.[36]

The commander-in-chief of the Egyptian Expeditionary Force, Archibald Murray, shared such misgivings as to the operational effectiveness of the irregular Arab forces. Even the stirring capture of the port-town of Aqaba in June 1917, where the defences had been designed to guard against a seaborne attack rather than a landward assault, owed much to the supporting bombardment by Royal Naval vessels.[37] It was only in 1918, with increased levels of allied manpower and materiel assistance, that the Northern Arab Army became slightly more effective as a combat force, whereupon it was divided into regular and irregular units, a British Section and a French Detachment. It also gained an intelligence capability and began providing Allenby's forces with useful information regarding developments on its southern and eastward flanks.[38] However, the only two meaningful instances of cooperation between the Northern Arab Army and Allenby's Egyptian Expeditionary Force – the two trans-Jordan raids that attempted to seize Amman in March and April 1918 – were resounding failures. These damaged Britain's hitherto rising prestige arising from military successes in Palestine and convinced wavering Arab tribes to remain loyal to the Ottoman Sultan.[39]

Over the intervening decades the Arab Revolt has entered into legend, largely due to the charisma of its leading personalities: Lawrence himself and Faisal bin Hussein, later the first King of Iraq. Moreover, while the Hashemite kings of Iraq were overthrown in 1958 and their hold on Syria lasted mere months in 1919, the dynasty they founded in Jordan remains one of the lynchpins of the pro-Western 'forces of moderation' in the modern Middle East. Not for nothing is the giant flagpole depicting the flag of the Arab Revolt over Aqaba one of the tallest in the world, visible from four countries – Egypt, Israel and Saudi Arabia, in addition to Jordan. And yet, the subsequent fame of the Arab Revolt is distinctly out of proportion to its contemporary significance, both militarily and – to the extent that Hussein succeeded neither in galvanising a general Arab revolt nor winning over prominent rivals such as the Al-Saud – politically. Instead, the most renowned historian of the Ottoman military in the First World War, Edward Erickson, offers the following pithy assessment:

…the Ottoman Army was able to deal with the mobile Arab rebel armies by largely ignoring them. Lawrence's bands raided isolated outposts and, more frequently, destroyed the Ottoman railway line to Medina. These losses were pinpricks to the Turks…Even in the final campaign in Syria the Turks deployed few military assets against the Arabs. Moreover, they never worried about an actual Arab uprising behind their lines as the rebels had little interaction with the civilian population in either Syria or Palestine…As a matter of record the Arab Revolt was never a movement that was broadly supported by the Arab population.[40]

Alongside the rise of an Arab political consciousness was the development and growth of Zionism as a competing national project. As the two laid claim to the same territory in Palestine, the emerging Arab nationalists and Zionists became locked in a struggle for land and resources. Like its Arab counterpart and the emergence of secular nationalisms in Europe, Zionism was inspired by the French Revolution and the Enlightenment's principles of the social contract and citizenship. Importantly, Zionism also grew as a response to escalating anti-Semitism in European society, such as the vicious series of pogroms in southern Russia in 1881. These and other instances of violent anti-Semitism triggered the drive to create a Jewish national home in the Biblical land of Israel. The first Aliyah (immigration) to Palestine took place from 1882 to 1903 as small groups of Zionists from Eastern Europe founded the first Jewish settlements at Rosh Pina, Petah Tikva, Rehovot and Rishon LeZion.[41] Concurrently, the publication of *Der Judenstaat* ('The Jewish State') by Theodore Herzl in 1896, and his convening of the first Zionist congress in Basle the following year, provided a 'practical and institutional framework' for the creation of a Jewish state. The Zionist congress brought together, for the first time, Eastern and Western European Zionists, and resulted in the establishment of the World Zionist Organisation, which was to be committed to the 'creation of a home for the Jewish people in Palestine to be secured by public law'. This was to be 'achieved incrementally through the purchase and settlement of land, on the one hand, and through diplomacy and the blessing of the Great Powers on the other'.[42]

Zionism was therefore a growing political and national force by 1914. A new wave of pogroms in Russia in the wake of the constitutional revolution of 1905 triggered a further surge in Jewish migration to Palestine. Until 1914 the headquarters of the World Zionist Organisation had been in Berlin, and its leading figures and thinkers had largely been of German and Austro-Hungarian origin.[43] A combination of Zionism's greater dynamism and strength, and desire to avoid losing the propaganda war to the enemy, gradually swung British governmental support behind Zionist aims and objectives. Moreover, Zionists had already become involved in the British war effort in the Middle East, as a Zion Mule Corps had been attached to the Mediterranean Expeditionary Force at Gallipoli, and several Jewish battalions had served with Allenby's forces in Palestine.[44] Especially noteworthy was the NILI espionage network of about forty Jewish agents based in Haifa in Palestine and dispersed across Palestine and Syria in 1917 before the group was discovered and rounded up.[45] The appointment of David Lloyd George as Prime Minister and Arthur Balfour as Foreign Secretary – both sympathetic to Zionism – in December 1916 sealed the shift in British policy at the highest level, if not among the Arabists in the Foreign Office.

Nevertheless, significant differences of opinion persisted among British Jews with regard to the proposal to create a Jewish homeland in Palestine. Herbert Samuel – the Home Secretary between January and December 1916, a close confidante of Weizmann, and later the first High Commission of Palestine between 1920 and 1925 – emerged as the leading architect of the creation of a Jewish national home in Palestine under British auspices. He was opposed by his own cousin, Edwin Montagu, who entered the Cabinet as Secretary of State for India in 1917. Montagu opposed the proposal for a Jewish home in Palestine as he feared that it would prove 'a rallying ground for anti-Semites in every country in the world'. Moreover, he believed that the proposed national project would undermine the position of Jews elsewhere in the Middle East and cast doubt upon the loyalty of Jewish communities in Europe. Montagu submitted a memorandum to his Cabinet colleagues setting out his objections to Zionism, in which he stated that 'I would almost be tempted to proscribe the Zionist organisation as illegal and against the national interest...I would ask of a British government sufficient tolerance to refuse a conclusion which makes aliens and foreigners by implication, if not by law, of all their Jewish fellow-citizens.'[46]

Montagu's intervention delayed the proposal but ultimately did not derail it. On 2 November 1917, Balfour sent a letter to Chaim Weizmann, the chairman of the British Zionist Organisation. Later the first President of Israel in 1948, Weizmann was during the First World War a professor of chemistry at the University of Manchester with impeccable access to the upper echelons of the British Government. These were based in part on Weizmann's pioneering wartime research into the production of acetone for artillery shells. His contacts allowed Weizmann to advocate the Zionist cause and search for a Jewish homeland to Balfour and Lloyd George.

The painstaking process of building support for Zionism culminated in the issuing of the historic Balfour Declaration, which stated that:

His Majesty's Government view with favour the establishment in Palestine of a national home for the Jewish people, and will use their best endeavours to facilitate the achievement of this object, it being clearly understood that nothing shall be done which may prejudice the civil and religious rights of existing non-Jewish communities in Palestine, or the rights and political status enjoyed by Jews in any other countries.[47]

British motives for issuing the Balfour Declaration included the desire to win the support of influential Jewish communities in the United States and in Russia and also to undermine the German war effort by alienating key participants within it. By 1917, 'the Zionists were a dynamic and expanding force' among the Jewish communities in both countries, which 'the British Government badly needed to influence and in which, apart from propaganda, it had few means of influence to hand'.[48] Further, the declaration of British support for the realisation of the Zionist objective in Palestine also generated a drive to ensure that the territory would be allocated to Britain rather than to France. Allenby's capture of and entry into Jerusalem five weeks later cemented Britain's control over Palestine and signalled that the internationalisation of Palestinian status (as mandated by the Sykes–Picot Agreement) was dead.[49]

By the time the Soviets began to release details of the secret wartime agreements, Britain therefore had to balance three competing and conflicting sets of commitments. At the heart of each was the reordering of political authority in the post-Ottoman Middle East. The vague promise of an independent Arab state made by McMahon to Hussein was counterbalanced by the equally vague promise of a Jewish national home in Palestine, while both were themselves undermined by the territorial pledges contained in the Sykes–Picot Agreement. But by 1917, the fluidity and uncertainty of the balance of force and interest in the Middle East was complicated further as the battlefronts suddenly sprang into life. The Palestinian historian Rashid Khalidi has recounted how the Balfour Declaration 'started the process of disillusionment with the Allies among the Arabs generally', in part because it was publicly announced 'only a few weeks before Allenby's troops entered Jerusalem in December 1917, at a time when it had become clear that the British would be the new rulers of the country'.[50] Thus, at almost the same time that the British made their pledge supporting the creation of a Jewish homeland, they also acquired the power on the ground in Palestine to be able to implement it.[51]

The Fourteen Points, the Declaration to the Seven, and the Anglo-French agreement

The Soviets' publication of the secret wartime agreements threw the British Government into disarray. The widespread anger that the revelations provoked in the Middle East and among Britain's allies prompted the Prime Minister, Lloyd George, to make a significant 'war aims' speech to the Trades Union Congress on 5 January 1918. As David Woodward has noted, the mounting defensive pressure to counter the negative reaction to the secret agreements resulted in 'the most significant wartime British statement on the objectives of the war' and 'represented an attempt to moderate his country's war aims'.[52] Its candour and 'liberal orientation' certainly surprised the speech's main audience, namely US policy-makers led by President Woodrow Wilson, who himself was preparing to make his famous 'Fourteen Points' speech just three days later. In his speech, Lloyd George promised the 'recognition of their separate national conditions' to the subject peoples of the Ottoman Empire, and affirmed the British Government's support for a post-war territorial settlement 'based on the right of self-determination or the consent of the governed'. However, he immediately watered down this bold aspiration as he added the caveat that 'What the exact form of that recognition in each particular case should be need not here be discussed, beyond stating that it would be impossible to restore to their former sovereignty…'[53]

Three days later, President Wilson delivered a speech to a Joint Session of Congress, in which he articulated his vision of American war aims and a sustainable post-war political order. The speech represented the outcome of a wide-ranging study group that Wilson had convened in September 1917 to develop the United States' formal war aims. Headed by Wilson's close foreign policy adviser Edward M. House, the group was known as 'The Inquiry' and involved some 150 academics and international affairs specialists. The fourteen dimensions to Wilson's speech covered a wide range of issues from freedom of the seas to removal of economic barriers and the conduct of open diplomacy rather than secret negotiation. Crucially, Wilson also went into the details of the territorial readjustments that he believed should underpin any peace agreement. After detailing the outlines of such agreements in Europe, the twelfth point focused on the Ottoman Empire and its Middle Eastern territories:

XII. The Turkish portion of the present Ottoman Empire should be assured a secure sovereignty, but the other nationalities which are now under Turkish rule should be assured an undoubted security of life and an absolutely unmolested opportunity of autonomous development, and the Dardanelles should be permanently opened as a free passage to the ships and commerce of all nations under international guarantees.[54]

Wilson introduced the principle of self-determination of peoples as the principle on which the post-war structure of international relations should be based. Although the President had not consulted with his allies prior to the speech, both he and Lloyd George had – publicly, at least – committed to the policy of self-determination in the Middle East, although the devil lay in the detail, or lack of it, concerning specific territories in the Ottoman sphere.

British and French officials in London, Paris and their colonial outposts immediately acknowledged the significance of the changed international situation, and realised that it would have implications for their own plans to reorder the Middle

East. Together with the Soviets' release of the secret agreements, the Fourteen Points ushered in a paradigm shift in the international relations of the First World War, prompting official policy in Britain and France to shift in response. Some officials, such as the commander-in-chief of Britain's Mesopotamian Expeditionary Force, General William Marshall, were openly dismissive of the 'twaddle about self-determination and the rights of small nations' which was 'the parrot-cries of the moment'.[55] Others, such as the acting British Civil Commissioner in Mesopotamia in 1918, Arnold Wilson, expressed dismay at Lloyd George's and President Wilson's new approach, which introduced 'disturbing elements into the situation' in the Middle East. Accordingly, Wilson refused to accept the change in policy and simply disregarded it as 'inconsistent with the traditional aims of British policy in the Middle East'.[56]

Furthermore, the President's enunciation of the outlines that a post-war settlement should take clashed with prevailing assumptions in London and Paris. Quite apart from the emerging rivalry to carve out competing spheres of influence in the Middle East, French President Georges Clemenceau favoured a decisive military defeat of Germany and the imposition of strong punitive measures upon the aggressor, while Lloyd George's government sought to protect and extend its interests in the Middle East. Neither government embraced the Fourteen Points, although each realised that the changing international relations of the conflict necessitated a new approach toward diplomacy and policy-making. Hence, the two major developments of 1917 – namely the American entry into the war and the Russian revolutions and subsequent exit from the conflict – had major implications for the enunciation of Allied states' war aims and post-war objectives. Put simply, the replacement of a fellow imperial state by an idealistic republic meant that the right of conquest could no longer be regarded as sufficient grounds for territorial acquisition.

In London in particular, senior officials accordingly began to formulate new policies that would deepen and secure British control over the military gains made in the Middle East. Policy-makers at the India Office and the Foreign Office searched for new ways of justifying post-war control of Mesopotamia and Egypt and Palestine respectively. They were assisted by Sir Percy Cox, who was temporarily recalled to London from his post as Civil Commissioner in Baghdad for consultations. The India Office reassessment was led by the outgoing Political Secretary, Sir Arthur Hirtzel, and his successor, Sir John Shuckburgh. Hirtzel acknowledged that 'the great change that has taken place in the general political situation' required 'an early reconsideration and readjustment of the policy to be pursued in the occupied territory'. Acknowledging the radically different international context, the Political Department of the India Office now argued that any claim to post-war control must be based 'on other grounds than mere right of conquest'. It thus recommended that British policy should aim at 'placing British interests and influence in the country… on so secure a basis as to guarantee their maintenance under any administrative system that may ultimately be introduced'.[57] This, they suggested, would involve the entrenching of British commercial interests in Mesopotamia behind an 'Arab facade' in Baghdad. In April 1918, the Eastern Committee set up by the War Cabinet in London, as well as the Foreign Secretary, Sir Arthur Balfour, formally adopted this reorientation of British policy.[58]

Later in 1918, the unexpectedly rapid end of the war that followed the failure of the Germans' spring offensives and the rapid succession of British and French breakthroughs on the Western Front injected still greater urgency into the search for territorial control after the end of hostilities. Whereas in the first half of the year, the focus of British and French wartime policy shifted to the desperate fight for survival in the face of the German onslaught, the dramatic change in the momentum of the war from August onwards opened up dizzying new possibilities of military advancement and territorial gain. Meanwhile, throughout the year, national groups across the Middle East began to formulate and advance political platforms as news of President Wilson's Fourteen Points spread, in spite of the strenuous efforts of British and French censors. The stage was thus primed for a growing clash between rising nationalist aspirations and deepening Anglo-French attempts to fortify their power and extend it into the post-war period. At the forefront of the minds of each group were the opportunities – as well as the challenges – posed by the impending end of hostilities.

One important development occurred in Syria, where a new Party of Syrian Unity was established late in 1917, soon after the Balfour Declaration and the Bolsheviks' publication of the Sykes–Picot Agreement. The intellectual heart of the burgeoning Arab national movements, activists both in Syria and among the sizeable Syrian community in Cairo responded to news of the Balfour Declaration by issuing counter-demands of their own. Two leading Syrian and Lebanese activists in Cairo (Fawzi al-Bakri and Sulayman Nasif) visited the Arab Bureau to deliver a telegram signed by them and two other notables which declared that Palestine was an inseparable part of Syria. However, British officials refused to forward the letter to London and also advised the activists to cease their protests.[59] Concerned by these developments, and also increasingly dissatisfied with Sharif Hussein's leadership of the Arab Revolt, on 28 April 1918 seven leading Syrian notables belonging to the Party of Syrian Unity issued a memorandum that requested a 'guarantee of the ultimate independence of Arabia'. In it, they claimed to represent various Arab clubs and societies who 'have been given full power to voice the expression of their tongues'. Indeed, the seven spanned most of the major societies active in Syria, and between them they represented 'all layers of the nation, and especially the intellectuals, the religious leaders, and the aristocracy' and also 'had ties with the chiefs of the Bedouin tribes'.[60]

The memorandum of the seven Syrians requested the British Government to respond to a series of questions and clarifications. At their core was the demand that Britain publicly confirm its intention to grant full independence to Arab lands, defined as the Arabian Peninsula, Syria, Mesopotamia and parts of south-eastern Turkey. The seven also asked the British Government to elaborate on the structures of political control that it envisaged for the above-mentioned territories.[61] This time, the British authorities in Cairo acknowledged the significance of the memorandum and its signatories and forwarded it on to London. It fell to Mark Sykes to draft the government's response on 11 June 1918, in what became known as the 'Declaration to the Seven' after it was read out to the seven notables at a meeting in Cairo on 16 June. The declaration divided the Arab territories into four categories: 1) areas that had been free and independent before the outbreak of the war; 2) areas emancipated from Ottoman control by Arab actions during the war; 3) areas formerly under Ottoman control occupied by Allied forces during the war; and 4) areas still under Ottoman control. In the first and second categories, the British Government pledged to 'recognise the complete and sovereign independence' of the Arab inhabitants; while in the third, 'the future government of these regions should be based upon the principle of the consent of the governed'; and in the fourth category, 'it is the wish and desire of His Majesty's Government that the oppressed peoples of these areas should obtain their freedom and independence…'.[62]

The Declaration to the Seven was notable primarily as it constituted the first British pronouncement to the Arab world that explicitly articulated the principle of national self-determination. In the influential post-war view of George Antonius, it was 'by far the most important declaration of policy publicly made by Great Britain in connexion with the Arab Revolt' as it confirmed Britain's 'previous pledges to the Arabs in plainer language than in any former public utterance' and provided 'an authoritative enunciation of the principles on which those pledges rested'.[63] It thus went further than Lloyd George's 'war aims' speech of January 1918, but like that earlier declaration, its significance was watered down by qualifications and ambiguities.[64]

However, the Declaration to the Seven was not widely publicised, and soon it was overtaken by the fast-unfolding chain of events as the Central Powers' resistance finally collapsed in the autumn of 1918. Nevertheless, it stood as testimony both to the rising political consciousness among Arab political societies and their mounting anticipation that the international context had changed the parameters (and acceptability) of traditional forms of colonial rule. It highlighted the impetus that the war provided to aspirations of local autonomy among the emerging nationalist classes throughout the Ottoman Empire and across the British and French domains in North Africa. However, this local mobilisation quickly clashed with the rapid British advances in Syria and Mesopotamia in September and October 1918, making urgent a final and definitive declaration of British and French policy.[65]

The outcome of the delicate triangulation of British, French and Arab interests was the Anglo-French Declaration issued on 7 November 1918. This went furthest of all in renouncing colonialism based on annexation and in aligning British and French policy with the principle of national self-determination, at least on paper. It emerged as officials in London sought to redefine their claim on large swathes of the Middle East in a manner consistent with the prevailing intellectual wind. British officials also were cognisant of the new-found constraints of the Sykes–Picot Agreement, now that the military situation on the ground had been transformed to their advantage.[66] Lord Robert Cecil, a member of the War Cabinet's Eastern Committee which advised

Lloyd George on how to derive maximum advantage from the military successes, had acknowledged as much in a memorandum he sent to French officials on 8 October 1918 (with the full approval of the Prime Minister), stating that:

With regard to the future direction of the other territories mentioned in the Anglo-French Convention of 1916, His Majesty's Government think it right to point out that the general position has so much changed since that agreement was entered into that its provisions do not...appear suitable to present conditions.[67]

British officials were thus faced both with French recalcitrance over reopening the territorial settlement agreed in 1916, and Arab aspirations that the sudden end to the war would lead to concessions that reflected their wartime support for London. Thus, the Anglo-French Declaration represented an attempt to reconcile the increasingly divergent pressures on policy-making. Drafted, as ever, by Sykes himself, it began with the bold assertion, completely at odds with the secret wartime agreements, that British and French goals in the Middle East throughout the war had aimed at securing 'the complete and final liberation of the peoples who have for so long been oppressed by the Turks, and the setting up of national governments, and administrations, deriving their authority from the free exercise of the initiative and choice of the indigenous populations'.[68] The Declaration went on to pledge that:

In pursuit of those intentions, France and Great Britain agree to further and assist in the establishment of indigenous Governments and administrations in Syria and Mesopotamia which have already been liberated by the Allies, as well as in those territories which they are engaged in securing and recognising these as soon as they are actually established. Far from wishing to impose on the populations of those regions any particular institutions they are only concerned to ensure by their support and by adequate assistance the regular workings of Governments and administrations freely chosen by the populations themselves...[69]

As the First World War span towards a rapid end, the contradictory paths of wartime pronouncements and promises inevitably rose to the surface. However, another interest that came of age in 1918 profoundly restructured the nature of the interaction between the Middle East and the international system over the course of the twentieth century. This was the growing awareness of the importance of oil as a fuel for powering the modern world, as well as the geopolitical significance of controlling the world's known or potential oil reserves. Together, oil and geopolitics emerged as a core Allied objective in the Middle East in 1918 at the same time that the sudden collapse of the Central Powers opened up new possibilities for Western intervention and control.

Oil and geopolitics

Developments during the final year of the war focused the attention of policy-makers on the potential of oil reserves located in the Middle East. This set in train the geostrategic importance that the region would maintain throughout the rest of the twentieth century and beyond. Oil was discovered by British concession-holders in the Middle East at Masjed-e-Soleyman in Persia (modern-day Iran) in May 1908. This landmark discovery was followed a year later by the creation of the Anglo-Persian Oil Company (APOC) and the construction of a large oil refinery at Abadan on the Persian coastline of the Gulf. The refinery opened in 1913, the same year that APOC negotiated with the First Lord of the Admiralty in London, Winston Churchill, to substitute oil for coal as the fuel for the Royal Navy. At that time the major oil-producing countries were the United States, Romania, Russia, the Dutch East Indies and Mexico, and the Admiralty lacked a source of supply under British control or at least influence. Before 1914, the United States accounted for wholly 62.3 per cent of oil supplies to the United Kingdom, followed by Romania (11.6 per cent), Russia (7.7 per cent), the Dutch colonies (7.7 per cent) and Mexico (4.1 per cent), with 'other countries' providing the remaining 6.5 per cent. This included Canada, the only sizeable oil-producing source within the British imperial system in 1914.[70] However, the British Empire only produced 2.5 per cent of world oil, and in a House of Common debate on the issue in July 1913, Churchill identified the crux of the problem as follows:

...while it is not desirable to draw all our supplies from one source it is essential that the fields over which His Majesty's Government will have control shall be so developed that in times of emergency they will be able to supply at short notice any deficiencies that may arise through the failures of deliveries elsewhere.'[71]

Simultaneously, the British Government established a Royal Commission on Fuel and Engines under Lord Fisher, who had retired as First Sea Lord in 1910 only to resume his position in 1914 before resigning in protest at Churchill's Gallipoli campaign in 1915.[72] The commission was mandated to examine 'the means of supply and storage of liquid fuel in war and peace' with a view to converting the Royal Navy from coal-fired to oil-powered vessels. It made three confidential reports which recommended that large oil reserves be accumulated in the United Kingdom and across the British Empire. At the same time, the aim was expressed that the Admiralty should become the independent owner and producer of its own supplies of oil.[73]

Technological advances made the possession of abundant sources of oil all the more pressing. Oil-burning vessels were both more economical to operate and could move faster than coal-fired ones. With Britain and Germany engaged in a naval arms race before 1914, officials in London and Berlin were quick to seize upon any advantage they could get. Germany's proximity to Romanian oilfields offered a convenient source of supply that culminated eventually in the German occupation of the country in 1916. Britain had no such equivalent, and the loss of Romanian and also Russian supplies during the war meant that by 1917 some 80 per cent of all supplies came from a single source, the United States, leading to an unhealthy over-dependence that was itself highly vulnerable to enemy disruption. Indeed, by 1918, the United Kingdom required 10 million tons of imported oil each year, while each cruiser in the Royal Navy required 6,000 tons of oil a day to operate.[74]

Churchill's conversion of the Royal Navy to oil was soon followed by the British Government's acquisition of a majority stake in APOC. In April 1914, an Admiralty report noted that APOC's existing field was capable of 'supplying a large proportion of the requirements of the Admiralty for a considerable period' and recommended that 'the whole concession judiciously worked would probably safeguard the fuel supply of His Majesty's Navy'.[75] On 20 May 1914, the British Government purchased a 51 per cent shareholding in APOC and on 10 August – six days after Britain declared war on Germany – the Anglo-Persian Oil Co. (Acquisition of Capital) Bill received royal assent.[76] Thereafter, as Chapter 6 made clear, the defence of the APOC oilfields, refinery and pipelines at Abadan became one of Britain's objectives in sending forces to Basra in October 1914, initiating the Mesopotamian campaign. During the war itself, the vast expansion in motorised transport in all theatres of the conflict revolutionised the position of oil in the military machine. In *Feeding Mars: Logistics in Western Warfare from the Middle Ages to the Present*, John Lynn described how the rapid technological changes brought about by the industrial revolution transformed 'both the means of transport and the items consumed' in industrialised conflict, which he argued 'redefined modern logistics' and the nature of warfare itself.[77] Meanwhile, Martin van Creveld suggested persuasively that a 'revolution of logistics' occurred during the war as factory-produced goods replaced food and fodder as the major items of consumption, placing immense strain on mechanised transportation systems and tying armies to their networks of supply and transport.[78]

With this in mind, it is perhaps surprising that oil did not emerge as a defining geopolitical interest for the Allies in the Middle East until very late on in the war. The need for securing control over the Persian oilfields and the reserves thought to exist in Mesopotamia (prior to the actual discovery of oil in 1927) suddenly exploded onto the British Government's agenda at the end of July 1918. This occurred as the Foreign Secretary, Arthur Balfour, prepared to make a statement on war aims to a meeting of the Imperial War Cabinet in London on 13 August. In the run-up to the meeting, the influential Secretary to the Imperial War Cabinet (which included leaders and representatives from the Colonies and Dominions of the British Empire), Sir Maurice Hankey, actively promoted to ministers a memorandum that had been prepared by Admiral Sir Edmond Slade, a former director of the Naval Intelligence Division and the leading advocate of the British Government's acquisition of the controlling stake in APOC in 1914, whereupon he also joined the company as a director. Slade's paper was entitled 'The Petroleum Situation in the British Empire' and it was forwarded by the Admiralty to the Imperial War Cabinet on 30 July 1918 for urgent consideration by ministers.

Slade began his memorandum by describing how 'There are two main points of view from which the study of the Petroleum situation in the British Empire must be considered. The first and most important is the strategic and the second is that of supply.'[79] He continued:

...It is no exaggeration to say that our life as an Empire is largely dependent upon our ability to maintain the control of bunker fuel...Oil fuel used as a means of raising steam is about twice as economical as coal and, used in an internal combustion engine, about four times. Oil must therefore gradually take the place of coal for all marine purposes and it is consequently of paramount importance to us to obtain the undisputed control of the greatest amount of Petroleum that we can.[80]

Turning his attention to the Middle East, Slade stated that:

In Persia and Mesopotamia lie the largest undeveloped resources at present known in the world... There are also many known deposits of oil in other parts of Persia and Mesopotamia which will form reserves for the future, when they are once developed so as to bring them into bearing. It is not too much to estimate that the oil lands of Persia and Mesopotamia which will extend over an area of 360,000 square miles, or more than twice the size of the oil lands of Russia, should not in the future provide a supply equal to that now given by the US. If this estimate is anywhere near the truth, then it is evident that the Power that controls the oil lands of Persia and Mesopotamia will control the sources of supply of the majority of the liquid fuel of the future.[81]

Slade concluded his explosive memorandum by recommending that 'We must therefore at all costs retain our hold on the Persian and Mesopotamian oil fields' and 'must not allow the intrusion in any form of foreign interests, however disguised they may be'. Such physical control of oilfield territory was, he considered, absolutely necessary, as he claimed that 'Conventions and Treaties are only paper and can be torn up and are not sufficient safeguard.'[82]

The note of urgency that runs through Slade's memorandum was immediately picked up by Hankey, who forwarded it to the First Lord of the Admiralty, Sir Eric Geddes, on 30 July, along with a note that stated that 'if this information is correct, the retention of the oil-bearing regions in Mesopotamia and Persia in British hands, as well as a proper strategic boundary to cover them, would appear to be a first-class British War Aim'. Hankey added that 'it would appear desirable that before we come to discuss peace, we should obtain possession of all the oil-bearing regions in Mesopotamia and Southern Persia, wherever they may be', and ended by stating that 'the matter is of the utmost urgency'.[83] In a separate letter to the Prime Minister, Hankey implored Lloyd George to take action: 'there may be reasons other than purely military for pushing on in Mesopotamia where the British have an enormous preponderance of force. Would it not be an advantage, before the end of the war, to secure the valuable oil wells in Mesopotamia?'[84] And to the Foreign Secretary, Hankey wrote, 'I do hope you will be able to read it [Slade's memorandum] as it really is a most vitally important paper', before reiterating that control of the Persian and Mesopotamian oil-bearing territories should be 'a first class British War Aim'. Accordingly, Hankey suggested to Balfour that 'in your statement to the Imperial War Cabinet, you should rub this in'.[85]

Doubtless to Hankey's dismay, his advocacy did not yield the positive results he expected. In a short conversation with Balfour, the Foreign Secretary commented that any retention or extension of British control over the Mesopotamian and Persian oilfields 'was a purely Imperialist War Aim'. This drew a defensive response from Hankey, who penned a further letter to Balfour on 12 August, the day before the Imperial War Cabinet was to meet to discuss war aims:

I suppose that if the matter is put as crudely as I put it, it is Imperialistic, and though this does not shock me, I suppose it would shock President Wilson and some of our Allies. Nevertheless, it appears to me, even from the point of view of the idealist, that it is almost unavoidable that we should acquire the Northern regions of Mesopotamia.[86]

Revealingly, Hankey posited the alternative to British control as 'handing back' the territories occupied in the Middle East to the 'devastating rule of the Turks'.[87] The notion that the peoples of the region might be allowed to choose their form of rule was entirely absent, as British policy-makers wedded to the 'old way of doing business' struggled to come to terms with the new international consensus forming around national self-determination. Similar disregard was shown by Britain's man in Mesopotamia, Arnold Wilson, who recalled in his post-war memoir how the looming end of hostilities led him to urge 'every effort…to score as heavily as possible on the Tigris before the whistle blew'. Thus, the city of Mosul, widely (and correctly) believed to be in the heartland of the richest oilfields in Mesopotamia, was occupied as late as 10 November 1918. This may have been one day before the end of the war in Europe, but it was eleven days after the Armistice of Mudros had (theoretically) ended the hostilities with the Ottoman Empire in the Middle East.[88]

Hankey's persistent advocacy ultimately paid off as Balfour told the Imperial War Cabinet meeting on 13 August that Britain could not allow Mesopotamia to revert to Ottoman control or come under Arab rule. Instead, it would become the exception to Britain's declared policy pronouncements concerning the future of the Middle East.[89] Yet, as the previous section indicated, this was itself superseded by the subsequent Anglo-French Declaration on 7 November 1918. The glaring contradictions inherent in British policy towards the region were thus encapsulated in Mesopotamia, where ideational concepts of national self-determination ran up against imperial strategic and commercial interests. It is instructive to note that the Anglo-French Declaration was proclaimed at the same time as Arnold Wilson's units were racing north to secure their gains in Mosul while they could get away with such forward action. France, too, responded to the British moves by looking towards embedding its own post-war interests in Syria, which would bring it into direct conflict with the Arab national movement. The final chapter in this book examines these political manoeuvres in full, as the uneasy consensus that had been forged during the war between British, French and Arab interests gave way to outright contestation between 1919 and 1922.

8

THE POST-WAR SETTLEMENTS, 1919-1923

The previous chapter documented the tangled webs of wartime diplomacy, secret agreements and conflicting pledges that had already started to unravel in 1918. These contradictory processes were greatly accelerated by the unanticipated collapse of the Central Powers between August and November 1918. The ending of hostilities on the battlefield gave way to competing aspirations for the peace settlement among combatants and host populations exhausted by four years of conflict. At their core lay a clash between British and French attempts to secure and extend wartime gains into the post-war period and surging national demands across the Arab world. President Wilson's concept of self-determination further added to the heady mix of political consciousness and nationalist expression. The result was a sustained period of unrest that rocked the grand pretensions of the fading imperial powers in the Middle East from 1919 to 1922, as local elites and local agendas emerged from the shadow of colonial control to exert a powerful influence on decision-making processes across the region.

This final chapter begins by focusing on two major trends in the immediate post-war period. The first explores the impact of the myriad wartime hardships on peoples and movements across the region. The cumulative effect of four years of social displacement and economic dislocation created deep grievances that found an outlet in the movements of individual and collective resistance to the structure and balance of political power. Socio-economic factors intersected in turn with the second trend, which was the disappearance of the Ottoman-era elites as new national figures competed with a fresh class of British and French colonial administrators for local and regional influence. The second trend picks up from the examination in Chapter 7 of the changing climate of international politics. It explores how this percolated throughout the Middle East in spite of the British and French attempts to suppress it after 1918. As officials in London and Paris and on the ground sought to recalibrate their regional policies to justify the extension of their wartime powers into the post-war period, they increasingly came into conflict with erstwhile local allies.

Rising nationalist hopes were subsequently dashed during the Paris Peace Conference in 1919. The chapter will therefore continue by describing how local anger at the imperial powers' attempts to legitimise and deepen their rule converged with the socio-economic hardships that afflicted virtually every grouping in the region. The result was a toxic alignment of shifting coalitions around a vague platform of protecting local resources from further predatory demands and maximising the political dividends from wartime choices and accommodations. This set the scene for developments in the Middle East and North Africa up until 1922. This was the year of the unilateral British declaration of Egyptian independence as well as the signing of the first Anglo-Iraqi treaty a year after the infamous Cairo Conference set the parameters for the modern state system in the Middle East. The same period also encompassed the French removal of Faisal bin Hussein from Syria, and the establishment of the post-war mandate system for the new political entities of Trans-Jordan and Palestine.

Exposure to, and participation in, the First World War and its turbulent aftermath thus contributed to the making of the modern Middle East. This was most visible in the decline of the Ottoman Empire and the emergence of the modern states-system (albeit under mandatory rule). This radically altered the political landscape of the region, but other forms of reordering also took place, ranging from the rise of a new type of nationalism that was able to mobilise a wider coalition of support and integrate economic and industrial components, the splintering and fragmentation of wartime alliances and agreements that still trigger bitter memories a century on, to the interjection of oil as a 'Western' policy objective with its geostrategic consequences, and a set of policy decisions that continue to reverberate across the region a century later. After a decade that has seen renewed Western intervention in Iraq as well as the Arab Spring upheaval which threatens to unravel the post-1918 political settlement, it is apparent that major issues of contention trace their roots to the decisions taken between 1914 and 1922.

The legacy of wartime hardships

The First World War has rightly been analysed in terms of a revolution in military affairs. From technological advances and the industrialisation of warfare to the relationship between political and military authority and the planning and execution of operations, the war did mark a watershed moment in modern military affairs. In the Middle East, although the fighting was neither as intense nor as concentrated as that on the Western Front, the cumulative impact of four years of conflict nevertheless was at least as devastating for the peoples and regions involved. The advent of modern, industrialised warfare made the fighting very different from pre-1914 colonial campaigns, which had made much more limited demands on host societies. During the First World War, by contrast, local resources were mobilised and ruthlessly exploited on an altogether different scale in order to meet the inexorable demands for logistical and administrative support. The extraction of local man- and animal-power, the requisitioning of crops for food and fodder, and the economic dislocation caused to regional commerce and trade routes, all magnified the impact of a form of 'total war' on the Middle East that involved the broad utilisation of both civil and military resources, however peripheral the campaigns were to the European combatants. In the case of the genocide of the Armenians and the redrawing of political boundaries that cut across long-established economic and commercial hinterlands and contributed to conditions of famine in the Levant and in Persia, the 'total' nature of the war became tragically real.[1]

The impact of four years of fighting therefore touched every part of life. The wartime mobilisation of local resources contributed greatly to the accumulation of grievances that afflicted groups across the economic and social spectrum. In rural regions, the requisitioning of manpower, camels and donkeys as well as food and fodder severely disrupted patterns of agricultural employment and production, while recruitment and fixed pricing also denied agriculturalists the chance to share in the higher wages and commodity prices that occurred as demand outstripped supply. In the food shortages that subsequently resulted, local producers began to protect and hoard supplies in order to prevent their diversion to urban and military markets. This affected the transfer of resources to urban centres and had a particularly debilitating impact on societies where the margin of subsistence over survival was already thin. Thus, the economic impact of the war involved a complex interplay of socio-economic and political factors on a recalcitrant local population. It also magnified the differences between collaborative networks of local agents, many of whom profited from their wartime activities, and the mass of peoples and communities who lacked such proximity to power to relieve or deflect the voracious demands of warfare.

By the start of 1918, nearly a full year before the end of hostilities, much of the Middle East and North Africa was gripped by conditions of real hardship. Previous chapters have documented the devastating famine that hit Syria and Lebanon from 1915 on. As the war continued into its third and then a fourth year, however, localised shortages of food and basic commodities became more widespread across the region. The implantation of armies consisting of hundreds of thousands of combatants and associated non-combatant support units caused a surge in military demands for civilian resources that were already becoming scarcer under wartime conditions. In Egypt, severe shortages of food were felt in urban areas in 1917 due to heavy military demands, a drop in imported European supplies, and the replacement of cereal by cotton crops. This led to, and subsequently was compounded by, rising inflationary pressures that accelerated sharply in 1917-18 after increasing steadily in 1915-16. As Joel Beinin and Zachary Lockman note in *Workers on the Nile*, the combined impact of scarcities and inflation drove many Egyptians to the edge of subsistence by 1918.[2] By the autumn, the food shortages were spreading into rural areas of Egypt as well, and the situation became critical as peasants began to withhold supplies of wheat for their own consumption because the maize they normally consumed had been requisitioned.[3]

Deteriorating conditions in Egypt were replicated across the regional zones of conflict. The division of Mesopotamia into competing spheres of British and Ottoman control cut urban areas off from their traditional agricultural hinterlands. As in Egypt, rising prices interacted with growing shortages, but were compounded by the effects of economic blockade by the warring armies of both sides. The city and province of Mosul was in a state of famine by November 1918 as thousands of inhabitants died from hunger. The Iraqi historian and sociologist Ghassan Atiyyah observed that in northern Mesopotamia, 'people were keen to see an end to the struggle because they hoped that the end of the war would bring them food from the southern districts under British control'.[4] Controversially, British officials only succeeded in averting the threat of famine in Baghdad – which would have been politically disastrous – by diverting much-needed food supplies from the tribal agricultural districts and villages astride the Tigris and Euphrates rivers. Thus, 'Baghdad [was] secured at the cost of the smaller towns', which in the case of Najaf had severe consequences, as mounting local anger at escalating prices led to the murder of the British agent there in March 1918.[5]

Conditions in Kurdistan and north-west Persia also deteriorated sharply in 1917 as scarcities of wheat and other forms of bread became more widespread. By November that year, people were dying on a daily basis of malnutrition in the Persian city of Tabriz, and throughout 1918 increasing numbers of British and Indian forces in Mesopotamia were being diverted to 'famine relief' operations across the Persian boundary, following a series of crop failures and a sustained period of drought. Caught in the periphery of the ferocious campaigns between the Russians and the Ottomans in the Caucasus and the voracious demands of the war economy imposed by both sides, northern Persia and Kurdistan were badly affected by the resulting economic disruption to regional trade. This caused a collapse in incoming tariff revenues that subsequently was magnified by a British decision to impose tariffs of their own on Persian trade with Mesopotamia, and additionally by a controversial decision to withhold the payment of oil royalties to the government of Persia. Recent research has estimated that up to one-quarter of the inhabitants of northern Persia died in the famine between 1917 and 1919.[6]

The economic impact of the war on the Ottoman Empire was no less dramatic. Figures compiled by Turkish economic historian Sevket Pamuk estimate that GDP (gross domestic product) declined by up to 40 per cent during the war, while private consumption collapsed by 35 to 45 per cent. Similar falls were registered in wheat production, sheep and goats (40 per cent), and the numbers of draught animals (more than 50 per cent).[7] Meanwhile, the cost of living in Constantinople increased by more than twenty times between 1914 and 1918 and inflation peaked at 600 per cent in 1917, a figure comparable to that of Russia immediately prior to the revolutions. Pamuk also identifies and calculates the immense human cost of the series of conflicts and upheaval that gripped the Ottoman Empire in its cathartic final decade of existence. This period covered the 1912-13 Balkan Wars, the First World War and the 1922 war of Turkish independence, during which 'as a result of these massive changes, the population of Turkey stood at around 13 million at the end of 1924; of the decrease of about 20 per cent on a decade previously, more than half had died and the rest had fled or emigrated'.[8] Pamuk eloquently summarised the decade of catastrophic upheaval:

Many of the commercialised, export-oriented farmers of western Anatolia, as well as the artisans, leading merchants, and moneylenders, who linked the rural areas with the port cities and the European trading houses in the long century before the war, had gone. In addition, agriculture, industry, and mining were affected adversely by the deterioration and destruction of equipment, draught animals, and vegetation during this decade.[9]

Erik Zurcher gives broadly comparable figures, estimating that the population of the Ottoman Empire's Anatolian heartland declined by up to 17.7 per cent during this decade of disaster between 1912 and 1922, compared with a figure of 'only' 3.5 per cent mortality for France during the war years. He added that:

If we use the more useful definition of 'population loss' – the difference between the actual population and what would have been the population total had normal growth continued during the war years – the difference is even more striking: 26 per cent loss in Turkey compared to 1 per cent in France…There were twelve provinces, most of them in the West, where the percentage of widows among the female population exceeded 30 per cent…[10]

With this in mind, John Darwin's description of post-war Egypt as an economic and social battleground is an accurate reflection of the traumatic impact of the First World War on local society.[11] In addition to the onerous military requirements for scarce civilian resources, the global influenza pandemic was beginning to hit hard among communities that already were living near the edge of subsistence. To these conditions of real hardship were added the feverish atmosphere of hope and anticipation that the end of the war would result in significant political changes across the Middle East. These factors intersected immediately after hostilities came to an end in November 1918.

The Peace Conference and the emergence of modern Turkey

Leaders and officials from across the world gathered in Paris in 1919 for the series of peace conferences that officially brought the First World War to an end. The scene was captured vividly by Margaret MacMillan in the opening paragraph of her account of the conference:

The Peace Conference was the world's most important business, the peacemakers the world's most powerful people. They met day after day. They argued, debated, quarrelled, and made it up again. They made deals. They wrote treaties. They created new countries and new organizations…Paris was at once the world's government, its court of appeal and parliament, the focus of its fears and hopes.[12]

The four 'victorious' powers – Britain, France, the United States and Italy – dominated the proceedings, although the Italians later pulled back from the conference. Although the Treaty of Versailles signed with a vanquished Germany on 28 June 1919 (the fifth anniversary of the assassination in Sarajevo of Archduke Franz Ferdinand that triggered the slide to war) is by far the most well-known outcome of the conference, four other treaties were formulated to address different regional aspects of the conflict. These were, in chronological order, the Treaty of Saint-Germain with Austria on 10 September 1919, the Treaty of Neuilly with Bulgaria on 27 November 1919, the Treaty of Trianon with Hungary on 4 June 1920, and finally the Treaty of Sèvres with the Ottoman Empire on 10 August 1920 (subsequently superseded by the Treaty of Lausanne with the new Republic of Turkey on 24 June 1923).

It took more than sixteen months of tortuous negotiation for the Treaty of Sèvres to come to fruition. Following the initial meetings in Paris in the spring and summer of 1919, the negotiations continued into 1920 with substantive meetings at the Conference of London (12-24 February) and the San Remo Conference (19-26 April). In addition to formulating a punitive treaty on the rump of the Ottoman Empire, the victorious powers also faced the task of reconciling their divergent wartime objectives and agreements. Against the backdrop of rising nationalist movements across the Middle East and an assertive Turkish military and nationalist alliance sweeping away the final vestiges of Ottoman rule, the wartime allies attempted to maintain political control by devising and distributing a system of mandates for administering the region. The result was the formation of the boundaries of the modern Middle East, albeit in the face of concerted public and political opposition from local populaces.

The Treaty of Sèvres concerned the partitioning of the Ottoman Empire and determining the nature of the post-war political entities that took its place. In addition to raising Kurdish and Armenian hopes that some form of conditional independence might be granted them, the treaty imposed swingeing political and financial terms on Istanbul. France, Italy and Greece were all given zones of influence in southern, western and central Anatolia, while Greece also made large territorial gains in Thrace. These effectively removed the Ottoman Empire from the European landmass, while Istanbul itself remained under the direct British, French and Italian occupation that had started on 12 November 1918.

Yet the ink on the treaty was hardly dry before it was rendered obsolete by radical shifts in the situation on the ground. A Turkish National Movement orchestrated by the legendary victor of Gallipoli, Mustapha Kemal 'Atatürk', was going from strength to strength as it capitalised on popular feelings of anger and humiliation and organised political and military resistance to the occupation. What began as a loose umbrella of nationalist groups across the country quickly swelled into a unifying national movement against the occupying powers. A series of congresses were convened in the second half of 1919 at which delegates from all over Turkey drew up a political manifesto. In March 1920, in the run-up to the final deliberations of the Treaty of Sèvres, the Turkish National Movement formally split with the Ottoman state and established its own parliament, the Grand National Assembly, in Ankara. It met for the first time on 23 April, while the Allied powers were meeting in San Remo to finalise the terms of the post-war settlement.[13]

Relations between the Turkish National Movement and the Ottoman Government broke down irretrievably in October 1920. By that stage, much of the country was afflicted by multiple and overlapping conflicts for territorial control and geostrategic influence. French, Greek and Armenian forces all engaged with units directed by the Grand National Assembly in separate parts of Turkey. As a steady stream of desertions increased the strength of Kemalist forces, they overwhelmed Armenian forces in November 1920. In March 1921, Turkey signed the Treaty of Moscow with the Soviet Union that incorporated the rump of Armenia as a Soviet republic and returned the two 'lost' Ottoman provinces of Kars and Ardahan to Turkey. Allied support for Kurdish independence also slipped away in the face of Turkish gains. Meanwhile, French forces withdrew from the southern Turkish region of Cilicia in 1921, following a gruelling conflict with Turkish nationalists that cost France heavily in lives and money. Finally, Greek troops fighting to realise Eleftherios Venizelos' 'Megali Idea' (Big Idea) initially made large gains as they pushed inland through Anatolia towards Ankara in 1921. However, Kemal's counter-attack in August 1922 shattered the morale of a hopelessly over-extended Greek army, and pushed them back into the coastal city of Smyrna. After Kemal entered Smyrna in September, the city was burned and looted and its Greek and Armenian communities forced to flee; representatives of the great powers were powerless to intervene.[14]

Aside from settling the modern boundaries of Turkey and Greece (and in the process unleashing a humanitarian catastrophe as hundreds of thousands of Greeks and Turks were forcibly 'exchanged'), the resolution of the Greco-Turkish war had another consequence. It led to the political downfall of Britain's wartime leader, David Lloyd George, whose Liberal party remained in its post-1915 alliance with the Conservatives. This occurred as a result of the 'Chanak Crisis' in October 1922. The resounding defeat of Greek forces in Anatolia opened the way for Kemal to march north towards Istanbul. To prevent this, Lloyd George's government in London called on the British Empire and its allies to hold the line at Chanak, on the Asiatic shore of the Dardanelles. However, in a humiliating development, only New Zealand supported the call for bellicosity, while France and Italy both refused to support Lloyd George. As criticism of Lloyd George mounted, his Conservative coalition partners voted to withdraw from the government, triggering a general election that the Conservatives won in a landslide on 15 November.[15]

As the last of the victorious 'triumvirate' still in power after Georges Clemenceau resigned in January 1920 and an incapacitated Woodrow Wilson stepped down in January 1921, Lloyd George's sudden departure from office was the last decisive break with the wartime era. Recognising that the Treaty of Sèvres was unenforceable, it was replaced by the Treaty of Lausanne in July 1923. This treaty extended international recognition of Turkish sovereignty in return for the abandonment of territorial claims for all non-Turkish regions of the Ottoman Empire. Allied forces also ended their military occupation of Istanbul (in September 1923) and Ankara was declared the new capital of the Republic of Turkey on 29 October, still celebrated wildly as Turkey's national day. In March 1924, the new Turkish Government headed by Atatürk (Mustapha Kemal) formally abolished the Caliphate, the last remaining Ottoman symbol, and embarked upon a process of reshaping Turkey into a modern, secular, European nation-state.[16]

Revolt in Egypt

The turmoil unfolding in Turkey was one factor that undermined the Allies' plans for reordering the Middle East after the war. The other was the widespread public and political opposition from local actors angry at the extension of wartime powers into the post-war period. This and the next two sections explore the nationalist backlashes in Egypt, Syria and Mesopotamia in order to make the point that the formulation of policy could no longer be conducted in smoky backrooms by imperial representatives. In the febrile atmosphere of 1919, with widespread anticipation of major political changes in line with the Allies' various pronouncements, rising national consciousness was reflected in the formation of genuinely national movements for the first time. These made possible the intersection of localised feelings of frustration and anger with hitherto elite-led and relatively inaccessible political narratives and platforms. The resulting politicisation made untenable the status quo so desired by British and French administrators as they struggled to manage their imperial possessions in the Middle East and North Africa.

On 13 November 1918, just two days after the Armistice signed at Versailles finally brought the First World War to an end, a delegation of three Egyptian nationalist politicians met with Sir Reginald Wingate, the British High Commissioner in Cairo. Led by Sa'ad Zaghloul, the *Wafd* (delegation) demanded that they be allowed to proceed to London to present their case for Egyptian self-government to the British Government. Nationalist opinion in Egypt fully expected the opportunity to participate in the Paris Peace Conference, particularly after they received news that a delegation from the Hejaz, led by Emir Faisal bin Hussein, the son of the Sharif of Mecca, would travel to Paris. In addition, they were enraged by the report of a British commission that proposed to introduce a bicameral legislature that would, for the first time, bring Egypt's foreign communities into the official decision-making process. These political grievances intersected with wartime-related issues, which included the enforced recruitment of hundreds of thousands of Egyptians into the Egyptian Labour Corps and the Camel Transport Corps, as well as the forced purchasing of cotton and foodstuffs for military use at prices far below prevailing market rates.[17]

The continuation into the post-war period of heavy-handed British actions in Egypt provided the trigger for these various strands of local anger to come together. Sir William Brunyate's report was bitterly opposed by Egypt's hitherto pro-British Sultan as well as by their Prime Minister, Husayn Rushdi, who resigned in anger and left Egypt without a government in the three critical months between the end of the war in November 1918 and the outbreak of the Egyptian Revolt in March 1919. Two pillars of Egyptian society that propped up the British colonial state were also alienated by the commission, namely civil servants and lawyers. Their influence became clear in the lead-up to the March revolt when both groups went on strike in protest at the subsequent arrest of the *Wafd* leadership, paralysing the functioning of the state apparatus as a result. The British advisers who assumed responsibility for the day-to-day running of Egypt instead failed to anticipate or observe the build-up of these incendiary pressures.[18]

British officials thus responded dismissively to Egyptian demands that the wartime arrangements, which had been seen by Egyptians as a temporary expediency in 1914, be reviewed and revised now that hostilities had ceased. In London, the Foreign Secretary, Arthur Balfour, ruled that 'no useful purpose would be served by allowing Nationalist leaders to come to London and advance immoderate demands which cannot be entertained'. He also questioned the very validity of Zaghloul's delegation, which he argued could not be considered representative of Egyptian people, and added that the British protectorate remained in force as peace had not yet been declared.[19] Splitting hairs between the end of active hostilities and the signing of a peace agreement was a delaying tactic that was also used by British officials in Mesopotamia in July 1919 to justify the observance of Peace Day celebrations commemorating the signing of the Treaty of Versailles. In the absence of a peace treaty with the Ottoman Empire (which was signed at Sèvres in August 1920), one British officer sought to explain to his men in the 11th (Bombay) Indian Labour Corps that 'this was Peace between the ALLIES and GERMANY only and that we are still at war'.[20]

News that Faisal bin Hussein, the charismatic son of the Sharif of Mecca, would be permitted to lead an Arab delegation from the Hejaz to the Paris Peace Conference enflamed Egyptian opinion still further. It also caused considerable friction with French officials who were intent on securing their influence in Syria as per the Sykes–Picot Agreement, in spite of Faisal's Arab Army's occupation of Damascus in October 1918.[21] In addition to Parisian mutterings about British perfidy, Egyptian nationalists started to question the apparent hypocrisy behind the decision to allow British allies to proceed to Paris in some instance but not others. Notably, they pointed to the staunch support that Egypt had provided as a base for the British campaigns in Sinai and Palestine as support for their demand to revisit the terms of the November 1914 proclamation of British protectorate status. In the words of a senior British judge on Egypt's Court of Appeal, in 1914 it had been a 'Colossal mistake to prefer the vague and indefinite Protectorate…Our angle of vision was faulty, and the chance of putting relations between ourselves and Egypt on a really satisfactory basis was lost.'[22]

Meanwhile Laurence Grafftey-Smith, a junior British official in the High Commission in Cairo, later acknowledged that London was too busy with preparations for dealing with Germany, and consequently 'the priority of an Egyptian grievance in this welter of preoccupation seemed invisibly low'.[23]

The carefully constructed edifice of wartime British control in Egypt crumbled away between November 1918 and March 1919. After Rushdi resigned, the country remained without a prime minister, and the British authorities lost a valuable political ally as well a means of testing the rising political temperature. Yet, a more fundamental issue among British officials both in Cairo and in London concerned their inability to identify or understand the deeper reconfiguration of the political landscape brought about by the war and its pledges. Both individually and as a collective, they failed to identify the extent to which the *Wafd* managed to mobilise the support of such a wide (and disparate) range of socio-economic groups. This, again, was a region-wide phenomenon, evidenced in, for example, the (albeit short-lived) proclamation of a Tripolitanian Republic by young Arab nationalists in Libya in 1918. This first attempt to establish a republican form of government in the Arab world was largely inspired by the revival of Arab political consciousness in Egypt itself during the war. One of its leaders, Abd al-Rahman Azzam Bey, was in fact an Egyptian nationalist who later became the first Secretary General of the Arab League in 1945.[24] It was in this context of intense trans-national connections that the spread of ideas took root with great speed following the conclusion of hostilities.

In early March 1919, the decision by British officials in Cairo to arrest Said Zaghloul and two other members of the *Wafd* and deport them to Malta provided the spark that lit the Egyptian revolt. Wingate, the British High Commissioner, confidently expected that their arrest would lead to a 'temporary reaction in our favour', his outlook conditioned by the institutional memory of pre-1914 displays of strength.[25] Then, the detention of nationalist leaders had frequently proved sufficient to quell any putative uprisings. However, in the very different conditions of 1919, the decision represented a serious miscalculation that severely underestimated the depth and extent of popular sympathy and support for the national movement. British complacency similarly failed to spot signs of increasing unrest among the units of the Egyptian Expeditionary Force impatiently awaiting their demobilisation orders. A large demonstration against the slow pace of demobilisation took place on 5 April 1919 at the main British base at Qantara on the Suez Canal, and when initial grievances were not addressed, units went on strike on Easter Sunday, 20 April. Lasting for one week and occurring contemporaneously with the nationalist revolt across Egypt, the military unrest rattled Allenby and the British high command. Allenby initially blamed the protests on 'some trade union microbe [that] has got into them' and lamented that 'I can't shoot them all for mutiny; so I must carry on as best I can, and I must resume demobilisation.' Yet the unrest continued, and by 17 May 1919 Allenby was writing in desperation to the newly appointed Chief of the Imperial General Staff in London, General Sir Henry Wilson, that 'There is great unrest and discontent in my army, and, in the case of the administrative services, unrest verges on mutiny.'[26]

Student demonstrations began in Cairo and Alexandria on 9 March and quickly escalated into a wave of strikes involving transport workers, judges and lawyers. The famous Al-Azhar mosque in Cairo opened its doors to Coptic preachers in a display of inter-communal solidarity, anticipating similar cooperation between Sunni and Shiite mosques in Mesopotamia the following year. Within six days, the unrest spread from the towns to locations throughout rural Egypt and more than 1,000 people were killed in the rioting that followed. Countrywide protests brought Egypt to a standstill as urban violence meshed with rural discontent and campaigns of assassination of British officers and officials. Disaffected civil servants and lawyers played a pivotal role in transmitting nationalist ideals from the cities to the provinces, as labour social clubs and organisations spread the activist message far and wide. The wives of leading *Wafd* figures, including Safiyya Zaghloul, led protests of veiled Egyptian women in solidarity with the nationalist movement, in addition to coordinating the production of banners and the circulation of petitions outlining their objectives. The actions of these women, especially the marches and demonstrations, unnerved British officials who did not know how to respond.[27] British control temporarily broke down once protesters targeted the communications and transport networks in many provinces. Ellis Goldberg argues convincingly that these actions amounted to a strategy to safeguard peasants' control of meagre food supplies by preventing the seizure and transfer of scarce commodities to the cities during a period of widespread human suffering and real hunger in rural Egypt.[28]

Egyptian nationalism as espoused in 1919 thus differed fundamentally from its pre-war guise. Exposure to, and participation in, the war facilitated the fusion of economic and political demands that gave greater depth to nationalist platforms and popular support. As noted by Albert Hourani, the defining legacy of Egypt's participation in the war effort was the transformation of Egyptian nationalism from a movement largely of the educated urban elite into one that could command the active or passive support of a broad cross section of socio-economic groups.[29] This new nationalism shed the pan-Islamic and pro-Ottoman beliefs of its pre-war predecessors and instead articulated a positivist doctrine that was rooted in the framework of a liberal political philosophy.[30] Egyptian historian Afaf Lutfi Al-Sayyid-Marsot noted also how 'colonial occupations have invariably prompted the rise of nationalist movements underlining the economic, legal, and political discrimination inseparable from foreign rule'. This intensified as large numbers of rural Egyptians became economically displaced by the diversion of civilian resources to military use and the requisitioning of their crops, labour and draft animals.[31]

Crucially, the formulation of a political vision for Egyptian independence enabled the *Wafd* to survive the initial rejection of its demands. This reflected another distinguishing factor in nationalist development, which was the recognition that a strong economic platform was instrumental to political advancement. Once again, this broke decisively with the earlier pre-1914 nationalist movements. The *Wafd's* membership was dominated by landowners, financiers, administrators, lawyers, civil servants and other urban professionals. Cumulatively, they provided the nucleus of a landed and commercial bourgeoisie with an economic stake in political autonomy. This emerging business class wished to build on the beginnings of import-substitution that had developed in Egypt as a result of the dislocation of global markets during the war. Additionally, they wished to take advantage of the significant shift in Egypt's external financial position, which had left the country with a substantial trade surplus. A notable example of the new business class was the Egyptian economist Talaat Harb, who led the call for the creation of a genuinely Egyptian bank (which came to fruition with the creation of Banque Misr in 1920) that would challenge the British and non-Egyptian monopoly on financial and industrial institutions in Egypt, such as the British-controlled National Bank of Egypt.[32] These efforts to construct a viable political and economic alternative to the British-influenced governing class distinguished the *Wafd* from the older Turco-Albanian circles of political elites in Egypt, in which the former Prime Minister Rushdi had been prominent.[33]

As a result, when the *Wafd* agitation came to a head in March 1919, the British authorities' reaction was unprepared for the changed circumstances of the time. The contested legacy of wartime grievances greatly facilitated the politicisation of Egyptian society that enabled the *Wafd* to tap into deep veins of popular frustration, anger and support. The resulting mass movement of resistance, based on grassroots mobilisation and involvement, took the British completely by surprise. The patrician leadership of the *Wafd* succeeded in fusing the nationalism of ideals espoused in intellectual circles with the social and economic objectives of large swathes of the Egyptian population. Hence, it was the *Wafd's* demonstrated ability to broaden its appeal far beyond the ranks of the educated urban notables that marked the real break with the past and shook the foundations of British policy in Egypt to their core. In desperation, the Foreign Office dismissed Wingate and replaced him as Special High Commissioner with General Sir Edmund Allenby, the conqueror of Palestine. He was given an extraordinary mandate to restore law and order and set about achieving this through a combination of military pacification in rural Egypt and judicious concession to nationalist opinion in the cities. These included the release of Zaghloul and his associates and permission for them to travel on to Paris for the peace conference. By 29 April 1919, Allenby was able to report to London that the situation was 'much improved', although his successor as commander-in-chief in Egypt, General Edward Bulfin, still claimed to identify 'Bolshevist tendencies among the extremists here'.[34]

The scale and ferocity of the unrest that convulsed Egypt in March and April 1919 led the British Government to despatch a commission, led by the arch imperialist figure (and Secretary of State for the Colonies) Alfred Milner, to examine the causes of the trouble and determine the future status of Egypt. However, the commission was met by an upsurge in political agitation and violence and a blanket refusal to participate by nationalist figures. Faced with this resolute rejection of the status quo, by February 1921 Milner concluded that the protectorate was no longer viable. This formed the basis of the recommendation made to the British Foreign Secretary, Lord Curzon, that the protectorate be replaced by a treaty of alliance with a nominally independent Egypt.

This notwithstanding, a chasm still remained between British desires to maintain secure control of such strategic infrastructure as the Suez Canal and the surrounding area, and the staunch public and political support in Egypt for far-reaching changes to the structure and balance of power in the country. The depth of these diverging expectations became evident in the heavily proscribed conditions under which Britain was only prepared to cede Egyptian 'independence'. As the security of Britain's imperial lines of communications was considered paramount, the conditions included the maintenance of British responsibility for foreign and defence policy in addition to the continuing occupation of the strategically vital Suez Canal zone. Negotiations then broke down as Zaghloul continued on a campaign of political resistance, before Allenby forced the issue on 28 February 1922 by persuading the British Government in London to make a unilateral declaration of Egyptian independence. The resulting Anglo-Egyptian Treaty declared Egypt 'a sovereign independent state' with four important exceptions: 'the security of the communications of the British Empire in Egypt', 'the defence of Egypt against all foreign aggression or interference, direct or indirect', 'the protection of foreign interests in Egypt and the protection of minorities' and 'the Sudan'.[35]

Denouement in Syria

In Syria and Lebanon, the fiercest confrontation occurred between local and international plans for the post-war settlement. Damascus and Beirut had formed the intellectual heartbeat of the Arab nationalist movement that drew strength from the wartime struggle against the Ottoman Empire. Yet, both areas had been apportioned to France under the terms of the Sykes–Picot Agreement in 1916, and came under Allied military occupation following Allenby's whirlwind advance in 1918. Between 1919 and 1921, a series of sharp clashes illustrated the complexity of the competing regional claims. These included an acrimonious falling-out between the erstwhile wartime allies as British and French officials harboured divergent visions for Syria, and mounting Arab anger at Allied actions that culminated eventually in the Syrian Revolt in 1919. This triangular imbalance of power and interest had lasting consequences as it led to the embedding of Arabism at the core of Syrian national identity, while also resulting in the establishment of the Hashemite kingdom in Iraq rather than in Syria itself.

The capture of Damascus by Allied and Arab forces on 1 October 1918 set in motion a protracted struggle for power and influence between French and Arab interests. The breakdown of relations among the erstwhile (reluctant) partners began to emerge before the city had even fallen and became increasingly bitter during 1919, culminating in a series of military clashes that extended into 1920. The encirclement of Damascus by both the Desert Mounted Corps and units of Faisal bin Hussein's

Arab Army was followed immediately by negotiations over which group would enter first and by attempts to set up an Arab administration in the city. Travelling with Faisal's Arab forces, T. E. Lawrence vividly described the Arabs' entry into Damascus in *Seven Pillars of Wisdom*:

Every man, woman and child in this city of a quarter-million souls seemed in the streets, waiting only the spark of our appearance to ignite their spirits. Damascus went mad with joy. The men tossed up their tarbushes to cheer, the women tore off their veils. Householders threw flowers, hangings, carpets, into the road before us: their wives leaned, screaming with laughter, through the lattices and splashed us with bath-dippers of scent...over the local cries and the shrilling of women came the measured roar of men's voices, chanting, 'Faisal, Nasir, Shukri, Urens', in waves which began here, rolled along the squares, through the market, down long streets to East gate, round the wall, back up the Meidan; and grew to a wall of shouts around us by the citadel.[36]

The commander-in-chief of the Egyptian Expeditionary Force, General Allenby, notified the War Office on 6 October 1918 that:

The Arabs proclaimed an Arab Government under King Hussein and hoisted the Arab flag immediately the Turkish evacuation of Damascus began, and before the Turkish troops had left the city an Arab Governor of Damascus was appointed. When my troops entered the city, therefore, an Arab administration was in being and the Arab flag was flying from the Government buildings.[37]

Allenby quickly found himself caught between diverging French and Arab views on the future of Syria even as he oversaw the creation of the Occupied Enemy Territory Administration (OETA). He met with Faisal at the Hotel Victoria in Damascus on 6 October and ordered him to 'moderate his aims and await decisions from London', adding that 'the French and British governments had agreed to recognise the belligerent status of the Arab forces fighting in Palestine and Syria, as Allies against the common enemy'.[38] The meeting did not go down well with Faisal, who objected to the prospect of French control over Syria and Lebanon, and claimed that Lawrence had assured him of post-war Arab control over the region. Relations soured rapidly as British, French and Arab officials contested each other's recollections of wartime promises, and French troops began to create 'facts on the ground' in Syria that clashed with simultaneous negotiations taking place in Paris and London. Cracks thus opened up the contradictory lines of policy as acts of violent resistance against French forces in Syria started to occur with increasing frequency. One particularly violent battle that took place on 15 December 1918 resulted in the defeat of French forces by Arab irregulars mobilised by local notables who were angered at the movement of occupying French troops inland from the coastal towns and deeper into Syria. Further clashes took place throughout 1919 as localised uprisings against foreign influence erupted in Aleppo, Damascus and Antioch (in modern-day Turkey).[39]

Simultaneous to the manoeuvrings in Syria were growing expressions of Arab nationalism in neighbouring Lebanon, also under Allied military control after the defeat of Ottoman forces in the autumn of 1918. An Administrative Council of Mount Lebanon met on 9 December 1918 to formulate the terms it wished to present at the Paris Peace Conference. Although the platform ultimately advocated a Lebanese political entity under French protection, they were opposed by other, pro-Syrian factions within Lebanese society, such as the Sunni Muslim communities of the coastal cities and the Arab nationalist circles in Beirut. A Syrian Congress was convened in Damascus on 6 June 1919, at which twenty-two delegates were elected to represent Lebanon. This congress gathered political and intellectual representatives from all across the Levant in order to convey the national aspirations of the Syrian people to the Paris conference.[40] It included Palestinian members in addition to the above-mentioned members from Lebanon. It was established by Faisal bin Hussein in the hope that it would gain him the international legitimacy he believed he needed in support of his case against the French.[41]

Against this backdrop, the British and French leaders met in London over 1-4 December 1918 to hammer out a new settlement in the Middle East. During a private meeting between President Georges Clemenceau and Prime Minister David Lloyd George, which even the British Foreign Office was unaware of until June 1919, the latter sought revisions to the Sykes–Picot Agreement that would transfer the oil-rich province of Mosul to the British sphere of influence and also ensure British interests in Palestine. In return, Clemenceau sought a free hand for France in Syria as well as a share in the Turkish Petroleum Company, which held the oil concession for Mosul. Notably, Clemenceau also wished to extend French control from Lebanon into Syria by occupying the Syrian heartland around the cities of Damascus, Homs, Hama and Aleppo. However, final agreement between the two leaders on Syria was not forthcoming at the meeting, setting the scene for the recriminations that followed during and after the Paris Peace Conference in 1919.[42]

French manoeuvring against British plans for Syria started as soon as Prince Faisal bin Hussein arrived at Marseilles with T. E. Lawrence in November 1918. The fact that Lawrence was accompanying the prince caused great concern among French officials as to his role and objective in the ensuing peace negotiations. Lawrence himself was in an extremely delicate position as his self-declared commitment to Faisal's Arab claim on Syria coexisted uneasily with the high-level bargaining between British and French leaders. During a visit to London in January 1919, Faisal came under pressure from the Foreign Office to accept French designs on Syria, and also to sign an agreement with Chaim Weizmann, the leader of the World Zionist Organization, which would recognise the Zionist presence in Palestine. This Faisal did grudgingly, only to suffer further slights once the Paris Peace Conference opened, coming under attack by French officials as a 'British puppet'. The label was not entirely without substance owing to the ubiquitous presence of Lawrence of Arabia, who acted, in Margaret Macmillan's words, as 'chaperon, translator, and paymaster, because Faisal was receiving a subsidy from the Foreign Office'.[43]

During the conference itself, French officials repeatedly attempted to obstruct or belittle Faisal and question the validity of his presence at the table. The French Foreign Office threw its support behind a hitherto obscure group called the Central Syrian Committee, which claimed to represent the Syrian diaspora in calling for a greater Syria under French protection.[44] In addition, they sought to drive a wedge between him and British officials by playing up perceived differences in approaches, agendas and lines of policy-making. This tactic reflected the growing sense of French unease at the weakness of their position in the Middle East (and elsewhere). Unlike the British and American delegations, which each arrived in Paris with detailed plans for what they wished to achieve, French preparations for the conference lagged far behind to the point of non-existence. In the words of historians Christopher Andrew and Alexander Kanya Forstner, 'All she possessed were the individual programmes of colonialist societies and of the foreign and colonial ministries.'[45]

With the Sykes–Picot Agreement unravelling before its eyes and Britain embedded militarily across the Levant and Mesopotamia, French sensitivities and uncertainties rose volubly to the surface. Having (wrongly) believed that Clemenceau and Lloyd George had personally 'settled' the 'Syria question' at their private meeting in London in December 1918, the focus of French attention shifted to the punitive treaty they wished to impose on Germany. Yet, as Matthew Hughes has noted, 'French concessions in the Middle East had the effect of whetting rather than sating Britain's appetite for expansion in the region.'[46] Meanwhile, local Arab aspirations were notable by their absence in official sympathies in London or in Paris, as the wartime agreements and promises were given short thrift once the specific war-related exigencies were removed.

During the course of 1919, two trends developed in parallel in Syria as they did elsewhere in the Middle East. The first was the aforementioned escalation of nationalist opposition to British and French plans to maintain their hold on the region; while the second was the growing realisation among imperial planners that the military occupation of the Middle East could not continue indefinitely. As in Egypt (and in Mesopotamia the following year), the volatile intersection of these patterns determined the shape of the fractured post-war settlement that emerged. By September 1919, the prospect of military and financial overstretch in the Middle East forced Lloyd George to acknowledge that Britain could not afford to maintain occupying troops in Syria and Lebanon in addition to Palestine and Mesopotamia. In a meeting with Faisal in Downing Street on 23 September, the Prime Minister told the prince that the British government was 'bringing home troops from every country where we did not intend permanently to remain' as doing otherwise 'would involve so gigantic a burden on the British taxpayer, that the country would never accept it'.[47] Thus, under the twin strains of rapid demobilisation (which saw the size of Britain's armed forces shrink from 3.5 million in November 1918 to 800,000 in November 1919 and then fall further to 370,000 by November 1920[48]) and financial retrenchment, the decision was taken to evacuate British forces from Syria and halve the wartime subsidy that was still being paid to Faisal. These two decisions stripped

Faisal of his major source of revenue and any lingering notion of external protection, leaving him exposed and vulnerable to the completion of French designs on Syria.[49]

The denouement in the triangular struggle for Syria took place in the ten months between September 1919 and July 1920. An American-led commission under Henry King and Charles Crane visited Syria as part of a broader visit to the Middle East that was intended to ascertain whether the region was ready for self-determination. Appointed personally by President Wilson, the King–Crane Commission spent forty-two days in Syria, Lebanon, Palestine, Mesopotamia and Asia Minor, gathering local opinions on the desired form of government and the degree to which outside intervention would be tolerated. Perhaps unsurprisingly, given the regional perception that the United States was not interested in territorial expansion in the Middle East, in August 1919 they reported an overwhelming consensus in favour of an American mandate for the region rather than see it fall under British or French tutelage. Yet, they also recommended that Faisal become the head of a united Syria under mandatory rule, as they found that 'This is expressly and unanimously asked for by the representative Damascus Congress in the name of the Syrian people, and there seems to be no reason to doubt that the great majority of the population of Syria sincerely desire to have Amir Faisal as ruler.' Their conclusion was categorical: 'The Peace Conference may take genuine satisfaction in the fact that an Arab of such qualities is available for the headship of this new state in the Near East.'[50]

The King–Crane recommendations were never taken up. They were fatally undermined by a combination of Anglo-French opposition to the report, a growing spirit of isolationism within the United States Congress, and the failing health of President Wilson himself. Moreover, a change of leadership in France in January 1920 signalled a hardening position towards Syria on the part of the new Prime Minister, Alexandre Millerand.[51] British retrenchment therefore intersected with American indifference and a renewed French drive to secure its wartime gains in the Middle East. The same month (January 1920), President Clemenceau met with Faisal and concluded a secret agreement whereby Syria would accept a French mandate (and acknowledge a separate mandate for Lebanon) as well as military and economic assistance in return for French guarantees of Syrian independence. Opinion in France was swinging towards a military solution in the Middle East as French forces also embarked upon a twenty-month campaign against the Turkish National Movement that lasted until September 1921. However, when word of the deal reached Faisal's supporters in Damascus, it met with staunch opposition from the Syrian Congress, and particularly from the influential Young Arab Society (*Jam'iyat al-'Arabiya al-Fatat*), a secret nationalist organisation that had been founded in Paris in 1911.[52]

On 7 March 1920, the Congress reconvened and unilaterally declared an independent Arab kingdom of Syria (including Lebanon and Palestine) with Faisal as its king. This action triggered an immediate response from France (and Britain), which both repudiated the unilateral declaration of independence and hastily convened a meeting of the European powers in the Italian town of San Remo to discuss how to regain the initiative in the face of this challenge to their authority. At the San Remo conference, the British, French and Italian prime ministers allocated among themselves the mandates for the former territories of the Ottoman Empire. Britain and France agreed to recognise the provisional independence of Mesopotamia and Syria respectively, but claimed the mandates – and crucial international recognition by the newly formed League of Nations – for their administration. Although somewhat along the lines of Faisal's January agreement with Clemenceau, this latest display of external intervention in regional affairs merely reinforced the more radical elements within Syria (and Mesopotamia) that rejected any further accommodation with the powers.[53]

The stage was thus set for the final, unhappy action in the struggle for Syria. Hardening attitudes both in Damascus and in Paris made it impossible to reach a peaceful settlement to Syria's political future. On 27 May, the French commander in Syria, General Henri Gouraud, was ordered to 'prepare for military action which the Sharifian government's increasingly insolent and threatening attitude has made indispensable'. After awaiting reinforcements from France and warning Britain not to interfere in the coming conflict, Gouraud's 24th Division routed Faisal's army of several hundred soldiers at the Battle of Maysalun on 23 July, and besieged and occupied Damascus the following day. Faisal was deposed and sent into temporary exile (before being appointed the first King of Iraq by the British in 1921), and the short-lived period of Hashemite rule of Syria formally came to an end.[54]

Eclipse of the Sharifian moment

Faisal's defeat and expulsion from Syria was one of a number of setbacks for the movement that his father headed. Although (as will subsequently be described) both Faisal and his brother Abdullah bin Hussein became kings in the British mandates of Iraq and Transjordan, the balance of tribal power in the Arabian Peninsula was moving decisively against the Sharif. Following a series of skirmishes between Sharifian forces and those of his arch-rival, Ibn Saud, in the eastern Hejaz in early 1919, Abdullah bin Hussein suffered a crushing defeat at the Battle of Turaba in May. The engagement proved to be the tipping-point as the Saudi forces grew progressively stronger after capturing the province of Asir, nestled between the Hejaz and Yemen, in 1920. This, in turn, was followed a year later by Ibn Saud's final defeat of his long-standing rival claimant to power in Arabia (the Rashidi dynasty). With the Hashemite hold over Hejaz looking increasingly fragile, Ibn Saud invaded the Hejaz and took Mecca, Medina and Jeddah in 1924. Two years later, he was proclaimed King of Hejaz with British recognition, leading to the eventual establishment of the modern kingdom of Saudi Arabia in 1932.[55]

The Hashemite fate illustrated the capricious and short-term nature of the wartime entanglements, as well as the difficulties of settling mutually incompatible claims once the war ended. With Britain having supported both the Sharif of Mecca and Ibn Saud through differing means, and with officials in London and Paris determined to safeguard their imperial interests in the Middle East, the post-war 'carve-up' of the Ottoman Empire became a trial of strength and raw power capabilities rather than an inclusive process that involved or respected local concerns. Idealistic documents such as the Fourteen Points or the Anglo-French Declaration were shown to be valueless pieces of paper when confronted with the messy realities on the ground, as competing interests fought for local and regional supremacy. This extended even to the 'appointment' of Hashemite monarchs in Iraq and Transjordan as compensation for their ejection from Syria and eclipse in the Arabian Peninsula.

Still more momentous was the legacy of British pronouncements in Palestine, which reverberate to this day. Although the Balfour Declaration of November 1917 had contained the reassurance that 'nothing shall be done which may prejudice the civil and religious rights of existing non-Jewish communities in Palestine',[56] facts on the ground soon rapidly acquired a momentum – and a tension – of their own. Substantial numbers of Zionist immigrants immediately began to move to Palestine, with over 18,500 arriving between 1919 and 1921. This occurred as petitions flooded in to the King–Crane Commission during their visit to Palestine in June 1919 which overwhelmingly expressed their authors' opposition to Zionism. The first Palestine Arab Congress was convened in Jerusalem in January and February 1919 to press for the inclusion of Palestine as part of an independent Syrian state governed by Faisal bin Hussein, and to demand the renunciation of the Balfour Declaration. However, their proposed delegation to the Paris Peace Conference was prevented from leaving Palestine, while on the ground, the purchase of large tracts of land by Jewish organisations triggered further resentment when it involved the displacement of indigenous Arab farmers who had worked as sharecroppers for generations. Subsequent Palestine Arab congresses took place in Haifa in 1920, Jerusalem in 1921, Nablus in 1922, and Jaffa in 1923 to register intense Arab opposition to British plans for Palestine. Furthermore, rising tensions led to major riots in Jerusalem in 1920 and in Jaffa in 1921, setting the scene for the continuing escalation of Arab–Jewish tensions as Zionist immigration accelerated over the coming decade.[57]

Britain formally assumed mandatory responsibility for Palestine in June 1922. One year later, the final piece of the post-war jigsaw fell into place when the territory covered by the mandate for Palestine was divided into two sub-regions. In 1923, the land to the east of the Jordan River (the 'East Bank') was separated to form the state of Transjordan. This new, wholly unplanned entity was created in 1922 in meetings in Jerusalem and London between the Secretary of State for the Colonies, Winston Churchill, and Abdullah bin Hussein, the brother of Prince Faisal. Paradoxically, the Hashemite kingdom implanted in Amman proved the most durable of all the regimes created by the mandatory powers after the war. Abdullah's eponymous great-grandson remains on the throne of Jordan a century later, in stark contrast to the fate of his cousins in Iraq, who were forced from power in a bloody revolution in July 1958. In addition, the British ceded a part of the Golan Heights to the French mandate in Syria. These final territorial adjustments left a truncated state in Palestine but laid down the essential state-system that has largely endured, under very different regime-types (with the exception of Jordan and the creation of Israel in 1948), to this day.

Uprising in Mesopotamia

The final act of the post-war reordering took place in Mesopotamia, where grandiose British objectives had to be substantially modified and scaled back following a nationalist uprising in 1920. Known in modern-day Iraq as *al-thawra al-iraqiyya al-kubra* (the great Iraqi revolution), the tribal rebellion that shook the foundations of British rule to its core had similar dynamics to those across the region. In Mesopotamia, too, the period leading up to the granting of the League of Nations mandate to the United Kingdom at the San Remo conference in April 1920 featured a steady divergence between nationalist aspirations for self-rule and the gradual accretion of responsibilities by the colonial power. This occurred as Britain's acting Civil Commissioner, Arnold Wilson, took advantage of the lack of policy supervision as officials in London readied for the peace conference to extend and sharpen the reach of his administrative apparatus. As with Egypt, the signs that British officials were preparing to formalise and extend their wartime powers enraged local opinion and triggered a wide-ranging nationalist backlash.

British officials in Mesopotamia faced similar challenges to their counterparts in Egypt in reconciling the Anglo-French Declaration of November 1918 and the news that a delegation from the Hejaz would be allowed to participate in the Paris Peace Conference with their unwillingness to make similar concessions locally. The Anglo-French Declaration provoked much discussion among local political leaders and notables in Mesopotamia, even though Arnold Wilson believed it to be a 'disastrous error' forced on the allies by President Wilson. Its impact was also magnified by the fact that news of the Anglo-French Declaration became public at the same time as President Wilson's Fourteen Points, which until October 1918 had been tightly censored by the Civil Commission in Baghdad.[58] Unlike his presidential namesake, Arnold Wilson confidently declared that 'the country as a whole neither expects nor desires any such sweeping schemes of independence'.[59] In this he enjoyed the support of his influential Oriental Secretary, Gertrude Bell, who stated categorically in December 1918 that nobody in Mesopotamia wanted self-rule; instead, 'they want us and no one else'.[60]

Senior officials in London, if not in Baghdad, did at least recognise that the changing international situation required a new approach to colonial acquisition, and thus sought to construct a watertight case for maintaining British control over Mesopotamia. Just over two weeks after the Armistice, on 26 November 1918, the Political Secretary at the India Office in London, Sir John Shuckburgh, stated that the Anglo-French Declaration 'clearly does not preclude close British control' provided the people elect for it. As a result, he suggested that 'the first step is to procure a local pronouncement in our favour' in Mesopotamia.[61] Two days later, the British Government, through the Secretary of State for India (through whom control over Mesopotamia was exercised), instructed Wilson to obtain a 'genuine expression of local opinion' on the creation of 'a single Arab state under British tutelage'. Such an 'authoritative statement' would, it was believed in London, enable the British Government to present it 'before the world as [an] unbiased pronouncement by [the] population of Mesopotamia'.[62]

The need to cloak British designs in a pseudo-democratic mandate resulted in Wilson authorising and overseeing a severely flawed survey of 'local opinion'. He instructed his (British) political officers to canvass the views of selected notables and tribal sheikhs, but omitted from his instructions any mention of the need to obtain a 'genuine expression of local opinion'.[63] What followed was a highly selective and manipulative series of interviews with sheikhs and notables who owed their positions largely to British patronage. Their overwhelmingly positive responses ensured that only favourable opinions were passed on to the Civil Commission in Baghdad. Wilson himself travelled to Najaf and Karbala in December 1918 to meet with local notables. He recorded how 'they wished for maintenance of present system of administration, but hoped it would be improved and elaborated by addition of more British officials'.[64] The background to this convenient finding, and the sanitised nature of the verdict as a whole, became clearer as Wilson acknowledged that the responses, which he claimed were 'unanimous and delivered with an emphasis which it is difficult to convey in writing', had in fact been 'thought out beforehand as the result of conversations with [the] Political Officer'.[65]

Two major consequences flowed from Wilson's manipulation of local opinion. First, it enabled British officials in Baghdad and London to misrepresent the results as a 'plebiscite' that exaggerated the level of support for continued British control. This, in turn, enabled the government in London to claim that the results fell in line with the policy of promoting 'indigenous governments' as per the Anglo-French Declaration. It also gave the Civil Commission in Baghdad the space to continue entrenching and expanding its range of powers and functions, in the process deepening nationalists' fears that Britain was preparing to flout the ambiguous promises of self-determination and local rule. The unfolding events in Syria, and the mounting signs that Britain and France would thwart Faisal's ambitions, also played heavily on local nationalist opinion in Mesopotamia, where the influence of Sharifian officers who had participated in the Arab Revolt was high.[66]

In this regard, the formation of a Revenue Secretariat in Baghdad became the lightning-rod of local resentment against the extension of British authority. In addition to visibly extending the realities of British control to rural regions of Mesopotamia, it also enabled the administration to become considerably more effective in its assessment of crops and its collection of revenue. However, its controller, E. B. Howell, was notably hostile to the transfer of any form of authority to local institutions and, in the opinion of Gertrude Bell, unable to 'envisage anything which is not on English lines'.[67] During the immediate run-up to the outpouring of nationalist feeling in 1920, he played a role similar to that of William Brunyate in Egypt, by alienating local opinion and reinforcing suspicions of the nature of British policy in Mesopotamia. Such feelings of ambivalence and animosity were further stimulated by the introduction of the Indian rupee as the unit of currency and by the continuing dominance of Indians among the lower ranks of the civil administration in Mesopotamia, to the exclusion of local Arabs. These developments meant that, throughout 1919, Mesopotamia remained firmly within the grip of a centralising British–Indian administration, with very limited local participation.[68]

Thus, the second consequence of Arnold Wilson's misrepresentation of local opinion was that his administration completely failed to identify or appreciate the degree of local opposition to Britain's post-war policy of deepening control over Mesopotamia. Although some discordant views were expressed among the respondents to Wilson's 'survey' of local opinion, they were dismissed as unrepresentative opinions coming from individuals 'whose views are theoretical and who are far less in touch than we are with the country as a whole and never take its interests into consideration'.[69] This remarkable display of arrogance and condescension illustrated the extent to which Wilson, and the officials who surrounded him, were out of touch with the real currents of local opinion. The persistence of such feelings also meant that the British administration lacked widespread political legitimacy as it sought to extend and deepen its control over Mesopotamia in 1919 and 1920.[70]

The flawed sets of assumptions and analyses of local conditions ensured that British officials completely misread the growth of new nationalist groups in Mesopotamia. A combination of their attitudes and training prevented officials such as Arnold Wilson from acknowledging that the highly charged atmosphere might provide the enabling environment for the many political, social and economic grievances that permeated Mesopotamian society. One prominent example appeared in February 1919 when a new political group formed in protest at the British authorities' refusal to allow a delegation from Mesopotamia to proceed to Paris for the peace conference. Similar to the *Wafd* in Egypt, the Iraq Guards for Independence (*Haras al-Istiqlal al-'Iraqiyin*) included more socially diverse members than existing national groups such as *al-'Ahd* ('the Covenant', a secret nationalist society founded in Istanbul by Arab officers in the Ottoman Army in 1913).[71] As early as August 1914, before the Ottoman war even started, British officials in Egypt had rebuffed an offer by the founder of *al-'Ahd*, Aziz Ali al-Masri, to recruit an armed force that, he claimed, would liberate Mesopotamia in exchange for British funding and arms. At that time, Gilbert Clayton, then the head of British Intelligence in Cairo, dismissed the offer as too 'vague': 'the details do not seem to have been thought out'.[72]

A major difference distinguishing *al-Istiqlal* from *al-'Ahd* was that the former rejected the latter's call for maintaining ties with the British during the struggle for independence. This was a world away from al-Masri's 1914 declaration that *al-'Ahd* sought 'a united Arabian state, independent of Turkey and every other power except England, whose tutelage and control of foreign affairs they invite'.[73] Furthermore, the Independence Guards benefited from the more propitious contextual circumstances of the time. They contained a large number of young educated nationalists who actively disseminated pro-independence propaganda, and worked to align Sunni and Shiite communities into a genuinely national, non-sectarian movement against the British. This was a significant new development that enabled *al-Istiqlal* to expand its activities and influence beyond Baghdad's urban, largely Sunni elite to encompass the Shiite holy cities of Najaf and Karbala, as well as the strongly Shiite regions around the Euphrates that had suffered some of the greatest rural hardships during the war.[74]

While *al-Istiqlal* lacked any real central cohesion or political programme, it nevertheless performed much the same role as the *Wafd* did in Egypt. This was to act as the focal point around which socially and economically diverse groups of discontented individuals and communities, Sunni and Shiite or town and tribal, could rally in a loose coalition. Inasmuch as there was any common objective that united these groups, it was that they had all suffered from wartime dislocation and resented the ongoing British demands for resources and taxation. Four distinct elements of Mesopotamian society came together during the first half of 1920 to trigger the set of three tribal uprisings that occurred between July and September. These were the tribal communities, Sunni urban notables and intellectuals, the Shiite religious hierarchy, and an officer class that consisted primarily of disillusioned Mesopotamian soldiers returning from Faisal's Arab army in Syria.[75]

Each of these groups nursed specific grievances relating to the war and the conduct of the continuing British occupation. Much tribal anger focused on the perceived heavy-handedness of the British occupying forces and their over-zealous officers. Particular resentment was directed against the political officer of the Diwaniyah division, Major Charles Daly, and Gertrude Bell subsequently commented that the fact that the tribal rebellion started in his division was akin to ice breaking at its thinnest point.[76] Daly's annual report for 1919 also illustrated the depth of British ignorance of the rising political temperature in Mesopotamia, as he wrote that 'the close of the year is marked by the absence of any disturbing element and a more satisfactory tribal situation than has ever before existed within living memory'.[77]

The other three broad disaffected groups also held particular grievances that underpinned their recourse to violence in the summer of 1920. The largely Sunni educated urban elites in Baghdad and Basra viewed with growing resentment the divergence between the lofty declarations of Allied policy and the realities of political entrenchment on the ground.[78] Writing in January 1919, Gertrude Bell responded dismissively to local aspirations by labelling the British and Allied proclamations as 'gusts of hot air emitted from home in the shape of international declarations'.[79] Only too late, in October 1920, did Bell retrospectively acknowledge that 'we had promised self-governing institutions and not only made no step toward them but were busily setting up something entirely different'.[80] Moreover, a potent further source of unease among groups of urban leaders was the British Government's preoccupation with the peace conference (and the revolt in Egypt and uprising in India) and consequent failure to make a substantive policy decision on Mesopotamia's future. This drift in policy in London opened up the space for Arnold Wilson to dictate events in Baghdad. However, as local suspicions about British intentions arose in 1920, many hitherto collaborative elements of urban society began to hedge their bets and tone down their support for local British officials to avoid offending any potential Arab administration that might eventually come to power.[81]

Shiite notables had long been excluded from positions of power and influence by the Sunni Ottomans, and the British continued this policy of marginalisation. In another curious parallel with the post-2003 invasion of Iraq, British officials viewed the pan-Islamic rhetoric of the Shiite religious hierarchy with deep distrust and suspected them of holding trans-national Persian loyalties and posing a direct challenge to British influence. Mutual distrust increased further in December 1918 when a leading Shiite theologian in Karbala, Mohammed Taqi al-Shirazi, published a *fatwa* that warned Muslims not to participate in selecting a non-Muslim to rule over Mesopotamia.[82] Again, direct parallels can be drawn between this intervention into political life and that of Grand Ayatollah Ali al-Sistani's ruling in 2003 that forced the US-led occupying forces to hold elections in post-Saddam Iraq.

The politicisation of the Shiite communities in Mesopotamia made them far more responsive to the Baghdadi nationalists' outreach. The holy month of Ramadan fell in April and May in 1920 and coincided with the aforementioned Allied conference at San Remo in Italy. The month was marked by unprecedented levels of cooperation between Shiites and Sunnis, with the use of mosques and other holy places as meeting-points and rallying-grounds. The Shiite holy centre of Kadhimayn became a geographically important pivot that connected the urban Sunni and rural Shiite elements of the nascent coalition together.[83] Furthermore, al-Istiqlal organised both Sunni celebrations and Shiite lamentations on the occasion of the Prophet's birthday in an unprecedented show of religious solidarity. Printing presses in Najaf and Karbala were set up to produce and distribute leaflets that urged the local tribes to prepare for the upcoming revolt.[84]

Finally, a combination of regional and international developments in 1919 and 1920 sowed doubts over Britain's overarching aims across the Middle East region. These chiefly impacted the many army officers from Mesopotamia who had served in Faisal's Northern Arab Army during the Arab Revolt. Many of the men had remained in Syria with Faisal and had become increasingly disillusioned and cynical about external pledges of support during the steady (aforementioned) breakdown in relations between Faisal and the French. In addition, the Mesopotamian officers became further embittered by Arnold Wilson's reluctance to allow them to return from Syria to Mesopotamia after the Battle of Maysalun. These experiences drove many of them to transfer their support from the moderately nationalist al-'Ahd to the more resolute al-Istiqlal.[85]

The inexorable build-up of tension and discontent intersected in the spring of 1920 with the San Remo meeting, at which Britain was awarded the League of Nations mandate for Mesopotamia, and with a recommendation by the (British) Judicial Secretary that a constitution be drawn up to regularise British rule. Parallels can again be drawn with the similar attempt in Egypt to legitimise and secure Britain's wartime extension of powers. Just as Sir William Brunyate's actions provoked a backlash in Egypt, so too did Sir Edgar Bonham Carter's in Mesopotamia. His proposal envisaged setting up a Council of State in which executive authority remained firmly in British hands. This was described by a British junior officer at the time (but writing retrospectively after concluding a long and senior administrative career in Iraq) as 'well in advance of [Arnold] Wilson's own original views'.[86]

Following the month of Ramadan and a series of mass peaceful demonstrations in Baghdad throughout May and June 1920, the tribal revolt finally broke out on 2 July. It started after Sha'lan Abu al-Jon, the Sheikh of the Zawalim clan of the Bani Hajim tribe, was arrested because he refused to pay taxes to the occupation authority. His arrest enraged his tribesmen who stormed the police station where he was being held and killed several policemen in the course of setting him free. The incident proved to be the flashpoint that triggered the pent-up frustrations which had been building among rural and urban groups alike. A cycle of momentum developed whereby the initial success of the first tribes that mobilised encouraged other tribes to participate in insurgent 'hit-and-run' grabs for local booty or resources. Within two weeks, thousands of armed tribesmen were squaring up with British units at Rumaytha, with each side suffering dozens of casualties.[87]

Three major tribal uprisings occurred between July and November 1920. These involved the tribes of the mid Euphrates region, the Baquba region on the Diyala river north of Baghdad, and the Falluja area west of Baghdad. Collectively, the events became known as the Great Iraqi Revolution (*al-thawra al-iraqiyya al-kubra*). However, for all their disruptive ferocity in localised theatres, the risings lacked central organisation and a common objective. Instead, they reflected a series of local backlashes to specific socio-economic hardships, and were severely compromised when tribes belonging to the powerful Muntafik confederation did not participate. Furthermore, the uprisings failed to spread to many urban areas, as the Sunni notable class chose to remain loyal to the British administration. Alarm at the expression of raw Shiite and tribal power led them pragmatically to opt to safeguard their existing privilege and place in the social order. Consequently, the uprisings eventually fizzled out as a local product of the mid-Euphrates tribes.[88]

The 1920 revolt has nevertheless been memorialised as one of the great founding-points of modern Iraqi nationhood. The events of that summer have been 'seen by most Iraqi political activists and social scientists as the first historical act by which "the Iraqis" fought the British, thereby creating the Iraqi state'.[89] Ever since Iraq became an independent state in 1932, the uprising has been subjected to potent (and politicised) myth-making. The enduring results of this process of appropriation of historical fact can be seen in the decision of one of the major Sunni insurgent groups that emerged in the deadly Anbar province after the 2003 US-led occupation of Iraq to call itself the 'Brigades of the Revolution of [19]20' (*Kata'ib Thawrat al-'Ashrin*).[90] This ignores the fact that it was the Sunni notables' refusal to join the Shiite-led uprising that contributed to its eventual failure. The ramifications of the different calculations made in 1920 reverberated throughout the modern state of Iraq. The distinction between the comparative loyalty of many Sunni communities and the predominantly Shiite insurrection had powerful political consequences. It confirmed the prejudices of British officials who were predisposed to continue the Ottomans' practice of working with Sunni notables as they constructed the modern state of Iraq and gradually transferred responsibilities to local partners.[91]

That said, the ferocity of the Mesopotamian uprising took the British civil and military authorities completely by surprise. Just three weeks before it began, Bell had confidently declared that 'I personally don't think that there will be an outbreak either here [Baghdad] or in the provinces.'[92] Military leaders were caught similarly unprepared. The new commander-in-chief in Mesopotamia, Aylmer Haldane, was felt by many of his colleagues to be ignorant of local opinions, and was on summer leave in the Persian hills, along with his general headquarters, when the revolt began.[93] Another senior officer, the commander of the 17th Indian Division, Major-General G. A. Leslie, was preoccupied with merging the Baghdad Racing Club with the Basra Racing Club in the immediate run-up to the trouble. Even after the tribal revolts were in full swing, his efforts at equine administration were such that he organised the inaugural Euphrates Gold Cup at Hillah on 17 October 1920, even as large parts of the surrounding area were still in revolt.[94]

Eighteen additional Indian Army battalions had to be rushed to Mesopotamia to join the nearly 100,000 troops that were still present on the ground nearly two years after the end of the war. The eventual quelling of the revolt came at the cost of 312 dead and 1,228 wounded British and Indian soldiers and the expenditure of an average of £591,700 per week between 1 July and 1 October 1920.[95] Even Winston Churchill, the Secretary of State for War in London, savaged the 'vicious system' under which 'a score of mud villages, sandwiched in between a swampy river and a blistering desert, inhabited by a few half-naked families, usually starving, are now occupied'.[96] His characteristically blunt and decidedly robust assessment underscored how London could no longer afford such high levels of expenditure of financial and military resources at a time of economic difficulty at home and political unrest throughout the empire. In consequence, policy-makers in London began finally to formulate a plan for reducing their direct control over Mesopotamia and drawing down their continuing post-war footprint.

Creation of the interwar order

The waves of violence that swept through the Middle East in 1919 and 1920 exposed the fragility of the post-war order that Britain and France were attempting to impose on the region. In the Caucasus, too, the end of the Russo-Ottoman war was not followed by a durable political settlement. Instead, a new set of localised conflicts consumed much of the region as first the Russians' withdrawal and then the Ottomans' defeat caused a vacuum in political authority across the region. Thus, Georgians and Armenians fought a border war in December 1918 while Armenians and Azeris engaged in a series of violent clashes over Baku and Karabakh that began in mid 1918 and continued until 1922. Growing ethnic and religious tensions led to further expulsions, of Muslims from Baku, and massacres, including one in September 1918 of between 10,000 and 20,000 Armenians by Ottoman forces and their Azeri allies and the large-scale killing of Armenians in the Karabakhi city of Shusha in March 1920; this also brought about the destruction of the Armenian quarters of the city and the end of centuries of Armenian economic and cultural vibrancy in the region. The period of regional fragmentation brought about by the reawakening of national movements in the Caucasus ended with the imposition of Soviet control in 1920 and the demise of the short-lived First Republic of Armenia and the Azerbaijan Democratic Republic.[97]

Localised backlashes such as these revealed how nationalist movements were moving far beyond the limited capabilities of their pre-war predecessors, in part because the demise or decline of imperial control opened up new possibilities for national groups. The rise of populist political figures capable of mobilising an increasingly nationwide constituency meant that they could no longer be dismissed as unrepresentative of local opinion, however much British and French officials tried to do so. Moreover, the nationalists' resentment at Western plans to reorder the region was not limited to the Middle East alone. The British Empire was roiled by large-scale disturbances ranging from Ireland to India and Afghanistan, imparting added urgency to the need to prioritise commitments. The widespread unrest in India was particularly momentous as it demonstrated to British officials that their use of Indian troops could no longer underwrite imperial policing in the Middle East and elsewhere. At the very moment when the British Empire reached its maximal territorial extent in the brief period of triumphalism that followed the wartime conquests, Gandhi's escalating campaign of civil disobedience introduced a powerful reality check on the exercise of British power in India. By June 1921, the British Viceroy of India had to inform the British Government that 'Public opinion in India will not tolerate any longer a system under which our troops are used…to suit the fluctuating requirements of His Majesty's Government.'[98]

In North Africa, simmering unrest in Morocco exploded into violent conflict between the Berbers of the Rif Mountains and their Spanish occupiers in 1921. More than 10,000 Spanish soldiers were killed in May and June alone as Berber forces led by a charismatic judge named Mohammed ibn Abd al-Karim al-Khattabi inflicted what Eugene Rogan has described as 'the worst defeat of a colonial army in Africa in the twentieth century'.[99] Moreover, the conflict spilled across into the French sphere of control in Morocco – which had seen significant violence before the First World War – dragging thousands of French troops into a counter-insurgency campaign in North Africa. More than 34,000 Moroccan soldiers had fought on the Western Front during the war and suffered very high casualty rates, and the desire for a return on that sacrifice and to share in the spirit of self-determination was strongly articulated.[100]

In the highly politicised context of the immediate post-war period, when expectations of substantive political advancement were running high, news travelled fast from region to region. The unrest in India and Ireland resonated with nationalists in Egypt and vice versa. Similarly, the news that the Hejaz would be permitted to send a delegation headed by Faisal to the Paris Peace Conference became a flashpoint for disgruntled Egyptian, Syrian and Mesopotamian nationalists who demanded why their delegations could not also attend. Such trans-regional linkages abounded and were magnified in the Middle East and North Africa by commonalities in language and the rapid rise in print media. They also reflected the interconnected political economies of the Middle East and North Africa, both with each other but also with India, as a result of their positioning within the imperial systems of Great Britain and France. Writing in 1981, the late historian of empire John Gallagher noted that the heart of the post-war 'crisis of empire' lay in the interconnected set of problems and responses to the hardships that the war had wrought. These led him to conclude that 'it is the issues themselves, rather than the regions, which need to be studied' since 'no analysis of any of these crises will be complete without establishing its interplay with the others'.[101]

The Cairo Conference that took place in the Egyptian capital in March 1921 provides a suitable end point for the analysis of the post-war reordering of regional affairs. Although final 'closure' was not reached until 1923 (in the case of the Treaty of Lausanne that replaced the short-lived and ill-fated Treaty of Sèvres with newly independent Turkey) or even 1925 (in the case of the resolution of the competing claims to the province of Mosul and its incorporation into the kingdom of Iraq), the decisions taken in Cairo laid the basis for the interwar order that followed. In undoing the majority of the decisions that had been taken immediately after the end of war, it reflected the rapidity with which the influence and reach of the Allied wartime powers had shrunk in the face of domestic contestation and region-wide backlash. The readjustment was a belated attempt to realign Western objectives in order to 'manage' the Middle East through cheaper mechanisms of governance and the more targeted deployment of coercive power. Gone were the grandiose imperial objectives of 1919 amid a more sober – albeit through gritted teeth – assessment that policy could no longer simply be formulated without involving local participants or partners.

In Cairo, the regional conference called by Winston Churchill – now the Secretary of State for the Colonies – and T. E. Lawrence, newly named his special adviser, was convened at the Semiramis Hotel on 12 March 1921. It was attended by the British civil and military leaderships in Palestine and Mesopotamia along with the Sharif of Mecca's two most prominent sons, Faisal and Abdullah. Most of the luminaries of British Arabism were also present, besides Lawrence, including Gertrude Bell, General Allenby, Arnold Wilson, Sir Percy Cox and Sir Herbert Samuel, the first High Commissioner for Palestine. The only Iraqi representative permitted to attend was Jafar al-Askari, a former Governor of Aleppo in Syria and now a leading figure in the Sharifian (Hashemite) movement, who was prepared to work with the British in Iraq. The conference met to approve hastily redrawn British plans for offering the thrones of the new kingdoms of Iraq and Transjordan to Faisal and Abdullah respectively, although most of the details had already been worked out in private meetings with Faisal in London beforehand.[102]

THE POST-WAR SETTLEMENTS, 1919–1923

The major decisions rubber-stamped in Cairo sealed the geopolitical map of the modern Middle East. Regimes may have changed in nature and political boundaries shifted with the series of Arab–Israeli wars, but the basic regional state-system remained in place. The delegates agreed that France would retain its mandates and influence over Syria and Lebanon, and Britain would do the same over Palestine, while continuing to support the creation of a Jewish homeland there. Meanwhile, the formalisation of the kingdoms of Iraq and Transjordan under Hashemite (and pro-British) control constituted a blow to the regional ambitions of Abdul-Aziz Al-Saud, who now found himself surrounded by three Hashemite rivals (the Sharif of Mecca in the Hejaz being the third), in part hastening the resolution of the Hashemite–Saudi bid for hegemony through brute force. With no tribal or familial connections to Mesopotamia, Faisal became King of Iraq after a carefully arranged 'plebiscite' conveniently showed a 96 per cent return in his favour, even as local candidates for the throne, such as the Naqib of Baghdad or the ever-prominent Sayid Talib in Basra (who was in fact deported to India a month before Faisal arrived), were passed over.[103]

This lack of local roots had consequences for the Iraqi monarchy as it struggled to establish itself as the legitimate political authority in Iraq. Ultimately, the roots that successive monarchs laid down were insufficient to save the institution from violent overthrow in 1958. The Hashemite rulers of Transjordan (and later Jordan) fared better, assisted by the stability imparted by the lengthy reigns both of Abdullah (1921-51) and his charismatic grandson, Hussein (1952-99), as well as high levels of external military and financial support that somewhat improbably enabled the resource-poor kingdom to survive to become a rock of stability in an otherwise volatile area. The British and French legacies in Palestine and Syria were far more controversial, and remain bitterly contested to this day. Indeed, Charles Tripp has noted recently how the 'violence of the colonial legacy' forged during and after the First World War has since 'provided a powerful framework for imagining power' throughout the region.[104] These memories, and the battles over the volatile and turbulent 'birth pangs' of the state-system that emerged from the crucible of the post-war turmoil, still resonate across the Middle East nearly a century on.

CONCLUSION

The impact on the societies and peoples of the Middle East of exposure to, and participation in, the First World War was colossal. Four years of fighting involved the entire region, either directly or indirectly, in some shape or form, in the localised conflicts that emerged from the initial struggle among the imperial powers for strategic gain. From the cramped beachheads of Gallipoli to the frozen mountain plateaus in the Caucasus and the sweltering desert of Sinai and Mesopotamia, battles raged over harsh and unforgiving terrain and exacted a terrible toll on the soldiers and non-combatant support units alike. Moreover, the implantation of vast armies and support units interfered with civilian patterns of economic and agricultural activity and made unsustainable demands on increasingly scarce local resources. Inflationary pressures and food shortages began causing real hardship as early as 1915 and evolved into deadly famines in large parts of the region, compounded by harsh extractive measures to feed voracious military machines.

A new dynamic also developed as the pressure of wartime exigencies led the imperial powers to seek out and work through local partners, and also, explosively, to reach secret agreements among themselves that divided the Middle East into spheres of influence and control. Whether formal or informal, these deals or promises quickly started to unravel and have formed the basis for anguished debates that have raged ever since. As their details became public knowledge against the wishes of colonial officials, they also accelerated the rise of new oppositional movements and created a reservoir of deep-rooted political and socio-economic grievances. These laid the basis for the significant and prolonged unrest that afflicted the Middle East directly after the war, revealing the limitations of externally imposed efforts to reorder the region to fit Western interests.

It is thus no exaggeration to note that the First World War was pivotal to the creation of the modern Middle East. It hastened the demise of the Ottoman Empire and paved the way for the emergence of a state-system (albeit under mandatory rule) that remains largely in place today. The entire political landscape of the region was reshaped as the legacy of the war sapped the ability of imperial 'outsiders' to dominate and influence events, and nationalist groups succeeded in mobilising mass movements around distinctly national identities. Yet, this occurred just as the actual and potential value of Middle Eastern oil became a permanent feature of a new set of Western geostrategic considerations. The advent of large-scale mechanisation not only revolutionised the conduct of industrialised warfare but also injected a degree of urgency into the search for reliable and controllable sources of supply.

The Middle East in 1923 was therefore unrecognisable from the Middle East in 1914. New political movements and mass ideologies were intermixed with emergent debates around the identities and developmental trajectories of nation-states. The focal point of decision-making shifted from the fading grandeur of imperial to the frenetic activity of national governments. A new political class chafed against and tested the boundaries of the mandatory system of the post-war settlement, while British and French colonial administrators struggled to adapt to new realities of diminished control. Turkey also changed beyond recognition as Atatürk embarked upon a wide-ranging programme of socio-political modernisation that involved reorienting the new republic towards Europe and turning its back on the Middle East. In the Arabian Peninsula, the competition between the Saudi and Hashemite dynasties was resolved in favour of Abdul Aziz Al-Saud, with lasting consequences for the state that took his familial name in 1932.

As the major participants mark the centenary of the First World War, most attention will focus on the commemoration of the battles of Gallipoli. Thousands of 'pilgrims' from Australia and New Zealand will flock to the peninsula in April 2015 to pay homage to the legacy of the campaign that so powerfully forged their national identity. Turkey will also mark the campaign, albeit in the midst of the first sustained challenge to the political order laid down by Atatürk after 1923 and amid accusations that the Islamist government in Ankara is engaging in 'neo-Ottoman' outreach. Yet, beyond historical curiosity on the hundredth anniversaries of the capture of Baghdad and Jerusalem in March and December 2017, it is likely that public interest in the centenary will be far more muted in the Middle East than elsewhere. In large part, this is unsurprising. With the region in the throes of renewed political turmoil and having experienced decades of regional and international crises, many attributable to the decisions taken during and after the First World War, the complicated legacies of the war have more immediacy and relevance than they do in Europe or Russia.

A parallel may be drawn with the divided Europe up until 1989, where the ramifications of the Second World War remained highly visible across multiple generations. In this context, it is harder to establish historical distance from events whose legacy continues to resonate throughout the region. So much has occurred in the intervening century that, while the connection to the First World War may not be immediately made, issues such as the Sykes–Picot Agreement and the Balfour Declaration are widely spoken about as if they refer to contemporary controversies. The US Ambassador to Syria between 1988 and 1991, Edward Djerejian, recalled how Syrian President Hafiz al-Assad 'subjected me to countless narratives about how the Sykes–Picot Agreement was the origin of all the ills of the contemporary Middle East'.[1] This explains also the references in commentary and the media to how the bitter civil war currently taking place in Syria is contributing to 'unmaking' the Sykes–Picot Agreement. Thus, an article in Beirut's *Daily Star* newspaper in June 2013 reported how 'one part of that legacy…is coming to a brutally violent end', while in the *London Review of Books*, the veteran Middle East correspondent, Patrick Cockburn, headlined a lengthy report from Syria 'Is it the End of Sykes–Picot?' Cockburn recorded how this was a sentiment expressed repeatedly to him while travelling through Iraq, adding that 'The feeling that the future of whole states is in doubt is growing across the Middle East – for the first time since Britain and France carved up the remains of the Ottoman Empire after the First World War.'[2]

With the passing of the last surviving participants, the First World War has moved from the fringes of personal experience into the history books. For many, the centenary will be an opportunity to pause and reflect on the enormity of human suffering involved. Those with ancestors who fought and died in the campaigns retain emotional and physical links with the past through letters, diaries and personal effects. In the case of a history professor at the University of Cambridge, these included an Ottoman bayonet that added a frisson of interest to student seminars. At Gallipoli, the shallow (and in some cases reconstructed) remains of wartime trench systems are still visible to people who leave the road and walk a few metres into the pine forests. British war cemeteries dot the landscape of the Middle East, some immaculately tended and others in various states of disrepair. The Gaza War Cemetery was extensively damaged in January 2009 during the Israeli bombardment of Gaza, while in Baghdad, the North Gate Cemetery, which contains the remains of more than 4,000 British, Indian and Ottoman soldiers, including the captor of the city, Lieutenant General Sir Frederick Maude, was damaged by a nearby car bomb in 2009. Gertrude Bell lies nearby, interred in the crumbling cemetery of Baghdad's Anglican church.

Signs of the First World War are everywhere and nowhere in the Middle East. Overlain by subsequent conflicts and decades of bitter contestation, the legacies of the wartime experience continue to reverberate long after the conflict entered into history in Europe. Seen by many as 'sideshows' to the main fighting on the Western Front, the Middle Eastern campaigns had monumental consequences for the entire region. As the same region now stands on the cusp of another period of transformative (though highly uncertain) change, it is more important than ever before to understand the processes that exerted such an influence on the contemporary development of states and societies in the Middle East.

NOTES

INTRODUCTION

1. See Chapter 6.
2. Edward Erickson, *The History of World War I: Gallipoli and the Middle East 1914-1918: From the Dardanelles to Mesopotamia* (London: Amber Books, 2008), p.217.
3. Kristian Coates Ulrichsen, *The Logistics and Politics of the British Campaigns in the Middle East, 1914-22* (Basingstoke: Palgrave Macmillan, 2010), p.47.
4. Sevket Pamuk, 'The Ottoman Economy in World War I', in Stephen Broadberry and Mark Harrison (eds.), *The Economics of World War I* (Cambridge: Cambridge University Press, 2009), p.120; Erik Zurcher, 'Little Mehmet in the Desert: The Ottoman Soldier's Experience', in Hugh Cecil and Peter Liddle (eds.), *Facing Armageddon: The First World War Experienced* (London: Leo Cooper, 1996), p.238.
5. 'First World War Centenary Plans Unveiled', *Daily Telegraph*, 9 June 2013.
6. http://www.gallipoli2015.dva.gov.au/Pages/default.aspx (accessed 18 July 2013).
7. http://ww100.govt.nz/rfp-scoping-gallipoli-heritage-site-interpretation#. UebIwMBwYhk (accessed 18 July 2013).
8. Notably Peter Hart, *Gallipoli* (London: Profile Books, 2011).
9. Notably Charles Townshend, *When God Made Hell: The British Invasion of Mesopotamia and the Creation of Iraq* (London: Faber and Faber, 2010).
10. Personal observation, London: The National Archives, February 2005.
11. Sir Jeremy Greenstock's book was entitled *The Cost of War*.
12. 'Greenstock Finally Delivers His Barb on Iraq', *Daily Telegraph*, 12 March 2007.

1: THE POLITICAL ECONOMY OF DIFFERENT EMPIRES IN 1914

1. Albert Hourani, *A History of the Arab Peoples* (London: Faber and Faber, 1991 [2002]), p.7.
2. D. T. Potts, 'The Archaeology and Early History of the Persian Gulf', in Lawrence Potter (ed.), *The Persian Gulf in History* (New York: Palgrave Macmillan, 2009), pp.39-41.
3. John Keegan, *A History of Warfare* (London: Pimlico, 1994), p.70.
4. Barry Strauss, *The Trojan War: A New History* (London: Simon & Schuster, 2006), p.18.

5. Fred Halliday, *The Middle East in International Relations: Power, Politics and Ideology* (Cambridge: Cambridge University Press, 2005), p.37.

6. C. A. Bayly, *The Birth of the Modern World 1780-1914* (Oxford: Blackwell Publishing, 2004), p.1.

7. Thomas Metcalf, *Imperial Connections: India in the Indian Ocean Arena, 1860-1920* (Berkeley, CA: University of California Press, 2007), p.1.

8. Patricia Risso, 'India and the Gulf: Encounters from the Mid-Sixteenth to the Mid-Twentieth Centuries', and William Beeman, 'Gulf Society: An Anthropological View of the Khalijis – Their Evolution and Way of Life', both in Potter (ed.), *The Persian Gulf in History*.

9. B. R. Tomlinson, *The Political Economy of the Raj: The Economics of Decolonisation in India* (London: Macmillan, 1979), pp.1-3.

10. James Onley, *The Arabian Frontier of the British Raj: Merchants, Rulers and the British in the Nineteenth Century Gulf* (Oxford: Oxford University Press, 2009).

11. John Willis, 'Maritime Asia, 1500-1800: The Interactive Emergence of European Domination', *American Historical Review*, 98(1), 1993, pp.84-5.

12. Sugata Bose, *A Hundred Horizons: The Indian Ocean in the Age of Global Empire* (Cambridge, MA: Harvard University Press, 2006), p.6.

13. Marc Valeri, *Oman: Politics and Society in the Qaboos State* (London: Hurst & Co., 2009), p.18.

14. Ibid. p.22; Beatrice Nicolini, 'The Baluch Role in the Persian Gulf during the Nineteenth and Twentieth Centuries', *Comparative Studies of South Asia, Africa and the Middle East*, XVII (2007), p.396.

15. Alan Villiers, *Sons of Sindbad* (London: Arabian Publishing Limited, 2006), pp.10-11.

16. For an original contribution to discussion of British imperial strategy, see Brock Millman, *Pessimism and British War Policy, 1916-1918* (London: Frank Cass, 2001).

17. Kristian Coates Ulrichsen, *The Logistics and Politics of the British Campaigns in the Middle East, 1914-1922* (Basingstoke: Palgrave Macmillan, 2010).

18. Reidar Visser, *Basra: The Failed Gulf State: Separatism and Nationalism in Southern Iraq* (Munster: Lit Verlag, 2005), pp.18-21.

19. David Fieldhouse, *Western Imperialism in the Middle East 1914-1958* (Oxford: Oxford University Press, 2006), p.15.

20. Virginia Aksan, 'The Ottoman Military and State Transformation in a Globalizing World', *Comparative Studies of South Asia, Africa and the Middle East*, XVII (2007), p.259.

21. Phebe Marr, *The Modern History of Iraq* (Boulder, CO: Westview Press, 1985), p.22.

22. Christopher Clay, 'The Origins of Modern Banking in the Levant: the Branch Network of the Imperial Ottoman Bank, 1890-1914', *International Journal of Middle East Studies*, XVI (1994), p.591.

23. Engin Deniz Akarli, 'The Tangled Ends of an Empire: Ottoman Encounters with the West and Problems of Westernisation – An Overview', *Comparative Studies of South Asia, Africa and the Middle East*, XVI (2006), p.359.

24. Ibid., p.362.

25. Metin Heper, 'Center and Periphery in the Ottoman Empire: With Special Reference

to the Nineteenth Century', *International Political Science Review*, I (1980), p.87.

26. Aksan, 'Military and State Transformation', pp.268-9.

27. Joel Migdal, *Strong Societies and Weak States: State-Society Relations and State Capabilities in the Third World* (Princeton, NJ: Princeton University Press, 1988), pp.54-5.

28. Nevn Cosar and Sevtap Demre, 'Incorporation into the World Economy: From Railways to Highways (1850-1950)', *Middle Eastern Studies*, 45 (2009), p.19.

29. Visser, *Failed Gulf State*, p.17.

30. Afaf Lutfi Al-Sayyid-Marsot, 'The British Occupation of Egypt from 1882', in Wm Roger Louis and Andrew Porter (eds.), *The Oxford History of the British Empire, Volume III: The Nineteenth Century* (Oxford: Oxford University Press, 2001), p.652.

31. E. E. Evans-Pritchard, *The Sanusi of Cyrenaica* (Oxford: Oxford University Press, 1949), pp.107-8.

32. Dirk Vandewalle, *A History of Modern Libya* (Cambridge: Cambridge University Press, 2006), pp.22-3.

33. Caesar E. Farah, *The Sultan's Yemen: Nineteenth-Century Challenges to Ottoman Rule* (London: I. B. Tauris, 2002), p.272.

34. Owen Pearson, *Albania in the Twentieth Century, A History, Volume I: Albania and King Zog: 1908-1939* (London: I. B. Tauris, 2006), p.12.

35. Edward Erickson, *Defeat in Detail: The Ottoman Army in the Balkans, 1912-1913* (Westport, CT: Greenwood, 2003), pp.332-4.

36. Hew Strachan, *The First World War, Volume I: To Arms* (Oxford: Oxford University Press, 2001), pp.680-83.

37. Feroz Ahmad, *The Young Turks: The Committee of Union and Progress in Turkish Politics, 1908-14* (London: Hurst & Co., 2010), pp.141-2.

38. cf. Thomas Pakenham, *The Scramble for Africa* (London: Abacus, 1992).

39. Roger Owen, *State, Power and Politics in the Making of the Modern Middle East* (London: Routledge, 1992), pp.10-11.

40. Fieldhouse, *Western Imperialism*, pp.246-7.

41. Hourani, *History of the Arab Peoples*, pp.282-5.

42. Alfred Cobban, *A History of Modern France, Volume 3: 1871-1962* (London: Penguin, 1990 edn), p.92.

43. Gary Wilder, *The French Imperial Nation-State: Negritude and Colonial Humanism between the Two World Wars* (Chicago, IL: University of Chicago Press, 2005), p.25.

44. Eugene Rogan, *The Arabs: A History* (London: Allen Lane, 2009), p.211.

45. Fieldhouse, *Western Imperialism*, p.247.

46. Wilders, *French Imperial Nation-State*, p.27.

47. Christopher Andrew and Andrew Sanya Kanya-Forstner, 'France, Africa and the First World War', *Journal of African History*, XIX (1978), pp.14-16.

48. Kenneth Perkins, *A History of Modern Tunisia* (Cambridge: Cambridge University Press, 2004), pp.74-5.

49. Keith Neilson, 'For Diplomatic, Economic, Strategic and Telegraphic Reasons: British Imperial Defence, the Middle East and India, 1914-1918', in Keith Neilson and Greg Kennedy (eds.), *Far-Flung Lines: Studies in Imperial Defence in Honour of Donald Mackenzie Schurman* (London: Frank Cass, 1997), p.102.

50. Robin Moore, 'Imperial India, 1858-1914,' in Louis and Porter, *Oxford History of the British Empire,* Vol. III, p.442.

51. Ibid.

52. Walter Reid, *Architect of Victory: Douglas Haig* (Edinburgh: Birlinn, 2006), p.149.

53. A. J. Stockwell, 'The War and the British Empire', in John Turner (ed.), *Britain and the First World War* (London: Unwin Hyman, 1988), p.38.

54. Al-Sayyid-Marsot, *British Occupation of Egypt*, p.653.

55. Nathan Brown, *Peasant Politics in Modern Egypt: The Struggle against the State* (New Haven: Yale University Press, 1990), p.196.

56. Roger Owen, *Lord Cromer: Victorian Imperialist, Edwardian Proconsul* (Oxford: Oxford University Press, 2004), p.233.

57. P. J. Cain, 'Character and Imperialism: The British Financial Administration of Egypt, 1878-1914', *Journal of Imperial and Commonwealth History*, XXXIV (2006), p.183.

58. M. W. Daly, 'The British Occupation, 1882-1922', in M. W. Daly (ed.), *The Cambridge History of Egypt, Volume 2: Modern Egypt: From 1517 to the End of the Twentieth Century* (Cambridge: Cambridge University Press, 1998), p.240.

59. Gabriel Baer, *A History of Landownership in Modern Egypt 1800-1950* (Oxford: Oxford University Press, 1962), p.57.

60. Al-Sayyid-Marsot, *British Occupation of Egypt*, p.658.

61. Ronald Hyam, 'The Primacy of Geopolitics: The Dynamics of British Imperial Policy, 1763-1963', in Robert King and Robin Kilson (eds.), *The Statecraft of British Imperialism: Essays in Honour of Wm Roger Louis* (London: Routledge, 1999), p.40.

62. David Gilmour, *Curzon: Imperial Statesman* (London: John Murray, 2003), p.203.

63. James Onley and Sulayman Khalaf, 'Shaikhly Authority in the Pre-Oil Gulf: An Historical-Anthropological Study', *History and Anthropology*, XVII (2006), p.202.

64. Coates Ulrichsen, *Logistics and Politics*, p.25.

65. Helmut Mejcher, *Imperial Quest for Oil: Iraq 1910-1928* (London: St Antony's Middle East Monographs No. 6, 1976), foreword by Elizabeth Monroe.

66. Daniel Yergin, *The Prize: The Epic Quest for Oil, Money and Power* (New York: Free Press, 2008 edn), pp.144-5.

67. Benjamin Slot, *Mubarak Al-Sabah: Founder of Modern Kuwait 1896-1915* (London: Arabian Publishing Limited, 2005), p.296.

68. Quoted in Philip Graves, *The Life of Sir Percy Cox* (London: Hutchinson, 1941), p.173.

69. Jacob Landau, *The Politics of Pan-Islam: Ideology and Organization* (Oxford: Oxford University Press, 1990), p.97.

70. Coates Ulrichsen, *Logistics and Politics*, p.26.

71. Strachan, *First World War*, pp.664-7.

72. Cf. Sean McMeekin, *The Berlin–Baghdad Express: The Ottoman Empire and Germany's Bid for World Power* (Cambridge, MA: Harvard University Press, 2010).

73. Ulrich Trumpener, 'Liman von Sanders and the German–Ottoman Alliance', *Journal of Contemporary History*, I (1966), pp.180-81.

74. Ibid., p.14.

75. Strachan, *First World War*, pp.700-704.

76. Bayly, *Birth of the Modern World*, p.199.

77. Hourani, *History of the Arab Peoples*, pp.302-4.
78. George Antonius, *The Arab Awakening: The Story of the Arab National Movement* (London: Hamish Hamilton, 1938), pp.68-9.
79. Ziad Fahmy, 'Francophone Egyptian Nationalists, Anti-British Discourse, and European Public Opinion, 1885-1910: The Case of Mustafa Kamil and Ya'qub Sannu", *Comparative Studies of South Asia, Africa and the Middle East*, XXVIII (2008), pp.181-2.
80. Vandewalle, *History of Modern Libya*, p.27.
81. Bayly, *Birth of the Modern World*, pp.206-7.
82. Hourani, *History of the Arab Peoples*, pp.309-10.
83. Shareen Blair Brysac and Karl Meyer, *Kingmakers: The Invention of the Modern Middle East* (New York: W. W. Norton & Co., 2008), p.18.
84. Frederick Anscombe, *The Ottoman Gulf: The Creation of Kuwait, Saudi Arabia, and Qatar* (New York: Columbia University Press, 1997), p.171.
85. Madawi Al-Rasheed, *Politics in an Arabian Oasis: The Rashidi Tribal Dynasty* (London: I. B. Tauris, 1990), pp.215-21.
86. Mohammad Gholi Majd, *Iraq in World War I: From Ottoman Rule to British Conquest* (Lanham, MD: University Press of America, 2006), pp.36-9.
87. Thair Karim, 'Tribes and Nationalism: Tribal Political Culture and Behaviour in Iraq, 1914-1920', in Faleh Abdul-Jabar and Hosham Dawod (eds.), *Tribes and Power: Nationalism and Ethnicity in the Middle East* (London: Saqi, 2003), p.288.
88. Ibid., p.291.
89. P. G. Elgood, *Egypt and the Army* (Oxford: Oxford University Press, 1924), p.85; P. G. Elgood, *The Transit of Egypt* (London: Edward Arnold, 1928), p.218.
90. Antonius, *Arab Awakening*, pp.115-16.
91. Malcolm Yapp, *The Making of the Modern Near East 1792-1923* (London: Longman, 1987), p.266.
92. Strachan, *First World War*, pp.678-80.
93. Yapp, *Making of Modern Near East*, p.274.
94. Matthew Hughes, *Allenby and British Strategy in the Middle East, 1917-1919* (London: Frank Cass, 1999), p.40.
95. Erik Zurcher, 'Ottoman Labour Battalions in World War I', internet essay (undated), available at http://www.arts.yorku.ca/hist/tgallant/documents/zurcherottomanlaborbattalions.pdf (accessed 8 October 2013).
96. Erickson, *Gallipoli and the Middle East*, p.19.
97. Steven Heydemann, 'War, Institutions, and Social Change in the Middle East', in Steven Heydemann (ed.), *War, Institutions, and Social Change in the Middle East* (Berkeley, CA: University of California Press, 2000), p.8.

2: MILITARY CAMPAIGNING IN THE MIDDLE EAST

1. Stuart Robson, *The First World War* (Harlow: Pearson Education Limited, 2nd edn, 2007), pp.37-9.
2. Niall Barr, 'The Desert War Experience', in Peter Liddle, Ian Whitehead and John Bourne (eds.), *The Great World War, 1914-45: Lightning Strikes Twice* (London:

HarperCollins, 2002), p.128.

3. W. M. Parker, 'Supply Services in Mesopotamia', *Royal United Services Corps Quarterly*, 9(2), 1921, p.422.
4. David Lloyd George extract from *War Memoirs*, quoted in David Woodward, *Lloyd George and the Generals* (London: Frank Cass, 2004), p.167.
5. Douglas Wilson Johnson, *Topography and Strategy in the War* (New York: Henry Holt, 1917), p.iii.
6. Hew Strachan, *The First World War, Volume I: To Arms* (Oxford: Oxford University Press, 2001), pp.716, 729.
7. Letter No.105 in 'The First World War Letters of Lt J. W. McPherson', Volume XI, London: Imperial War Museum, 80/25/I.
8. H. S. Gullett, *The Official History of Australia in the War of 1914-1918, Volume 7: Sinai and Palestine. The Australian Imperial Force in Sinai and Palestine 1914-1918* (St Lucia, Queensland: University of Queensland Press, 1925), p.47.
9. Kristian Coates Ulrichsen, *The Logistics and Politics of the British Campaigns in the Middle East, 1914-22* (Basingstoke: Palgrave Macmillan, 2011), p.43.
10. Aylmer Haldane, *The Insurrection in Mesopotamia, 1920* (London: Blackwood, 1922), p.120.
11. Hubert Young, *The Independent Arab* (London: John Murray, 1933), p.44.
12. Edmund Candler, *The Sepoy* (London: John Murray, 1920), pp.50, 102.
13. Coates Ulrichsen, *Logistics and Politics*, p.44.
14. Alan Moorehead, *Gallipoli* (Ware, Herts: Wordsworth Editions, 1997), pp.127-8.
15. Ellis Ashmead-Bartlett, *The Uncensored Dardanelles* (London: Hutchinson, 1920), p.81.
16. Robert Rhodes James, *Gallipoli* (London: B. T. Batsford, 1965), pp.334-7.
17. Ross Anderson, *The Forgotten Front: The East African Campaign 1914-1918* (Stroud: Tempus Publishing, 2004), pp.296-7.
18. Coates Ulrichsen, *Logistics and Politics*, p.44.
19. John Lynn, *Feeding Mars: Logistics in Western Warfare from the Middle Ages to the Present* (Oxford: Westview Press, 1993), p.183.
20. Martin van Creveld, 'World War I and the Revolution in Logistics', in Roger Chickering and Stig Forster (eds.), *Great War, Total War: Combat and Mobilization on the Western Front, 1914-1918* (Cambridge: Cambridge University Press, 2000), pp.60-69.
21. Matthew Hughes, *Allenby and British Strategy in the Middle East, 1917-1919* (London: Frank Cass, 1999), p.50.
22. Coates Ulrichsen, *Logistics and Politics*, pp.33-4.
23. Ulrich Trumpener, 'The Turkish War, 1914-1918', in John Horne (ed.), *A Companion to World War I* (Chichester: Wiley-Blackwell, 2010), p.99.
24. Coates Ulrichsen, *Logistics and Politics*, p.28.
25. G. F. Davies, 'Lecture on Supplies and Transport – Egyptian Expeditionary Force', *Army Service Corps Quarterly*, 8 (1920), p.103.
26. Letter from John Maxwell to Sir Ian Hamilton, 31 March 1915, London: Liddell Hart Centre for Military Archives (LHCMA), Papers of Sir Ian Hamilton, 7/1/15.
27. Peter Hart, *Gallipoli* (London: Profile Books, 2011), p.55.

28. Letter from Sir Ian Hamilton to Lord Kitchener, 15 July 1915, London: LHCMA, Hamilton papers, 7/1/6.
29. Letter from Sir Ian Hamilton to Sir John Cowans, 2 July 1915, London: LHCMA, Hamilton papers, 7/1/7.
30. Erickson, *Gallipoli and the Middle East*, pp.18-19.
31. Sevket Pamuk, 'The Ottoman Economy in World War I', in Broadberry and Harrison, *Economics of World War I*, p.116.
32. Matthew Hughes, 'General Allenby and the Palestine Campaign, 1917-18', *Journal of Strategic Studies*, 19(4), 1996, pp.68-9.
33. Pamuk, 'Ottoman Empire in World War I', p.131.
34. Martin Gilbert, *A History of the Twentieth Century, Volume One: 1900-1933* (London: HarperCollins, 1997), pp.355-6.
35. Strachan, *First World War*, p.715.
36. Kaushik Roy, 'Equipping Leviathan: Ordnance Factories of British India, 1859-1913', *War in History*, 10(4), 2003, pp.400-401.
37. M. D. Morris, 'The Growth of Large-Scale Industry to 1947', in D. Kumar and T. Raychaudhuri (eds.), *The Cambridge Economic History of India, Volume 2: c.1757-c.1970* (Cambridge: Cambridge University Press, 1983), pp.601-2.
38. Roy, 'Equipping Leviathan', p.400.
39. Coates Ulrichsen, *Logistics and Politics*, p.46.
40. Stephen Broadberry and Mark Harrison (eds.), *The Economics of World War I* (Cambridge: Cambridge University Press, 2005), p.1.
41. Avner Offer, *The First World War: An Agrarian Interpretation* (Oxford: Oxford University Press, 1989), p.402.
42. Chris Wrigley, 'The War and the International Economy', in Chris Wrigley (ed.), *The First World War and the International Economy* (Cheltenham: Edward Elgar, 2000), p.4.
43. William Robertson, *Soldiers and Statesmen 1914-1918, Volume II* (London: Cassell, 1926), p.166.
44. Pamuk, 'Ottoman Economy', p.115.
45. Coates Ulrichsen, *Logistics and Politics*, p.45.
46. Wilfred Nunn, *Tigris Gunboats: The Forgotten War in Iraq 1914-1917* (London: Chatham Publishing, 2007 [1923]), p.88.
47. Paolo Coletta, *Allied and American Naval Operations in the European Theatre, World War I* (Lewiston, NY: Lampeter, 1996), pp.311-18.
48. Private letter from General Sir Archibald Murray to Field Marshal Lord Kitchener, 11 December 1915, in the Papers of Sir Archibald Murray, London: Imperial War Museum, 79/48/3.
49. Ibid., p.318.
50. Robertson, *Soldiers and Statesmen*, p.166.
51. Paul Halpern, *The Naval War in the Mediterranean* (London: HarperCollins, 1987), p.324.
52. Michael Neiberg, *Fighting the Great War: A Global History* (London: Harvard University Press, 2005), pp.133-4.
53. B. J. C. McKercher, 'Economic Warfare', in Hew Strachan (ed.), *World War I: A History*

(Oxford: Oxford University Press, 1999), p.128.

54. Halpern, *Naval War in the Mediterranean*, p.312.

55. Ibid., p.345.

56. Coates Ulrichsen, *Logistics and Politics*, p.65.

57. John Darwin, *Britain, Egypt and the Middle East: Imperial Policy in the Aftermath of War 1918-1922* (London: Macmillan, 1981), p.12.

58. Ellis Goldberg, 'Peasants in Revolt – Egypt 1919', *International Journal of Middle East Studies*, 24(2), 1992, p.268.

59. Coates Ulrichsen, *Logistics and Politics*, p.142.

60. Gideon Biger, 'The Turkish Activities in Palestine During World War I Revised', in Yigal Sheffy and Shlaul Shai (eds.), *The First World War: Middle Eastern Perspective* (Tel Aviv: Israel Society for Military History), pp.60-62.

61. Coates Ulrichsen, *Logistics and Politics*, p.123.

62. Peter Gatrell, *Russia's First World War. A Social and Economic History* (Harlow: Pearson, 2005), pp.188-90.

63. John Horne, 'Introduction', in John Horne (ed.), *State, Society and Mobilization in Europe During the First World War* (Cambridge: Cambridge University Press, 2002), p.12.

64. Avner Offer, 'The Blockade of Germany and the Strategy of Starvation, 1914-1918: An Agency Perspective', in Roger Chickering and Stig Forster (eds.), *Great War, Total War: Combat and Mobilisation on the Western Front, 1914-1918* (Cambridge: Cambridge University Press, 2000), p.176.

65. Ian Beckett (ed.), *1917: Beyond the Western Front* (Leiden: Brill, 2009), pp.xii-xiii.

66. Judith Brown, 'War and the Colonial Relationship: Britain, India and the War of 1914-18', in M. R. D. Foot (ed.), *War and Society: Historical Essays in Honour and Memory of J. R. Western, 1928-1971* (London: Elek, 1973), p.85.

67. Roger Owen, *Lord Cromer: Victorian Imperialist, Edwardian Proconsul* (Oxford: Oxford University Press, 2004), p.233.

68. Richard Meinertzhagen, *Army Diary 1899-1926* (London: Oliver & Boyd, 1960), p.58.

69. Andrew Lambert, 'The Royal Navy, 1856-1914: Deterrence and the Strategy of World Power', in Keith Neilson and Elizabeth Jane Errington (eds.), *Navies and Global Defence: Theories and Strategy* (Westport, CO: Greenwood, 1995), p.87.

70. George Morton Jack, 'The Indian Army on the Western Front, 1914-1915: A Portrait of Collaboration', *War in History*, 13(3), pp.339-40.

71. Coates Ulrichsen, *Logistics and Politics*, p.28.

72. Keith Jeffery, '"An English Barrack in the Oriental Sea?" India in the Aftermath of the First World War', *Modern Asian Studies*, 15(3), 1981, p.369.

73. Benjamin Schwarz, 'Divided Attention: Britain's Perception of a German Threat to her Eastern Frontier in 1918', *Journal of Contemporary History*, 28(1), 1993, p.104.

74. Dharma Kumar, 'The Fiscal System', in Dharma Kumar and Tapan Raychaudhuri (eds.), *The Cambridge Economic History of India, Volume 2: c.1757-c.1970* (Cambridge: Cambridge University Press, 1983), p.921.

75. K. N. Chaudhuri, 'Foreign Trade and Balance of Payments (1757-1947)', in Kumar and Raychaudhuri, *Cambridge Economic History of India, Vol. 2*, p.807.

3: THE CAUCASUS CAMPAIGNS

1. Jennifer Keene and Michael Neiberg (eds.), *Finding Common Ground: New Directions in First World War Studies* (Leiden: Brill, 2011).
2. Malcolm Yapp, *The Making of the Modern Near East 1792-1923* (London: Longman, 1987), p.274.
3. Edward Erickson, *The History of World War I: Gallipoli and the Middle East, 1914-1918: From the Dardanelles to Mesopotamia* (London: Amber Books, 2008), p.39.
4. C. A. Bayly, *The Birth of the Modern World 1780-1914* (Oxford: Blackwell Publishing, 2004), pp.206-7.
5. Engin Deniz Akarli, 'The Tangled Ends of an Empire: Ottoman Encounters with the West and Problems of Westernisation – An Overview', *Comparative Studies of South Asia, Africa and the Middle East*, XVI (2006), pp.359-62.
6. Noel Malcolm, *Kosovo: A Short History* (London: Macmillan, 1998), p.201.
7. Hew Strachan, *The First World War, Volume I: To Arms* (Oxford: Oxford University Press, 2001), pp.712-13.
8. Ibid., p.714.
9. Erickson, *Gallipoli and the Middle East*, pp.24-5.
10. Ibid., p.35.
11. Lawrence Sondhaus, *World War One: The Global Revolution* (Cambridge: Cambridge University Press, 2011), pp.91-2.
12. John Keegan, *The First World War* (New York: Alfred A. Knopf, 1999), p.223.
13. Sondhaus, *World War One*, p.92.
14. Hew Strachan, *First World War*, p.728.
15. David Stevenson, *1914-1918: The History of the First World War* (London: Allen Lane, 2004), pp.115-16.
16. Alan Kramer, 'Combatants and Noncombatants: Atrocities, Massacres, and War Crimes', in John Horne (ed.), *A Companion to World War I* (Oxford: Wiley-Blackwell, 2010), pp.191-2.
17. Ibid.
18. Gerard Libaridian, *Modern Armenia: People, Nation, State* (New York: Transaction Publishers, 2007), p.106.
19. Martin Gilbert, *A History of the Twentieth Century, Volume 1: 1900-1933* (London: HarperCollins, 1997), pp.132-3.
20. Vahakn Dadrian, 'The Armenian Genocide: An Interpretation', in Jay Winter (ed.), *America and the Armenian Genocide of 1915* (New York: Cambridge University Press, 2003), p.52.
21. Feroz Ahmad, *The Young Turks: The Committee of Union and Progress in Turkish Politics, 1908-14* (London: Hurst & Co, 2010), pp.143-4.
22. Taner Akçam, *From Empire to Republic: Turkish Nationalism and the Armenian Question* (London: Zed Books, 2004), p.133.
23. Strachan, *First World War*, p.718.
24. Guenter Lewy, *The Armenian Massacres in Ottoman Turkey: A Disputed Genocide* (Salt Lake City, UT: Utah University Press, 2005), p.32.

25. Sean McMeekin, *The Russian Origins of the First World War* (Cambridge, MA: Harvard University Press, 2011), pp.151-2.

26. Ibid., pp.153-4.

27. Peter Balakian, *The Burning Tigris: The Armenian Genocide and America's Response* (New York: HarperCollins, 2003), p.178.

28. Henry Morgenthau, *Ambassador Morgenthau's Story* (Detroit, MI: Wayne State University Press, 2003 edn), p.204.

29. Akçam, *From Empire to Republic*, p.162.

30. Gilbert, *History of the Twentieth Century*, pp.356-7.

31. David Fieldhouse, *Western Imperialism in the Middle East: 1914-1958* (Oxford: Oxford University Press, 2006), pp.40-41.

32. Balakian, *Burning Tigris*, p.187.

33. Donald Miller and Lorna Touryan Miller, *Survivors: An Oral History of the Armenian Genocide* (Berkeley, CA: University of California Press, 1993), p.84.

34. Ibid.

35. Ibid., p.96.

36. Lewy, *Armenian Massacres*, p.213.

37. Christopher Walker, *Armenia: The Survival of a Nation* (London: Palgrave Macmillan), 1990, p.210.

38. 'Armenians Are Sent to Perish in Desert; Turks Accused of Plan to Exterminate Whole Population; People of Karahissar Massacred', *New York Times*, 18 August 1915.

39. Erickson, *Gallipoli and the Middle East*, p.125.

40. Gilbert, *History of the Twentieth Century*, p.357.

41. Balakian, *Burning Tigris*, p.280.

42. Gilbert, *History of the Twentieth Century*, p.394.

43. Erickson, *Gallipoli and the Middle East*, p.119.

44. Ibid.

45. Yapp, *Making of the Modern Near East*, p.274.

46. McMeekin, *Russian Origins*, pp.190-91.

47. Erickson, *Gallipoli and the Middle East*, p.154.

48. John Buchan, *Greenmantle* (Oxford: Oxford University Press, 1993 edn), p.272.

49. Gilbert, *History of the Twentieth Century*, p.406.

50. Cyril Falls, *The First World War* (London: Longman, 1960), pp.192-3.

51. Eric Lohr, 'Russia', in John Horne (ed.), *A Companion to World War I* (Oxford: Wiley-Blackwell, 2010), p.484.

52. Peter Gatrell, *A Whole Empire Walking: Refugees in Russia During World War I* (Indianapolis, IN: Indiana University Press, 1999), pp.52-4.

53. Stephen Broadberry and Mark Harrison (eds.), *The Economics of World War I: An Overview* (Cambridge: Cambridge University Press, 2009), p.18.

54. Peter Gatrell, *Russia's First World War: A Social and Economic History* (Harlow: Pearson, 2005), p.189.

55. Ibid., p.190.

56. Ibid.

57. Gilbert, *History of the Twentieth Century*, pp.440-41.

58. Ibid.
59. Ibid.
60. Ibid.
61. McMeekin, *Russian Origins*, p.225.
62. Ibid., pp.225-6.
63. Yapp, *Making of the Modern Near East*, p.274.
64. Erik Zurcher, 'Little Mehmet in the Desert: The Ottoman Soldier's Experience', in Hugh Cecil and Peter Liddle (eds.), *Facing Armageddon: The First World War Experienced* (London: Leo Cooper, 1996), pp.233-4.
65. Ibid., pp.234-5.
66. Matthew Hughes, *Allenby and British Strategy in the Middle East, 1917-1919* (London: Frank Cass, 1999), p.50.
67. Ibid., pp.50-51.
68. Quoted in John Fisher, *Curzon and British Imperialism in the Middle East 1916-1919* (London: Frank Cass, 1999), p.164.
69. Ibid., p.165.
70. Benjamin Schwarz, 'Divided Attention: Britain's Perception of a German Threat to her Eastern Position in 1918', *Journal of Contemporary History*, 28(1), 1993, p.105.
71. Ibid., p.106.
72. George Barrow, *The Life of General Sir Charles Carmichael Monro* (London: Hutchinson, 1921), p.169.
73. Fisher, *Curzon and British Imperialism*, p.166.
74. Kramer, 'Combatants and Noncombatants', pp.192-3.

4: GALLIPOLI AND SALONIKA

1. Robin Prior, *Gallipoli: The End of the Myth* (Kensington, NSW: UNSW Press, 2009), p.252.
2. Jeff Hopkins-Weisse, 'Blood Brothers', *Australian Literary Review*, 1 April 2009, and Jeff Hopkins-Weisse, *Blood Brothers: The Anzac Generals* (Adelaide: Wakefield Press, 2009).
3. 'Those heroes who shed their blood and lost their lives, you are now lying in the soil of a friendly country. Therefore rest in peace. There is no difference between the Johnnies and the Mehmets to us where they lie side by side in this country of ours. You, the mothers who sent their sons from far away countries, wipe away your tears, your sons are now lying in our bosom and are in peace. After having lost their lives on this land they become our sons as well.'
4. Sean McMeekin, *The Russian Origins of the First World War* (Cambridge, MA: Harvard University Press, 2011), p.115.
5. Quoted in McMeekin, *Russian Origins*, p.98.
6. Sean McMeekin, *The Berlin–Baghdad Express: The Ottoman Empire and Germany's Bid for World Power* (Cambridge, MA: Harvard University Press, 2010), p.342.
7. Hew Strachan, *The First World War, Volume I: To Arms* (Oxford: Oxford University Press, 2001), pp. 644-51, 670-73.
8. Albert Hourani, *A History of the Arab Peoples* (London: Faber and Faber, 1991), p.309.

9. M. M. Ruiz, 'Manly Spectacles and Imperial Soldiers in Wartime Egypt, 1914-19', *Middle Eastern Studies*, 45(3), 2009, p.356.

10. Benjamin Slot, *Mubarak Al-Sabah: Founder of Modern Kuwait, 1896-1915* (London: Arabian Publishing, 2005), p.134.

11. Kjetil Selvik and Stig Stenslie, *Stability and Change in the Modern Middle East* (London: I. B. Tauris, 2011), pp.27-8.

12. David French, 'The Dardanelles, Mecca and Kut: Prestige as a Factor in British Eastern Strategy, 1914-1916', *War and Society*, 5(1), 1987, p.50.

13. Peter Hart, *Gallipoli* (London: Profile Books, 2011), p.7.

14. Kathleen Burk, 'Wheat and the State During the First World War', in Michael Dockrill and David French (eds.), *Strategy and Intelligence: British Policy During the First World War* (London: Hambledon Press, 1996), pp.120-22.

15. Hart, *Gallipoli*, pp.12-13.

16. Ibid.

17. Letter from Winston S. Churchill to H. H. Asquith, 29 December 1914, in Martin Gilbert (ed.), *Winston S. Churchill, Companion Volume III: Part I July 1914-April 1915* (Boston, MA: Houghton Mifflin, 1973), p.343.

18. Lawrence Sondhaus, *World War One: The Global Revolution* (Cambridge: Cambridge University Press, 2011), p.133.

19. French, 'Dardanelles, Mecca and Kut', p.51.

20. John Grigg, *Lloyd George: From Peace to War 1912-1916* (London: Penguin, 1985), p.200.

21. Basil Liddell Hart, *A History of the World War, 1914-1918* (London: Faber and Faber, 1938), p.218.

22. Martin Gilbert, *A History of the Twentieth Century,. Volume 1: 1900-1933* (London: HarperCollins, 1997), pp.362-3.

23. Hart, *Gallipoli*, pp.51-2.

24. George Cassar, *The French and the Dardanelles: A Study of Failure in the Conduct of War* (London: George Allen & Unwin, 1971), pp.48, 54.

25. Michael S. Neiberg, *Fighting the Great War: A Global History* (Cambridge, MA: Harvard University Press, 2005), p.99.

26. Cassar, *The French and the Dardanelles*, pp.60-61.

27. Both quotes contained in Alan Moorehead, *Gallipoli* (Ware, Herts: Wordsworth Editions, 1997), p.50.

28. Trumbull Higgins, *Winston Churchill and the Dardanelles* (London: Heinemann, 1963), p.118.

29. Quoted in Hart, *Gallipoli*, p.37.

30. Ibid., p.46.

31. Ibid., p.76.

32. Royal Dublin Fusiliers Association, 'Irish Battalions – Major Battles: Helles Landings, Gallipoli, April 1915.'

33. Edward Erickson, *Ordered to Die: A History of the Ottoman Army in the First World War* (London: Praeger, 2000), p.83.

34. Ibid., p.84.

35. Kristian Coates Ulrichsen, *The Logistics and Politics of the British Campaigns in the Middle East, 1914-22* (Basingstoke: Palgrave Macmillan, 2010), p.111.

36. Letter from Sir Ronald Graham to the Viceroy of India, 6 May 1915, Cambridge University Library (CUL), Papers of Sir Charles Hardinge, volume 94.

37. Letter from Sir Henry McMahon to the Viceroy of India, CUL, Hardinge papers, volume 94.

38. Letter from General Sir Ian Hamilton to Lord Kitchener, 15 July 1915, London: Liddell Hart Centre for Military Archives (LHCMA), Papers of General Sir Ian Hamilton, 7/1/6.

39. Letter from General Sir Ian Hamilton to Sir John Cowans, 2 July 1915, LHCMA, Hamilton papers, 7/1/7.

40. Hart, *Gallipoli*, pp.233-4.

41. Sondhaus, *The Global Revolution*, p.137.

42. Gavin Roynon (ed.), *A Prayer for Gallipoli: The Great War Diaries of Chaplain Kenneth Best* (London: Simon & Schuster, 2011), p.141.

43. Hart, *Gallipoli*, p.270.

44. Robert Rhodes James, *Gallipoli* (London: B. T. Batsford, 1965), p.221.

45. Ibid., pp.236-7.

46. Ibid., pp.246-7.

47. Ellis Ashmead-Bartlett, *The Uncensored Dardanelles* (London: Hutchinson, 1924), p.165.

48. John Lee, 'Sir Ian Hamilton and the Dardanelles, 1915', in Brian Bond (ed.), *Fallen Stars: Eleven Studies of Twentieth Century Military Disasters* (London: Brassey's, 1991), pp.45-6.

49. Hart, *Gallipoli*, p.327.

50. Ashmead-Bartlett, *Uncensored Dardanelles*, p.203.

51. Ronald Robinson, 'Imperial Theory and the Question of Imperialism After Empire', *Journal of Imperial and Commonwealth History*, 12(2), 1984, p.44.

52. French, 'Dardanelles, Mecca and Kut', p.46.

53. Letter from Sir Ronald Graham to the Viceroy of India, 16 November 1915, CUL, Hardinge papers, volume 94.

54. Cited in French, 'Dardanelles, Mecca and Kut', p.54.

55. Ibid.

56. Telegram from Sir Austen Chamberlain to the Viceroy of India, 21 October 1915, CUL, Hardinge papers, volume 94.

57. Evidence of Sir Arthur Hirtzel to the Mesopotamia Commission of Inquiry, 7 September 1916, London: The National Archives (TNA), PRO CAB 19/8.

58. Hart, *Gallipoli*, p.395.

59. Ibid., pp.406-8.

60. George H. Cassar, 'Monro, Sir Charles Carmichael, baronet (1860–1929)', *Oxford Dictionary of National Biography*, Oxford University Press, 2004; online edn, May 2008 [http://www.oxforddnb.com/view/article/35068, accessed 11 July 2012].

61. Ibid.

62. Hart, *Gallipoli*, p.399.

63. Ibid.

64. Winston Churchill, *The World Crisis 1911-1918* (London: Penguin Classics, 2005 abridged and revised edn), p.526.

65. Hart, *Gallipoli*, pp.399-400.

66. Letter from Sir Henry McMahon to the Viceroy of Egypt, 3 December 1915, CUL, Hardinge papers, volume 94.

67. Ulrich Trumpener, 'The Turkish War, 1914-18', in John Horne (ed.), *A Companion Volume to World War I* (Oxford: Wiley-Blackwell, 2010), pp.102-3.

68. Churchill, *The World Crisis*, p.541.

69. Ashmead-Bartlett, *Uncensored Dardanelles*, p.257.

70. Edward Erickson, *Gallipoli: The Ottoman Campaign* (Barnsley, Yorks: Pen & Sword, 2010) pp.xiv-xv.

71. Ibid.

72. Martin Gilbert, *A History of the Twentieth Century, Volume 1: 1900-1933* (London: HarperCollins, 1997, pp.381-2.

73. Mark Mazower, *Salonica: City of Ghosts. Christians, Muslims and Jews 1430-1950* (London: HarperCollins, 2004), pp.308-9.

74. Gilbert, *History of the Twentieth Century, Volume 1*, pp.421-2.

75. Allain Bernede, '"The Gardeners of Salonika": The Lines of Communication and the Logistics of the French Army of the East, October 1915-November 1918', *War and Society*, 16, 1998, pp.54-5.

76. Mazower, *City of Ghosts*, pp.315-16.

77. Trevor Wilson, *The Myriad Faces of War* (Cambridge, Polity Press, 1986), p.619.

78. Ibid., p.620.

79. Gilbert, *History of the Twentieth Century, Volume One*, pp.510-11.

5: EGYPT AND PALESTINE

1. Evidence of Commander A. Hamilton (Principal Maritime Transport Officer, Indian Expeditionary Force 'D') to the Mesopotamia Commission, 26 October 1916. London: The National Archives, PRO CAB 19/8.

2. Malcolm Yapp, *The Making of the Modern Middle East 1792-1923* (London: Longman, 1987), p.274.

3. Matthew Hughes, *Allenby and British Strategy in the Middle East, 1917-1919* (London: Frank Cass, 1999), p.40.

4. David Fieldhouse, *Western Imperialism in the Middle East 1914-1958* (Oxford: Oxford University Press, 2005), p.45.

5. Kjetil Selvik and Stig Stenslie, *Stability and Change in the Modern Middle East* (London: I. B. Tauris, 2011), pp.29-31.

6. Jukka Nevakivi, *Britain, France and the Arab Middle East, 1914-1920* (London: Athlone Press, 1969), p.43.

7. Afaf Lutfi Al-Sayyid-Marsot, 'The British Occupation of Egypt from 1882', in Andrew Porter (ed.), *The Oxford History of the British Empire, Volume 3: The Nineteenth Century* (Oxford: Oxford University Press, 1999), pp.660-64.

8. A. J. Stockwell, 'The War and the British Empire', in John Turner (ed.), *Britain and the First World War* (London: Unwin Hyman, 1988), p.46.
9. David French, 'The Dardanelles, Mecca and Kut: Prestige as a Factor in British Eastern Strategy, 1914-1916', *War and Society*, 5 (1987), p.46.
10. Alfred Milner, *England in Egypt* (London: Edward Arnold, 1892), p.24.
11. P. G. Elgood, *Egypt and the Army* (Oxford: Oxford University Press, 1924), p.10.
12. J. C. B. Richmond, *Egypt 1798-1952: Her Advance Toward a Modern Identity* (London: Methuen, 1977), p.169.
13. Kristian Coates Ulrichsen, *The Logistics and Politics of the British Campaigns in the Middle East, 1914-22* (Basingstoke: Palgrave Macmillan, 2010), p.85.
14. Telegram from Sir Milne Cheetham to Sir Edward Grey, 18 November 1914, in London, National Archive, file PRO FO 407/183/274.
15. Keith Neilson, 'For Diplomatic, Economic, Strategic, and Telegraphic Reasons: British Imperial Defence, the Middle East and India, 1914-1918', in Keith Neilson and Gregory Kennedy (eds.), *Far Flung Lines: Essays on Imperial Defence in Honour of Donald MacKenzie Schuman* (London: Routledge, 1997), pp.118-19.
16. M. W. Daly, *The Sirdar: Sir Reginald Wingate and the British Empire in the Middle East* (Philadelphia, PA: American Philosophical Society, 1997), p.203.
17. Coates Ulrichsen, *Logistics and Politics*, p.30.
18. Frederick Clarke, 'The Memoirs of a Professional Soldier in Peace and War by Musketeer' (Unpublished memoir, 1968), p.24. London: Liddell Hart Centre for Military Archives (LHCMA), Papers of Brigadier Frederick Arthur Stanley Clarke.
19. Ronald Wingate, *Wingate of the Sudan* (London: John Murray, 1955), p.206.
20. 'Memorandum on Martial Law in Egypt' by General Sir Archibald Murray, 26 November 1916, London, National Archive, file FO 371/2930.
21. E. W. Poulson Newman, *Great Britain in Egypt* (London: Cassell, 1928), p.210.
22. Djemal Pasha, *Memories of a Turkish Statesman – 1913-1919* (London: Hutchinson, 1922), p.154.
23. Coates Ulrichsen, *Logistics and Politics*, p.32.
24. A. Forbes, *A History of the Army Ordnance Services, Volume 3: The Great War* (London: Medici Society, 1929), p.211.
25. Letter from General Ian Hamilton to General Reginald Wingate, 2 October 1915, in Papers of Sir Ian Hamilton, London: LHCMA, 7/1/26.
26. Coates Ulrichsen, *Logistics and Politics*, p.56.
27. G. F. Davies, 'Lecture on Supplies and Transport – Egyptian Expeditionary Force', *Army Service Corps Quarterly*, 8 (1920), p.103.
28. Dirk Vandewalle, *A History of Modern Libya* (Cambridge: Cambridge University Press, 2006), p.27.
29. Ali Abdullatif Ahmida, *The Making of Modern Libya: State Formation, Colonization, and Resistance, 1830-1932* (New York: State University of New York, 1994), pp.115, 121.
30. Ibid., pp.121-2.
31. Letter from Sir John Maxwell to Sir William Robertson (Chief of the Imperial General Staff, London), 4 March 1916, in Papers of Sir William Robertson, London: LHCMA, 4/5/1.

32. Elgood, *Egypt and the Army*, p.230.
33. Jonathan Newell, 'British Military Policy in Egypt and Palestine, August 1914-June 1917', PhD thesis, University of London (1990), p.162.
34. Cyril Falls and George MacMunn, *Official History: Military Operations. Egypt and Palestine, Volume I* (London: HMSO, 1928), p.173.
35. The analogy of the umbilical cord was made in W. Elliot and A. Kinross, 'Maintaining Allenby's Armies: A Footnote to History', *Royal Army Service Corps Quarterly*, 13 (1925), p.119.
36. Coates Ulrichsen, *Logistics and Politics*, p.58.
37. Ibid.
38. Gideon Biger, 'The Turkish Activities in Palestine during WW1 Revisited', in Yigal Sheffy and Shaul Shai (eds.), *The First World War: Middle Eastern Perspective* (Tel Aviv: Israel Society for Military History, 2000), p.62.
39. Laurence Grafftey-Smith, *Bright Levant* (London: John Murray, 1970), p.21.
40. Matthew Hughes, 'General Allenby and the Palestine Campaign, 1917-1918', *Journal of Strategic Studies* (19), 1996, p.62.
41. Anthony Bruce, *The Last Crusade: The Palestine Campaign in the First World War* (London: John Murray, 2002), p.87.
42. Phillip Chetwode, 'Secret Notes on Operation of Desert Column', 15 March 1917, in London: Imperial War Museum (IWM), Papers of Field Marshal Lord Chetwode, P183, folder 2.
43. Brock Millman, *Pessimism and British War Policy, 1916-1918* (London: Frank Cass, 2001), p.1.
44. Spencer Tucker (ed.), *The Encyclopaedia of World War I: A Political, Social, and Military History* (Santa Barbara, CA: ABC-CLIO, 2005), p.249.
45. William Robertson, *Soldiers and Statesmen 1914-1918* (London: Cassell, 1928), p.163.
46. Yigal Sheffy, 'The Introduction of Chemical Weapons in the Middle East', in Sheffy and Shai, *First World War*, pp.78-9.
47. Falls and MacMunn, *Egypt and Palestine Official History I*, pp.293-303.
48. Gullett, *Official History Sinai and Palestine*, p.394.
49. Telegram from the Commander-in-Chief of the Egyptian Expeditionary Force to the Chief of the Imperial General Staff, 28 March 1917, in Papers of Sir William Robertson, London: LHCMA, box 4/5.
50. Sheffy, 'Introduction of Chemical Weapons', pp.79-80.
51. Coates Ulrichsen, *Logistics and Politics*, p.71.
52. Alan MacDonald, *A Lack of Offensive Spirit? The 46th (North Midland) Division at Gommecourt, 1st July 1916* (Eastbourne, E. Sussex: Iona Books, 2008), p.505.
53. Peter Simkins, 'Haig and the Army Commanders', in Brian Bond and Nigel Cave (eds.), *Haig: A Reappraisal 70 Years On* (Barnsley: Leo Cooper, 1999), p.84.
54. 'Report on Railway Situation – GS Z/31', sent from the Commander-in-Chief of the Egyptian Expeditionary Force to the Chief of the Imperial General Staff in London, 7 May 1917, London: IWM, Chetwode Papers, P183, folder 3.
55. Yigal Sheffy, 'Institutionalized Deception and Perception Reinforcement: Allenby's Campaign in Palestine', in Michael Handel (ed.), *Intelligence and Military Operations*

(London: Routledge, 1990), p.180.

56. Philip Chetwode, 'Notes on the Palestine Operations', 21 June 1917, in Papers of Sir William Bartholomew, London: LHCMA, box 1/2.

57. Matthew Hughes, *Allenby and British Strategy in the Middle East, 1917-1919* (London: Frank Cass, 1999), pp.50-51.

58. Yigal Sheffy, 'Chemical Warfare and the Palestine Campaign, 1916-1918', *Journal of Military History*, 73(3), 2009, pp.834-5.

59. Quoted in Jean Bou, 'Cavalry, Firepower, and Swords: The Australian Light Horse and the Tactical Lessons of Cavalry Operations in Palestine, 1916-1918', *Journal of Military History*, 71(1), 2007, p.108.

60. John Grainger, *The Battle for Palestine, 1917* (Woodbridge, Suffolk: Boydell & Brewer, 2006), pp.146-7.

61. Hughes, 'Allenby and the Palestine Campaign', p.70.

62. Bou, 'Cavalry, Firepower, and Swords', p.109.

63. John Keay, *Sowing the Wind: The Seeds of Conflict in the Middle East* (London: John Murray, 2003), p.84.

64. Matthew Hughes, 'Command, Strategy and the Battle for Palestine, 1917', in Ian Beckett (ed.), *1917: Beyond the Western Front* (Leiden: Brill, 2009), pp.125-6.

65. Ulrich Trumpener, 'The Turkish War, 1914-18', in John Horne (ed.), *A Companion to World War I* (Oxford: Wiley-Blackwell, 2010), p.104.

66. Stefan Goebel, *The Great War and Medieval Memory: War, Remembrance and Medievalism in Britain and Germany, 1914-1940* (Cambridge: Cambridge University Press, 2007), p.115.

67. Quoted in Hughes, *Allenby and British Strategy*, p.41.

68. Hikmet Ozdemir, *The Ottoman Army 1914-1918: Disease and Death on the Battlefield* (Salt Lake City, UT: University of Utah Press, 2008), pp.156-7.

69. Eugene Rogan, *The Arabs: A History* (London: Allen Lane, 2009), p.149.

70. Peter Sluglett, 'Aspects of Economy and Society in the Syrian Provinces: Aleppo in Transition, 1880-1925', in Leila Fawaz and C. A. Bayly, *Modernity and Culture: From the Mediterranean to the Indian Ocean* (New York: Columbia University Press, 2002), p.147.

71. William Cleveland, *A History of the Modern Middle East* (Boulder, CO: Westview Press, 1994).

72. United States Library of Congress Exhibition: The American Colony in Jerusalem: World War I, http://www.loc.gov/exhibits/americancolony/amcolony-ww1.html (accessed 24 October 2011).

73. 'Report on Palestine and Syria Situation by William Yale', 10 July 1917, London: National Archive, file FO 371/2784.

74. George Antonius, *The Arab Awakening: The Story of the Arab National Movement* (London: Hamish Hamilton, 1938), pp.241-2.

75. 'Arabia in Asia (No.XVIIIA) – Week Ending 5th June 1916', London: The National Archives, PRO/CAB/17/175.

76. Ronald Storrs, *Orientations* (London: Nicholson & Watson, 1943), pp.324, 335-6.

77. Eran Dolev, *Allenby's Military Machine: Life and Death in World War I Palestine*

(London: I. B. Tauris, 2007), p.102.

78. Hughes, *Allenby and British Strategy*, p.82.

79. Coates Ulrichsen, *Logistics and Politics*, p.73.

80. J. M. House, *Combined Arms Warfare in the Twentieth Century* (Lawrence, KS: University Press of Kansas, 2001), p.58.

81. Hughes, *Allenby and British Strategy*, pp.97-8.

82. T. E. Lawrence, *Seven Pillars of Wisdom* (Ware, Herts: Wordsworth Editions, 1997 edn), p.652.

83. Cyril Falls, *Armageddon 1918* (London: Weidenfeld & Nicolson, 1964), pp.94-100

84. Storrs, *Orientations*, p.335.

85. Hughes, *Allenby and British Strategy*, p.93.

86. John Fisher, *Curzon and British Imperialism in the Middle East* (London: Routledge, 1999), p.286.

87. Hatem Shareef Abu-Lebdeh, *Conflict and Peace in the Middle East* (Lanham, MD: University Press of America, 1997), pp.47-8.

88. Steven Heydemann, 'War, Institutions, and Social Change in the Middle East', in Steven Heydemann (ed.), *War, Institutions, and Social Change in the Middle East* (Berkeley, CA: University of California Press, 2000), pp.2-3.

6: MESOPOTAMIA

1. Quoted in Robert Fisk, *The Great War for Civilisation: The Conquest of the Middle East* (London: Fourth Estate, 2005), p.172.

2. Thair Karim, 'Tribes and Nationalism: Tribal Political Culture and Behaviour in Iraq, 1914-20', in Faleh Abdul-Jabar and Hosham Dawod (eds.), *Tribes and Power: Nationalism and Ethnicity in the Middle East* (London: Saqi Books, 2003), p.283.

3. Charles Townhsend, *When God Made Hell: The British Invasion of Mesopotamia and the Creation of Iraq, 1914-1921* (London: Faber and Faber, 2010), p.i.

4. James Barr, *A Line in the Sand: Britain, France and the Struggle that Shaped the Middle East* (London: Simon & Schuster, 2011).

5. Arnold Wilson, *Mesopotamia 1917-1920: A Clash of Loyalties* (Oxford: Oxford University Press, 1931), p.11.

6. Kristian Coates Ulrichsen, 'The British Occupation of Mesopotamia, 1914-1922', *Journal of Strategic Studies*, 30(2), 2007, pp.377-8.

7. Phebe Marr, *The Modern History of Iraq* (Boulder, CO: Westview Press, 2004), p.22.

8. Reidar Visser, *Basra: The Failed Gulf State: Separatism and Nationalism in Southern Iraq* (Munster: Lit Verlag, 2005), pp.18-19.

9. Kristian Coates Ulrichsen, 'Basra, Southern Iraq and the Gulf: Challenges and Connections', *LSE Kuwait Programme Working Paper No.21*, January 2012, p.2.

10. Kristian Coates Ulrichsen, *The Logistics and Politics of the British Campaigns in the Middle East, 1914-22* (Basingstoke: Palgrave Macmillan, 2010), p.25.

11. Quoted in J. E. Peterson, 'Britain and the Gulf: At the Periphery of Empire', in Lawrence Potter (ed.), *The Persian Gulf in History* (New York: Palgrave Macmillan, 2009), p.281.

12. Keith Surridge, 'The Ambiguous Amir: Britain, Afghanistan and the 1897 North-West Frontier Uprising', *Journal of Imperial and Commonwealth History*, 36(3), 2008, pp.422-3.
13. Briton Cooper Busch, *Britain, India and the Arabs, 1914-1921* (Berkeley, CA: University of California Press, 1971), p.35.
14. Mohammad Gholi Majd, *Iraq in World War I: From Ottoman Rule to British Conquest* (Lanham: MD, University Press of America, 2006), p.51.
15. Ibid., p.52.
16. Ibid., p.59.
17. Coates Ulrichsen, *Logistics and Politics*, p.33.
18. Townshend, *When God Made Hell*, pp.4-5.
19. 'Report by Brigadier-General W. S. Delamain on the Operations of Indian Expeditionary Force 'D' up to the 14th November 1914', London: India Office Library (IOL), IOR/L/MIL/17/88.
20. Evidence of Commander A. Hamilton to the Mesopotamia Commission, 26 October 1916, London: The National Archives (TNA), PRO/CAB/19/8.
21. Coates Ulrichsen, *Logistics and Politics*, p.37.
22. Wilfred Nunn, *Tigris Gunboats: The Forgotten War in Iraq 1914-1917* (London: Chatham Publishing, 2007 edn), pp.39-40.
23. 'Dalit', 'The Campaign in Mesopotamia – The First Phase', *Journal of the Royal United Services Institute*, 69 (1924), p.520.
24. Nunn, *Tigris Gunboats*, p.44.
25. Gholi Majd, *Iraq during World War I*, p.91.
26. Ghassan Atiyyah, *Iraq: 1908-1921. A Socio-Political Study* (Beirut: Arab Institute for Research and Publishing, 1973), p.41.
27. 'Dalit', 'Campaign in Mesopotamia', p.520.
28. Letter from Lord Hardinge of Penshurst to Lieutenant-General Sir James Willcocks, 10 February 1916, Papers of Viscount Hardinge, Cambridge University Library, volume 102.
29. Stephen Longrigg, *Iraq, 1900 to 1950: A Political, Social and Economic History* (London: Oxford University Press, 1953), p.78.
30. 'Short Memorandum on the Inception, Difficulties and Results of the Mesopotamian Campaign', September 1916, London: IOL, IOR L/MIL/15/15/76.
31. Evidence of Sir Arthur Hirtzel to the Mesopotamia Commission, 7 September 1916, London: TNA, PRO CAB 19/8.
32. Note by Sir Edmund Barrow, Military Secretary, India Office, 'Persian Gulf Operations', 27 November 1914, London: TNA, WO 106/54.
33. Ibid.
34. Letter from Sir Beauchamp Duff to Lord Hardinge of Penshurst, 28 November 1914, Hardinge papers, CUL, volume 102.
35. 'Despatch by Lieutenant-General Sir A. A. Barrett, Commanding I.E.F. D, Regarding the Operations Resulting in the Capture of Qurnah, 9th December 1914' (Simla: Government of India Centre Press, 1915), in London: IOL, IOR/L/MIL/17/15/89.
36. Coates Ulrichsen, *Logistics and Politics*, p.36.

37. Longrigg, *Iraq 1900 to 1950*, pp.80-81.

38. David French, 'The Dardanelles, Mecca and Kut: Prestige as a Factor in British Eastern Strategy, 1914-1916', *War and Society*, 5(1), 1987, pp.54-5.

39. Townshend, *When God Made Hell*, p.71.

40. Hubert Young, *The Independent Arab* (London: John Murray, 1933), p.44.

41. Ibid., p.47.

42. George MacMunn, *Behind the Scenes in Many Wars* (London: John Murray, 1930), pp.215-16.

43. Coates Ulrichsen, *Logistics and Politics*, p.91.

44. Quoted in Paul Davis, 'British–Indian Strategy and Policy in Mesopotamia, November 1914 to April 1916', PhD dissertation, University of London (1981), p.250.

45. Evidence of Sir Robert Carlyle to the Mesopotamia Commission, 28 September 1916, London: TNA, PRO/CAB/19/8.

46. Coates Ulrichsen, *Logistics and Politics*, p.91.

47. Kaushik Roy, 'Equipping Leviathan: Ordnance Factories of British India, 1859-1913', *War in History*, 10(4), 2003, p.405.

48. Townshend, *When God Made Hell*, p.65.

49. Telegram from Sir Beauchamp Duff to General Sir Percy Lake, 20 January 1916, London: TNA, PRO/CAB/19/20.

50. Coates Ulrichsen, *Logistics and Politics*, p.47.

51. Karim, 'Tribes and Nationalism', p.288.

52. Coates Ulrichsen, *Logistics and Politics*, p.99.

53. Atiyyah, *Iraq, 1908-1921*, p.250.

54. Fanar Haddad, *Sectarianism in Iraq: Antagonistic Visions of Unity* (New York: Columbia University Press, 2011), p.2.

55. Gokhan Cetinsaya, *Ottoman Administration of Iraq, 1890-1908* (New York: Routledge, 2006).

56. Hanna Batatu, *The Old Social Classes and the Revolutionary Movements of Iraq: A Study of Iraq's Old Landed and Commercial Classes* (Princeton, NJ: Princeton University Press, 1978), p.13.

57. Ibid., p.16.

58. Atiyyah, *Iraq, 1908-1921*, p.14.

59. Toby Dodge, *Inventing Iraq: The Failure of Nation-Building and a History Denied* (London: Hurst & Co., 2003), p.92.

60. 'Administrative Report of Suq Al-Shuyukh and District for Year 1916-1917' by Captain H. R. P. Dickson, Assistant Political Officer, Suq Al-Shuyukh, 9 May 1917, London: TNA, FO/371/3059.

61. Coates Ulrichsen, *Logistics and Politics*, p.98.

62. Telegram from Viscount Hardinge of Penshurst to Austen Chamberlain, 25 July 1915, Hardinge papers, CUL, volume 103.

63. Letter from Viscount Hardinge of Penshurst to Lieutenant-General Sir James Willcocks, 15 June 1915, Hardinge papers, CUL, volume 103.

64. Townshend, *When God Made Hell*, p.139.

65. 'Mesopotamian Expeditionary Force: Despatch of Operations by Lieutenant-General

Sir W. R. Marshall, 1918 April 1 – October 31', London: TNA, WO/106/916.

66. Coates Ulrichsen, *Logistics and Politics*, p.48.
67. Gholi Majd, *Iraq in World War I*, p.184.
68. Telegram from the Viceroy to the Secretary of State for India, 6 October 1915, Hardinge papers, CUL, volume 103.
69. Telegram from the Secretary of State for India to the Viceroy, 8 October 1915, Hardinge papers, CUL, volume 103.
70. Telegram from the General Officer Commanding, Force D, to the Secretary of State for India, October 1915, Hardinge papers, CUL, volume 103.
71. Telegram from the Secretary of State for India to the Viceroy, 21 October 1915, Hardinge papers, CUL, volume 103.
72. Coates Ulrichsen, *Logistics and Politics*, p.48.
73. F. J. Moberly, *History of the Great War Based on Official Documents. The Campaign in Mesopotamia, 1914-1918* (London: HMSO, 1923), volume II, p.167.
74. Coates Ulrichsen, *Logistics and Politics*, pp.48-9.
75. Ibid., p.49.
76. Moberly, *Official History*, vol. II, p.278.
77. Ibid., p.280.
78. Telegram from General Sir Percy Lake to the Chief of the General Staff in India, 8 February 1916, London: TNA, WO 106/905.
79. Coates Ulrichsen, *Logistics and Politics*, p.50.
80. Telegram from General Sir Percy Lake to the Chief of the General Staff in India, 15 February 1916, London: TNA, WO 106/905.
81. Coates Ulrichsen, *Logistics and Politics*, p.51.
82. Gholi Majd, *Iraq During World War I*, p.209.
83. Telegram from General Sir Percy Lake to the Chief of the General Staff in India, 22 April 1916, London: TNA, WO 106/905.
84. Telegram from Field Marshal Lord Kitchener to General Sir Beauchamp Duff, 25 April 1916, London: TNA, WO 106/906.
85. Townshend, *When God Made Hell*, pp.332-5.
86. Ibid., p.335.
87. Coates Ulrichsen, *Logistics and Politics*, p.52.
88. Ibid.
89. Ibid.
90. Sir George Buchanan, 'Port Administration and River Conservancy Department, MEF – Report for Month Ending June 30th, 1916', London: TNA, WO 95/4993.
91. 'Report by Major-General H. F. E. Freeland on the Working and Future Development of the Port of Basra and of the River and Railway Communications in Mesopotamia', April 1918, London: TNA, MUN 4/6517, p.9.
92. Cf. Coates Ulrichsen, *Logistics and Politics*, chapters 4-6.
93. Michael Casey, *The History of Kuwait* (Westport, CT: Greenwood, 2007), p.52.
94. David Roberts, 'Kuwait', in Christopher Davidson (ed.), *Power and Politics in the Persian Gulf* (London: Hurst & Co., 2011), p.90.
95. Casey, *History of Kuwait*, p.53.

96. Steven Wright, 'Foreign Policies with International Reach: The Case of Qatar', in David Held and Kristian Coates Ulrichsen (eds.), *The Transformation of the Gulf: Politics, Economics and the Global Order* (London: Routledge, 2011), pp.297-8.

97. 'Abd al-Fattah Hasan Abu Aliyya, 'Early Roots of Projects to Settle the Bedouins in the Arabian Peninsula', in Fahd al-Semmari (ed.), *A History of the Arabian Peninsula* (London: I. B. Tauris, 2010), pp.207-8.

98. Joseph Kechichian, *Faysal: Saudi Arabia's King for all Seasons* (Gainesville, FL: University Press of Florida Press, 2008), p.17.

99. Coates Ulrichsen, *Logistics and Politics*, p.67.

100. Lieutenant General F. S. Maude, 'Report on Operations 28 August 1916 to 31 March 1917', London: TNA, WO 32/5206.

101. 'Sketch of Military Operations in Mesopotamia 1917', London: TNA, WO 106/912.

102. Ibid.

103. H. V. F. Winstone, *Leachman: 'OC Desert': The Life of Lieutenant-Colonel Gerard Leachman* (London: Quartet, 1982), p.203.

104. Benjamin Schwarz, 'Divided Attention: Britain's Perception of a German Threat to Her Eastern Frontier in 1918', *Journal of Contemporary History*, 28 (1993), pp.106-9.

105. Coates Ulrichsen, *Logistics and Politics*, p.69.

106. 'Mesopotamian Expeditionary Force: Despatch of Operations by Lieutenant-General Sir W. R. Marshall, 1918 1 October – 31 December', London: TNA, WO 106/917.

107. Coates Ulrichsen, *Logistics and Politics*, p.159.

108. Ibid.

109. Gertrude Bell, 'Report on the Najaf-Karbala District', London: TNA, FO 371/3060.

110. Coates Ulrichsen, *Logistics and Politics*, p.157.

111. Telegram from Lieutenant-General Sir Frederick Maude to the Chief of the General Staff in India, 9 July 1917, London: IOL, L/MIL/5/758.

112. Telegram from Sir Percy Cox to the India Office in London, 25 May 1917, London: IOL, L/P&S/10/666.

113. Atiyyah, *Iraq*, p.158.

114. Oil had been seeping to the surface in areas around Mosul and Kirkuk, so its existence was more than mere conjecture; nevertheless, the first major strike of oil only occurred in October 1927.

115. Letter from Sir Maurice Hankey to Sir Eric Geddes, 30 July 1918, London: TNA, CAB 21/119.

116. Paper by Admiral Sir Edmond Slade on the Petroleum Situation in the British Empire, 29 July 1918, London: TNA, CAB 21/119.

117. Major General F. H. Sykes, 'Petroleum Situation in the British Empire: Notes by the Chief of the Air Staff', 9 August 1918, London: TNA, CAB 21/119.

118. Letter from Sir Maurice Hankey to Sir Arthur Balfour, 12 August 1918, London: TNA, CAB 21/119.

119. Coates Ulrichsen, *Logistics and Politics*, p.89.

7: THE STRUGGLE FOR POLITICAL CONTROL IN THE MIDDLE EAST

1. Telegram from the Viceroy of India to the Secretary of State for India, 7 December 1914, in the Papers of Viscount Hardinge of Penshurst, Cambridge University Library (CUL), volume 98.

2. Telegram from the Secretary of State for India to the Viceroy of India, 16 December 1914, London: India Office Library (IOL), L/P&S/10/514.

3. Kristian Coates Ulrichsen, *The Logistics and Politics of the British Campaigns in the Middle East, 1914-22* (Basingstoke: Palgrave Macmillan, 2010), p.85.

4. George Cassar, *The French and the Dardanelles: A Study of Failure in the Conduct of War* (London: George Allen & Unwin, 1971), p.48.

5. Quoted in ibid., pp.54-5.

6. David Dutton, 'Britain and France at War, 1914-1918', in Alan Sharp and Glyn Stone (eds.), *Anglo-French Relations in the Twentieth Century: Rivalry and Cooperation* (Abingdon: Routledge, 2000), p.84.

7. Quoted in Sean McMeekin, *The Russian Origins of the First World War* (Cambridge, MA: Harvard University Press, 2011), pp.110-11.

8. Ibid.

9. Eugene Rogan, *The Arabs: A History* (London: Penguin, 2009), p.150.

10. Isaiah Friedman, *British Pan-Arab Policy 1915-1922: A Critical Appraisal* (New Brunswick, NJ: Transaction Publishers, 2010), pp.15-16.

11. V. H. Rothwell, 'Mesopotamia in British War Aims, 1914-1918,' *Historical Journal* (13:2), 1970, p.279.

12. David French, 'The Rise and Fall of 'Business as Usual'', in Kathleen Burk (ed.), *War and the State: The Transformation of British Government, 1914-1919* (London: Allen & Unwin, 1982), p.22.

13. Roger Adelson, *London and the Invention of the Middle East: Money, Power, and War, 1914-1922* (New Haven, CT: Yale University Press, 1995), p.4.

14. Quoted in Friedman, *British Pan-Arab Policy*, p.18.

15. Paula Mohs, *British Intelligence and the Arab Revolt: The First Modern Intelligence War* (London: Routledge, 2008), p.33.

16. Jukka Nevakivi, *Britain, France and the Arab Middle East, 1914-1920* (London: Athlone Press, 1969), pp.18, 43.

17. John Fisher, *Curzon and British Imperialism in the Middle East, 1916-1919* (London: Frank Cass, 1999), p.117.

18. John Keay, *Sowing the Wind: The Seeds of Conflict in the Middle East* (London: John Murray, 2003), pp.42-3.

19. Quotes taken from David Fieldhouse, *Western Imperialism in the Middle East 1914-1958* (Oxford: Oxford University Press, 2006), p.53.

20. Bruce Westrate, *The Arab Bureau: British Policy in the Middle East, 1916-1920* (Pennsylvania, PA: University of Pennsylvania Press, 1992).

21. Bernard Reich, *Political Leaders of the Contemporary Middle East and North Africa: A Biographical Dictionary* (Westport, CT: Greenwood, 1990), pp.17-18.

22. Christopher Andrew, *The Climax of French Imperial Expansion, 1914-1924* (Stanford, CA: Stanford University Press, 1981), p.66.

23. Keay, *Sowing the Wind*, p.59.
24. Rogan, *The Arabs*, p.153.
25. Quoted in Keith Jeffery, *The British Army and the Crisis of Empire, 1918-22* (Manchester: Manchester University Press, 1984), p.122.
26. Ibid.
27. Fieldhouse, *Western Imperialism in the Middle East*, p.58.
28. Rashid Khalidi, 'The Arab Experience of the War', in Hugh Cecil and Peter Liddle (eds.), *Facing Armageddon: The First World War Experienced* (London: Leo Cooper, 1996), p.648.
29. Rogan, *The Arabs*, p.178.
30. Thair Karim, 'Tribes and Nationalism: Tribal Political Culture and Behaviour in Iraq', in Faleh Abdul-Jabar and Hosham Dawod (eds.), *Tribes and Power: Nationalism and Ethnicity in the Middle East* (London: Saqi Books, 2003), p.288.
31. Lawrence James, *The Golden Warrior: The Life and Legend of Lawrence of Arabia* (London: Abacus, 2000 edn), p.151.
32. David Stevenson, *1914-1918: The History of the First World War* (London: Allen Lane, 2004), p.124.
33. Keay, *Sowing the Wind*, p.65.
34. T. E. Lawrence, *Seven Pillars of Wisdom* (Ware, Herts: Wordsworth Editions, 1997 edn), p.42.
35. James, *Golden Warrior*, p.160.
36. Ibid., p.162.
37. Keay, *Sowing the Wind*, p.70.
38. David Murphy, *The Arab Revolt 1916-1918* (London: Osprey Publishing, 2008), pp.57-9.
39. Matthew Hughes, *Allenby and British Strategy in the Middle East 1917-1919* (London: Frank Cass, 1999), pp.71-6.
40. Edward Erickson, *The History of World War I: Gallipoli and the Middle East 1914-1918: From the Dardanelles to Mesopotamia* (London: Amber Books, 2008), p.193.
41. Antony Best, Jussi Hanhimaki, Joseph Maiolo, Kirsten Schulze, *International History of the Twentieth Century* (London: Routledge, 2004), p.107.
42. Ibid., p.108.
43. David Stevenson, *The First World War and International Politics* (Oxford: Oxford University Press, 1988), p.177.
44. Best et al., *International History of the Twentieth Century*, pp.111-12.
45. Yigal Sheffy, 'Institutionalized Deception and Perception Reinforcement: Allenby's Campaign in Palestine', in Michael Handel (ed.), *Intelligence and Military Operation* (London, Routledge, 1990), p.180.
46. Quoted in John Grigg, *Lloyd George: War Leader* (London: Allen Lane, 2002), p.354.
47. Quoted in Rogan, *The Arabs*, p.154.
48. Stevenson, *First World War and International Politics*, p.177.
49. Fieldhouse, *Western Imperialism in the Middle East*, p.58.
50. Khalidi, 'The Arab Experience of the War', p.652.
51. Stevenson, *First World War and International Politics*, p.176.

52. David Woodward, 'The Origins and Intent of David Lloyd George's January 5 War Aims Speech', *The Historian*, 34(1), 1971, p.22.
53. Grigg, *War Leader*, p.382.
54. 'President Wilson's Fourteen Points', delivered in Joint Session, 8 January 1918, text available at http://wwi.lib.byu.edu/index.php/President_Wilson%27s_Fourteen_Points (accessed 28 March 2013).
55. William Marshall, *Memories of Four Fronts* (London: Ernest Benn, 1929), p.329.
56. Philip Ireland, *Iraq: A Study in Political Development* (London: Jonathan Cape, 1937), p.136.
57. 'Future of Mesopotamia – Note by Political Department, India Office, on Points for Discussion with Sir P. Cox, 3 April 1918', London: India Office Library, L/P&S/10/686.
58. Fisher, *Curzon and British Imperialism*, p.130.
59. Eliezer Tauber, *The Arab Movements in World War I* (London: Frank Cass, 1993), pp.173-4.
60. Ibid., p.181.
61. Ibid.
62. George Antonius, *The Arab Awakening* (London: Hamish Hamilton, 1938), pp.433-4
63. Ibid., pp.272-3.
64. Timothy Parrs, *Britain, the Hashemites, and Arab Rule, 1920-1925: the Sherifian Solution* (London: Frank Cass, 2003), p.50.
65. Hughes, *Allenby and British Strategy*, p.115.
66. Ibid., p.117.
67. Quoted in Hughes, *Allenby and British Strategy*, p.117.
68. Keay, *Sowing the Wind*, p.100.
69. Ibid.
70. 'Paper by Admiral Sir Edmond Slade on the Petroleum Situation in the British Empire', 29 July 1918, London: The National Archives (TNA), CAB 21/119.
71. Quote taken from B. S. McBeth, *British Oil Policy 1919-1939* (London: Frank Cass, 1985), p.11.
72. See Chapter 4.
73. Ibid.
74. Helmut Mejcher, *Imperial Quest for Oil: Iraq 1910-1928* (London: Ithaca Press, 1976), pp.37-8.
75. McBeth, *British Oil Policy*, p.11.
76. Ibid., p.12.
77. John Lynn, *Feeding Mars: Logistics in Western Warfare from the Middle Ages to the Present* (Oxford: Westview Press, 1993), p.183.
78. Martin van Creveld, 'World War I and the Revolution of Logistics', in Roger Chickering and Stig Forster (eds.), *Great War, Total War: Combat Mobilization on the Western Front* (Cambridge: Cambridge University Press, 2000), p.67.
79. 'Paper by Admiral Sir Edmond Slade on the Petroleum Situation in the British Empire', 29 July 1918, London: TNA, CAB 21/119.
80. Ibid.

81. Ibid.
82. Ibid.
83. Letter from Maurice Hankey to Sir Eric Geddes, 30 July 1918, London: TNA, CAB 21/119.
84. Letter from Maurice Hankey to David Lloyd George, 1 August 1918, London: TNA, CAB 21/119.
85. Letter from Maurice Hankey to Sir Arthur Balfour, 1 August 1918, London: TNA, CAB 21/119.
86. Letter from Maurice Hankey to Sir Arthur Balfour, 12 August 1918, London: TNA, CAB 21/119.
87. Ibid.
88. Arnold Wilson, *Mesopotamia 1917-1920: A Clash of Loyalties* (Oxford: Oxford University Press, 1930), p.11.
89. Ritchie Ovendale, *The Middle East Since 1914* (London: Longman, 1992), p.44.

8: THE POST-WAR SETTLEMENTS, 1919-1923

1. Martin Navias and Tim Moreman, 'Limited War and Developing Countries', in Laurence Freedman (ed.), *War* (Oxford: Oxford University Press, 1994), p.309.
2. Joel Beinin and Zachary Lockman, *Workers on the Nile: Nationalism, Communism, Islam and the Egyptian Working Class, 1882-1954* (Princeton, NJ: Princeton University Press, 1987), p.85.
3. Ellis Goldberg, 'Peasants in Revolt – Egypt 1919', *International Journal of Middle East Studies*, 24 (1992), p.263.
4. Ghassan Atiyyah, *Iraq: 1908-1921: A Socio-Political Study* (Beirut: Arab Institute for Research and Publishing, 1973), p.220.
5. Ibid.
6. Mohammad Gholi Majd, *The Great Famine and Genocide in Persia, 1917-1919* (Lanham, MD: University Press of America, 2003), p.44.
7. Sevket Pamuk, 'The Ottoman Economy in World War I', in Stephen Broadberry and Mark Harrison (eds.), *The Economics of World War I* (Cambridge: Cambridge University Press, 2009), p.120.
8. Ibid., p.132.
9. Ibid.
10. Erik Zurcher, 'Little Mehmet in the Desert: The Ottoman Soldier's Experience', in Hugh Cecil and Peter Liddle (eds.), *Facing Armageddon: The First World War Experienced* (London: Leo Cooper, 1996), p.238.
11. John Darwin, *Britain, Egypt and the Middle East: Imperial Policy in the Aftermath of War 1918-1922* (London: Macmillan, 1981), p.73.
12. Margaret MacMillan, *Peacemakers: The Paris Conference of 1919 and Its Attempt to End War* (London: John Murray, 2001), p.1.
13. David Fieldhouse, *Western Imperialism in the Middle East, 1914-1958* (Oxford: Oxford University Press, 2006), p.65.
14. MacMillan, *Peacemakers*, pp.460-62.

15. Ibid., pp.462-3.
16. Fieldhouse, *Western Imperialism in the Middle East*, p.65.
17. Kristian Coates Ulrichsen, *The Logistics and Politics of the British Campaigns in the Middle East, 1914-22* (London: Palgrave Macmillan, 2010, p.178).
18. Ibid., p.89.
19. Ibid., p.179.
20. War Diary of 11th Indian Labour Corps, London: The National Archives (TNA), PRO WO 95/5036.
21. Efraim Karsh, *Empires of the Sand: The Struggle for Mastery in the Middle East 1789-1923* (Cambridge, MA: Harvard University Press, 2001), p.175.
22. J. E. Marshall, *The Egyptian Enigma: 1890-1928* (London: John Murray, 1928), p.142.
23. Laurence Grafftey-Smith, *Bright Levant* (London: John Murray, 1970), p.59.
24. Dirk Vandewalle, *A History of Modern Libya* (Cambridge: Cambridge University Press, 2006), p.27.
25. 'Note by Wingate on Deportation of Egyptian Nationalists', 9 March 1918, London: TNA, FO 371/3714.
26. Matthew Hughes, *Allenby and British Strategy in the Middle East 1917-1919* (London: Frank Cass, 1999), p.143.
27. Nabila Ramdani, 'Women in the 1919 Egyptian Revolution: From Feminist Awakening to Nationalist Political Activism', *Journal of International Women's Studies*, 14(2), 2013, pp.45-7.
28. Goldberg, 'Peasants in Revolt', p.261.
29. Albert Hourani, *Arabic Thought in the Liberal Age, 1798-1939* (London: Royal Institute of International Affairs, 1962), p.209.
30. Nadav Safran, *Egypt in Search of a Political Community: An Analysis of the Intellectual and Political Evolution of Egypt* (Oxford: Oxford University Press, 1961), p.92.
31. Afaf Lutfi Al-Sayyid Marsot, 'The British Occupation of Egypt from 1882', in Wm Roger Louis and Andrew Porter (ed.), *The Oxford History of the British Empire, Volume III: The Nineteenth Century* (Oxford: Oxford University Press, 1999), p.663.
32. Hourani, *Arabic Thought*, p.209.
33. Malcolm Yapp, *The Making of the Modern Near East* (London: Longman, 1995), p.295.
34. Coates Ulrichsen, *Logistics and Politics*, pp.181-3.
35. P. J. Vatikiotis, *The Modern History of Egypt* (London: Weidenfeld & Nicolson, 1969), p.263.
36. T. E. Lawrence, *Seven Pillars of Wisdom* (Ware, Herts: Wordsworth Editions, 1997 edn), p.644.
37. Matthew Hughes (ed.), *Allenby in Palestine: The Middle East Correspondence of Field Marshal Viscount Allenby June 1917 – October 1919* (Stroud: Sutton Publishing, 2004), p.201.
38. Ibid., p.202.
39. Sami Moubayed, *Steel and Silk: Men and Women Who Shaped Syria 1900-2000* (Seattle: Cune Press, 2006), pp.363-4.
40. Eugene Rogan, *The Arabs* (London: Penguin, 2009), p.214.
41. Adel Beshara (ed.), *The Origins of Syrian Nationhood: Histories, Pioneers and Identity*

(CRC Press, 2012).

42. Hughes, *Allenby and British Strategy*, pp.124-6.
43. MacMillan, *Peacemakers*, pp.400-401.
44. Ibid.
45. Christopher Andrew and Alexander Sydney Kanya Forstner, *France Overseas: The Great War and the Climax of French Imperial Expansion* (London: Thames & Hudson, 1981), p.165.
46. Hughes, *Allenby and British Strategy*, p.128.
47. Ibid., p.154.
48. Keith Jeffery, 'Sir Henry Wilson and the Defence of the British Empire 1918-22', *Journal of Imperial and Commonwealth History*, 5(3), 1977, p.271.
49. Fieldhouse, *Western Imperialism*, pp.251-2.
50. Text of the 'Recommendations of the King–Crane Commission with Regard to Syria–Palestine and Iraq (August 29, 1919)' available at http://unispal.un.org/UNISPAL.NSF /0/392AD7EB00902A0C852570C000795153.
51. Hughes, *Allenby and British Strategy*, p.147.
52. Fieldhouse, *Western Imperialism*, p.253.
53. Hughes, *Allenby and British Strategy*, p.155.
54. Andrew and Kanya Forstner, *France Overseas*, p.119.
55. Fieldhouse, *Western Imperialism*, p.63.
56. See Chapter 7.
57. Rogan, *The Arabs*, p.198.
58. Peter Sluglett, *Britain in Iraq 1914-1922* (London: Ithaca Press, 1976), p.19.
59. Arnold Wilson, *Mesopotamia 1917-1920: A Clash of Loyalties* (Oxford: Oxford University Press, 1931), p.103.
60. Letter from Gertrude Bell to Sir Hugh Bell, 27 December 1918, Papers of Gertrude Bell, University of Newcastle-upon-Tyne, www.gerty.ncl.ac.uk.
61. Minute by 'J.E.S.', 26 November 1918, London: India Office Library (IOL), IOR L/MIL/5/761.
62. Telegram from Edwin Montagu to Arnold Wilson, 28 November 1918, London: IOL, IOR L/MIL/5/761.
63. Atiyyah, *Iraq*, p.180.
64. Telegram from Arnold Wilson to the India Office, 14 December 1918, London: TNA, FO 371/3386.
65. Ibid.
66. Coates Ulrichsen, *Logistics and Politics*, p.185.
67. Letter from Gertrude Bell to Sir Hugh Bell, 24 October 1920, Newcastle: Bell papers, www.gerty.ncl.ac.uk.
68. Philip Ireland, *Iraq: A Study in Political Development* (Oxford: Jonathan Cape, 1937, p.100.
69. Telegram from Arnold Wilson to Edwin Montagu, 11 December 1918, London: TNA, FO 371/3386.
70. Coates Ulrichsen, *Logistics and Politics*, p.186.
71. Charles Tripp, *A History of Iraq* (Cambridge: Cambridge University Press, 2007), p.28.

72. Charles Townshend, *When God Made Hell: The British Invasion of Mesopotamia and the Creation of Iraq, 1914-1921* (London: Faber and Faber, 2010), p.56.
73. Quoted in Paula Mohs, *Military Intelligence and the Arab Revolt: The First Modern Intelligence War* (London: Routledge, 2008), p.16.
74. Atiyyah, *Iraq*, p.278.
75. Coates Ulrichsen, *Logistics and Politics*, p.187.
76. Letter from Gertrude Bell to Sir Hugh Bell, 11 July 1920, Newcastle: Bell papers, www.gerty.ncl.ac.uk.
77. 'Administrative Report of the Diwaniyah Division for the Year 1919', by Major C. K. Daly, London: IOL, IOR L/P%S/10/622.
78. Coates Ulrichsen, *Logistics and Politics*, p.189.
79. Letter from Gertrude Bell to Sir Hugh Bell, 10 January 1919, Newcastle: Bell papers, www.gerty.ncl.ac.uk.
80. Letter from Gertrude Bell to Sir Hugh Bell, 10 October 1920, Newcastle: Bell papers, www.gerty.ncl.ac.uk.
81. Coates Ulrichsen, *Logistics and Politics*, p.189.
82. Laurence Louer, *Transnational Shia Politics: Religious and Political Networks in the Gulf* (London: Hurst & Co., 2008), p.81.
83. Atiyyah, *Iraq*, p.328.
84. Townshend, *When God Made Hell*, p.466.
85. Atiyyah, *Iraq*, p.283.
86. Stephen Longrigg, *Iraq: 1900 to 1950: A Political, Social and Economic History* (London: Oxford University Press, 1953), p.120.
87. Thair Karim, 'Tribes and Nationalism: Tribal Political Culture and Behaviour in Iraq, 1914-20', in Faleh Abdul-Jabar and Hosham Dawod (eds.), *Tribes and Power: Nationalism and Ethnicity in the Middle East* (London: Saqi Books, 2003), p.292.
88. Coates Ulrichsen, *Logistics and Politics*, p.191.
89. Karim, 'Tribes and Nationalism', p.284.
90. Charles Tripp, *The Power and the People: Paths of Resistance in the Middle East* (Cambridge: Cambridge University Press, 2003), p.41.
91. Coates Ulrichsen, *Logistics and Politics*, p.191.
92. Letter from Gertrude Bell to Sir Hugh Bell, 14 June 1920, Newcastle: Bell papers, www.gerty.ncl.ac.uk.
93. Coates Ulrichsen, *Logistics and Politics*, p.191.
94. Letter from Major General G. A. Leslie to his wife, 19 October 1920, London: IOL, Papers of G. A. Leslie, Mss Eur F462.
95. Haldane, *Insurrection*, p.331.
96. Townshend, *When God Made Hell*, p.453.
97. Michael Croissant, *Armenia–Azerbaijan Conflict: Causes and Implications* (Westport, CT: Praeger, 1998, p.15).
98. A. J. Stockwell, 'The War and the British Empire', in John Turner (ed.), *Britain and the First World War* (London: Unwin Hyman, 1998), p.45.
99. Rogan, *The Arabs*, p.221.
100. Ibid.

101. John Gallagher, 'Nationalisms and the Crisis of Empire, 1919-1922', *Modern Asian Studies*, 15, 1981, p.355.
102. David Fromkin, *A Peace to End All Peace* (New York: Henry Holt, 1989), p.503.
103. Michael Asher, *Lawrence: The Uncrowned King of Arabia* (New York: Overlook Press, 1999), p.356.
104. Tripp, *Power and the People*, p.28.

CONCLUSION

1. Edward Djerejian, *Danger and Opportunity: An American Ambassador's Journey Through the Middle East* (New York: Threshold Editions, 2008), p.90.
2. 'Arming Syrian Rebels Could Create a Legacy as Harmful as Sykes–Picot', *The Daily Star*, 22 June 2013; 'Is It the End of Sykes–Picot? Patrick Cockburn on the War in Syria and the Threat to the Middle East', *London Review of Books*, volume 35 no. 11, 6 June 2013.

BIBLIOGRAPHY

Primary Sources

Cambridge University Library

Papers of Viscount Hardinge of Penshurst

Imperial War Museum

Papers of Sir Archibald Murray
Papers of Field Marshal Philip Chetwode

India Office Library (British Library)

L/MIL/5 series
L/MIL/15 series
L/MIL/17 series
L/P&S/10 series
Papers of G. A. Leslie

Liddell Hart Centre for Military Archives (King's College London)

Papers of Sir William Bartholomew
Papers of Sir Ian Hamilton
Papers of Sir Ian Robertson

The National Archives (London)

CAB 17 series
CAB 19 series
CAB 21 series
FO 371 series
MUN 4 series
WO 32 series
WO 95 series
WO 106 series

University of Newcastle-upon-Tyne

Papers of Gertrude Bell

BIBLIOGRAPHY

Secondary sources

Books

Abu-Lebdeh, Hatem Shereef, 1997. *Conflict and Peace in the Middle East*. Lanham, MD: University Press of America.

Adelson, Roger, 1995. *London and the Invention of the Modern Middle East: Money, Power, and War, 1914-1922*. New Haven, CT: Yale University Press.

Ahmad, Feroz, 2010. *The Young Turks: The Committee of Union and Progress in Turkish Politics, 1908-14*. London: Hurst & Co.

Ahmida, Ali Abdullatif, 1994. *The Making of Modern Libya: State Formation, Colonization, and Resistance, 1830-1932*. New York: State University of New York.

Akçam, Taner, 2004. *From Empire to Republic: Turkish Nationalism and the Armenian Question*. London: Zed Books.

Al-Rasheed, Madawi, 1990. *Politics in an Arabian Oasis: The Rashidi Tribal Dynasty*. London: I. B. Tauris.

Anderson, Ross, 2004. *The Forgotten Front: The East African Campaign 1914-1918*. Stroud: Tempus Publishing.

Andrew, Christopher, 1981. *The Climax of French Imperial Expansion, 1914-24*. Stanford, CA: Stanford University Press.

Andrew, Christopher and Alexander Sydney Kanya Forstner, 1981. *France Overseas; The Great War and the Climax of French Imperial Expansion*. London: Thames & Hudson.

Anscombe, Frederick, 1997. *The Ottoman Gulf: The Creation of Kuwait, Saudi Arabia, and Qatar*. New York: Columbia University Press.

Antonius, George, 1938. *The Arab Awakening: The Story of the Arab National Movement*. London: Hamish Hamilton.

Asher, Michael, 1999. *Lawrence: The Uncrowned King of Arabia*. New York: Overlook Press.

Ashmead-Bartlett, Ellis, 1920. *The Uncensored Dardanelles*. London: Hutchinson.

Atiyyah, Ghassan, 1973. *Iraq: 1908-1921: A Socio-Political Study*. Beirut: Arab Institute for Research and Publishing.

Baer, Gabriel, 1962. *A History of Landownership in Modern Egypt 1800-1950*. Oxford: Oxford University Press.

Balakian, Peter, 2003. *The Burning Tigris: The Armenian Genocide and America's Response*. New York: HarperCollins.

Barr, James, 2011. *A Line in the Sand: Britain, France and the Struggle that Shaped the Middle East*. London: Simon & Schuster.

Barrow, George, 1921. *The Life of General Sir Charles Carmichael Monro*. London: Hutchinson.

Batatu, Hanna, 1978. *The Old Social Classes and the Revolutionary Movements of Iraq: A Study of Iraq's Old Landed and Commercial Classes*. Princeton, NJ: Princeton University Press.

Bayly, C.A., 2004. *The Birth of the Modern World 1780-1914*. Oxford: Blackwell Publishing.

Beckett, Ian, 2009, ed. *1917: Beyond the Western Front*. Leiden: Brill.

Beinin, Joel and Zachary Lockman, 1987. *Workers on the Nile: Nationalism, Communism, Islam and the Egyptian Working Class, 1882-1954*. Princeton, NJ: Princeton University Press.

Beshara, Adel, 2012 edn. *The Origins of Syrian Nationhood: Histories, Pioneers and Identity*. CRC Press.

238

BIBLIOGRAPHY

Best, Anthony, Jussi Hanhimaki, Joseph Maiolo and Kirsten Schulze, 2004. *International History of the Twentieth Century*. London: Routledge.

Bose, Sugata, 2006. *A Hundred Horizons: The Indian Ocean in the Age of Global Empire*. Cambridge, MA: Harvard University Press.

Broadberry, Stephen and Mark Harrison, eds. 2009. *The Economics of World War I*. Cambridge: Cambridge University Press.

Brown, Nathan, 1990. *Peasant Politics in Modern Egypt: The Struggle Against the State*. New Haven, CT: Yale University Press.

Bruce, Anthony, 2002. *The Last Crusade: The Palestine Campaign in the First World War*. London: John Murray.

Brysac, Shareen Blair and Karl Meyer, 2008. *Kingmakers: The Invention of the Modern Middle East*. New York: W. W. Norton & Co.

Buchan, John, 1993 edn. *Greenmantle*. Oxford: Oxford University Press.

Candler, Edmund, 1920. *The Sepoy*. London: John Murray.

Casey, Michael, 2007. *The History of Kuwait*. Westport, CT: Greenwood.

Cassar, George, 1971. *The French and the Dardanelles: A Study of Failure in the Conduct of War*. London: George Allen & Unwin.

Cetinsaya, Gokhan, 2006. *Ottoman Administration of Iraq, 1890-1908*. New York: Routledge.

Churchill, Winston, 2005 edn. *The World Crisis 1911-1918*. London: Penguin Classics.

Cleveland, William, 1994. *A History of the Modern Middle East*. Boulder, CO: Westview Press.

Coates Ulrichsen, Kristian, 2010. *The Logistics and Politics of the British Campaigns in the Middle East, 1914-22*. Basingstoke: Palgrave Macmillan.

Cobban, Alfred, 1990 edn. *A History of Modern France, Volume 3: 1871-1962*. London: Penguin.

Coletta, Paolo, 1996. *Anglo-American Naval Operations in the European Theatre, World War I*. Lewiston, NY: Lampeter.

Cooper Busch, Briton, 1971. *Britain, India and the Arabs, 1914-1921*. Berkeley, CA: University of California Press.

Croissant, Michael, 1998. *Armenia–Azerbaijan Conflict: Causes and Implications*. Westport, CT: Praeger.

Daly, M. W., 1997. *The Sirdar: Sir Reginald Wingate and the British Empire in the Middle East*. Philadelphia, PA: American Philosophical Society.

Darwin, John, 1981. *Britain, Egypt and the Middle East: Imperial Policy in the Aftermath of War 1918-1922*. London: Macmillan.

Djerejian, Edward, 2008. *Danger and Opportunity: An American Ambassador's Journey Through the Middle East*. New York: Threshold Editions.

Dodge, Toby, 2003. *Inventing Iraq: The Failure of Nation-Building and a History Denied*. London: Hurst & Co.

Dolev, Eran, 2007. *Allenby's Military Machine: Life and Death in World War I Palestine*. London: I. B. Tauris.

Elgood, P. G., 1924. *Egypt and the Army*. Oxford: Oxford University Press.

Elgood, P. G., 1928. *The Transit of Egypt*. London: Edward Arnold.

Erickson, Edward, 2000. *Ordered to Die: A History of the Ottoman Army in the First World War*. London: Praeger.

Erickson, Edward, 2003. *Defeat in Detail: The Ottoman Army in the Balkans, 1912-1913*. Westport, CT: Greenwood.

BIBLIOGRAPHY

Erickson, Edward, 2008. *The History of World War I: Gallipoli and the Middle East, 1914-1918: From the Dardanelles to Mesopotamia*. London: Amber Books.

Erickson, Edward, 2010. *Gallipoli: The Ottoman Campaign*. Barnsley, Yorks: Pen & Sword.

Evans-Pritchard, E. E., 1949. *The Sanusi of Cyrenaica*. Oxford: Oxford University Press.

Falls, Cyril, 1960. *The First World War*. London: Longman.

Falls, Cyril, 1964. *Armageddon 1918*. London: Weidenfeld & Nicolson.

Falls, Cyril and George MacMunn, 1928. *Official History: Military Operations. Egypt and Palestine, Volume I*. London: HMSO.

Farah, Caesar E., 2002. *The Sultan's Yemen: Nineteenth-Century Challenges to Ottoman Rule*. London: I. B. Tauris.

Fieldhouse, David, 2006. *Western Imperialism in the Middle East 1914-1958*. Oxford: Oxford University Press.

Fisher, John, 1999. *Curzon and British Imperialism in the Middle East 1916-1919*. London: Frank Cass.

Fisk, Robert, 2005. *The Great War for Civilisation: The Conquest of the Middle East*. London: Fourth Estate.

Forbes, A., 1929. *A History of the Army Ordnance Services, Volume 3: The Great War*. London: Medici Society.

Friedman, Isaiah, 2010. *British Pan-Arab Policy 1915-1922: A Critical Appraisal*. New Brunswick, NJ: Transaction Publishers.

Fromkin, David, 1989. *A Peace to End All Peace*. New York: Henry Holt.

Gatrell, Peter, 2005. *Russia's First World War: A Social and Economic History*. Harlow: Pearson.

Gatrell, Peter, 2009. *A Whole Empire Walking: Refugees in Russia During World War I*. Indianapolis, IN: Indiana University Press.

Gholi Majd, Mohammad, 2003. *The Great Famine and Genocide in Persia, 1917-1919*. Lanham, MD: University Press of America.

Gholi Majd, Mohammad, 2006. *Iraq in World War I: From Ottoman Rule to British Conquest*. Lanham, MD: University Press of America.

Gilbert, Martin, 1973, ed. *Winston S. Churchill, Companion Volume III: Part I July 1914-April 1915*. Boston, MA: Houghton Mifflin.

Gilbert, Martin, 1997. *A History of the Twentieth Century, Volume 1: 1900-1933*. London: HarperCollins.

Gilmour, David, 2003. *Curzon: Imperial Statesman*. London: John Murray.

Goebal, Stefan 2007. *The Great War and Medieval Memory: War, Remembrance and Medievalism in Britain and Germany, 1914-1940*. Cambridge: Cambridge University Press.

Grafftey-Smith, Laurence, 1970. *Bright Levant*. London: John Murray.

Grainger, John, 2006. *The Battle for Palestine, 1917*. Woodbridge, Suffolk: Boydell & Brewer.

Graves, Philip, 1941. *The Life of Sir Percy Cox*. London: Hutchinson.

Grigg, John, 1985. *Lloyd George: From Peace to War 1912-1916*. London: Penguin.

Grigg, John, 2002. *Lloyd George: War Leader*. London: Allen Lane.

Gullett, H. S., 1925. *The Official History of Australia in the War of 1914-1918, Volume 7: Sinai and Palestine: The Australian Imperial Force in Sinai and Palestine 1914-1918*. St Lucia, Queensland: University of Queensland Press.

Haddad, Fanar, 2011. *Sectarianism in Iraq: Antagonistic Visions of Unity*. New York: Columbia University Press.

Haldane, Aylmer, 1922. *The Insurrection in Mesopotamia, 1920*. London: Blackwood.

BIBLIOGRAPHY

Halliday, Fred, 2005. *The Middle East in International Relations: Power, Politics and Ideology*. Cambridge: Cambridge University Press.

Halpern, Paul, 1987. *The Naval War in the Mediterranean*. London: HarperCollins.

Hart, Peter, 2011. *Gallipoli*. London: Profile Books.

Higgins, Trumbull, 1963. *Winston Churchill and the Dardanelles*. London: Heinemann.

Hopkins-Weisse, Jeff, 2009. *Blood Brothers: The Anzac Generals*. Adelaide: Wakefield Press.

Hourani, Albert, 1991 [2002]. *A History of the Arab Peoples*. London: Faber and Faber.

House, J. M., 2001. *Combined Arms Warfare in the Twentieth Century*. Lawrence, KS: University Press of Kansas.

Hughes, Matthew, 1999. *Allenby and British Strategy in the Middle East 1917-1919*. London: Frank Cass.

Hughes, Matthew, 2004. *Allenby in Palestine: The Middle East Correspondence of Field Marshal Viscount Allenby June 1917 – October 1919*. Stroud: Sutton Publishing. Ireland, Philip, 1937. *Iraq: A Study in Political Development*. Oxford: Jonathan Cape.

James, Lawrence, 2000 edn. *The Golden Warrior: The Life and Legend of Lawrence of Arabia*. London: Abacus.

Jeffery, Keith, 1984. *The British Army and the Crisis of Empire, 1918-22*. Manchester: Manchester University Press.

Karsh, Ephraim, 2001. *Empires of the Sand: The Struggle for Mastery in the Middle East 1789-1923*. Cambridge, MA: Harvard University Press.

Keay, John, 2006. *Sowing the Wind: The Seeds of Conflict in the Middle East*. London: John Murray.

Kechichian, Joseph, 2008. *Faysal: Saudi Arabia's King for all Seasons*. Gainesville, FL: University of Florida Press.

Keegan, John, 1994. *A History of Warfare*. London: Pimlico.

Keegan, John, 1999. *The First World War*. New York: Alfred A. Knopf.

Keene, Jennifer and Michael Neiberg, 2011, eds. *Finding Common Ground: New Directions in First World War Studies*. Leiden, Brill.

Landau, Jacob, 1990. *The Politics of Pan-Islam: Ideology and Organization*. Oxford: Oxford University Press.

Lawrence, T. E., 1997 edn. *Seven Pillars of Wisdom*. Ware, Herts: Wordsworth Editions.

Lewy, Guenter, 2005. *The Armenian Massacres in Ottoman Turkey: A Disputed Genocide*. Salt Lake City, UT: University of Utah Press.

Libaridian, Gerard, 2007. *Modern Armenia: People, Nation, State*. New York: Transaction Publishers.

Liddell Hart, Basil, 1938. *A History of the World War, 1914-1918*. London: Faber and Faber.

Longrigg, Stephen, 1953. *Iraq: 1900 to 1950: A Political, Social and Economic History*. London: Oxford University Press.

Louër, Laurence, 2008. *Transnational Shia Politics: Religious and Political Networks in the Gulf*. London: Hurst & Co.

Lynn, John, 1993. *Feeding Mars: Logistics in Western Warfare from the Middle Ages to the Present*. Oxford: Westview Press.

MacDonald, Alan, 2008. *A Lack of Offensive Spirit? The 46th (North Midland) Division at Gommecourt, 1st July 1916*. Eastbourne, E. Sussex: Iona Books.

MacMillan, Margaret, 2001. *Peacemakers: The Paris Conference of 1919 and Its Attempt to End War*. London: John Murray.

MacMunn, George, 1930. *Behind the Scenes in Many Wars*. London: John Murray.

BIBLIOGRAPHY

Malcolm, Noel, 2008. *Kosovo: A Short History*. London: Macmillan.

Marr, Phebe, 2005. *The Modern History of Iraq*. Boulder, CO: Westview Press.

Marshall, J. E., 1928. *The Egyptian Enigma: 1890-1923*. London: John Murray.

Mazower, Mark, 2004. *Salonica: City of Ghosts: Christians, Muslims and Jews 1430-1950*. London: HarperCollins.

McBeth, B. S., 1985. *British Oil Policy 1919-1939*. London: Frank Cass.

McMeekin, Sean, 2010. *The Berlin–Baghdad Express: The Ottoman Empire and Germany's Bid for World Power*. Cambridge, MA: Harvard University Press.

McMeekin, Sean, 2011. *The Russian Origins of the First World War*. Cambridge, MA: Harvard University Press.

Meinertzhagen, Richard, 1960. *Army Diary 1899-1926*. London: Oliver & Boyd.

Mejcher, Helmut, 1976. *Imperial Quest for Oil: Iraq 1910-1928*. London, Ithaca Press: St Antony's Middle East Monographs No. 6.

Metcalf, Thomas, 2007. *Imperial Connections: India in the Indian Ocean Arena 1760-1820*. Berkeley, CA: University of California Press.

Migdal, Joel, 1988. *Strong Societies and Weak States: State–Society Relations and State Capabilities in the Third World*. Princeton, NJ: Princeton University Press.

Miller, Donald and Lorna Touryan Miller, 1993. *Survivors: An Oral History of the Armenian Genocide*. Berkeley, CA: University of California Press.

Millman, Brock, 2001. *Pessimism and British War Policy, 1916-1918*. London: Frank Cass.

Milner, Alfred, 1892. *England in Egypt*. London: Edward Arnold.

Moberly, F. J., 1923. *History of the Great War Based on Official Documents. The Campaign in Mesopotamia, 1914-1918*. London: HMSO.

Mohs, Paula, 2008. *British Intelligence and the Arab Revolt: The First Modern Intelligence War*. London: Routledge.

Moorehead, Alan, 2007. *Gallipoli*. Ware, Herts: Wordsworth Editions.

Morgenthau, Henry, 2003 edn. *Ambassador Morgenthau's Story*. Detroit, MI: Wayne State University Press.

Moubayed, Sami, 2006. *Steel and Silk: Men and Women Who Shaped Syria 1900-2000*. Seattle, WA: Cune Press.

Murphy, David, 2008. *The Arab Revolt 1916-1918*. London: Osprey Publishing.

Neiberg, Michael, 2005. *Fighting the Great War: A Global History*. London: Harvard University Press.

Nevakivi, Jukka, 1969. *Britain, France and the Arab Middle East, 1914-1920*. London: Athlone Press.

Nunn, Wilfred, 2007 edn. *Tigris Gunboats: The Forgotten War in Iraq 1914-1917*. London: Chatham Publishing.

Offer, Avner, 1989. *The First World War: An Agrarian Interpretation*. Oxford: Oxford University Press.

Onley, James, 2009. *The Arabian Frontiers of the British Raj: Merchants, Rulers and the British in the Nineteenth Century*. Oxford: Oxford University Press.

Ovendale, Ritchie, 1992. *The Middle East Since 1914*. London: Longman.

Owen, Roger, 1992. *State, Power and Politics in the Making of the Modern Middle East*. London: Routledge.

Owen, Roger, 2004. *Lord Cromer: Victorian Imperialist, Edwardian Proconsul*. Oxford: Oxford University Press.

BIBLIOGRAPHY

Ozdemir, Hikmet, 2008. *The Ottoman Army 1914-1918: Disease and Death on the Battlefield*. Salt Lake City, UT: University of Utah Press.

Pakenham, Thomas, 1992. *The Scramble for Africa*. London: Abacus.

Parrs, Timothy, 2003. *Britain, the Hashemites, and Arab Rule, 1920-1925: the Sherifian Solution*. London: Frank Cass.

Pasha, Djemal, 1922. *Memories of a Turkish Statesman – 1913-1922*. London: Hutchinson.

Pearson, Owen, 2006. *Albania in the Twentieth Century, A History, Volume I: Albania and King Zog: 1908-1939*. London: I. B. Tauris.

Perkins, Kenneth, 2004. *A History of Modern Tunisia*. Cambridge: Cambridge University Press.

Poulson Newman, E. W., 1928. *Great Britain in Egypt*. London: Cassell.

Prior, Robin, 2009. *Gallipoli: The End of the Myth*. Kensington, NSW: UNSW Press.

Reich, Bernard, 1990. *Political Leaders of the Contemporary Middle East and North Africa: A Biographical Dictionary*. Westport, CT: Greenwood.

Reid, Walter, 2006. *Architect of Victory: Douglas Haig*. Edinburgh: Birlinn.

Rhodes James, Robert, 1965. *Gallipoli*. London: B. T. Batsford.

Richmond, J. C. B., 1977. *Egypt 1798-1952: Her Advance Toward a Modern Identity*. London: Methuen.

Robertson, William, 1926. *Soldiers and Statesmen 1914-1918, Volume II*. London: Cassell.

Robson, Stuart, 2007 edn. *The First World War*. Harlow: Pearson Education Limited.

Rogan, Eugene, 2009. *The Arabs: A History*. London: Allen Lane.

Roynon, Gavin, 2011 edn. *A Prayer for Gallipoli: The Great War Diaries of Chaplain Kenneth Best*. London: Simon & Schuster.

Safran, Nadav, 1961. *Egypt in Search of a Political Community: An Analysis of the Intellectual and Political Evolution of Egypt*. Oxford: Oxford University Press.

Selvik, Kjetil and Stig Stenslie, 2011. *Stability and Change in the Modern Middle East*. London: I. B. Tauris.

Slot, Benjamin, 2005. *Mubarak Al-Sabah: Founder of Modern Kuwait 1896-1915*. London: Arabian Publishing Limited.

Sluglett, Peter, 1976. *Britain in Iraq 1914-1922*. London: Ithaca Press.

Sondhaus, Lawrence, 2011. *World War One: The Global Revolution*. Cambridge: Cambridge University Press.

Stevenson, David, 1988. *The First World War and International Politics*. Oxford: Oxford University Press.

Stevenson, David, 2004. *1914-1918: The History of the First World War*. London: Allen Lane.

Storrs, Ronald, 1943. *Orientations*. London: Nicholson & Watson.

Strachan, Hew, 2001. *The First World War, Volume I: To Arms*. Oxford: Oxford University Press.

Strauss, Barry, 2006. *The Trojan War: A New History*. London: Simon & Schuster.

Tauber, Eliezer, 1993. *The Arab Movements in World War I*. London: Frank Cass.

Tomlinson, B.R., 1979. *The Political Economy of the Raj: the Economics of Decolonisation in India*. London: Macmillan.

Townshend, Charles, 2010. *When God Made Hell: The British Invasion of Mesopotamia and the Creation of Iraq, 1914-1921*. London: Faber and Faber.

Tripp, Charles, 2007, *A History of Iraq*. Cambridge: Cambridge University Press.

Tripp, Charles, 2013. *The Power and the People: Paths of Resistance in the Middle East*. Cambridge: Cambridge University Press.

BIBLIOGRAPHY

Tucker, Spencer, 2005 edn. *The Encyclopaedia of World War I: A Political, Social, and Military History*. Santa Barbara, CA: ABC-CLIO.

Valeri, Marc, 2009. *Oman: Politics and Society in the Qaboos State*. London: Hurst & Co.

Vandewalle, Dirk, 2006. *A History of Modern Libya*. Cambridge: Cambridge University Press.

Vatikiotis, P.J. 1969. *The Modern History of Egypt*. London: Weidenfeld & Nicolson.

Villiers, Alan, 2006 edn. *Sons of Sindbad*. London: Arabian Publishers Limited.

Visser, Reidar, 2005. *Basra: The Failed Gulf State: Separatism and Nationalism in Southern Iraq*. Munster: Lit Verlag, 2005.

Walker, Christopher, 1990. *Armenia: The Survival of a Nation*. London: St Martin's Press.

Westrate, Bruce, 1992. *The Arab Bureau: British Policy in the Middle East, 1916-1920*. Pennsylvania, PA: University of Pennsylvania Press.

Wilder, Gary, 2005. *The French Imperial Nation-State: Negritude and Colonial Humanism between the Two World Wars*. Chicago, IL: University of Chicago Press.

Wilson, Arnold, 1930. *Mesopotamia 1917-1920: A Clash of Loyalties*. Oxford: Oxford University Press.

Wilson Johnson, Douglas, 1917. *Topography and Strategy in the War*. New York: Henry Holt.

Wilson, Trevor, 1986. *The Myriad Faces of War*. Cambridge: Polity Press.

Wingate, Ronald, 1955. *Wingate of the Sudan*. London: John Murray.

Winstone, H. V. F., 1982. *Leachman: 'OC Desert': The Life of Lieutenant-Colonel Gerald Leachman*. London: Quartet.

Woodward, David, 2004. *Lloyd George and the Generals*. London: Frank Cass.

Yapp, Malcolm, 1987. *The Making of the Modern Middle East 1792-1923*. London: Longman.

Yergin, Daniel, 2008 edn. *The Prize: The Epic Quest for Oil, Money & Power*. New York: Free Press.

Young, Hubert, 1933. *The Independent Arab*. London: John Murray.

Chapters

Abu Aliyya, 'Abd al-Fattah Hasan, 2010. 'Early Roots of Projects to Settle the Bedouins in the Arabian Peninsula.' In Fahd al-Semmari, ed. *A History of the Arabian Peninsula*. London: I. B. Tauris.

Al-Sayyid Marsot, Afaf Lutfi, 2001. 'The British Occupation of Egypt from 1882.' In Wm Roger Louis and Andrew Porter, eds. *The Oxford History of the British Empire, Volume III: The Nineteenth Century*. Oxford: Oxford University Press.

Barr, Niall, 2002. 'The Desert War Experience.' In Peter Liddle, Ian Whitehead and John Bourne, eds. *The Great World War, 1914-45: Lightning Strikes Twice*. London: HarperCollins.

Beeman, William, 2009. 'Gulf Society: An Anthropological View of the Khalijis – Their Evolution and Way of Life.' In Lawrence Potter, ed. *The Persian Gulf in History*. New York: Palgrave Macmillan.

Biger, Gideon, 2000. 'The Turkish Activities in Palestine During World War I Revised.' In Yigal Sheffy and Shlaul Shai, eds. *The First World War: Middle Eastern Perspective*. Tel Aviv: Israel Society for Military History.

Brown, Judith, 1973. 'War and the Colonial Relationship: Britain, India and the War of 1914-18.' In M. R. D. Foot, ed. *War and Society: Historical Essays in Honour and Memory of J. R. Western, 1928-1971*. London: Elek.

BIBLIOGRAPHY

Burk, Kathleen, 1996. 'Wheat and the State During the First World War.' In Michael Dockrill and David French, eds. *Strategy and Intelligence: British Policy During the First World War*. London: Hambledon Press.

Chaudhuri, K. N., 1983. 'Foreign Trade and Balance of Payments (1757-1947).' In Dharma Kumar and Tapan Raychaudhuri, eds. *The Cambridge Economic History of India, Volume 2: c.1757-c.1970*. Cambridge: Cambridge University Press.

Dadrian, Vahakn, 2003. 'The Armenian Genocide: An Interpretation.' In Jay Winter, ed. *America and the Armenian Genocide of 1915*. New York: Cambridge University Press.

Daly, M. W., 1998. 'The British Occupation, 1882-1922.' In M. W. Daly, ed. *The Cambridge History of Egypt, Volume 2: Modern Egypt: From 1517 to the End of the Twentieth Century*. Cambridge: Cambridge University Press.

Dutton, David, 2000. 'Britain and France at War, 1914-1918.' In Alan Sharpe and Glyn Stone, eds. *Anglo-French Relations in the Twentieth Century: Rivalry and Cooperation*. London: Routledge.

French, David, 1982. 'The Rise and Fall of "Business as Usual".' In Kathleen Burk, ed. *War and the State: The Transformation of British Government, 1914-1919*. London: Allen & Unwin.

Heydemann, Steven, 2000. 'War, Institutions, and Social Change in the Middle East.' In Steven Heydemann, ed. *War, Institutions, and Social Change in the Middle East*. Berkeley, CA: University of California Press.

Horne, John, 2002. 'Introduction.' In John Horne, ed. *State, Society and Mobilization in Europe During the First World War*. Cambridge: Cambridge University Press.

Hughes, Matthew, 2009. 'Command, Strategy and the Battle for Palestine, 1917.' In Ian Beckett, ed. *1917: Beyond the Western Front*. Leiden: Brill.

Hyam, Ronald, 1999. 'The Primacy of Geopolitics: The Dynamics of British Imperial Policy, 1763-1963.' In Robert King and Robin Wilson, eds. *The Statecraft of British Imperialism: Essays in Honour of Wm Roger Louis*. London: Routledge.

Karim, Thair, 2003. 'Tribes and Nationalism: Tribal Political Culture and Behaviour in Iraq, 1914-1920.' In Faleh Abdul-Jabar and Hosham Dawod, eds. *Tribes and Power: Nationalism and Ethnicity in the Middle East*. London: Saqi Books.

Khalidi, Rashid, 1996. 'The Arab Experience of the War.' In Hugh Cecil and Peter Liddle, eds. *Facing Armageddon: The First World War Experienced*. London: Leo Cooper.

Kramer, Alan, 2010. 'Combatants and Noncombatants: Atrocities, Massacres, and War Crimes.' In John Horne, ed. *A Companion to World War I*. Chichester: Wiley-Blackwell.

Kumar, Dharma, 1983. 'The Fiscal System.' In Dharma Kumar and Tapan Raychaudhuri, eds. *The Cambridge Economic History of India, Volume 2: c.1757-c.1970*. Cambridge: Cambridge University Press.

Lambert, Andrew, 1995. 'The Royal Navy, 1856-1914: Deterrence and the Strategy of World Power.' In Keith Neilson and Elizabeth Jane Errington, eds. *Navies and Global Defence: Theories and Strategy*. Westport, CO: Greenwood.

Lee, John, 1991. 'Sir Ian Hamilton and the Dardanelles, 1915.' In Brian Bond, ed. *Fallen Stars: Eleven Studies of Twentieth Century Military Disasters*. London: Brassey's.

Lohr, Eric, 2010. 'Russia.' In John Horne, ed. *A Companion to World War I*. Chichester: Wiley-Blackwell.

McKercher, B. J. C., 1999. 'Economic Warfare.' In Hew Strachan, ed. *World War I: A History*. Oxford: Oxford University Press.

Moore, Robin, 2001. 'Imperial India, 1858-1914.' In Wm Roger Louis and Andrew Porter, eds. *The Oxford History of the British Empire, Volume III: The Nineteenth Century*. Oxford: Oxford University Press.

Morris, M. D., 1983. 'The Growth of Large-Scale Industry to 1947.' In D. Kumar and T. Raychaudhuri, eds. *The Cambridge Economic History of India, Volume 2: c.1757-c.1970*. Cambridge: Cambridge University Press.

Neilson, Keith, 1997. 'For Diplomatic, Economic, Strategic and Telegraphic Reasons: British Imperial Defence, the Middle East and India, 1914-1918.' In Keith Neilson and Greg Kennedy, eds. *Far-Flung Lines: Studies in Imperial Defence in Honour of Donald Mackenzie Schurman*. London: Frank Cass.

Nevias, Martin and Tim Moreman, 1994. 'Limited War and Developing Countries.' In Lawrence Freedman, ed. *War*. Oxford: Oxford University Press.

Offer, Avner, 2000. 'The Blockade of Germany and the Strategy of Starvation, 1914-1918: An Agency Perspective.' In Roger Chickering and Stig Forster, eds. *Great War, Total War: Combat and Mobilisation on the Western Front, 1914-1918*. Cambridge: Cambridge University Press.

Pamuk, Sevket, 2009. 'The Ottoman Economy in World War I.' In Stephen Broadberry and Mark Harrison, eds. *The Economics of World War I*. Cambridge: Cambridge University Press.

Peterson, J.E., 2009. 'Britain and the Gulf: At the Periphery of Empire.' In Lawrence Potter, ed. *The Persian Gulf in History*. New York: Palgrave Macmillan.

Potts, D.T., 2009. 'The Archaeology and Early History of the Persian Gulf.' In Lawrence Potter, ed. *The Persian Gulf in History*. New York: Palgrave Macmillan.

Risso, Patricia, 2009. 'India and the Gulf: Encounters from the Mid-Sixteenth to the Mid-Twentieth Centuries.' In Lawrence Potter, ed. *The Persian Gulf in History*. New York: Palgrave Macmillan.

Roberts, David, 2011. 'Kuwait.' In Christopher Davidson, ed. *Power and Politics in the Persian Gulf*. London: Hurst & Co.

Sheffy, Yigal, 1990. 'Institutionalized Deception and Perception Reinforcement: Allenby's Campaign in Palestine.' In Michael Handel, ed. *Intelligence and Military Operations*. London: Routledge.

Sheffy, Yigal, 2000. 'The Introduction of Chemical Weapons in the Middle East.' In Yigal Sheffy and Shlaul Shai, eds. *The First World War: Middle Eastern Perspective*. Tel Aviv: Israel Society for Military History.

Simkins, Peter, 1999. 'Haig and the Army Commanders.' In Brian Bond and Nigel Cave, eds. *Haig: A Reappraisal 70 Years On*. Barnsley, Yorks: Leo Cooper.

Sluglett, Peter 2002. 'Aspects of Economy and Society in the Syrian Provinces: Aleppo in Transition, 1880-1925.' In Leila Fawaz and C. A. Bayly, eds. *Modernity and Culture: From the Mediterranean to the Indian Ocean*. New York: Columbia University Press.

Stockwell, A. J., 1988. 'The War and the British Empire.' In John Turner, ed. *Britain and the First World War*. London: Unwin Hyman.

Trumpener, Ulrich, 2010. 'The Turkish War, 1914-1918.' In John Horne, ed. *A Companion to World War I*. Chichester: Wiley-Blackwell.

Van Creveld, Martin, 2000. 'World War I and the Revolution in Logistics.' In Roger Chickering and Stig Forster, eds. *Great War, Total War: Combat and Mobilization on the Western Front, 1914-1918*. Cambridge: Cambridge University Press.

BIBLIOGRAPHY

Wright, Steven, 2011. 'Foreign Policies with International Reach: The Case of Qatar.' In David Held and Kristian Coates Ulrichsen, eds. *The Transformation of the Gulf: Politics, Economics and the Global Order*. London: Routledge.

Wrigley, Chris, 2000. 'The War and the International Economy.' In Chris Wrigley, ed. *The First World War and the International Economy*. Cheltenham: Edward Elgar.

Zurcher, Erik, 1996. 'Little Mehmet in the Desert: The Ottoman Soldiers' Experience.' In Hugh Cecil and Peter Liddle, eds. *Facing Armageddon: The First World War Experienced*. London: Leo Cooper.

Journal articles

Akarli, Engin Deniz, 2007. 'The Tangled Ends of an Empire: Ottoman Encounters with the West and Problems of Westernisation – An Overview.' *Comparative Studies of South Asia, Africa and the Middle East*, 12.

Aksan, Virginia, 2007. 'The Ottoman Military and State Transformation in a Globalizing World.' *Comparative Studies of South Asia, Africa and the Middle East*, 12.

Andrew, C. M. and Kanya-Forstner, A. S., 1978. 'France, Africa and the First World War.' *Journal of African History*, 19.

Bernede, Allain, 1998, '"The Gardeners of Salonika": The Lines of Communication and the Logistics of the French Army of the East, October 1915-November 1918.' *War and Society*, 16.

Bou, Jean, 2007. 'Cavalry, Firepower, and Swords: The Australian Light Horse and the Tactical Lessons of Cavalry Operations in Palestine, 1916-1918.' *Journal of Military History*, 71.

Cain, P. J., 2006. 'Character and Imperialism: The British Financial Administration of Egypt, 1878-1914.' *Journal of Imperial and Commonwealth History*, 34.

Clay, Christopher, 1994. 'The Origins of Modern Banking in the Levant: the Branch Network of the Imperial Ottoman Bank, 1890-1914.' *International Journal of Middle East Studies*, 16.

Coates Ulrichsen, Kristian, 2007. 'The British Occupation of Mesopotamia, 1914-1922.' *Journal of Strategic Studies*, 30.

Coates Ulrichsen, Kristian, 2012. 'Basra, Southern Iraq and the Gulf: Challenges and Connections.' *LSE Kuwait Programme Working Paper*, 21.

Cosar, Nevn and Demre, Sevtap, 2009. 'Incorporation into the World Economy: From Railways to Highways (1850-1950).' *Middle Eastern Studies*, 45.

'Dalit', 1924. 'The Campaign in Mesopotamia – The First Phase.' *Journal of the Royal United Services Institute*, 69.

Davies, G. F., 1920. 'Lecture on Supplies and Transport – Egyptian Expeditionary Force.' *Army Service Corps Quarterly*, 8.

Elliot, W. and A. Kinross, 1925. 'Maintaining Allenby's Armies: A Footnote to History.' *Royal Army Service Corps Quarterly*, 1925.

Fahmy, Ziad, 2008. 'Francophone Egyptian Nationalists, Anti-British Discourse, and European Public Opinion, 1885-1910: The Case of Mustafa Kamil and Ya'qub Sannu'.' *Comparative Studies of South Asia, Africa and the Middle East*, 28.

French, David, 1987. 'The Dardanelles, Mecca and Kut: Prestige as a Factor in British Eastern Strategy, 1914-1916.' *War and Society*, 5.

BIBLIOGRAPHY

Gallagher, John, 1981. 'Nationalisms and the Crisis of Empire, 1919-1922.' *Modern Asian Studies*, 15.

Goldberg, Ellis, 1992. 'Peasants in Revolt – Egypt 1919.' *International Journal of Middle East Studies*, 24.

Heper, Metin, 1980. 'Center and Periphery in the Ottoman Empire: With Special Reference to the Nineteenth Century.' *International Political Science Review*, 1.

Hughes, Matthew, 1996. 'General Allenby and the Palestine Campaign, 1917-18.' *Journal of Strategic Studies*, 19.

Jack, George Morton, 2006. 'The Indian Army on the Western Front, 1914-1915: A Portrait of Collaboration.' *War in History*, 13.

Jeffery, Keith, 1977. 'Sir Henry Wilson and the Defence of the British Empire 1918-22.' *Journal of Imperial and Commonwealth History*, 5.

Jeffery, Keith, 1981. '"An English Barrack in the Oriental Sea?" India in the Aftermath of the First World War.' *Modern Asian Studies*, 15.

Nicolini, Beatrice, 2007. 'The Baluch Role in the Persian Gulf During the Nineteenth and Twentieth Centuries.' *Comparative Studies of South Asia, Africa and the Middle East*, 12.

Onley, James and Khalaf, Sulayman, 2006. 'Shaikhly Authority in the Pre-Oil Gulf: An Historical-Anthropological Study.' *History and Anthropology*, 17.

Parker, W. M., 1921. 'Supply Services in Mesopotamia.' *Royal United Services Corps Quarterly*, 9.

Ramdani, Nabila, 2013. 'Women in the 1919 Egyptian Revolution: From Feminist Awakening to Nationalist Political Activism.' *Journal of International Women's Studies*, 14.

Robinson, Ronald, 1984. 'Imperial Theory and the Question of Imperialism After Empire.' *Journal of Imperial and Commonwealth History*, 12.

Rothwell, V.H., 1970. 'Mesopotamia in British War Aims, 1914-1918.' *Historical Journal*, 13.

Roy, Kaushik, 2003. 'Equipping Leviathan: Ordnance Factories of British India, 1859-1913.' *War in History*, 10.

Ruiz, M.M., 2009. 'Manly Spectacles and Imperial Soldiers in Wartime Egypt, 1914-1919.' *Middle Eastern Studies*, 45.

Schwarz, Benjamin, 1993. 'Divided Attention: Britain's Perception of a German Threat to her Eastern Frontier in 1918.' *Journal of Contemporary History*, 28.

Sheffy, Yigal, 2009. 'Chemical Warfare and the Palestine Campaign, 1916-1918.' *Journal of Military History*, 73.

Surridge, Keith, 2008. 'The Ambiguous Amir: Britain, Afghanistan and the 1897 North-West Frontier Uprising.' *Journal of Imperial and Commonwealth History*, 36.

Trumpener, Ulrich, 1966. 'Liman von Sanders and the German–Ottoman Alliance.' *Journal of Contemporary History*, 1.

Willis, John, 1993. 'Maritime Asia, 1500-1800: The Interactive Emergence of European Domination.' *American Historical Review*, 89.

Woodward, David, 1971. 'The Origins and Intent of David Lloyd George's January 5 War Aims Speech.' *The Historian*, 34.

INDEX

INDEX

Anglo-Persian Oil Company (APOC): 145, 169; Abadan facility, 122–4, 168; creation of, 168; shareholders of, 23

Anglo-Qatar Treaty (1916): provisions of, 140

Anglo-Russian Convention (1907): provisions of, 70; signing of, 23–4, 76

Antonius, George: 114–15

Arab Bureau: 154, 165; creation of (1915), 156

Arab Congress (1913): 28

Arab League: personnel of, 26, 182

Arab Spring: 1, 157, 174

Arabic (language): 28–9, 102

Arabism: British, 200; role in Syrian national identity, 185

Armenia: Erevan, 59; government of, 63; independence of (1991), 73

Armenian-Azerbaijani War (1918–20): casualties of, 199; Khaibalikend Massacre (1919), 198–9; September Days (1918), 198–9; Shusha Massacre (1920), 199

Armenian Democratic Liberal Party: launch of (1885), 59

Armenian Genocide (1915): 2, 54, 56–7, 61; attempts to recognise, 73; casualty figures of, 63; media coverage of, 62–3; Meskene camp, 63

Armenian Revolutionary Federation: support for Ottoman Empire, 61

Armenian Revolutionary Movement: emergence of, 59

Armenians: 178–9, 198–9; persecution of, 2, 54, 56–7, 59; territory inhabited by, 30, 56, 58–60

Ashmead-Bartlett, Ellis: 37, 92

al-Askari, Jafar: 200

Asquith, Herbert Henry: 79, 109, 152

al-Assad, Hafiz: 204

Atiyyah, Ghassan: 144, 176

Australia: 1, 6, 14, 27, 48, 80, 101, 105, 204; government of, 3–4

Australian and New Zealand Army Corps (ANZAC): 6, 102, 143; role in Gallipoli Campaign (1915–16), 36–7, 83, 88; role in Sinai and Palestine Campaign (1915–18), 108; role on Western Front, 75

Australian Mounted Division: 116

Austria: 54, 178

Austria-Hungary: 25, 41, 60, 64, 66, 69, 95; Brody, 64; Czernowitz, 64; navy of, 44; territory of, 17, 56; Vienna, 95

Aylmer, Sir Fenton: Adjutant General of Indian Army, 128, 135; Commander-in-Chief of Tigris Corps, 136

Azerbaijan: Baku, 54, 59, 72, 143, 146; Karabakh, 198; oil reserves of, 72

Azzam, Abd al-Rahman: Secretary General of Arab League, 26, 182

Babylon: 13

Bahrain (Tylos): 13, 23, 122, 139

al-Bakri, Fawzi: visit to Arab Bureau (1917), 165

Balakian, Peter: 62

Balfour, Sir Arthur: 145–6, 161–2; British Foreign Secretary, 145, 150, 161, 165, 169–71, 181

Balfour Declaration (1917): 6–7, 99; contents of, 162, 191

Baluch (tribe): migration of, 14

Baluchistan: 14; British annexation of (1876–9), 21

Bani Hajim (tribe): Zawalim (clan), 197

Bani Lam (tribe): 124; territory inhabited by, 132

Banque Misr: creation of (1920), 184

Baratov, Major General Nikolai: 69; military forces led by, 65

Baring, Sir Evelyn (Lord Cromer): Agent General of Egypt, 47

Barr, James: 119

Barrow, Sir Edmund: Military Secretary at India Office, 122, 129

INDEX

INDEX

Druze: territory inhabited by, 19–20
Dual Control: 21
Duff, General Sir Beauchamp: 135, 138; Commander-in-Chief of Indian Army, 125, 128–9; suicide of (1918), 136, 138
Dunsterville, General Lionel: military forces led by, 143
Dutch East Indies: 168
Dutton, David: 93, 151

East Africa Campaign (1914–18): 45
Eastern Front: 31, 42, 66; Battle of Tannenberg (1914), 57; Brusilov Offensive (1916), 67
Eastern Question: 54
Egypt: 2, 7, 24, 35, 45–8, 67, 77, 89, 103, 106, 127–8, 138, 149, 153, 175–6, 181, 192, 195; Alexandria, 21–2, 84, 103–5, 151, 183; British Occupation of (1882–1952), 6, 17, 21, 26, 54, 99–100, 102, 104; British Protectorate of (1914–22), 28, 102, 174, 185; Cairo, 26, 84, 89, 101–2, 104, 114, 121, 151–6, 159, 165–6, 182–3, 194, 200–1; Court of Appeal, 181; Denshawai Massacre (1906), 26, 104; El-Arish, 35, 107; government of, 22, 84, 101; Khedivate of (1867–1914), 17, 22; Legislative Assembly, 101–2; Mersa Matruh, 105; Port Said, 102, 111; Qantara, 35, 107, 111, 182; Revolt (1919), 181–5, 195; Romani, 107–8; Sollum, 105; Suez, 102; Suez Canal, 6, 14, 17, 21, 23, 35, 48, 101, 103–4, 107–9, 121, 182, 185; 'Urabi Revolt (1879–82), 21, 26; Western Desert, 104–6
Egyptian Expeditionary Force (EEF): 35, 104, 112–17, 137; Eastern Force, 108, 110–11; formerly MEF, 97, 106; personnel of, 49, 110–11, 117, 159, 182, 186; ration strength of, 98

Egyptian Labour Corps: 104, 108, 180; personnel of, 105
Egyptian Works Battalion: 104
Elgood, Percival: political career of, 28
Erickson, Edward: 92, 160
d'Esprey, General Louis Franchet: 116
Euphrates, River: 35, 97, 125–7, 129, 142, 145, 176, 197
Evert, General Alexei: Commander of Russian Western Army Group, 66

von Falkenhayn, General Erich: military forces led by, 111–12
Ferdinand, Archduke Franz: assassination of (1914), 56, 178
Finland: 70
First Balkan War (1912–13): 3, 177; belligerents of, 18, 81; political impact of, 15, 17–18
First World War (1914–18): 1, 3–5, 7, 11–12, 15–16, 20–1, 27, 40, 46–7, 49–50, 60, 70, 73, 75, 97, 119, 149, 154, 174–5, 177, 201, 203, 205; Armistice at Compiègne (1918), 31, 192; Armistice of Mudros (1918), 116, 171; Battle of Jutland (1916), 45; belligerents of, 1–2, 25, 29, 31, 38–9, 41–2, 44–5, 47–8, 57, 76–7, 123, 168, 200; casualties of, 2, 41, 58, 112; industrial impact of, 37–8; logistical efforts in, 39–40; Paris Peace Conference (1919), 7, 150, 174, 177–8, 180, 187–9, 191–2, 194, 200; Treaty of Brest-Litovsk (1918), 30, 38, 41, 50, 70–1, 143; Treaty of Bucharest (1918), 71; Treaty of Saint-Germain (1919), 178; Treaty of Sèvres (1920), 178–81, 200; Treaty of Trianon (1920), 178; Treaty of Versailles (1919), 178, 180; US entry into (1917), 45, 164
Fisher, Admiral John: First Sea Lord, 80, 168
Forstner, Alexander Kanya: 188

253

INDEX